FAMINE IN NORTH KOREA

FAMINE IN NORTH KOREA

Markets, Aid, and Reform

STEPHAN HAGGARD AND
MARCUS NOLAND

FOREWORD BY AMARTYA SEN

Columbia University Press   New York

Columbia University Press
Publishers Since 1893
New York, Chichester, West Sussex
Copyright © 2007 by Stephan Haggard and Marcus Noland
All rights Reserved

Library of Congress Cataloging-in-Publication Data

Haggard, Stephan.
Famine in North Korea : markets, aid, and reform /
Stephan Haggard and Marcus Noland.
p. cm.
Includes bibliographical references and index.
ISBN 10: 0-231-14000-2 (clothbound : alk. paper) —
ISBN 13: 978–0-231-14000-3 (clothbound : alk. paper)
ISBN 10: 0-231-51152-3 (e-book)
ISBN 13: 978–0-231-51152-0 (e-book)

1. Famines—Korea (North) 2. Food supply—Korea (North)
3. Food relief—Korea (North) 4. Korea (North)—Economic conditions.
5. Korea (North)—Economic policy.
6. Korea (North)—Social conditions.
I. Noland, Marcus, 1959– II. Title.

Columbia University Press books are printed on
permanent and durable acid-free paper

Printed in the United States of America

c 10 9 8 7 6 5 4 3 2

To Sharon Crasnow and Christina Wood

CONTENTS

List of Figures   ix
List of Tables   xi
List of Abbreviations   xiii
Foreword by Amartya Sen   xv
Preface   xxi

1. Introduction: Famine, Aid, and Markets in North Korea   1

PART I. PERSPECTIVES ON THE FAMINE

2. The Origins of the Great Famine   21
3. The Distribution of Misery: Famine and the Breakdown
   of the Public Distribution System   51

PART II. THE DILEMMAS OF HUMANITARIAN ASSISTANCE

4. The Aid Regime: The Problem of Monitoring   79
5. Diversion   108
6. The Political Economy of Aid   126

PART III: DEALING WITH A CHANGING NORTH KOREA

7. Coping, Marketization, and Reform: New Sources
   of Vulnerability   165
8. Conclusion: North Korea in Comparative and
   International Perspective   209

Appendix 1: Illicit Activities   245
Appendix 2: The Scope of the Humanitarian Aid Effort   249
Appendix 3: The Marketization Balance Sheet   259

Notes   263

References   283

Index   303

LIST OF FIGURES

2.1. Trade with USSR/Russia, 1985–2004   28

2.2. Fertilizer (NPK) Consumption, 1989–2004   33

2.3. Estimates of North Korean Grain Production, 1982–2005   35

2.4. North Korean Food Imports and Aid, 1990–2004   43

2.5. North Korean Commercial Food Imports and Total Imports, 1993–2003   43

2.6. Scenarios of Food Supply and Minimum Human Need, 1990–2004   45

2.7. Scenarios of Food Supply and Normal Human Demand, 1990–2004   47

2.8. Scenarios of Food Supply and Normal Total Demand, 1990–2004   48

3.1. Estimates of Daily Per Capita PDS Rations   60

3.2. PDS Rations, January 2000–May 2004   61

4.1. Sources of Food Supply, 1990–2004   82

4.2. WFP Targets by Appeal   91

4.3. Accessible and Restricted Counties, 1995–96   93

4.4. Accessible and Restricted Counties, February 2000   94

4.5. Accessible and Restricted Counties, October 2005   95

4.6. Number of Monthly Monitoring Visits, June 1999–March 2005   98

5.1. Effect of Food Aid on the Market Price of Food   113

6.1. Total Food Aid by Major Donors, 1996–2004   128

6.2. Japan's Trade with North Korea   137

6.3. Commercial Trade Between North and South Korea   141

6.4. China's Trade with North Korea   156

6.5. Volume of Cereal Shipments to North Korea, Total and
From China, 1990–2004   157

6.6. Value of Cereal Imports From China, 1992–2004   157

6.7. Fuel Imports From China, 1992–2004   159

6.8. Food Aid to North Korea, 1996–2004   161

7.1. North Korea's Composition of Output   167

7.2. Price Trends, 1998–2003   180

7.3. North Korean GDP   187

7.4. Child Nutritional Status   196

7.5. Stunting, 2004   200

7.6. Underweight, 2004   200

7.7. Wasting   202

LIST OF TABLES

1.1. Estimated Mortality in Major Twentieth-century Famines 7

2.1. Grain Imports, 1991–97 32

2.2. Domestic Production Estimates, 1990–96 36

3.1. PDS Allocations and Population Estimates by Occupation 54

3.2 Answers to the Question "When Did Regular Food Distribution Stop?" September 1997–May 1998 59

3.3. Provincial Grain Production, 1989–97 63

3.4. Government Estimates of Population by Province and Food Category 64

3.5. Monthly PDS Allocations, November 1997–April 1999 69

3.6. Mortality Rate by Occupation 71

4.1. Results of UN Consolidated Appeals Process 83

4.2. Total Humanitarian Assistance, by Donor Organization 86

4.3. Developments in the Monitoring Regime 99

5.1. Price Wedges 116

6.1. U.S. Assistance to North Korea, 1995–2005 131

6.2. U.S. Food for Talks, 1995–2005 132

6.3. Japanese Food Aid to North Korea, 1994–2005 138

6.4. South Korean Humanitarian Assistance, 1995–2005 142

6.5. South Koreans' Opinions on the Nature of North Korea 149

6.6. European Humanitarian Assistance by Donor Organization, 1996–2005 151

7.1. Johns Hopkins 1999 Survey Results on Principal Source of Food, 1994–97   174

7.2. Johns Hopkins 2001 Survey Results on Principal Source of Food, 1995–98   174

7.3. State Consumer Prices Before and After the Price Reform of July 1, 2002   183

7.4. Monthly Incomes Before and After the Price Reform of July 1, 2002   184

7.5. Regional Price Differences   192

7.6. Nutritional Status by Region   199

Appendix 2.1. Total Humanitarian Assistance, by Sector   250

Appendix 2.2. Consolidated Appeal Humanitarian Assistance, by Agency   251

Appendix 2.3. Consolidated Appeal Humanitarian Assistance, by Sector   252

Appendix 2.4. WFP Target Groups, by Appeal   253

Appendix 3.1. Marketization, 1999–2003   261

LIST OF ABBREVIATIONS

Agricultural Recovery and Environmental Protection Plan	AREP
Consolidated Appeals Process	CAP
Democratic People's Republic of Korea	DPRK
European Commision Humanitarian Aid Office	ECHO
Flood Damage Rehabilitation Committee	FDRC
Food and Agricultural Organization	FAO
Food and Agricultural Organization and World Food Programme	FAO/WFP
Food and Agricultural Organization Statistical Databases	FAOSTAT
General Accounting Office	GAO
General Affairs and External Relations Council	GAERC
International Federation of Red Cross and Red Crescent Societies	IFRC
Korea Development Institute	KDI
Korea Institute for International Economic Policy	KIEP
Korea Institute for National Unification	KINU
Korean Buddhist Sharing Movement	KBSM
Korean Peninsula Energy Development Organization	KEDO
Médecins sans Frontières	MSF
metric ton	MT

normal trade relations	NTR
Office for the Coordination of Humanitarian Affairs	OCHA
Proliferation Security Initiative	PSI
public distribution center	PDC
Public Distribution System	PDS
state-owned enterprise	SOE
Supreme People's Assembly	SPA
United Nations Commodity Trade Statistics Database	UN-COMTRADE
United Nations Office for the Coordination of Humanitarian Affairs	UN-OCHA
United States Agency for International Development	USAID
United States Department of Agriculture Foreign Agricultural Service	USDAFAS
United Nations Development Program	UNDP
weapons of mass destruction	WMD
World Food Programme	WFP
World Food Programme International Food Aid Information System	WFPINTERFAIS

FOREWORD

Amartya Sen

In 1844 a young but fast advancing British politician, Benjamin Disraeli, described the unusual features of a famine-ridden Ireland: "you have a starving population, an absent aristocracy, and an alien Church, and in addition the weakest executive in the world." "That," Disraeli went to say, "is the Irish question." This remarkable book is a treatise on what can be called "the North Korean question."

Stephan Haggard and Marcus Noland have presented here a penetrating investigation of the North Korean famine that started almost exactly 150 years after the Irish famine. The famine in North Korea has already killed a great many people, possibly as many as a million (about the same as the Irish famine of the 1840s), and it may kill many more unless the underlying causes are addressed and overcome. The Irish famine also led to a massive emigration from Ireland, particularly to North America. Many North Koreans too have tried to move out of their stricken country, especially to China, but the political barriers to such movement make the process hazardous and often unsuccessful.

Like its notorious Irish predecessor, the North Korean question too cannot but lead to a many-layered answer. It involves *economics* (especially the proximate as well as long-run causes of the failure of a huge section of the population to command enough food for survival), *politics* (in particular the nature and operation of the government that influences—often adversely—the deprived people's ability to have enough food), *practical ethics* (including the dilemmas faced by the international community in providing humanitarian aid that would actually help), and *social organization* (varying from the old socialist entitlements to the newly emerging marketized allocation). Stephan Haggard and Marcus Noland have greatly advanced the understanding of these difficult issues in the specific context of North Korea, but their study is likely to be of wider interest as well, since starvation and famines associated with economic malfunctions, organizational quandary, and political authoritarianism have had other victims across the world and may continue to flourish in the future, unless the causal processes are arrested and reversed.

Despite many similarities in outcome, the societal process that led to the North Korean famine is, in many ways, very dissimilar (as one would expect) to what happened in British Ireland in the 1840s. And yet there are also some odd resemblances between the two famines, respectively in the most thriving empire in recent history and the most problematic communist state in the contemporary world, separated by a century and a half. Even though Haggard and Noland do not get into this comparison (they have other—more immediate as well as more basic—issues of the nature, causation, and consequences of the North Korean famine to address), it is instructive to see the similarities between two very different famines, drawing on the rich investigation of the North Korean famine presented in this book, in addition to other studies on the North Korean famine, and of course the comparatively voluminous literature on the Irish famine. (An illuminating and impressive study can be found in *The Great North Korean Famines* by Andrew S. Natsios, published in 2002.)

The dictatorial North Korean regime cannot certainly be described as "the weakest executive in the world," in the way that Disraeli described London's rule of Ireland. In fact, the North Korean administration is one of the most forceful and intrusive; it is also, as dissidents know chillingly well, extraordinarily fierce. And yet that ruthless state, with its well-oiled machinery of authoritarian repression, was also remarkably feeble in executing even the most elementary policies that could help the famine victims.

Haggard and Noland do not suggest that the leaders of the Korean regime were deliberately aiming at mass starvation and death, despite the contrary impression generated by the lack of any serious preventive action taken by the North Korean regime. The same, as it happens, can also be said about the Irish famine, since no one in office in London tried to kill the Irish—the rulers managed to do so merely through a mixture of negligence, obduracy, and confusion. And yet the suspicion that starvation was generated in Ireland by the British as a matter of policy would still color the way the British rule would be viewed by many in Ireland for a great many decades to come: Mr. Malone in George Bernard Shaw's *Man and Superman* articulates this thesis with much sharpness ("When a country of full o food and exporting it, there can be no famine. . . . Me father was starved dead, and I was starved out to America in me mother's arms"). The tenuous official attempts at remedying the respective famines did little in either country to eradicate the principal sources of adversity, and the real culprit is callousness, combined with a determination, again in both countries, by the rulers not to allow any political change in the respective regimes, nor any radical re-examination of the basic political agenda of the two ruling groups. In addition—and no less importantly—there was in each case a fairly comprehensive failure to understand what exactly causes starvation and famines.

Why, then, did the Irish and the Koreans starve? The question takes us to different levels of investigation, including the proximate economic factors and the underlying political causes. A family will certainly starve when it is unable to own enough food to eat. That issue of ownership—or more generally of entitlement (since there are economic and legal systems in which a person is entitled to get some food to eat even without actually owning that food)—can be distinguished from the question of availability of food in an economy, which a starving person can, as it were, "see" without being entitled to eat. The availability of food would typically be one influence among many that determines the entitlements of different persons. Sometimes a sharp fall in total food production would go hand in hand with a fall in the outputs of individual producers, leading to starvation of the families dependent on self-produced food. In other cases, even though there is no general decline of total food production, some individual producers may have a fall in their own production of food, or of other goods, by selling so that they could buy food in the market. So a disastrous failure of food entitlement on the part of a substantial section of the population can take place with or without any overall reduction in food availability for the country as a whole. And nevertheless, in almost all cases the total availability of food would tend to have some influence on the prices that prevail in the market, thereby influencing food entitlements of people to a varying extent.

In the Irish case the reliance on the market was very pervasive (as one would expect), supplemented—often very inadequately—by public distribution. The crisis in the production of potatoes, thus, contributed greatly to the emergence and continuation of the Irish famine. But here too it would be a mistake to concentrate only on the reduced food output, since the distribution of hardship and starvation calls for a fuller analysis of how the process of ownership and entitlement works, along with the many economic influences that shape them. At the height of the Irish famine, ship after ship sailed down the Shannon carrying expensive food items, from meats to dairy products, taking food from starving Ireland to well-fed England where the buyers could afford to pay a higher price than what these commodities could fetch in Ireland itself. Who can buy what—or get what through a public distribution system—is a central issue in all famines, and it is critically important in understanding the North Korean famine as well as Irish starvation.

Haggard and Noland investigate these issues quite extensively. They show the role of so-called socialist entitlements in North Korea, determined by the state (with fairly powerful biases in the distribution of food), the breakdown of the public distribution system, and the growing role of the market mechanism (emerging in a rather ad hoc way in response to the crisis, rather than as a determined and elaborately planned public policy, as in post-reform China). They also examine the policy failures that made agricultural production quite unreliable, generating recurrent supply problems, while the production of non-food goods was severely compromised by the regime's "rigid pursuit of self-sufficiency" in food, making it harder for North Korea to buy food from abroad through exchange based on selling non-food goods (thereby compromising the food entitlements that could be generated through trade with abroad, and not just through growing more food at home).

Revealing as the economic analysis is, the authors also identify why—and how—the roots of the famine extend deeply into politics and cannot be adequately assessed through economic analysis alone. Disraeli had noted that the alienation of the British rulers in Ireland was reinforced by "an absent aristocracy and an alien Church." North Korea did not have these problems, and yet the rulers clearly were quite firmly distanced from the more miserable of their subjects. The priority of the military was strong; regional diversities were very considerable; and the official faith in a centralized food distribution system remained strong even as it crumbled all around. The emergence of markets appeared threatening to the regime, though they had to settle for an uneasy equilibrium with it. Given the authoritarian nature of the government, there was no way of making the rulers change track, nor of course any hope that the rulers with fixed views and priorities would make way for a different government.

An important role in the hunger scene in North Korea has been played by humanitarian aid coming from abroad. But the aid agencies were troubled by the fact that the regime could not be made to allocate the received food in the way that humanitarian concerns would demand. There have been persistent wrangles between the givers and the receivers, and while the authors show how the dictatorial character of the regime—with a powerful personality cult—has been a major problem, they also discuss the infelicities of the aid arrangements, with difficulties on the donor side as well as on the side of the recipients.

There is a lot more in the story than can be quickly summarized here. But this is just as it should be. It is a book that must be read by people interested in the economics of poverty and hunger, or in the politics of authoritarianism, or in the role—and the difficulties—of international assistance in the miserable world in which we live. The North Korean question proves to be rich, and begins to parallel the seriousness of the old Irish question. This book goes a long way in pursuing that new question. It is an admirable contribution on a truly important subject.

PREFACE AND ACKNOWLEDGMENTS

This book is an outgrowth of an earlier report commissioned by the U.S. Committee for Human Rights in North Korea. We owe the committee, and its executive director, Debra Liang-Fenton, an enormous debt of gratitude.

In preparing that earlier report, and now this book, we have benefited enormously from a large virtual college of policy makers, humanitarian workers, and academics with an interest in North Korea. We would like to thank Jae-hoon Ahn, Jagdish Bhagwati, Jon Brause, Maria Castillo-Fernandez, Christine Chang, Nicholas Eberstadt, L. Gordon Flake, Ruediger Frank, Lola Gostelow, Cormac Ó Gráda, Han Ki-Soo, David Hawk, Amanda Hayes, Christopher Hughes, Erica Kang, Byung-kook Kim, Yeri Kim, Young-Hoon Kim, Tae-jin Kwon, Andrei Lankov, Sue Lautze, Suk Lee, Young-sun Lee, Wonhyuk Lim, Mark Manyin, Chun Sang Moon, Chung-in Moon, Sang-wook Nam, Takeshi Nagasawa, William Newcomb, Syungje Park, Raphael Perl, Ed Reed, Hazel Smith, and Jae-Jean Suh. David Kang, Miles Kahler, Hans Maretzki, Barry Naughton, and Scott Snyder took the time to read the entire manuscript and offered particularly valuable comments. We a special debt of gratitude to Daniel Pinkston, who not only provided detailed comments on the whole manuscript but provided assistance with romanization. We also benefited from the comments on our earlier report provided by three anonymous readers commissioned by the U.S. Committee for Human Rights in North Korea.

Among those we interviewed were members of the South Korean Ministry of Unification, the Korea Institute for National Unification, the Korea Rural Economic Institute, the Korea Institute for International Economic Policy, the Korea Development Institute Graduate School, and the World Food Programme. We also benefited enormously from off-the-record conversations with a number of current staff at official and nongovernmental relief agencies, who, for obvious reasons of political sensitivity, requested anonymity.

Earlier versions of this work profited from presentations at the East Asia Institute and the KDI School in Seoul and workshops organized by the Korea Economic Institute at the University of California, San Diego, and Portland State University; our thanks to Scott Rembrandt for his role in these efforts.

Haggard would also like to thank the students in his course on the North Korean nuclear issue at the Graduate School of International Relations and Pacific Studies in the spring of 2005 and an independent study group on food aid to North Korea that included Yeri Kim, Amanda Hayes, and Takeshi Nagasawa, who wrote insightful papers on the Chinese and Japanese aspects of the issue. Haggard would also like to thank Bob Kaufman for his forbearance.

Erik Zhang did additional fieldwork for a project with Tai Ming Cheung on the China–North Korea economic relationship that is reported here. Paul Karner's assistance in pulling together the data for this report was invaluable; we could not have done this without him. Yeon-Kyeong Kim, Yeri Kim, and Ketki Sheth also provided essential research assistance.

A NOTE ON ROMANIZATION

All Korean terms and proper names are transliterated according to the McCune-Reischauer system. North Korean and South Korea have separate romanization systems, which may cause confusion. All systems have imperfections, but the McCune-Reischauer system remains the standard for scholarly work in English. Readers might be more familiar with the North Korean or South Korean transliterations of the names of public figures Kim Il-sŏng (Kim Il Sung), Kim Jŏng-il (Kim Jong Il), No Mu-hyŏn (Roh Moo-Hyun), and No Tae-u (Roh Tae Woo) or common terms such as *chuch'e* (*juche*). We also follow the Korean tradition of family name preceding the given name, which is separated by a hyphen. In cases of North-South dialect differences regarding provincial names, we use standard South Korean spellings. Some maps were drawn from sources that did not adhere to the McCune-Reischauer system.

Some time later many of the people, both men and women, began to complain against their fellow Jews. Some said, "We have large families, we need grain to keep us alive."

Others said, "We have had to mortgage our fields and vineyards and houses to get enough grain to keep us from starving."

Still others said, "We have had to borrow money to pay the royal tax on our fields and vineyards. We are the same race as our fellow Jews. Aren't our children just as good as theirs? But we have to make slaves of our children. Some of our daughters have already been sold as slaves. We are helpless because our fields and vineyards have been taken away from us."

When I heard their complaints, I grew angry and decided to act. I denounced the leaders and officials of the people and told them "You are oppressing your brothers!"

—Nehemiah 5:1–7, *Good News Bible*

FAMINE IN NORTH KOREA

CHAPTER ONE

Introduction

Famine, Aid, and Markets in North Korea

Beginning sometime in the early 1990s and extending into 1998, North Korea experienced famine. We estimate that the great North Korean famine killed between six hundred thousand and one million people, between 3 and 5 percent of the entire population of the country. Such events are national traumas that live in the collective memory for generations. Famines produce countless personal tragedies: watching loved ones waste away from hunger and disease; making fateful choices about the distribution of scarce food; migrating to escape the famine's reach; and, all too often, facing the stark reality that these coping strategies are futile. A full understanding of such disasters can only be communicated through their human face: the individual experience of the suffering and humiliation that extreme deprivation brings to its victims. Through refugee accounts, this human face of the North Korean famine is slowly becoming available to us and speaks far more eloquently than we can here.

But famines also have causes as well as profound demographic, economic, and political consequences for the societies that experience them. Despite its rigidly authoritarian and closed nature, North Korea is no exception to this rule. The purpose of this book is to explore the political economy of this great famine through a number of different but ultimately complementary lenses. What does the North Korean case say about the causes of famines more generally? What lessons does it hold for the humanitarian community? What does it say about the transition from socialism? And how have recurrent food shortages played into the security equation and political dynamics on the Korean peninsula?

Sadly, our concerns are not simply historical ones, and we were first brought to these issues by contemporary concerns (Haggard and Noland 2005). As in far too many cases, famines are not necessarily followed by a return to abundance. Rather, the acute shortages of the mid-1990s turned into a chronic food emergency that persisted well into the first decade of the 21st century. Despite the efforts of the international humanitarian community, and despite—and even because of—a set of wide-ranging but ultimately flawed economic reforms, large portions of North Korea's highly urbanized society suffer from unreliable access to food. North Korean families continue to experience the ravages of malnutrition, most painfully evident in the admittedly partial and imperfect information we have on the nutritional status of children over time.

Famines bear a curious resemblance to genocides. As Samantha Powers (2002) has pointed out, outsiders' first response to genocides is denial. Given the horror of events, the natural reaction is that it can't be happening; it is not possible. During genocides, however, delay is fatal; where there is a will, masses of people can be killed quickly. Similarly, while we can procrastinate about many things, we cannot go for long without adequate sustenance (see Russell 2005). By the time the evidence of famine is clear, it is often too late to reverse its effects, and the worst damage has been done.

Yet the humanitarian effort in North Korea faced additional barriers. Until a series of great floods in the summer of 1995, the North Korean government was slow to respond to the warning signs that a famine was under way. The closed nature of the country made it even more difficult for outsiders to read the signals.

Once aid was fully mobilized in 1996, the North Korean government proved deeply suspicious of foreign intent and has to this day thrown roadblocks in the way of the relief effort. The delivery and monitoring of humanitarian assistance to North Korea is an ongoing negotiation and struggle, and for a good reason: there is ample evidence of things to hide. Large amounts of aid—we estimate as much as 30 percent or more—is diverted to the military and political elite, to other undeserving groups, and to the market.

Floods, subsequent natural disasters, and the hostile policy of outsiders constitute the official explanation for North Korea's food problems. Yet the chronic nature of North Korea's problems suggests that forces more systemic were at work. These included failed economic and agricultural policies but also a particular system of entitlements associated with the socialist economy and a political system that provided no channels for redress when these entitlements failed. Following the pioneering work of Amartya Sen (1981; 2000: chap. 6;

Dreze and Sen 1989), we suggest throughout this book that the ultimate and deepest roots of North Korea's food problems must be found in the very nature of the North Korean economic and political system. It follows almost as a matter of logic that those problems will not be definitively resolved until that regime is replaced by one that, if not fully democratic, is at least more responsive to the needs of its citizenry.

As we have suggested, however, the famine was not without its own consequences, and one of them was an increasing marketization of the economy and, beginning in 2002, the initiation of economic reforms. Marketization and reform remain the key unfolding story in the country, a work-in-progress that contains the small glimmers of hope we can hold out for an economically if not politically reformed North Korea. Yet through 2005 these signs of change remained largely hopes. The initiation of reform overlapped with renewed international political conflict over North Korea's nuclear ambitions—a crisis largely of North Korea's own making—which in turn had predictably mixed effects on the reform effort.

Moreover, the reforms themselves failed to return the country to sustainable growth and unleashed a stubborn inflation that contributed to the ongoing food problems in the country. By this time, North Korea was a society increasingly divided between those with access to foreign exchange and stable supplies of food and those vulnerable to an erratic public food distribution system and markets providing food and other goods at prices beyond the reach of the ordinary citizen.

We divide our account into three broad questions. In part 1 (chapters 2 and 3), we consider the contours of the famine of the mid-1990s: its underlying and proximate causes and its trajectory and more immediate consequences, including mortality. In these chapters, we are speaking both to a broader literature on famine and to important accounts of the North Korean case, on which we build.[1] The second section (chapters 4 and 5) is devoted to a discussion of the political economy of humanitarian assistance. These politics involve the humanitarian community and its norms, the political as well as economic interests of the North Korean government, and the sometimes congruent, sometimes conflicting interests of the donor governments. In the third section (chapter 6), we look at the famine through yet a third lens: what it says about North Korea as a socialist economy undergoing some sort of transition. The famine ultimately triggered a process of economic reform in the North. But as we now know from nearly twenty years of "transitology," the route to the market is not linear but strewn with partial reforms and a variety of intermediate models of which North Korea is certainly one.

In the remainder of this introduction, we outline these themes in somewhat more detail, returning in the conclusion to some of the broader policy issues posed by North Korea's famine and food shortages (the subject of chapters 7 and 8 in part 3). Before turning to those themes, however, we sketch a few features of the country's political history. Although this survey is admittedly cursory, we reference a number of works where these issues can be pursued in greater depth and focus primarily on those background conditions that are germane to our story.

The Setting

At the conclusion of the Second World War, the Japanese colony of Korea was partitioned into zones of U.S. and Soviet military occupation.[2] Unable to agree on a formula for a unified Korea, the Republic of Korea (ROK, or South Korea) declared independence under U.S. patronage in 1948, while the Democratic People's Republic of Korea (DPRK, or North Korea) was established under Soviet tutelage. In June 1950, North Korea invaded South Korea. The initial success of the invading forces was reversed with the support of a U.S.-dominated United Nations force, which in turn drove China to enter the war in October to prevent a North Korean defeat. Combat ended with an armistice in 1953. After tremendous physical destruction and loss of life, the war did little more than reestablish the original borders. No formal peace treaty was ever signed, and the combatants technically remain at war.

Kim Il-sŏng fully consolidated his power over rival factions in the DPRK after 1956 and began to articulate a distinctive national ideology called *chuch'e* (Armstrong 2002 and Lankov 2002). Typically translated as "self-reliance," North Korean ideology in fact combines a number of elements—extreme nationalism, Stalinism, even Confucian dynasticism—into a complex mix (Cumings 2003; Oh and Hassig 2000). The political order has exhibited a high degree of personalism. Kim Il-sŏng was deified as the "Great Leader." Similar efforts have been made to canonize his son, Kim Jŏng-il, who assumed the reins of political power when his father died in 1994.

Personalism was combined with an extreme, even castelike social regimentation. The government classified the population—and kept dossiers on them—according to perceived political loyalty and even the social standing of parents and grandparents. The share of the population deemed politically reliable is relatively small, on the order of one-quarter of the population, with a core political and military elite of perhaps two hundred thousand, or roughly 1 percent of the population.[3] As we will show, this political-cum-social structure also has important implications for the distribution of food and other goods.

A further feature of the political and economic system is extreme militarization (Kang 2003). By standard statistical measures such as the share of the population under arms or the share of national income devoted to the military, North Korea is the world's most militarized society. The bulk of its million-strong army is forward-deployed along the demilitarized zone (DMZ) separating it from South Korea, a highly destabilizing military configuration. Viewed with the benefit of hindsight, the division of the peninsula has proven surprisingly stable; a recurrence of full-scale war has been avoided. Yet underneath this apparent stability is a history of sustained military competition and recurrent crises. Moreover, militarization has important domestic effects. During external crises, the government reverts to *sŏn'gun*, or "military-first" politics. As we will argue, the expenditure priorities of the regime are also an important aspect of the hunger story, and the question of diversion of humanitarian supplies to the military is an ongoing political issue among donors.

In the early 1990s, North Korea experienced a rapid deterioration in its external security environment. The collapse of the Soviet Union and the ongoing reform efforts in China put North Korea at odds with its two most important patrons. The continued dynamism of the South Korean economy made it more and more difficult—and costly—to maintain the illusion of military parity. The acquisition of nuclear weapons no doubt seemed an inexpensive way to address these insecurities but resulted in a major crisis with the United States in 1992–94 (Sigal 1998; Wit, Poneman, and Galucci 2004). The nuclear crisis and the question of food aid became inextricably linked, but in unexpected ways, as the provision of assistance was used to induce North Korean participation in diplomatic negotiations. Similar issues arose after the 2002 nuclear standoff as the main aid donors—the United States, Japan, China, South Korea, and the European Union—diverged on how to deal with North Korea's nuclear ambitions; we return to these issues below.

Despite claims of self-reliance and the extremely closed nature of the economy, international assistance has long been crucial to North Korea's very survival. Before the 1990s, North Korea depended both militarily and economically on Soviet largesse. China subsequently has come to play a more important role. From a balance-of-payments standpoint, it appears that North Korea now derives roughly one-third of its revenues from aid, roughly one-third from conventional exports, and roughly one-third from unconventional sources (in estimated order of significance, missile sales, drug trafficking, remittances, counterfeiting, and smuggling; see appendix 1). The remittances come mostly from a community of pro-Pyongyang ethnic Koreans in Japan and increasingly from refugees in China, who may number one hundred thousand or more (KINU 2004).

North Korea is characterized by a complete absence of standard political freedoms and civil liberties. The political system is completely dominated by a deified leader, with the military complex, the Korean Workers' Party, and the state apparatus playing supporting roles that have shifted in importance over time. Independent political or social organizations are not weak in North Korea; they are virtually nonexistent. Any sign of political deviance, from listening to foreign radio broadcasts to singing South Korean songs to inadvertently sitting on a newspaper containing the photograph of Kim Il-sŏng, can be subject to punishment. Until the famine forced their breakdown, the government maintained complex controls on internal migration and foreign travel and even criminalized the very coping behaviors through which families sought to secure food.

The regime maintains a network of political prison camps that hold two hundred thousand or more political prisoners (Hawk 2003; KINU 2004; Kang 2002, a memoir by one camp survivor). Death rates in these camps are high, torture is practiced, and there are numerous eyewitness accounts of public executions, including cases of schoolchildren being forced to witness these killings (see United States Department of State 2005, Amnesty International 2004, and KINU 2004). A second network of smaller extrajudicial detention centers developed as an ad hoc response to coping behavior at the height of the famine, which included unauthorized internal movement and crossing into China.

In sum, the North Korean case exhibits a number of features that make it a particularly difficult target for humanitarian efforts. In contrast to civil war settings, the government exercises complete control over its territory. It has a well-developed ideology that has until recently been highly impervious to reform or outside advice. The political leadership exhibits an extreme wariness toward outside influences of any sort, a posture justified by an increasingly adverse security setting. These characteristics not only make North Korea a hard target for humanitarian assistance, but they help explain some of the underlying and proximate causes of the famine as well.

The Great Korean Famine: Causes, Trajectory, Consequences

Famines and food shortages have been a perennial feature of the human condition and, as the North Korean case suggests, have by no means been eliminated. Table 1.1, adapted from Devereux (2000) with our estimates for the

TABLE 1.1. Estimated Mortality in Major Twentieth-century Famines

Years	Location (epicenter)	Excess mortality	Causal triggers
1903–6	Nigeria (Hausaland)	5,000	Drought
1906–7	Tanzania (south)	37,500	Conflict
1913–14	West Africa (Sahel)	125,000	Drought
1917–19	Tanzania (central)	30,000	Conflict and drought
1920–21	China (Gansu, Shaanxi)	500,000	Drought
1921–22	Soviet Union	9,000,000	Drought and conflict
1927	China (northwest)	3,000,000–6,000,000	Natural disasters
1929	China (Hunan)	2,000,000	Drought and conflict
1932–34	Soviet Union (Ukraine)	7,000,000–8,000,000	Government policy
1943	India (Bengal)	2,100,000—3,000,000	Conflict
1943–44	Rwanda	300,000	Conflict and drought
1944	Netherlands	10,000	Conflict
1946–47	Soviet Union	2,000,000	Drought and government policy
1957–58	Ethiopia (Tigray)	100,000–397,000	Drought and locusts
1958–62	China	30,000,000–33,000,000	Government policy
1966	Ethiopia (Wollo)	45,000–60,000	Drought
1968–70	Nigeria (Biafra)	1,000,000	Conflict
1969–74	West Africa (Sahel)	101,000	Drought
1972–73	India (Maharashtra)	130,000	Drought
1972–75	Ethiopia (Wollo and Tigray)	200,000—500,000	Drought
1974–75	Somalia	20,000	Drought and government policy
1974	Bangladesh	1,500,000	Flood and market failure
1979	Cambodia	1,500,000—2,000,000	Conflict
1980–81	Uganda (Karamoja)	30,000	Conflict and drought
1982–85	Mozambique	100,000	Conflict and drought
1983–85	Ethiopia	590,000–1,000,000	Conflict and drought
1984–85	Sudan (Darfur, Kordofan)	250,000	Drought
1991–93	Somalia	300,000—500,000	Conflict and drought
1995–99	North Korea	600,000—1,000,000	Flood and government policy
1998	Sudan (Bahr el Ghazal)	70,000	Conflict and drought

Source: Adapted from Devereux 2000, table 1

North Korean case, suggests that roughly seventy million people died of famine in the twentieth century.[4] Yet a simple Malthusian picture of famine as a natural inevitability has become harder to sustain, because of changes both in the nature of famine and in our understanding of it. The postwar period has seen a gradual elimination of famine from virtually all parts of the world with the exception of Africa (North Korea, along with China and Cambodia, constitute important exceptions to this rule). One reason for this hopeful development is that famines caused by crop failure associated with natural disasters such as floods and droughts can be mitigated by the increasing ability of both the international community and national governments to respond to food shortages. Increasingly, famines and food shortages must be seen not as natural events but as complex man-made disasters. Civil conflict figures prominently in a large number of the famines listed in table 1.1, and, tellingly, the socialist famines—in the Soviet Union, Cambodia, China, Ethiopia, and North Korea—rank among the most deadly.

In his early work on famine, Amartya Sen (1981) made the important observation that famine could occur even where aggregate supplies of food were adequate if there were failures in the distribution system, including through the market. Rather than focusing on the sheer quantity of food available, Sen's analysis delved into issues of distribution and entitlement and in doing so set in train many of the most important debates on the phenomenon of famine that continue to this day. To what extent can famines in general, and any given famine in particular, be attributed to food availability decline as opposed to questions of distribution and entitlement? If we do find evidence of a decline in food availability, is this in fact a result of natural disasters, or must we also look at other causes, such as incentives for production or failure to access external sources of supply? And if we do witness entitlement failures—the inability of individuals to command the resources to gain access to food that is in principle available—to what political economy factors do we owe this failure?

Chapter 2 takes up these questions. We show that for military, political, and ideological reasons that can be traced to the division of the peninsula, the North Korean regime has consistently pursued the goal of achieving agricultural self-sufficiency. Whatever its political rationale, the economic logic for doing so is dubious; arable land is scarce in North Korea, and the weather is far from hospitable for agriculture. Given these obstacles and the unwillingness to pursue a more market-oriented agricultural policy, the North Korean government pursued a "forced march" approach to agricultural production that included heavy reliance on industrial inputs. This agricultural strategy has proven problematic throughout the country's history, generating a recurrent pattern of shortages—in 1945–46, 1954–55, and 1970–73—of which the great famine and ongoing crisis is only the most recent example.

Moreover, for political as well as economic reasons, the North Korean government suppressed private production and trade in grain and monopolized distribution through the so-called Public Distribution System (PDS). This system was at the core of the socialist system of entitlements to food and constituted a powerful tool of social control, particularly for urban populations that were completely dependent on it. No understanding of the famine is possible without understanding the PDS and its virtual collapse.

In turning to the more proximate causes of the famine of the mid-1990s and the chronic food problems the country has faced since, we first address the official explanation offered by the North Korean government. That explanation attributes the famine to natural disasters—floods and drought—and indirectly to the decline in preferential trade relations with Russia and China. As can be seen, this interpretation bears a close family resemblance to theories of famine that stress declines in food availability and exogenous shocks, in this case including not only weather but the disruption of imported inputs.

We show that this interpretation is misleading in important respects. The change in North Korea's external economic relations was clearly permanent, not merely a transitory shock, and the decline in food production was visible well before the floods of 1995. Yet the government was slow to recognize the extent of the problem and take the steps necessary to guarantee adequate food supplies, whether through increases in domestic production or greater access to external sources of supply. To attribute the famine primarily to external causes is to neglect the fundamental failure of the government to respond to its changed circumstances in a timely and appropriate way, particularly through efforts to increase or conserve foreign exchange earnings that would have allowed commercial imports.

To elaborate this point, we construct food balance sheets for the country from 1990 to the present. We approach this task with the caution—and warnings—that it deserves, but the underlying purpose is to assess the overall availability of food from all sources and the shortfall between different estimates of supply and demand. To what extent have North Korea's food problems been the result of a decline in overall food availability, and what is the ultimate source of that decline? To what extent can North Korea's problems be traced to the distribution of food?

The evidence with respect to food availability is mixed; the country certainly experienced a decline in production, and under some assumptions about demand North Korea's famine could be treated as a classic food availability problem. But we also show that with some important adjustments—such as maintaining the ability to import food on commercial terms or aggressively seeking humanitarian assistance—the government could have avoided the worst of the great famine and the shortages that continue to this day. Indeed, we argue that in an increasingly integrated global market for basic foodstuffs, food availability must be seen in an open-economy context. If internal food availability declines but external sources of supply are available, then we have really identified a new sort of entitlement problem. Why do donors fail to respond to manifest need? Even more perplexing, why do governments not avail themselves of external sources of supply available through trade or aid?

A disturbing finding from this balance sheet exercise is that as humanitarian assistance responded to the crisis, commercial imports of food fell. Rather than using humanitarian assistance as an addition to supply, the government used it largely as balance-of-payments support, offsetting aid by cutting commercial food imports and allocating the savings to other priorities. Again, these findings cast particular doubt on arguments that food shortages after 1995 could be attributed to a decline in domestic food availability alone.

In chapter 3, we turn our attention to the system of socialist entitlements in more detail: the complex problem of who had—and who lost—access to food during the great famine. North Korea is a surprisingly urbanized country, a result of the regime's emphasis on heavy industrialization. Between 60 and 70 percent of the North Korean population depended on the PDS, and we show the importance of regional, urban-rural, and occupational differences in access to food. The regions directly affected by the floods of 1995 certainly suffered shortages, but so did remote mountain areas of the north and the industrial cities of the east coast. In contrast to famines elsewhere in the world, North Korea's was an urban as well as rural phenomenon. Pyongyang—the seat of government and of the ruling elite—was at least relatively protected.

These regional differences—and information suggesting that certain parts of the country were cut off from both aid and domestic distribution—suggest strongly that political decisions about distribution played an important role in the famine. We review a number of possible reasons why the government responded to the pattern of shortfalls as it did. While we find no evidence that · particular segments of the population were deliberately starved—as was the case in the Ukraine under Stalin (Conquest 1986) and Cambodia under Pol Pot (Short 2004)—there is evidence that informational failures and the lack of accountability characteristic of authoritarian regimes played a crucial role.

As is always the case, food shortages took a particular heavy toll on vulnerable groups such as children and the elderly, and deaths were the result not only

of starvation but of increased susceptibility to disease and the more general collapse of the public health-care system. We review the various efforts to estimate
the death toll, which range from a low of 220,000 excess deaths (by the North
Korean government) to as many as 3.5 million at the upper end. We argue that
the most plausible estimates fall in the range of 600,000 to 1 million deaths as
a result of the famine, or roughly 3 to 5 percent of the population.

The Humanitarian Response: The Political Economy of Aid

The 1948 Universal Declaration of Human Rights enshrined the right to adequate food. The 1966 International Covenant on Economic, Social and Cultural Rights elaborated this commitment as "the fundamental right of everyone
to be free from hunger." At the 1996 World Food Summit, official delegations
from 185 countries, including representatives from the governments of the
United States and the DPRK, reaffirmed "the right of everyone to have access
to safe and nutritious food, consistent with the right to adequate food and the
fundamental right of everyone to be free of hunger" (FAO 1996).

When these rights were first advanced, the international community did
not have the means to honor them; they were little more than pious wishes.
In today's world, however, many of the economic, administrative, and logistic
barriers to realizing these objectives have fallen away. Global food supplies are
adequate: there is plenty of food to go around. Global markets for basic grains
are well developed and highly integrated. Satellite technology and improved
forecasting mean that information on weather patterns and crop conditions is
now readily available, providing an effective early warning system of potential
shortfalls and crises. An effective set of international institutions is now capable
of soliciting food contributions and delivering emergency assistance to populations facing distress from natural disasters and economic dislocation. Logistics
capabilities have improved dramatically. This system is by no means perfect;
chronic food shortages still plague a number of countries (FAO 2003). But at
least one reason for the decline in the incidence of outright famine is the development of highly effective humanitarian aid institutions.

Just as the sources of food shortage and famine and the effectiveness of
relief efforts must be traced to human rather than natural causes, so must the
effectiveness of relief efforts. In a number of countries in Africa—the Great
Lakes region, Sudan, Somalia—both the source of shortages and the inability
of outsiders to provide timely relief can be traced to civil war or weak states
that do not control their territory. Humanitarian efforts face difficulties in these

cases largely because of the absence of centralized authority, a clear interlocutor for outside agencies.

A second, more rare set of cases includes those in which authoritarian governments exercise full control over their populations but fail to respond in a timely fashion to signs of food distress and limit external access for other political reasons. The socialist famines in the Ukraine, China, Cambodia, and North Korea all fall into this category. Such settings raise fundamental ethical questions for donors. It is impossible in such circumstances to guarantee that all aid is being used appropriately. Should the international community provide assistance even if it means prolonging the life of a despotic regime? Does aid prolong the very policies that led to the famine in the first place, creating a problem of moral hazard? Should donors provide assistance even if some portion of that assistance is diverted to undeserving groups, including the military and party cadre? If the decision is made to provide assistance, how can donors guarantee that food aid reaches vulnerable groups and achieves other objectives, such as inducing economic reforms or empowering new social groups?

These questions are partly ethical in nature, and in the conclusion of the book we consider some ways of thinking about them. But these questions also require attention to empirical issues of political economy, bargaining, and strategy. We can make a more informed judgment of the core ethical questions—how and even whether to aid North Korea—by shedding light on how the aid relationship actually works in practice.

The aid effort that began in 1995 consisted of three distinct components: aid channeled through multilateral institutions, the World Food Programme (WFP) in particular; bilateral aid outside the WFP; and assistance from the NGO sector. The NGO sector has made important contributions to easing the crisis; several excellent studies have reviewed this experience in some detail (Smith 2002; Flake and Snyder 2003; Reed 2004), and we provide an overview in chapter 4. But the bulk of food assistance has passed through multilateral and bilateral channels, and we focus most of our attention on them.

We consider this humanitarian response through two distinct lenses, the first having to do with the relationship between the donors and the North Korean government (chapters 4 and 5); the second looking in more detail at the donors themselves (chapter 6). A growing literature on the political economy of aid has underscored the mixed-motive nature of any aid relationship.[5] Donors give aid for a variety of political, economic, and humanitarian reasons and naturally want to assure that their objectives are being achieved. They do so through the imposition of conditions of various sorts (*ex ante* controls) and monitoring and review procedures (*ex post* controls). In the case of humanitarian assistance, these conditions involve efforts to target vulnerable populations and guarantee that they are being reached.

Aid recipients have their own reasons for taking aid, and while some conditions attached to aid may be perfectly acceptable—and incentives of donors and recipients therefore aligned—other conditions attached to aid entail costs of various sorts. These range from adopting politically difficult policies, as is the case with International Monetary Fund programs, to accepting external monitoring of aid, as is the case with humanitarian assistance.

An increasingly skeptical literature has argued that the incentives embodied in the aid relationship are almost by necessity perverse. Burnside and Dollar (1997) were among the first to challenge the notion that aid could induce policy change, arguing that aid should therefore only be extended where policy conditions were ripe. Yet the efficacy of aid even in countries with good policies is now in doubt as well (Easterly, Levine, and Roodman 2003). Aid may also have perverse political effects. It is a pure rent to the incumbent government, which (in the absence of adequate monitoring at least) can dole it out with the sole object of maintaining its incumbency. This issue of supporting the regime has been a recurrent one in discussions of North Korea, where most aid passes through the Public Distribution System. At least some humanitarian groups regarded the PDS, embodying a high degree of nominal centralization and direct state control, as a useful instrument for delivering aid. Recent research also suggests the aid may actually undermine the quality of governance by encouraging rent seeking and diversion (Knack 2000; Svensson 2000). Moreover, aid is only likely to be effective under a limited set of political conditions. For example, Svensson (1999) finds that the growth-promoting effects of aid are conditional on political rights, which needless to say are altogether absent in North Korea.

A central theme of our study is the incredible difficulty the humanitarian community has had in dealing with the North Korean government. In part for reasons of political accountability, in part because of concerns over effectiveness, the humanitarian effort has sought to target its assistance to North Korea to vulnerable groups, mainly children, pregnant and nursing women, and the elderly, as well as to monitor those priorities closely (chapter 4). At virtually every point, the government placed roadblocks in the way of the donor community's achieving this objective, which it met to the extent that it did only through extraordinary perspicacity and flexibility. We detail the restrictions placed on external monitoring and show that, as diligent as outside monitors are, it is virtually impossible for them to track food donations within the country from the port to the final consumer. This is not a secret; it is a well-known fact, and no one knows it better than the dedicated cadre of aid workers and NGOs themselves.

The question of monitoring is closely related to the third rail of humanitarian assistance: the perennial problem of diversion of aid to unintended purposes and undeserving recipients (chapter 5). We argue that the term "diversion" is used casually and in fact encompasses several quite different phenomena. The most common image is of the military seizing grain to feed the army and party cadre. But the political and military elite has a variety of channels for accessing food, including first draw on the domestic harvest, access to unmonitored imports from China and South Korea, and access to grain via the market. This type of large-scale centralized diversion no doubt occurs but is almost certainly exaggerated.

Much less attention has been given to the effect of the huge differences between controlled and market prices on the incentive to divert food for economic reasons: to sell it in the market. These incentives operate with respect to farmers, who can earn more by selling grain to the market than by surrendering it to the state. They operate with respect to those with access to imports, and they almost certainly operate with respect to aid as well. This aspect of diversion is almost certainly underestimated in standard accounts, and its effects are not straightforward. There is no question that such diversion reduces the amount of food going to intended beneficiaries. But ironically it also has the unintended, and presumably positive, long-term consequence of promoting the marketization of the economy and even lowering prices; in our discussion of reform, we consider who the winners and losers were from this process of diversion and marketization.

Before turning to those issues, however, we step back and consider the aid process from a macropolitical perspective. Although the World Food Programme is the immediate supplier of food, the WFP does not have its own stocks and ultimately depends on appeals issued to governments. Moreover, a number of governments deliver aid bilaterally, outside of the WFP channel. In addition to their humanitarian motives, what, if anything, were the donor governments trying to do by supplying aid to North Korea? This question is the subject of chapter 6.

Despite the continuing refrain that humanitarian objectives should be held separate from politics, particularly in the United States, this separation has proven impossible to maintain in practice; aid is closely tied up with shifting political objectives on the part of donor governments and the publics to which they are ultimately accountable. We begin with brief sketches of the aid behavior of the major donors: the United States, Japan, South Korea, the European

Union, and China. In a handful of instances, political factors have pushed governments to withhold aid; Japan provides some of the starkest examples of this political linkage. For the most part, however, political calculations have had the opposite effect, leading governments to maintain or increase food aid to entice North Korea into negotiations. This has even been the case since the onset of the current nuclear standoff in October 2002.

A consideration of donor interests cannot consider individual country programs in isolation, however; foreign assistance involves important issues of coordination. When donor objectives are not aligned, it becomes more difficult to maintain a united front vis-à-vis a recalcitrant recipient, and problems of moral hazard can quickly arise. In the early 2000s, patience with North Korea began to wane in the United States and Japan. Overall stresses on the emergency relief system made it harder to meet targets, and multilateral aid declined. Yet North Korea has been able to compensate partly if not fully for these losses by increasing EU involvement, continuing reliance on quasi-commercial imports of food and other inputs from China, and, above all, by the growing generosity of South Korea. Although we focus primarily on food, we show how South Korea's humanitarian assistance is but one aspect of the much broader shift in that country's foreign policy that began under President Kim Dae-jung (1998–2003) and has accelerated under President No Mu-hyŏn (2003–present): namely, to seek an improvement of political and military relations on the peninsula through a process—and a highly costly and unreciprocated one—of economic engagement.

Marketization and Reform: From Socialist Famine to the New Shortages

In chapter 7, we return to the domestic front by looking at the DPRK's response to the immediate aftermath of the famine. On the one hand, the government sought to reassert control over a country that had come apart during the great famine. On the other hand, the coping strategies that households pursued during the famine produced fundamental changes in the political economy of North Korea, including extensive marketization.

The emergence of markets is often associated with leadership decisions and top-down reforms, such as those launched in China in the late 1970s that finally came to North Korea twenty-five years later, in 2002. But the marketization fueled by the famine, we argue, can be traced in part to the coping strategies of local party, government, and military units together with individual enterprises and households. As the Public Distribution System collapsed and the market came to supply a greater and greater share of total consumption, a new divide appeared in North Korean society, between those who could augment their wages with foreign exchange and other sources of income and those who could not. A new poor emerged as a result, with the cities once again being among the most severely affected.

Marketization struck fear into the hearts of political authorities, who saw it as the opening wedge for the emergence of an economy and private sphere beyond the clutches of the state. We interpret the reforms of 2002 not simply as a progressive effort to move the North Korean economy in a new direction but also as a defensive move designed to reassert control. Whatever the intent of the reforms, however, they resulted in very high levels of inflation. Food prices rose far faster than nominal wages, resulting in a sharp decline in the welfare of those forced to purchase food in the market. Farmers probably benefited from this change in relative prices, but the result was to exacerbate the stark division we have noted between haves and have-nots.

What effect did marketization and the reforms have on welfare in North Korea? The same patterns of secrecy and obstruction that have hampered the implementation of relief activities militate against the evaluation of their effectiveness as well. We can, however, evaluate the four UN-sponsored nutrition surveys that have been done to date, as well as a variety of other sorts of evidence that has not been fully exploited in this context, including refugee interviews and data on prices. We conclude chapter 7 by using this information—sketchy as it is—as a guide to where North Korea stood ten years after the famine of the mid-1990s and roughly five years into the reforms. We find that, as of 2005, there had been some marginal improvement in nutritional status since the peak of the famine. There is also considerable cross-regional variation in nutritional status, however, as well as ample evidence that this major humanitarian disaster was by no means over.

Looking Forward

As we sent this manuscript to press in mid-2006, the Six-Party Talks remained stalled. Most analysts, however, could see the contours of the "grand bargain" that would resolve the standoff. In return for abandoning its nuclear weapons programs, returning to the Treaty on the Non-Proliferation of Nuclear Weapons, and accepting international safeguards inspections, the other parties to the talks—most importantly, the United States—would offer North Korea a security guarantee, a promise of recognition, and eventual entry into the international financial institutions. The deal would also include a package of additional humanitarian assistance as well as energy from South Korea in the form of electricity.

We would like to believe that the relaxation of North Korea's security concerns will provide an opportunity for a serious reform effort that will move North Korea, however gradually, toward a more market-oriented economy and a more liberal if not fully democratic polity. Unfortunately, we are skeptical on both counts. The reform process through mid-2006 appeared inauspicious, and there are no signs of political relaxation; to the contrary. Moreover, we anticipate that North Korea will rely heavily on international largesse for some time.

In the conclusion, we take up the ethical issues of dealing with a country like North Korea. The core of the ethical dilemma surrounding engagement with North Korea is the political leadership of the country's apparent lack of concern for the welfare of the people. As we document, the regime has acted with systematic recklessness and callousness. In this context, we take seriously the argument that the country should not be assisted at all and note, for example, that some of the most courageous survivors of North Korea's prison system have advocated a strategy of cutting North Korea off and seeking to hasten its decline (see, e.g., C. Kang 2005).

Few would rue the disappearance of the Kim Jŏng-il regime, but wishful thinking is not a substitute for policy. Given that North Korea has already survived a famine that ranks among the most destructive of the twentieth century, there is precious little evidence that denying it access to food—even if such an effort could be orchestrated—would produce regime change. In the interim, the innocent—who have no effective control over the policies and behavior of their government—would continue to suffer. We see no substitute for a policy of seeking to aid the North Korean people while engaging the government and encouraging its political as well as economic evolution.

Yet if the world is going to continue to provide aid, we should be clear-eyed about the terms on which it is provided. Two issues continue to loom for the humanitarian effort: coordination among the donors and the design of the relief effort itself. We make a practical as well as principled case for multilateralism. The supply of effectively unconditional aid by South Korea and China has undercut the effectiveness of the multilateral humanitarian effort through the World Food Programme. Bilateral development assistance runs the same risks of supporting ineffectual policies. Second, the WFP and the donors have the obligation to continue to bring to the world's attention not only the humanitarian conditions in North Korea—the ongoing shortages of food—but the conditions under which outside donors operate. It is an obligation of those who seek to engage with North Korea—as we believe we must—also to speak the truth about the conditions in which North Koreans live. This book is designed in some small way to further that objective.

PART I

Perspectives on the Famine

CHAPTER TWO

The Origins of the Great Famine

Tolstoy leads off *Anna Karenina* with the well-known observation that while happy families are all alike, unhappy families are all unhappy in their own ways. So it is with famines. The more closely we study these complex and rare social events, the more we have come to appreciate not only their intricacies but their idiosyncrasies; not all famines arise from similar causes. A central debate in the famine literature, however, concerns the relative influence of food availability decline versus problems in entitlement and distribution: the bundle of legal and moral rights that determine the access of particular groups or individuals to food. Amartya Sen's (1981) study of four major twentieth-century famines noted that the prefamine period was not necessarily characterized by inadequate aggregate food supply or a significant decline in the availability of food. Rather, he argued, the famine resulted from entitlement failures, particularly the failure of "exchange entitlements": the ability of certain groups to purchase food on the market (for a critical review, see Devereux 2001). Although Sen's initial formulation included reference to entitlements in the form of transfers from the state, only in subsequent work (Dreze and Sen 1989) did he and others begin to elaborate how work, production, and exchange entitlements were embedded in systems of political rights, what Appadurai (1984) called "enfranchisement," and de Waal (1997) captured in the idea of an "anti-famine political contract" (see also Ravallion 1987; Devereux 1993:76–82).

In adopting this entitlement framework to the study of the North Korean case, we make two amendments and extensions. First, it is critically important to begin the analysis of any famine with an understanding of the existing set of entitlements. The failure of socialist systems of entitlements is core to many of the greatest famines of the twentieth century, including those in the Soviet Union (1921–22, 1946–47, and in the Ukraine in 1932–34), China (1958–62), Cambodia (1979), and Ethiopia (1984–85), as well as in North Korea. Although we believe that these entitlement failures can be attributed in part to the authoritarian nature of political rule, socialist systems do have distinctive features that warrant elaboration.

The entitlement approach was initially formulated with respect to settings in which markets failed because the poor did not command adequate resources to purchase food. As we will show in chapters 3, 6, and 7, these circumstances came to pertain in North Korea as well as markets emerged in the wake of the famine and a succession of economic reforms. Yet in the prefamine and famine period, entitlement failures did not have to do with the market but with the socialist production and distribution system, or what might be called the socialist social contract. In socialist systems, the discrete types of entitlements that have been distinguished in other settings—for example, entitlements to work, to produce, to exchange, and to transfers from the government—are all determined very directly by the state (Kornai 1992). Assignment to a particular job and even work location is a function of manpower planning and, as we will see, political calculations. Cultivators do not have independent rights to their property or products, either; rather, any food that is available to them is a function of procurement and allocation decisions taken by the state. Markets are completely suppressed or tightly controlled, and so at least in theory there are no independent sources of supply; exchange entitlements in the sense Sen initially intended do not exist or emerge only as the economy marketizes.

As a result, to the extent that we can speak of entitlement failures, they are entirely and more immediately state failures: the failure to pursue sustainable agricultural policies (Walker 1989; Devereux 1993:133–137); the failure to procure adequate grain supplies from the agricultural sector; the failure to distribute food equitably, particularly in the context of shortages. In the next chapter, we argue that while the government did make efforts to equalize the distribution of food during the famine,[1] it ultimately failed to do so because of both a surprisingly decentralized system of distribution and deep-seated political biases in the distribution of food. We thus circle back to observations about the close relationship among political regime type, rights, and famine.

A second observation that we explore in more detail in this chapter is that the line between food availability and entitlements is particularly blurred in such a system. It is increasingly recognized that food availability cannot be treated as exogenous, for example, a result of weather-related shocks such as drought or floods. Rather, aggregate food availability is also strongly affected by a variety of government policy choices. We must thus consider decisions that affect patterns of production and risk in the domestic economy. Many of the problems that North Korea faced in the 1990s were the result of policy choices the regime made with respect to agriculture that substantially increased the risk of production shortfalls and even weather-related shocks.

In a closed-economy context, socialist governments facing a decline in food availability have little choice in the short run but to restrict consumption directly. However, this Hobson's choice sidesteps external sources of supply. When the early famine literature spoke of food availability, it did so with respect to some delimited geographic space, typically the nation-state or the relevant subnational unit within it, such as the region or province. In considering the history of famines, this made sense because political leaders have not traditionally been able to command resources outside their jurisdictions.

But as global markets not only for food but for other commodities and capital have become more integrated, countries are in principle able to command foreign food. They do this either by trading other products in exchange for it or by maintaining the capacity to borrow so that food can be purchased from abroad. Moreover, as international humanitarian institutions have evolved, countries increasingly have recourse to what might be called international humanitarian entitlements, however imperfectly defined these remain. De Waal (1997) has focused renewed attention on both the short- and longer-term failures of the humanitarian community in stopping famine, but we must also consider the responses of governments themselves. In the case of shortages, or even of the risk of shortages, governments have the obligation to exploit external sources of supply fully. Indeed, under the United Nation's International Covenant on Economic, Social and Cultural Rights, to which North Korea has been a party since 1981, states have an affirmative obligation to seek and facilitate international assistance to ensure the availability of food during times of shortage (Haggard and Noland 2005:app. B).

However, socialist governments that pursue policies of self-sufficiency limit their capacity to purchase food and frequently fail to avail themselves of international assistance as well. As a result, they effectively deny their citizens entitlements just as clearly as more localized entitlement or political contract failures do. When North Korea was faced with external shocks—and they were severe ones—the government failed to respond in ways that would increase its ability to purchase food, whether through earned foreign exchange or by borrowing. Moreover, the government was slow to appeal for outside support and even placed roadblocks on the delivery of foreign assistance (chapter 4). To under-stand the North Korean famine—and many others, we would suggest—we must consider why governments fail over both the long and short run to avail themselves fully of external sources of supply.

We tackle the causes of the great famine in two steps. In this chapter, we take up the question of food availability and possible government responses to a decline in production. In chapter 3, we consider the question of socialist entitle-ments by dissecting the public distribution system (PDS) and its collapse in the 1990s. Throughout, we focus on issues of human agency and political economy. Natural causes—even ones such as the weather—often gain their force because of prior political and policy choices. North Korea did experience severe floods in 1995 and a succession of natural disasters thereafter as well. But the country's vulnerability to those conditions was exacerbated at every point by decisions the government made that compounded risk.

Socialist Agriculture, North Korean Style

Following the Korean War, debates emerged within the Korean Workers' Party over the appropriate course of reconstruction. These debates closely mirrored those taking place in Moscow at the time. Revisionists argued for a more bal-anced strategy that would pay more attention to light industry, consumer goods, and food production (Okonogi 1994). With Kim Il-sŏng's rejection of de-Stalinization and his consolidation of complete political control vis-à-vis his factional rivals (Lankov 2005a), the government adopted the classic Stalinist strategy of promoting heavy industry. Socialist industrialization typically rests on the mobilization of rural labor into the industrial workforce; in addition to the squeeze on agriculture, this labor mobilization constitutes one important source of primitive accumulation in socialist systems. Yet this industrialization strategy conflicted with the equally important goal of achieving food self-suf-ficiency, an objective that was closely tied both to security concerns and the ideological commitment to *chuch'e* that first surfaced in the mid-1950s.

As a result of North Korea's industrial ambitions, the country exhibits a somewhat anomalous economic structure. Despite a relatively low per capita income, the country was fairly urbanized at the outset of the famine, with fully 61 percent of the population living in urban areas. Only 31 percent of the workforce was in agriculture, with fully 41 percent in industry and the remain-der in services and other activities (UNDP 1998).[2] This economic structure had important implications. In contrast to many other famines, vulnerability to food shortage was by no means limited to the countryside but struck urban workers particularly hard as well.

In pursuing a policy of food self-sufficiency, the most basic problem confronting the North Korean leadership was the inauspicious nature of the country's natural resource endowment. At the time of partition, Korean industry, and almost all heavy industry, was concentrated in the North, developed by the Japanese as a component of their larger strategy of controlling Manchuria. The southern part of the country was the rice bowl. Only some 20 percent of North Korean land can be cultivated; the rest comprises mountainous areas that offer extremely limited scope for agricultural expansion.[3] Given its northern latitude, weather conditions are also far from favorable. It is cold, and growing seasons are short.

Particularly after the peninsular war, the government set about establishing a thoroughly orthodox centrally planned economy, remarkable only in the degree to which markets were suppressed. Land belonging to Korean landlords and Japanese colonialists had been seized and redistributed to the peasantry during 1945–46. Land reform was accompanied by a particularly dramatic fall in agricultural output and the first of a succession of recurrent food shortages. Because of the increasingly rigid partition, the government was unable to draw on supplies from the South as the northern part of the country had historically done. The new administration responded by temporarily banning private trade in food and launching compulsory grain seizures in the rural areas during the winter of 1945–46. This policy of forcible rural grain seizures in response to urban shortages was to be repeated during subsequent food emergencies in 1954 (in conjunction with collectivization) and again in 1970–73. Efforts by the state to expand its take from the harvest undoubtedly constituted an important historical memory shaping the behavior of cultivators into the 1990s. Such seizures inevitably create perverse incentives, encouraging farmers to preharvest, hide and consume grain, and divert food toward the black market, barter, and other nonstate channels such as transfers within extended family networks; as we will show in the next chapter, all these factors came into play during the famine.

Following the Korean War, the government rapidly collectivized agriculture as a means of supporting the industrial push, introduced quantitative planning in production, established state marketing and distribution of grain, and in 1957 finally prohibited private production and trade of grain once and for all. Henceforth, co-ops would sell only to the state; merchants had to join cooperatives or find other employment to maintain eligibility for rations (Lankov 2005a:179). Beginning in 1959 and motivated by military as well as economic concerns, food security was pursued through self-sufficiency not only at the national level but also at the provincial and even county levels as well (Lee 2000; S. Lee 2003). This strategy resulted in a distribution system that was in fact decentralized in certain respects since local officials were responsible for coordinating demand and supply within their jurisdictions. Nonfarm households obtained grain and some other food items through a rationing system, the public distribution system or PDS, which we take up in more detail in the next chapter. It is only necessary to note here that for urban consumers, the PDS constituted their only access to food.

In pursuing the goal of self-sufficiency, the government sought to compensate for natural resource constraints and the relatively limited share of the workforce devoted to agriculture through three core strategies: expanding cropland; shifting output from traditional food crops such as tubers, millet, and potatoes in favor of higher-yield grains, namely, rice and corn; and, above all, adopting an industrial approach to agricultural production that paralleled the "big push" approach to industry. This last component of North Korean agriculture is key to understanding the country's subsequent vulnerability.

Particularly from the 1960s, the government aggressively pursued the "four modernizations" of "mechanization, electrification, irrigation, and chemicalization." The result was one of the world's most input-intensive agricultural systems, with unusually high use of chemical fertilizers and pesticides. Yields increased but were highly vulnerable to availability of these crucial inputs, either from imports or from the industrial sector, which also relied on imported inputs. Fertilizer provides the central example. North Korea developed its own capacity in fertilizer production with Soviet assistance, but these facilities in turn were dependent on petrochemical feedstock that came directly from imports or was dependent on imported oil.

In response to food shortages in 1970–73, the degree of centralization of agricultural planning intensified. Local authorities were increasingly marginalized with respect to supply management. Food production was subject to the same process of input-output standardization as any other economic activity. Instructions to state farms and cooperatives were specified down to the level of fertilizer usage by individual farm households. In 1973 a Cultural Revolution–type movement—the Three Revolutions Team Movement—dispatched young Communists to initiate ideological, cultural, and technical education of farm households. The movement established new rural educational institutions and reassigned existing rural extension officials, requiring them to enroll in *chuch'e* curriculum programs. This social engineering eroded knowledge of, respect for, and influence of traditional farming techniques and further stifled individual initiative (S. Lee 2003)

The External Environment Sours

The crisis of the 1990s had its origins in a complex set of external and internal developments that began to unfold in the late 1980s. Notwithstanding its claims to self-reliance, North Korea had in fact long been dependent on outside assistance, with first the Soviet Union and later China playing the role of patron. Not only did the Soviet Union finance North Korea's recurrent current account deficits, but Soviet pricing of coal and oil exports reflected additional subsidies (Eberstadt, Rubin, and Tretyakova 1995).

Facing economic constraints of its own and perhaps frustrated by North Korean unwillingness to repay accumulated debts, the Soviet Union began to cut aid and reduce its support beginning in 1987.[4] In 1990 the Soviet Union initiated a diplomatic breakthrough with South Korea and simultaneously demanded that North Korea pay world market prices—and in foreign exchange—for Soviet goods. The Soviets also began to terminate technology transfer in the military sphere; this proved important because the export of arms based on Soviet designs constituted an important source of foreign exchange.

This fundamental change in North Korea's external relations not only represented a profound political shock (see Oberdorfer 1997:chaps. 9 and 10); the end of barter and debt financing, and the subsequent collapse of the Soviet economy, constituted a profound economic shock as well. The decline in imports from Russia in 1991 was equivalent to 40 percent of all of North Korea's imports. By 1993 imports from Russia were only 10 percent of their 1987–90 average and subsequently declined to irrelevance (figure 2.1; Eberstadt, Rubin, and Tretyakova 1995). In the face of this massive trade shock, the North Korean industrial economy began to implode.

Under these conditions, the regime faced two basic options, and although we tell the story with respect to food, it applied to consumption more generally.[5] The country could either reduce domestic consumption to bring it into line with shrinking domestic supplies, or it could relieve the domestic supply constraint by importing food from abroad. The latter strategy in turn could be achieved through three non–mutually exclusive means: increasing exports to pay for needed imports, sustaining the ability to borrow on commercial terms, or seeking foreign aid.

The regime began to repress demand, initiating a "let's eat two meals a day" campaign in 1991.[6] In 1987 the government also substantially increased food imports and became a net food importer (S. Lee 2005:6). But the government proved unable to sustain the needed level of imports into the 1990s. Perhaps

$ US (millions)

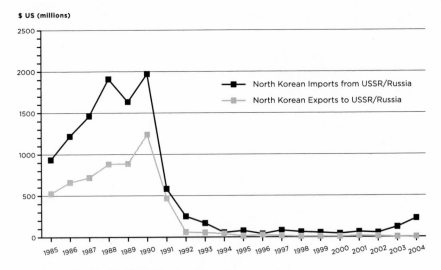

FIGURE 2.1. Trade with USSR/Russia, 1985–2004

Source: Eberstadt 2003 for 1985–2001; IMF 2006 for 2002–2004. *Note: Eberstadt data reported as exports from the Soviet Union/Russia. 10% c.i.f./f.o.b. adjustment made.*

because of the country's unrelenting emphasis on autarky and self-reliance, the political leadership seemed strangely unable to grasp the epochal nature of the changes around it and took only limited and woefully inadequate steps to boost exports or reestablish access to commercial borrowing.

Efforts with respect to expanding exports were not auspicious. During the cold war, North Korea's fraternal allies complained bitterly about the low quality of the North Korean manufactures they were forced to accept as part of politically determined barter trade. Arms sales, particularly to both Iran and Iraq during their decade-long war in the 1980s, had been an important source of revenue, a kind of franchise granted to North Korea by the Soviets. But entering the 1990s, North Korean arms exports fell victim to declining global demand, intensified competition from Eastern Europe, and the increasing obsolescence of Soviet-era designs as the new Russian government became less and less willing to support Pyongyang with the transfer of current technologies.

In 1991 the government took its first, tentative step toward mimicking the export processing zones that had sprung up throughout the Asia Pacific since the 1960s. Yet nearly every aspect of this effort—from the geographical location of the first zone in the isolated N'ajin-Sönbong corridor to the lack of a clear and credible legal foundation for the zone[7]—reflected lack of North Korean understanding of the needs of foreign investors. Not until the mid-1990s, when the famine was in full swing, would the leadership attempt to revive the virtually dormant N'ajin-Sŏnbong zone, and not until the late 1990s would it begin to explore other locations that made more economic sense, such as along the Chinese border (Sinŭiju) or more proximate to South Korea (Kaesŏng). Given the options investors had to choose from, it is not surprising that missions sent abroad to attract foreign investment into the zone in 1995–96—at the height of the famine—proved largely fruitless. North Korea attracted little investor interest beyond some speculative Hong Kong money, and the bulk of that was devoted not to manufacturing but to a resort and casino designed to attract Chinese tourists.

It could be argued that the export sector was vulnerable to the same constraints as those facing the economy as a whole, including the decline of reliable power supplies and the collapse of the transport infrastructure. There is certainly truth in this argument, yet these constraints were precisely what early export processing zones—whether in Korea and Taiwan in the 1960s or China in the 1980s—were trying to circumvent. Estimates vary, but between 1990 and 1995 North Korea's merchandise exports fell by 50 to 60 percent (Noland 2000). Over the same period, Vietnam, which suffered a similar trade shock with the collapse of the Soviet Union, nearly tripled its exports by reforming with alacrity and making itself attractive to foreign investors.[8] External shocks alone cannot explain these differences.

In the short run, the alternative to earning foreign exchange through exports would have been to borrow money on international capital markets. Financial markets are even less forgiving than other foreign investors, however, and North Korea had thoroughly burned its bridges in this regard. In the 1970s, the North Korean government contracted loans extended from foreign, mostly Japanese and French, banks as well as a flood of suppliers' credits extended by Western companies eager to do business. Erik Cornell (2002:5–6), Sweden's first ambassador to North Korea, describes how expensive machinery was left to rust in warehouses because of failure to coordinate its purchase with factory construction or power. Expensive prototypes were built largely to demonstrate technological capability, and great sums were squandered on luxurious cars for the nomenklatura and fancy electrical equipment for theaters and museums. Payments quickly lapsed, and North Korea effectively defaulted on its obligations Rarely, Cornell concludes, "have trading relations been established, and contracts and agreements of this scale and magnitude entered into, between parties wallowing in such monumental delusions with regard to each other's principles, intentions, priorities, production capacity and social mores" (2002:6).

The government had also accumulated a substantial foreign debt during the 1970s and 1980s to the Soviet Union and China. Virtually all that debt had fallen into arrears as well.[9] Reestablishment of access to Western financial markets was no doubt further constrained by growing tension over the regime's nuclear ambitions, which began to surface in the second half of 1992. As a result of its past behavior and mounting political tensions, the capacity of the government to borrow was limited to little more than trade credits, and even such short-term credits required substantial courage on the part of the lender. For many transactions, North Korea was reduced to paying cash out of dwindling foreign exchange reserves.

The aid option was also constrained, although again North Korea's own political and policy choices were an important component of that failure as well. As we have seen, the Soviet Union had already tired of providing endless, unrequited support. Once the transition to a new foreign policy occurred under Gorbachev and particularly with the coming of democratic rule throughout the Eastern bloc, support for North Korea quickly became an anachronism, championed in Russia, for example, by a dwindling faction of disaffected nationalists. Even China, as we will discuss in more detail in chapter 4, tired of providing assistance. North Korea lacked diplomatic relations with the West outside of the Scandinavian countries, foreclosing bilateral aid; not until the second half of the 1990s did it pursue an active diplomacy to build these ties and secure assistance through them. Nor was North Korea a member of the international financial institutions such as the World Bank, Asian Development Bank, and International Monetary Fund (IMF) that could have served as sources of assistance on concessional terms. Again, it was not until the aftermath of the famine in the mid-1990s that the country would begin exploratory contacts with these organizations.

Responsibility for North Korea's failure to gain entry into the international financial institutions lies in part with the advanced industrial states. Even in the late 1990s and early 2000s, North Korean efforts in this regard were blocked by the United States and Japan.[10] Even if these political constraints had not existed, however, the regime showed little willingness to subject itself to the conditionality, transparency, and monitoring associated with membership in the international financial institutions; to attribute North Korea's isolation to foreign actors alone is at least somewhat disingenuous. IMF staff report that during a 1996 informational mission—still the high-famine period—the North

Korean delegation lost interest when it became apparent that IMF funds would not be immediately forthcoming. At a roundtable on agricultural recovery convened by UNDP in 1998, discussed in more detail in chapter 3, North Korean representatives made it clear that they were unwilling to entertain any fundamental institutional changes in the system of cooperative farming. The purpose of the meeting in their view was simply to secure support for their rehabilitation efforts. Indeed, during one 1998 UN meeting on agricultural recovery, the North Korean delegation walked out when one of the foreign participants mentioned the word "reform."

A particularly revealing example of the challenges associated with North Korean participation in the IFIs concerns the availability and quality of data. In May 1997, when North Korea's membership fees to the United Nations were being assessed, North Korea dramatically lowered data on per capita GNP provided to the UN Budget and Finance Committee in order to decrease membership dues. A year later, to acquire UNDP and IMF support, the government reported very different statistics. In both cases, the data came from the same source: the Chosŏn Central Bureau of Statistics (KIEP 2004:25–26).

Instead of expanding legitimate commercial transactions or international borrowing, the 1990s witnessed an intensification of illicit activities, including smuggling and counterfeiting. These sorts of illicit activities, together with legal, though diplomatically contentious, missile sales, accounted for perhaps one-third of North Korean foreign exchange earnings and would later become the focus of U.S.-led interdiction activities and sanctions under the administration of George W. Bush (we provide a more detailed outline of these activities in appendix 1).

The difficulties North Korea faced in earning foreign exchange and its inability to borrow from commercial or international public sources had important implications for its capacity to import. Table 2.1 tracks North Korean grain imports by source in the first half of the 1990s and shows the dangerous instability of the country's commercial grain transactions. Canadian and Thai imports were volatile, and imports from other sources declined sharply in 1992.

Of particular interest is the course of North Korea's grain trade with China, a crucial episode that we take up in more detail in chapters 4 and 6. China quietly followed the Soviet Union by establishing diplomatic relations with South Korea in 1992. In the period immediately following the collapse of the Soviet Union, however, China had stepped into the economic breach and became North Korea's primary supplier of both oil and food, most of it almost certainly on "friendship" or concessional terms.[11] By 1993 China supplied North Korea

TABLE 2.1. Grain Imports, 1991–97 (thousands of metric tons)

	1991	1992	1993	1994	1995	1996	1997
China	300	620	740	305	153	547	867
Syria	–	–	–	–	–	140	34
Thailand	90	20	78	52	162	30	38
Canada	350	80	160	–	–	–	–
Japan	–	–	–	–	370	132	–
EU	–	–	–	–	–	–	115
Other	550	110	115	133	277	201	576
Total	1,290	830	1,093	490	962	1,050	1,630

Note: Other includes imports from other countries and food aid from international organizations.
Source: Cho and Zang 1999.

with 77 percent of fuel imports and 68 percent of food imports (Cho and Zang 1999:26, table 1). But in that same year, China began to demand that it be paid in cash as well, a demand that was increasingly difficult given the tightening of sanctions during the nuclear crisis. China also pulled back on crucial exports of corn to North Korea. In 1994 there was a second, sharp reduction in North Korean imports from China. Preferential relations were reestablished in the wake of the U.S.-DPRK Agreed Framework of that year, and North Korea got some assistance in the form of heavy oil shipments from the United States under the agreement. Nonetheless, North Korea's food situation was already extraordinarily precarious at this point. If there was a single proximate external trigger to the North Korean famine, Chinese trade behavior during these crucial years is a plausible candidate.

One way to grasp the extent and effect of these external shocks is to consider the decline in the availability of fertilizer. The Ministry of Agriculture has estimated that the annual requirement of fertilizer nutrients (nitrogen, phosphorus, and potassium, or NPK) needed to maintain adequate levels of productivity is around 700,000 tons. As can be seen in figure 2.2, the availability of fertilizer showed a steady decline over the first half of the 1990s, reflecting a decline in imports of both fertilizer and the petroleum feedstock needed by North Korean plants. By 2000, when total availability had recovered somewhat, to 210,000 tons, only 28,300 tons was supplied by domestic production; the remaining 181,700 tons came from commercial imports and particularly bilateral and multilateral fertilizer assistance.

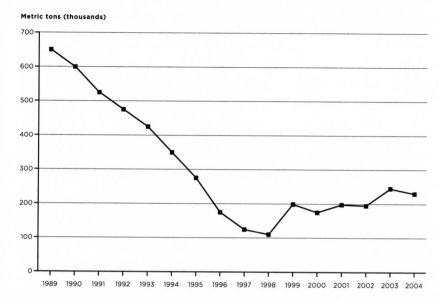

FIGURE 2.2. Fertilizer (NPK) Consumption, 1989–2004
Source: FAO/WFP 2004.

Domestic Response and the Debate over Proximate Causes

Faced with these shocks, the government did take a number of policy initiatives to increase domestic supplies. In December 1993, the government admitted that the Third Seven-Year Plan 1987–93 had not fulfilled its objectives. This admission was a surprising one for a government of this sort, although the failure was attributed to external shocks rather than any inherent problems in the socialist strategy. Some government actions marked departures from past policy and the first stirrings of the "reform from below" that occurred during the famine. The government increased the permissible scale of private gardens from 80 to 120 square meters, though the gardens remained merely privately tended, not privately owned, and were situated on marginal, nonirrigated land. Similarly, after an attempt to crack down on black markets before 1993, the government also extended the frequency and scope of farmers' markets. These markets were at least temporarily allowed to trade in grains, a major departure, as we will show in more detail below.

The dominant approach of the government, however, was to focus on technical fixes that reflected a continuation of past policy rather than policy reforms emphasizing producer incentives. Among the government's reforms were efforts to expand grain-sown areas, shift crop composition in favor of high-yield

rice and corn, maximize industrial inputs (subject to availability), and inten-
sify double-cropping and dense planting—in short, what it had done in the
past. Continuous cropping led to soil depletion, and the overuse of chemical
fertilizers contributed to acidification of the soil and eventually a reduction in
yields.[12] As yields declined, hillsides were denuded to bring more and more
marginal land into production. These measures contributed to soil erosion and
river silting and thus bear some responsibility for the catastrophic effects of the
flooding that occurred in 1995.

The increasing vulnerability associated with the government's strategy to increase
grain output provides the context for considering the effects of the succession of
natural disasters that struck the country from the middle of the decade (for a catalog of these, see Woo-Cumings 2002:27–29). Catastrophic floods hit the country
in July and August 1995. In mid-August, the North Korean government announced
that the floods had resulted in nearly two million tons of lost grain, the destruction
of over 300,000 hectares of cropland, and the displacement of 5.4 million people.[13]
The flooding played an important role in the politics of the crisis, since it provided
the opening for the government to portray the problem as a natural disaster, to
admit to catastrophic crop failures, and to seek international relief more openly.
For example, the government unit charged with obtaining international assistance
was renamed the Flood Damage Rehabilitation Committee (FDRC), a guise that
a number of foreign relief agencies found advantageous as well. The floods of 1995
were followed by less severe floods in July 1996 and by drought in 1997 and again
in 2000–2001 when the most serious postfamine shortages emerged.

In considering the effects of these various shocks, it is useful to start with
what we know about agricultural output. We know of serious food shortages in
1945–46, in 1954–55, and again in 1970–73 (see S. Lee 2003 for a discussion of
each of these episodes). Thereafter, the industrial approach to agriculture bore
some fruit before it started to reach limits in the late 1980s. We present the data
available in two ways. Figure 2.3 provides four official estimates of production
that are commonly used in discussions of North Korean food output: North
Korean official pronouncements and estimates from the Food and Agricultural
Organization (which most closely mirror official pronouncements), the United
States Department of Agriculture (USDA), and the South Korean Ministry of
Unification. Table 2.2 includes the same four sets of estimates shown in figure
2.3 but also all others by independent researchers of which we are aware.

As can be seen, these estimates differ on several crucial points. All four of the
series tracked in figure 2.3 show increases in production through most of the
1980s. They also all show a decline in output during the first half of the 1990s.
But differences in the timing and depth of this decline are highly consequential

Metric tons (millions)

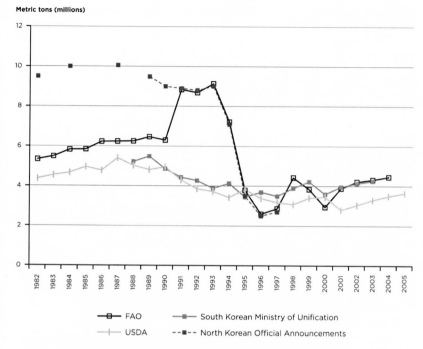

FIGURE 2.3. Estimates of North Korean Grain Production, 1982–2005
Sources: FAOSTAT; USDAFAS; Korean Ministry of Unification: Woo 2004.

for any interpretation of the famine. Those that appear to reflect more closely information provided by the government show a pattern of high initial output followed by a sharp collapse in 1995–96; Lee, Nakano, and Nabukuni (1995) also show an output collapse but from lower levels of production.

A number of factors, however, lead us to doubt the veracity of this "high initial output, rapid collapse" scenario or even the "steady output, sudden collapse" variant. First, there is evidence of several sorts (which we review in more detail in chapter 3) that the government was concerned about food availability well before the mid-1990s. This evidence includes stepped-up diplomatic efforts to secure external sources of supply, acknowledgment of difficulties and the tentative reforms noted above, hortatory campaigns to reduce consumption, and the first reports from defectors of food shortages in 1993. If domestic production really were as high as the official pronouncements or the FAO series show, there would have been no reason for food shortages in the absence of some fundamental change in entitlements. But there is no evidence of such a change.

TABLE 2.2. Domestic Production Estimates, 1990–96. (millions of metric tons in milled grain equivalent)

	1990	1991	1992	1993	1994	1995	1996
High initial output, rapid collapse							
Official announcements (UNDP 1998)	9.00	8.90	8.80	9.00	7.10	3.50	2.50
Roundtable	7.58	7.26	7.27	7.06	7.50	5.73	2.77
FAO	8.10	8.80	8.60	9.10	7.20	3.70	2.50
Steady output, sudden collapse							
Lee, Nakano, and Nabukuni 1995	5.79	5.72	5.84	5.82	5.85	5.90	2.84
Secular decline							
NUB	5.48	4.81	4.43	4.27	3.88	4.13	3.45
USDA/FAS	5.08	4.30	3.86	3.72	3.42	3.83	3.38
Kim 2003			4.43	3.90	2.92	3.77	2.60
WFP						4.08	2.84

Sources: Noland 2000, table 5.1; FAOSTAT n.d.

Second, there are strategic reasons for the government to present the estimates that it did. Caught up in a major foreign policy crisis in the first part of the decade, the political leadership did not want to reveal any signs of weakness or vulnerability to external pressure or sanctions. Once the government had admitted its difficulties, however, its incentives were almost exactly the opposite: the greater the production shortfall, the greater the humanitarian relief that would be warranted.

Third, there are some technical issues with the data that reflect the difficulty of dealing with a closed society. To this day, there is still some confusion about whether the North Korean numbers are reporting hulled grain. The high estimates for the earlier period might well be reporting harvests on an unhulled basis, thus overstating food availability. Conversely, for the political reasons noted above, the government may have switched to reporting hulled grain at some point to highlight the shortfall.

In our view, the "secular decline" story is much more plausible than those focusing simply on the short-run collapse of output. Agriculture, like the rest of the economy, saw a steady contraction over the first half of the decade, a result of declining inputs such as fertilizer (figure 2.2) and the limits of the government's industrial approach to food production. The estimates produced by the USDA and the South Korean Ministry of Unification indicate that grain production fell by more than 15 percent between 1990 and 1994, well before the floods. In our construction of a food balance sheet for the country, however, we entertain the possibility that these estimates might nonetheless still be high for 1996–97; as can be seen, it is in those two postflood years when there is the greatest divergence in the series since the mid-1990s. We therefore take that possibility into account.

Nonetheless, the review up to this point establishes two important points. First, as the situation deteriorated in the early 1990s, the government was fatally slow in adjusting to its changed economic circumstances. The deterioration in the country's external credit and balance of payments—not to mention its nuclear brinksmanship—made it difficult to pursue commercial sources of imports. But the government was also slow and secretive in exploring concessional sources of food as well. After a failed overture to the World Food Programme and South Korea in the early 1990s, it was not until the fall of 1994 that North Korea again opened an aid offensive by approaching the Japanese for assistance. In the absence of any sense of urgency emanating from the North Koreans themselves, it was unlikely that potential donors would respond aggressively. It was not until 1995 that the government openly appealed for outside support and even then the full magnitude of the crisis took some time to sink in. Not until 1996 did humanitarian assistance begin to flow into the country in any volume.

Second, this chronology, as well as information that we have on the timing of the onset of the famine (chapter 3), undermines the claim that the floods were the principal or even proximate determinant of food shortages (e.g., Woo-Cumings 2002, Smith 2005b). The flooding contributed to the food crisis both directly through the loss of stocks and the removal of farmland from production and indirectly through its impact on infrastructure and particularly the energy sector (Williams, von Hippel, and Hayes 2000). All the estimates reported in table 2.2 show a falloff of production in 1996, the year following the floods.

The agricultural sector, however, like the rest of the economy, had been in secular decline since the beginning of the decade, and the effects of the floods must be placed in the context of the other external shocks we have noted. On the basis of their econometric analysis of North Korean agricultural production, Heather Smith and Yiping Huang conclude that "the dominant triggering factor in the crisis was the sharp loss of supplies of agricultural inputs following the disruption of the trade with the socialist bloc from the late 1980s. . . . The contribution of climatic factors to the agricultural crisis, as stressed by North

Korea's policy-makers, was at most a secondary cause" (2003:756). This conclusion is supported by the computable general equilibrium model-based simulation of Marcus Noland, Sherman Robinson, and Tao Wang (2001), who find that restoration of flood-affected land and capital would have had but a minor impact on the availability of food.

Why the Delayed Adjustment?

Given our emphasis on the government's delay in making the necessary economic adjustments required to address the food shortages or seeking external assistance, we must ask the next logical question: why did the regime prove unable to adapt to its very changed circumstances? General arguments about the role of *chuch'e*, nationalism, and the ideological significance of self-reliance certainly constitute a general backdrop to understanding the regime's behavior.[14] But these ideas were quite plastic. Notwithstanding claims of self-reliance, the government had been highly dependent on socialist sources of aid for some time, and ultimately it did make a strong international appeal. Our answers to this crucial question are necessarily speculative, but it is worth reviewing some contending, although not mutually exclusive, hypotheses.

The first throws the responsibility back onto the international community. Under this interpretation, the government did in fact signal its distress and sent signals of its willingness to trade concessions of various sorts for economic assistance. But these appeals did not meet a favorable response and as a result may have discredited those within the North Korean government who were associated with them. The nuclear standoff of 1992–94 has been interpreted as an extended effort to secure not only security guarantees but economic assistance as well.[15] The failure of the International Atomic Energy Agency, South Korea, and the United States to resolve the crisis in a timely manner and the tightening of sanctions against the country constituted an important background condition for the famine.

Evidence supporting this hypothesis can be found in the 1991 opening of the N'ajin-Sonbŏng export-processing zone, which drew little investor interest, and a failed appeal to the World Food Programme in the same year (on the latter, see Natsios 1999:166). Most important for our purposes, however, are signs of more aggressive commercial diplomacy and "aid seeking" beginning in 1994. These proposals were initially either rebuffed or their significance ignored.[16] Particularly striking in this regard was a request made by the North Koreans at the end of the first round of postcrisis talks in Geneva for 2.5 million tons of food aid. This suggested a shortfall of staggering proportions, yet American negotiators do not appear to have appreciated the full implications of the admission (Wit, Poneman, and Galucci 2004:281). Selig Harrison (2002:142) reports that North Korea made a "food for peace" proposal as late as 1997 that was similarly ignored by the United States. Moreover, as we will show in our discussion of the aid regime below, the initial humanitarian response got caught up in efforts to use aid strategically as well as honest disagreements within the humanitarian community about the extent of the famine.

Before the second half of 1994, North Korean appeals were still not straightforward about the extent of the country's food distress. Even then, the North Korean authorities were trying to hide the extent of the problem, particularly as it affected the northeast of the country. The WFP mission of 1991 is revealing in this regard. After being called in, the assessment team was given no evidence that the country had any special food needs (Natsios 1999:166). From 1993 on, the growing evidence of famine leaking out of China was continually offset by mixed messages from the North Koreans. An additional problem arose from the fact that Pyongyang, to which foreigners had the most direct access, was protected from the worst of the food shortages by its highly privileged status. Subsequent accounts by resident foreigners note the emergence of shortages even in the foreign community (Harrold 2004:108–10), but even a highly trained observer could conclude in 1996 that malnutrition was not widespread (Nathanail 1996). In retrospect, of course, it is easy to see that the signs of famine were there, but the important point is that they were being read in spite of—not with the assistance of—the North Korean authorities.

Given the weakness of these signals, a second possible explanation for the delay focuses on divisions within the North Korean government itself over the priority that should be given to the military (hard-liners) and to economic reform (soft-liners); Selig Harrison (2002:chap. 4) offers this explanation most explicitly (see also Martin 2004:472–81). Harrison argues that Kim Jŏng-il was either a closet reformer at the time (which we strongly doubt) or forced to tolerate a certain degree of marketization as a result of the crisis (for which we provide more detailed evidence below). But according to Harrison, the government was riven between competing factions. Hard-liners ridiculed the idea that Pyongyang would get any help from Washington, Tokyo, and Seoul, which they believed were intent on bringing about the collapse of North Korea. Military and political concessions were therefore pointless and would not be reciprocated. The government's primary obligation was survival, which called for a strengthening of military capabilities, including through nuclear weapons if necessary. These calculations constituted the historical origin of the so-called military first politics—a new ideological emphasis under Kim Jŏng-il on the political role of the military in North Korean society—that we take up in more detail in chapter 8.

The reformers, by contrast, recognized that the nuclear issue was a stumbling block to normalization of relations with the United States and the liberalization of foreign economic policy. They were initially able to win concessions on opening the country to nuclear inspections, but the result was an uneasy internal compromise. As the international community came to doubt the veracity of North Korean claims and the United States began to exert pressure on the country, the reformers were discredited and forced onto the defensive.

As military tensions deepened, an additional security motive may have played a role in the decision to conceal the extent of the food problem. In December 1996, Kim Jŏng-il made a speech at Kim Il-sŏng University commemorating its fiftieth anniversary that was subsequently smuggled out of the country. While the veracity of such documents can always be challenged, the speech contains a wide-ranging review of the country's problems at the time that has the ring of authenticity to it. In it, Kim Jŏng-il explicitly states, "If the U.S. imperialists know that we do not have rice for the military they would immediately invade us" (1996). In the context of a severe crisis, such an admission of weakness might have been seen as risky. The very substantial appeal made to the United States at the end of the Geneva talks in 1994 could be interpreted in this light; with the crisis over, the government was in a position to reveal its true food needs (Wit, Poneman, and Galucci 2004:281).

The question of the responsibility for the nuclear standoff of 1992 and its subsequent escalation into full-blown crisis takes us far beyond our purposes here, but it is ultimately germane to any interpretation of the famine.[17] Were the North Koreans responding to the severe deterioration in their security environment, signs of aggressive intent from the United States, and botched negotiations? Or was the crisis ultimately of their own manufacture, an effort to extract concessions for fulfilling their obligations under the NPT and bilateral agreements with South Korea as well? If the latter is the case, as we are more inclined to believe, then the responsibility of the government only deepens. In either case, however, we can certainly imagine that the period of high international tension—followed almost immediately by the death of Kim Il-sŏng and a highly uncertain political transition—could result in a shift in favor of security considerations over preoccupation with economic issues and even food security.

But evidence from this period provided by defectors suggests yet another explanation for the slow adjustment and delay in seeking assistance, evidence that comports with the arguments and findings of Jean Dreze and Amartya Sen on the relationship between regime type and famine (Dreze and Sen 1989,

1991).[18] In a succession of steps stretching over two decades, Kim Jŏng-il took over political and administrative responsibilities from his father as well as being promoted within the military. Several journalistic accounts of the period based on defector interviews note that, during 1991 and 1992, Kim Il-sŏng—and perhaps Kim Jŏng-il as well—were being shielded from damaging information about the extent of economic deterioration.

Particularly interesting is Jasper Becker's reporting (2005:101–3) on the views of Yi Min-bok, a North Korean agricultural expert who defected in 1995. According to Yi, inspectors from Pyongyang were continually deceived by sycophantic local officials fearful of admitting grain shortfalls. These officials falsified reports on targets and even borrowed grain from one another to demonstrate their successes. These fears stemmed from the fact that the top political leadership had directly identified itself with particular farming techniques, down to the details of the inputs to be used and the spacing of plantings. To admit failure or to question these techniques was to question the top leadership itself—an action of potentially fatal consequence. In his speech at Kim Il-sŏng University in 1996, Kim Jŏng-il himself admitted that this sort of deception was a problem, a practice he labeled "pointism."

This deception was not revealed until one of Kim Il-sŏng's guerilla colleagues, Kang Sŏng-san—who not coincidentally had been governor of North Hamgyŏng Province, one of the hardest-hit regions—went directly to Kim Il-sŏng with information on the problems he had seen firsthand (Oberdorfer 1997:298; Natsios 1999:166–67). According to Kang Myŏng-do, Kang Sŏng-san's son-in-law and a defector, this information triggered a review of economic policy that ultimately led to the admission of failure and partial change in policy course in December 1993. But this change of course came as the nuclear confrontation was escalating and was in any case too late to stem the damage that had been done not only by external events but also by complacency at the top. The crucial importance of adjusting policy at this point in time is damning testimony to the incredible cost of the leadership's nuclear gamble as well as the deeper entitlement problems that can arise in totalitarian political systems.

Constructing Food Balances

The traditional approach to analyzing famines has been to construct an aggregate balance sheet of food supply and demand. This approach is inadequate standing on its own because it ignores the critical question of distribution. Nonetheless, it is a necessary exercise when assessing food availability and remains a staple of organizations such as the World Food Programme, which use it as a guide to overall need.

Total supply is equal to domestic production plus imports, either in the form of commercial purchases or aid receipts, minus exports. We have no evidence that North Korea exported grain during the famine—an anomaly that has arisen in a number of cases, most notably the Irish famine of 1846–50—so this last component can safely be ignored.[19] Before we can construct food balances, however, we need to address three issues: discrepancies among alternative reporting sources with respect to the production data; the apparent negative correlation between humanitarian assistance and commercial imports and domestic production; and the appropriate measure of domestic demand.

With respect to the first issue, we have reviewed in some detail the alternative estimates that exist and construct our presentation around estimates produced by the USDA. These are generally lower than the figures reported by the FAO, especially in the early 1990s. But we consider the implications of the FAO numbers to be right for two crucial years—1996 and 1997—when their estimates of production are substantially lower.

A second set of complications has to do with imports. The data suggest that there is a very close relationship between North Korea's receipt of concessional aid and its commercial imports. In the first half of the 1990s, commercial imports were highly erratic, varying by as much as 500,000 metric tons from one year to the next. As the famine broke, the government scrambled to secure grain, and commercial imports rose somewhat. But as the international aid campaign took off, rising aid inflows crowded out or replaced food imports on commercial terms (figure 2.4).[20]

Some have made the exculpatory argument that this decline in imports occurred in the context of an economic contraction and a decline in total imports (Lim 2006a). This is narrowly true but misleading: as shown in figure 2.5, both total imports and commercial food imports declined in the mid-1990s, but the decline in food imports was far greater—that is, there was a disproportionate fall in commercial food imports. Figure 2.5 also illustrates another striking point: that while total imports subsequently grew in the context of an overall economic recovery, commercial food imports remained essentially flat.

Put differently, the component of the total food supply coming from imports cannot be treated as a given; rather, imports appear to have been affected by policy and expenditure choices by the North Korean government. Rather than continuing to import on commercial terms and using humanitarian aid as a supplement to those imports, the government used humanitarian sources as a substitute for them. Aid was used as form of balance-of-payments support.

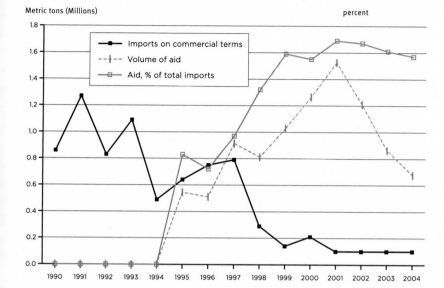

FIGURE 2.4. North Korean Food Imports and Aid, 1990–2004
Source: Imports: FAO/WFP (various publications); Aid: WFPINTERFAIS 2004, 2005b.

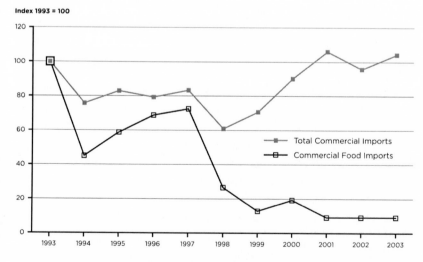

FIGURE 2.5. North Korean Commercial Food Imports and Total Imports, 1993–2003
Sources: Total imports: Lee, Young-Hoon 2005, table 2.2; Korean Ministry of Unification; Inter-Korean Cooperation, www.unikorea.go.kr/index.jsp.

This phenomenon is not unknown in other famines: food merchants, for example, may experience a significant increase in real income during short-ages, some of which may go into the consumption of luxury imports. What is different about socialist famines in general, and the North Korean case in particular, is that those resource allocation decisions were not made by decentralized economic actors via the market. Rather, they were political decisions made by the state, presumably reflecting some degree of conscious choice. As we discussed in chapter 1, one consequence of the suppression of markets and the assertion of control over production and distribution by the socialist state is the counterpart assumption of responsibility for managing entitlements to food.

Under certain circumstances, such a policy of treating humanitarian assis-tance as balance-of-payments support might have made sense. If humanitarian assistance and domestic production fully met domestic demand, then foreign exchange could be diverted from commercial imports of food to other pur-poses, such as capital goods and intermediate goods, or other inputs that would boost overall economic recovery. But domestic demand was not adequately met. Moreover, the conserved foreign exchange was used partly for military imports, which discouraged more aggressive efforts to earn foreign exchange through increased economic openness and exports.[21]

To complicate matters, it is misleading to assume that aid and commercial imports are unrelated. Had North Korea continued to import grain on com-mercial terms, it probably would not have received as much aid as it did. Rightly or wrongly, the humanitarian effort might have been adjusted downward.

In recognition of these difficulties, we have constructed two counterfactual food supplies in figure 2.6. The baseline is the supply that obtained in real-ity: local production plus imports and aid. The first counterfactual supply line is based on an assumption that commercial grain imports remained at their 1993 level instead of declining and that the country received no aid. This "go it alone" scenario provides a sense of how North Korea would have fared if it had relied solely on commercial imports without any humanitarian assistance. The second counterfactual assumes that commercial imports were maintained at their 1993 level *and* that the food aid North Korea actually received was fully additional, rather than crowding out imports.[22] By definition this supply line will exceed all others, since it embodies the (arguably unrealistic) assumption that North Korea continued to import substantial supplies of food on com-mercial terms *and* received the same level of assistance from the international community that it actually did.

Metric tons (millions)

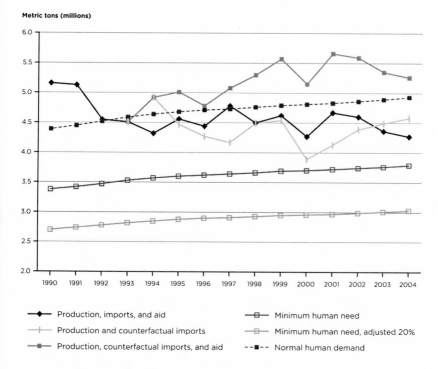

FIGURE 2.6. Scenarios of Food Supply and Minimum Human Need, 1990–2004

Note: Demand Figures based on population data taken from the Bank of Korea and annual per capita consumption of 167kg in cereal equivalent. Counterfactual supply keeps 1994–2003 imports held at 1993 level. Normal human demand derived from FAO/WFP 1995. *Sources:* Production: USDAFAS: PSD database; Imports: Noland 2003; WFPINTERFAIS 2004, 2005b.

As there is uncertainty about the supply of food in North Korea and how to think about imports, so there are also divergent estimates as to demand. In constructing food balances, the FAO and WFP use fixed estimates or targets that are adjusted for estimated spoilage. To derive a national minimum needs target, the FAO/WFP posits a per capita grain consumption figure and simply multiplies by the population; the calculation makes no reference to prices but is rooted in a postulated individual human need. To perform this exercise, one therefore needs data on both food consumption—or target consumption—and population. As with all North Korean data, population figures are of questionable accuracy, in part because of disagreements over the death toll during the famine, which we take up in more detail at the end of the next chapter (on the difficulty of assessing North Korea's population statistics, see Eberstadt and

Banister 1992 and Eberstadt 2000). For the sake of this exercise, we set aside these concerns and use the same figures as the FAO/WFP.

The second component of this calculation—the level of human need—is similarly problematic. The FAO/WFP estimates that minimum per capita human needs in North Korea are 167 kilograms of cereals such as rice and corn annually (FAO/WFP 1996). In a devastating critique written during the famine, however, Australian economist Heather Smith points out that this estimate—increased in the midst of the famine—was deficient in at least two ways (Smith 1998). First, the WFP analysts had underestimated the role of other food products in the North Korean diet, particularly noncereal grains such as pulses (beans) and starchy roots (potatoes and sweet potatoes). As a result, they overestimated North Korean cereal needs. Second, the 167 kilograms per annum figure was inconsistent with data reported both by the North Korean authorities and the FAO showing that North Koreans had historically consumed well under that target, as had other comparable populations. Smith argued that attaining this target would have implied the highest level of cereals consumption in North Korea since 1968! In combination, Smith concluded that the WFP had overestimated the minimum cereals target by approximately 20 percent. Figure 2.6 thus reports two levels of "minimum human needs," one taken directly from the WFP and one adjusted downward by 20 percent following Smith's observation about the North Korean diet and historical patterns of consumption.

As is immediately obvious, aggregate supply exceeds both of these targets for the entire decade of the 1990s *regardless of the production numbers used.* If the demand and supply figures are accurate, and food is distributed equally across the population, no one starves. If there is starvation, it must be due to inequalities in distribution, not inadequate aggregate supply.

Minimum human needs may be too modest a benchmark, however. The WFP has also published an estimate of normal human demand—that is, what was being consumed in North Korea before the famine (figure 2.7). Here the interpretation is more ambiguous. Starting in 1993, actual supply—production, imports, and aid—generally lies below the "normal human demand" line. However, this aggregate shortage disappears if one accepts Smith's criticism that demand has been overestimated or if the North Korean government had continued to import grains on commercial terms and had continued to receive aid at the volumes that were actually given. On the "normal human demand" criterion, the severity of the North Korean situation depends on what weight one puts on Smith's demand-side critique, the North Korean government's irresponsibility in not maintaining commercial food imports, and the extent to which the international community would have reduced aid if it had.

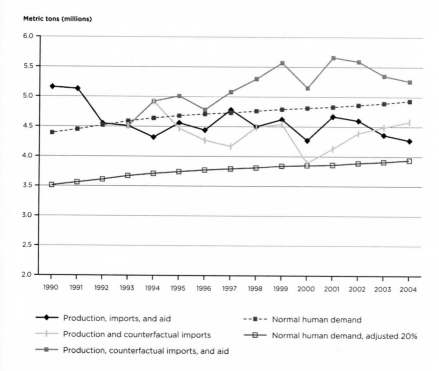

Metric tons (millions)

FIGURE 2.7. Scenarios of Food Supply and Normal Human Demand, 1990–2004
Note: Demand Figures based on population data taken from the Bank of Korea and annual per capita consumption of 167kg in cereal equivalent. Counterfactual supply keeps 1994–2003 imports held at 1993 level. Normal human demand derived from FAO/WFP 1995. *Sources:* Production: USDAFAS: PSD database; Imports: Noland 2003; WFPINTERFAIS 2004, 2005b.

One point is worth emphasizing strongly, however. Looking at the counterfactual supply figures, it appears that the additional imports required to close the supply gap were modest to the point of triviality. As we noted in the previous section, there is considerable disagreement on a critical variable—local production—and for the mid-1990s some sources generate substantially lower estimates of local output. But substituting the quasi-official FAO numbers for the USDA figures does not alter this analysis in any significant way. A modest effort to increase imports would have had a large ameliorative effect.

Finally, figure 2.8 reports an estimate of "normal total demand" constructed by taking the "normal human demand" figure and adding to it a generous provision of 2.3 million metric tons (MT) for nonfood purposes such as livestock feed, the production of liquor, and postharvest losses.[23] This figure is the maximum nonhuman use number ever cited by the FAO/WFP, and some analysts question whether it adequately takes into account reduced needs for livestock feed as a result of the herd culling that occurs in all famines; the inclusion of feed requirements probably biases the demand estimate upward (see Smith 1998 and Lintner 2005). Using these figures, demand always exceeds supply. But it is important to underline that this shortfall does not imply an inability to meet basic needs but rather would reflect a failure to meet basic needs because alternative uses were prioritized. On the basis of her extensive firsthand observation of the situation in the DPRK in 1995 and 1996, Susan Lautze reached exactly this conclusion and also confirmed our emphasis on the significance of foreign exchange earnings for meeting overall domestic demand: "The DPRK has the opportunity and capacity to meet survival consumption food requirements through commercial avenues, including the prioritization of its scarce foreign exchange reserves for the commercial import of food" (1996:6).

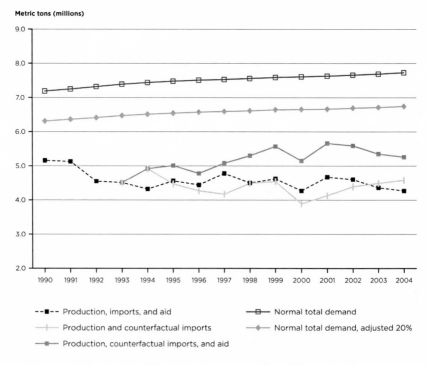

FIGURE 2.8. Scenarios of Food Supply and Normal Total Demand, 1990–2004

Note: Demand Figures based on population data taken from the Bank of Korea and annual per capita consumption of 167kg in cereal equivalent. Counterfactual supply keeps 1994-2003 imports held at 1993 level. Normal demand derived from FAO/WFP 1995. *Sources:* Production: USDAFAS: PSD database; Imports: Noland 2003; WFPINTERFAIS 2004, 2005b.

The analysis thus far has treated food as a nonstorable commodity that must be supplied annually. In fact, food is storable. The one institution in North Korea alleged to maintain substantial inventories is the military, with published estimates of military grain stockpiles ranging from around 400,000 metric tons to as high as 1.5 million metric tons, or something on the order of 5 percent to 20 percent of normal annual demand (Lautze 1996, Noland 2000).[24] If the military had large stockpiles entering the period of shortage, the government could have drawn these stocks down as an additional source of domestic supply. We cannot say for certain what the size of military inventories were, but if they existed and were not drawn down, it would only reinforce the argument that shortages were a function of distribution rather than a lack of aggregate supply. If military inventories were drawn down, then the domestic supply numbers are probably understated to some extent. But if the military was forced to disburse its accumulated stocks during the famine (as some contemporaneous reports claimed), it might also subsequently have sought to rebuild those inventories once conditions had eased. As a result, the supply figures following the worst of the famine may overstate effective supply in more recent periods as the military began to restock.

Conclusion

Famines are complex political and social as well as economic events. In this chapter, we have begun our analysis by focusing on some of the longer-run factors that affected overall food availability. The first lesson is painfully simple: North Korea does not have a comparative advantage in the production of grain, and any effort to go against that trend is likely to involve substantial inefficiencies. But the story of North Korean agriculture is not simply one of the sorts of inefficiencies that plague protected agriculture in a number of advanced industrial states or elsewhere in Asia, for example, in Japan and South Korea. Rather, North Korean strategy toward agriculture as well as toward the economy as a whole was based on a particularly rigid pursuit of self-sufficiency that had the unintended and sadly ironic effect of making the economy more rather than less vulnerable to external shocks.

North Korea did experience a number of political and economic shocks in the first half of the 1990s, and they were severe. These included the changing trade behavior of the Soviet Union and China as well as weather-related disasters. These shocks contributed to a secular decline in domestic output. But a central point of this chapter is that total supply is not a function of domestic output alone. It also depends on the ability and willingness of the country to maintain imports: by earning adequate foreign exchange through exports, by borrowing, or through timely appeals for international public assistance.

The supply data and food balances we have outlined suggest that the capacity of the government to secure adequate external supplies in the first half of the 1990s was erratic and tenuous. But even then, and with all the caution that should be used in approaching our balance sheet exercise, it is not clear that demand outstripped aggregate supply or that the country experienced a food availability famine. If the North Korean government had maintained access to commercial imports during the first half of the 1990s, the famine could have been avoided. Similarly, if it had treated the aid that it received as an additional increment to aggregate supply instead of offsetting aid receipts by cutting commercial imports, and if the international community had accommodated this decision, it could have quite easily serviced normal human demands. Similarly, if the country's priorities across alternative uses had been different, it is quite possible that it could have serviced normal human demand.

Regrettably, rather than using humanitarian assistance as an addition to domestic production and commercial sources of supply, the government used aid largely as balance-of-payments support, allowing it to allocate the savings in commercial imports to other priorities, including military ones and luxury imports for the elite. For example, in 1999, at the same time that it was cutting commercial grain imports to less than 200,000 metric tons, the government allocated scarce foreign exchange to the purchase of forty MiG-21 fighters and eight military helicopters from Kazakhstan. Moreover, this was a period during which North Korea's security situation had actually improved. The Agreed Framework ending the first nuclear standoff had been in place for nearly five years, and the country was making progress, albeit slowly, on negotiating a number of remaining issues with the United States—particularly with respect to missiles—that could have led to improved diplomatic and economic relations. It is this combination of failure to adjust, falling commercial imports in the face of rising aid, and continued military expenditures and luxury imports in the face of famine deaths that constitutes the first important piece of evidence in evaluating the government's response to the famine.

We again want to emphasize the caution with which our statistical analysis should be approached. Life in North Korea during the 1990s would have been difficult under any set of policy choices. But the evidence does not support the pessimistic conclusion that a famine that killed hundreds of thousands of people was an inevitable result of external shocks and adverse weather conditions. To understand why demands a more careful consideration of domestic distributional issues and the management of foreign aid; we take these issues up in the next three chapters.

CHAPTER THREE

The Distribution of Misery

Famine and the Breakdown of the Public Distribution System

The balance sheet approach laid out in the previous chapter provides the overall context for understanding the allocation of food in North Korea. Yet it does not get at the crucial distributional questions that are often at the heart of food emergencies and famines. We structure our discussion of these issues around a detailed analysis of the Public Distribution System (PDS) and its effective breakdown during the high famine period of 1994–98. The PDS was the major source of food for most North Koreans until the famine and thus implicitly a central pillar of political control. It remains an important if declining source of food to this day and also serves as the main conduit for the delivery of food aid. Understanding the PDS is therefore also crucial for our discussion of humanitarian assistance in chapter 4.

The main question we seek to address is how—and how equitably—food was distributed in the country. These issues are complex; access to food in North Korea has been a function of jobs and age, the season of the year, and, increasingly over time, cash income. We, however, place particular emphasis on the regional dimension of the crisis. Where people lived—in Pyongyang and the rice bowl of the country as opposed to the east coast and more remote mountain provinces of the north—made a big difference on how they fared. We show that the famine hit particularly hard at the urban working class of the cities and towns of the eastern provinces of the country (see also Smith 2005a, 2005b:83–87).

Perceived political reliability influenced virtually all the factors that in turn affected entitlements to food, including access to education, the nature of employment, and place of residence. A full consideration of entitlements thus requires a closer look at features of the political system, most notably its complex system of political stratification.

Differences in entitlements naturally influenced mortality. We close the chapter with the debate over the famine's overall death toll but also a consideration of how that mortality was distributed across different groups. Our analysis of the PDS serves one additional purpose. The collapse of the PDS marked a fundamental change in the socialist system of entitlements. Local political officials and households responded by developing a variety of coping strategies, from the diversion of food by cooperative farmers, to the stripping of enterprise assets, to internal migration and foraging, to various forms of trade. When the famine had run its course, the government sought to reassert control. But as a consequence of both policy and these coping strategies, markets began to play an increasingly important role in the allocation food. The reforms of 2002 that we take up in more detail in chapter 7 must be seen in this historical context. Reform should not necessarily be interpreted as an effort to liberalize the economy. Rather, it can be interpreted as an effort to control a process of decentralization and marketization that emerged out of the ashes of the PDS and was seen as a threat to the state's political as well as economic control.

The Public Distribution System and the System of Entitlements

Under the PDS, each of the twelve provinces and special province-level municipalities (Pyongyang, Namp'o, and Kaesŏng) has a Food Administration Department (FAO/WFP 1998b). Each of the more than two hundred counties and urban districts (seventeen cities and thirty-six urban districts) of the country also has a Food Administration Section and a warehouse. The county warehouse is the primary source of food supplies to the lower-level public distribution centers (PDCs) throughout the county as well as the distribution channel for food commodities specifically allocated to institutions such as nurseries, kindergartens, and hospitals. Outside of food going to these institutions, the PDCs are the final "retail" outlet for all cereal food distribution to the general public other than cooperative farmers. Each PDC covers a specific geographical area with population ranging from 1,500 to 3,000 families.

Although the North Korean political and administrative system appears centralized and hierarchical, it is in fact decentralized in several important respects and became more so as the food crisis deepened. One implication of the central government's push for self-sufficiency at the county and provincial levels was that local authorities had to coordinate not only the supply of food but its demand as well. As a result, local officials exercised considerable influence over the distribution of food in their jurisdiction.

The county level of government is an intermediary link between the provincial level authorities and those at the village level. As we have discussed, the agricultural strategy of the government encouraged self-sufficiency at fairly low levels of administrative organization. County-level warehouses are controlled by the county-level People's Committees, which are made up of party functionaries and senior administrative cadre. These committees played an important role both in the collection of food—by transmitting targets and supervising grain collection from the cooperatives in their jurisdictions—and in allocating food to the ultimate "retail" sites. County-level party and administrative officials were also at the front line in coping with the shortfalls that spread across the country as the famine deepened.

At the onset of the famine, the PDS distributed food to between 60 and 70 percent of the population at highly subsidized prices (FAO/WFP 1996).[1] The allocation of rations followed a complex system of occupational and age-related stratification; table 3.1 shows these allocations at the beginning of the 1990s as well as estimates of the population falling in each group. This hierarchy of entitlements broke down in the 1990s and therefore should not be treated as a guide to how different occupational groups fared; according to the first director of the WFP operations in Pyongyang, the famine reduced the number of distinct PDS categories to three (Becker 1996). Nonetheless, several general points about this system are worth noting.

First, for those in urban areas, the availability of food outside the PDS was extremely limited before the marketization of the 1990s and, more important, prohibitively costly. In 1992 a kilo of rice through the PDS cost .08 won; on the market, it sold for 25 won a kilo, over three hundred times the PDS price and approximately 35 percent of the average monthly wage (S. Lee 2003:table 8–11). Control over access to food thus constituted one of the central elements of overall political and social control.

Second, the distribution of food reflected quite openly the basic principles of stratification in the socialist system. At the top of the hierarchy of entitlements were the military and special security forces and high-ranking government officials, as well as those engaged in heavy labor. Yet table 3.1 does not fully capture the system of privilege because the top ranks of the political class were also centrally rather than generally supplied, receiving their rations through the party or special suppliers within the government (S. Lee 2003:255). This fact is important when we take up the issue of diversion of food to the

TABLE 3.1. PDS Allocations and Population Estimates by Occupation

Occupation and Age Group	Per Capita Daily Ration (grams)	Populatiion distribution (thousands)	(%)	Ratio of Rice to Corn Pyongyang Area	Other Areas
High-ranking government officials	700	4.8	0.02	10:0	10:0
Regular laborers	600	[4905.4]	37.14	6:4	3:7
Heavy-labor workers	800	[4905.4]	18.95	6:4	3:7
Office workers	600	1976.3	7.48	6:4	3:7
Special security	800	[603.3]	2.28	7:3	7:3
Military	700	[603.3]	2.28	6:4	3:7
College students	600	591.7	2.24	6:4	3:7
Secondary school students	500	2182.5	8.26	6:4	3:7
Primary school students	400	2397.5	9.08	6:4	3:7
Preschool students	300	1270.6	4.81	6:4	3:7
Children under 3 years	100–200	1866	7.06	6:4	3:7
Aged and disabled	300	104.9	0.40	6:4	3:7

Source: Adapted from Kim, Lee and Sumner 1998. Note: Figures in brackets appear as such in original source to indicate that they were calculated under assumptions of the population distribution. Population figures for preschool students correspond to "Children under 6 years" in original source.

military and political elite in chapter 4.[2] The military—which includes not only combat units but also an array of productive enterprises—maintained its own internal distribution system. The Provisions Bureau, under the General Rear Services Bureau of the Ministry of the People's Armed Forces, had responsibility both for supplying rations to military units and for managing the military's emergency war stockpiles of food and fuel. At the bottom of the hierarchy were children—who have lower caloric needs—but also the elderly and disabled. These vulnerable groups naturally became a central focus of the relief efforts.

Not noted in the table are the inmates of the country's vast political prison system, which probably held roughly two hundred thousand prisoners, or just under 1 percent of the population. By numerous refugee accounts, the rations allocated to prisoners were well below subsistence levels, suggesting a policy of deliberate starvation, and mortality levels were extremely high (see, e.g., Kang 2002; Hawk 2003:25).

These apparent principles of distribution do not fully capture the underlying system of entitlements, however, because assignment to these occupational categories in turn rested to some extent on political status.[3] Since the purges of the late 1950s, the Korean Workers' Party has undertaken a succession of efforts to investigate the class background of the population and to classify individuals in terms of their political reliability.[4] These efforts drew a basic distinction among "core," wavering," and "hostile" classes based on family background. The most recent effort at categorization rested on a highly differentiated set of fifty-one social groups. For example, families of workers, soldiers, or party members were considered core; families of middle peasants, traders, and owners of small businesses were considered wavering. The government classified twenty-nine distinct groups as hostile, from families of rich peasants, to individuals with clear religious identities, to the intelligentsia and even returning Chinese and Japanese Koreans.

Membership in these categories did not directly determine access to food, but it had powerful indirect effects. Class position influenced membership and promotion in the party, access to education and housing, and work assignments and subsequent mobility. Class position also had important implications for residence. Beginning in the late 1950s, members of the hostile class were relocated to remote parts of the country that experienced severe deprivation during the famine. Interestingly, many of the counties suspected of housing such internal exiles as well as the large-scale penal colonies for political prisoners have remained off-limits to external monitoring.[5] By contrast, members of the core class were much more likely to gain residence in Pyongyang. By all accounts, residency in Pyongyang—which constitutes roughly 15 percent of the population—is a privilege. Its residents fare much better than those living elsewhere in the country and were protected to at least some extent from the worst of the famine.

Finally, it is important to consider the question of the size and composition of the elite in North Korea: those whom the government would seek to protect. A recent South Korean estimate from the mid-1990s suggested that the core class constituted 28 percent of the population,[6] and the Korean Workers' Party is relatively large by Communist standards; Armstrong (2001) estimates membership as high as 15 percent of the population.

These relatively broad definitions of favored groups are much too inclusive, however. The core class includes families with working-class and peasant backgrounds who were by no means elite. The party includes low-level cadre at the village and work-unit level who were almost certainly not protected during the famine. The military, security, and high-ranking government and party officials constitute only 6 percent of all those receiving rations in this form. Nonetheless, there is ample evidence, including from a speech attributed to Kim Jŏngil himself, that the military was not fully protected from food shortages and hunger (1996). The very first reports to leak out of the country in 1993 came from military defectors who noted problems of malnutrition within the army (Associated Press 1993; Becker 1996). Nor was residency in Pyongyang a guarantee. Accounts by expatriates living in Pyongyang report signs of food shortages during the famine (e.g., Harrold 2004)—although not of starvation—and from at least 1998 if not before, the North Korean government has made efforts to reduce the size of Pyongyang and other provincial cities by relocating people to rural areas (KINU 2004:31–32).

It is impossible to say what the size of the protected population was; for the purpose of estimating the death toll, we estimate that four million people were probably protected from extreme deprivation through one means or another (residence in Pyongyang, party connections, being in the military). But it is too facile to say that the North Korean government simply protected the elite while allowing others to starve, unless by "elite" we mean a narrow circle of the very top party, government, and military leadership.[7] Many if not most of this group of four million almost certainly experienced food shortages and even hunger at some time during the famine. The food crisis of the 1990s thus cut at the very base of the regime's support and posed serious problems of political legitimacy and control.

The Distribution of Food in the Countryside

Two groups fell partly or entirely outside of the PDS. Workers on state farms that specialized in nongrain production received six months rations shortly after the harvest; for the other six months of the year, they relied on the PDS. The overwhelming share of farm households—roughly 90 percent—worked on the cooperative farms created through collectivization. Cooperatives are given production targets each year in the spring, although targets are adjusted—in effect, renegotiated—depending on the harvest. Cooperative farms paid the government for inputs, but individuals were allowed to supplement their rations by maintaining family plots.[8] Cooperative farms also retained the grain for annual farm household rations, which were distributed after the main harvest in October.[9] These rations, determined by the government, were subtracted from production before it was sold to the state at prescribed prices.[10] In addition, cooperatives retained prescribed quantities of cereals for seed and livestock.

This system is somewhat different from that in other socialist countries since farm households do not surrender all grain and thus have a direct claim on the harvest (S. Lee 2003). Of course, the government sets production targets, farmers' rations, and the prices cooperative and state farms have to pay for inputs; all these decisions are interdependent and affect the final availability of food to farmers. But the government faced several daunting strategic problems whenever they sought to increase procurement from cooperatives and farm households. These problems were particularly critical at the height of the famine but remain relevant to this day.[11]

First, and at the broadest level, the socialist grain procurement system rests on a fundamental exchange between the government and cultivators. The farmers surrender grain at prices well below what they could command on the market, but they receive in return an allotment of food and a bundle of inputs and consumer goods. Yet, as we have shown, the ability of the government to uphold its end of the bargain was severely impaired as external sources of inputs dried up and the industrial economy went into decline. The government was increasingly unable to provide the most basic inputs on which agricultural production depended: fertilizer and the energy required to maintain the country's irrigation system. Nor did the industrialization strategy historically favor the production of consumer goods. As a result, the terms of trade between agriculture and industry were increasingly unfavorable to the farmers as the economy contracted. The surrender of grain to the government no doubt looked more and more like a one-sided deal or confiscatory tax.

Second, the government historically allocated relatively generous rations for farmers, equivalent to those for heavy manual laborers. If the allocation to farmers were cut sharply—or if farmers had the expectation that it might be cut, for example, in response to reduced yields or adverse weather—households had strong incentives to protect themselves. They could do this by:

- preharvesting grain so that it would not be subject to the harvest time procurement;
- hiding and hoarding food once harvested;
- diverting effort into the private plots allowed to state and cooperative farmers and into altogether illegal plots that were maintained secretly on marginal lands;
- diverting food into various forms of exchange, either for cash or through barter, where they could earn very high returns as shortages became more severe;
- remitting food to family members in the city.

We only have hints at the magnitude of these behaviors, but they were almost certainly significant and constitute the main reason why the production numbers reviewed in chapter 2 are not reflective of the actual availability of grain. Production data do not speak to the crucial issue of the share of the harvest that actually finds its way into the distribution system. We analyze this issue quantitatively in chapter 4.

A final problem the government faced has to do with the way food is distributed to farmers as opposed to those dependent on the PDS. Once the allocation is made to farmers at the time of the harvest, they have the relative security of those stocks. Those dependent on the PDS, by contrast, receive their rations every two weeks and are at the mercy of government largesse. As a result, it is easier for the government to impose the costs of any disruption in supply on the PDS rather than on farmers, which it could only do by recollecting grain already allocated. Again, this is precisely what appeared to happen; the PDS became increasingly erratic in its delivery of food, with long stretches of very low rations or none at all.

The Breakdown of the PDS

Although we talk about the breakdown of the PDS system during the famine, there is evidence that it had not been functioning for some time before that. Choi and Koo (2005) document problems with the PDS extending well back into the 1980s. As Soviet aid was terminated after 1987, daily grain rations distributed through the PDS—which officially had been 600 to 700 grams for most urban dwellers and 700 to 800 grams for high officials, military personnel, and heavy laborers—were cut by 10 percent. In 1991, as economic difficulties worsened, the government launched a "let's eat two meals a day" campaign, though according to former East German ambassador Hans Maretzki, campaigns to suppress food consumption were already under way in the late 1980s. In 1992 rations were cut yet another 10 percent.[12]

The erratic performance of the PDS before the famine is confirmed by refugee interviews. The Korean Buddhist Sharing Movement conducted the earliest systematic refugee interviews in late 1997 through the first half of 1998 (KBSM 1998). This sample is biased in two important respects. First, just over half the respondents are from North and South Hamgyŏng provinces, which were hit particularly hard by the shortages. Second, their very refugee status suggests that they were among the most vulnerable—although perhaps the most entrepreneurial—in their particular locations.

Despite these possible sources of bias, it is revealing that almost 30 percent of the interviewees reported that regular food distribution had stopped by 1993 and that 93 percent said that such distribution had stopped by 1996 (table 3.2).

Similar evidence of the decline of the PDS is found in a pair of well-designed studies conducted by the Johns Hopkins School of Public Health, the first based on interviews of 440 adult refugees done in September 1998 (Robinson et al. 1999), the second based on a larger sample of 2,692 refugees conducted from July 1999 to June 2000 (Robinson et al. 2001). The first Hopkins study reported average daily rations for 1994 of only 150 grams per day. By 1997, however, average reported rations had fallen to only 30 grams per person per day. The 1999–2000 interviews yielded similar findings. For 1995 respondents reported receiving on average only 120 grams per person per day; by 1998 this had fallen to 60 grams.

Outside of these refugee interviews, we do not have consistent data on PDS deliveries from the government itself until the fall of 1995 when the international relief effort began. The data reported in figure 3.1 were provided by North Korean authorities to the World Food Programme/UN Food and Agricultural Organization assessment teams that began to visit the country regularly beginning in the fall of 1995. Unfortunately, they, too, are potentially subject to bias. The North Korean authorities arguably had incentives to understate food deliveries in order to maximize external support. Moreover, as with the food balance information we reviewed in chapter 2, these averages mask important distributional differences across regions and groups; we take these differences up in more detail below.

TABLE 3.2. Answers to the Question "When Did Regular Food Distribution Stop?" (September 1997–May 1998)

Year	People	Percent	Percent Providing Date	Cumulative Percent Providing Date
1992 or before	137	13.4	14.5	14.5
1993	136	13.3	14.4	28.9
1994	329	32.3	34.9	63.8
1995	287	28.2	30.4	94.2
1996 or after	55	5.4	5.8	100
Unknown	75	7.4	–	–
Total	1,019	100	–	–

Source: Korean Buddhist Sharing Movement (1998)

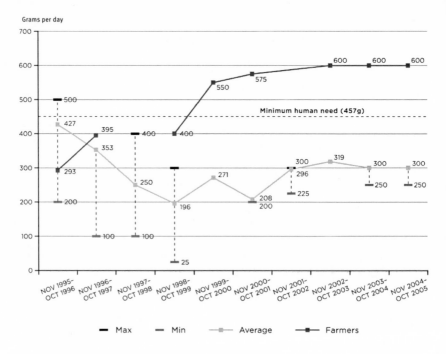

FIGURE 3.1. Estimates of Daily per Capita PDS Rations
Note: In most cases, averages are taken directly from the source. Otherwise, they are calculated as the simple average of the estimates for different cohorts throughout the marketing year. *Source:* NAO/ WFP (various publications); Natsios 2001.

Nonetheless, the overall picture of the evolution of the PDS suggested by this data is broadly consistent with that generated by the refugee interviews. Four points are worth noting. First, average distribution under the PDS for the period never reaches the absolute minimum need of approximately 457 grams per day necessary to provide 1,600 calories. Even if we make the 20 percent adjustment used in chapter 2 to account for the fact that the North Korean diet typically has other sources of calories—generating a minimum consumption figure of 365 grams per day—the average ration still consistently falls below it.

Second, while we would expect average rations to fall steadily from 1995–96 through 1998, the peak famine period, PDS rations do not recover after that point despite the increase in humanitarian assistance and the partial revival of production beginning in 1998. This can be seen in more detail in the monthly estimates we have extracted from WFP reports from 2000 through May 2004, when such reports were terminated (figure 3.2). In some months, rations get up to 350 grams, but in no month do they equal the 450-gram minimum.

Grams per day

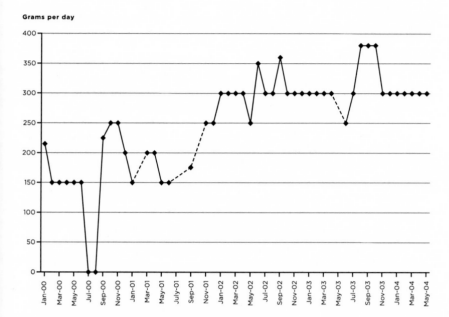

FIGURE 3.2. PDS Rations, January 2000–May 2004.
Source: Humanitarian Development Resource Center for DPR Korea.

A third point concerns farmers; the one important exception to the relatively constant PDS rations in the postfamine period pertains to this group. As figure 3.1 shows clearly, farmers' rations turn upward with the fall harvest in 1999. This change was almost certainly a conscious policy decision, as the very low rations allocated to farmers at the harvests of 1995 and 1996 were undoubtedly responsible for the difficulties the government had in procuring grain. If we consider that farmers also have easier access to other foodstuffs—not to mention any grain they can divert and cash income they can generate from trade—it is clear that at least some portion of the rural population ended up faring somewhat better in the wake of the famine, and perhaps even during it, than the urban populations. The obvious exception would have been those areas directly affected by the floods.

Finally, it is important to underscore that these numbers mask important seasonal fluctuations that constitute one of the most serious problems with the breakdown of the PDS. Historically, the months of April through June are the lean or hungry months in Korea: stocks from the previous fall harvest are running low, and early crops have not yet come in yet. In North Korea during the famine, this lean season would begin as early as December, and rations would fall to nominal amounts or nothing at all; this pattern was repeated in the spring of 1998 and again in 1999, when rations basically ceased. The period 2002–3 showed more even estimates of grain across seasons resulting from increased shipments from South Korea, although levels remained low. But the data in figure 3.2 for 2000 and 2001—well after the peak of the famine had passed—still show sharp seasonality in PDS deliveries.

The Famine Unfolds

A decline in food availability is not typically distributed across the population evenly. Food shortages among some sectors of the population, and even famine and starvation, can occur within the context of adequate aggregate food availability.[13] The distribution of shortages across groups thus tells us something about both de jure and de facto entitlements.

In tracing the unfolding of the famine, it is useful to focus in the first instance on its geographic incidence and spread.[14] As regionalized crises appeared, beginning in the northeast of the country, the government had to make strategic decisions about how to respond. In the absence of timely external supplies, the government would have had to reallocate grain aggressively across provinces.[15] The government, however, faced not only declining domestic production but also increasing difficulties in procuring grain and the simultaneous breakdown of the country's transport system. As a result, the capability of the government to move food across provinces was severely impaired.

Despite the earlier shortages noted above, 1994 probably marked the onset of famine conditions. As we indicated in chapter 2, that year was characterized not only by a continuing deterioration in North Korea's economy and external position but a sharp reduction in maize imports from China. Moreover, table 3.3 suggests a second, equally important problem: a weak harvest in the northeast of the country. The data on regional production come from North Korea's report to the first roundtable discussions at the United Nations in 1998 (UNDP 1998), a meeting with donors designed to outline a broad rehabilitation program. The North Koreans might have exaggerated the extent of the overall drop in production. Nonetheless, we see no clear reason why they would misrepresent the *relative* performance of different provinces. The northeast provinces (South and North Hamgyŏng and Yanggang) are colder, have shorter growing seasons, and produce less rice. Yields for maize, the dominant food crop, have historically been lower than in other regions. If per capita production in the northeastern provinces dropped to 153 kilograms per person as official data suggests, it would fall below the ability of these provinces even to meet the reduced ration of the time (S. Lee 2003:238).

TABLE 3.3. Provincial Grain Production, 1989–97 (Index, 1989–92 = 100)

	1989–92	1993	1994	1995	1996	1997
Pyongyang, Namp'o and Kaesŏng	100	116	69	48	36	37
South and North P'yŏng'an	100	113	91	33	24	29
South and North Hamgyŏng	100	61	73	44	28	18
South and North Hwanghae	100	111	70	42	25	38
Kangwŏn	100	86	89	50	22	19
Total	100	104	80	40	27	31

Source: S. Lee 2003.

But the problem was even more severe than these numbers suggest because of the economic geography of this part of the country. Two issues stand out, one having to do with the urban populations of the northeast, the other with rural ones. Table 3.4 shows the government's estimate of the distribution of population by province and the share of the population in each province dependent on the PDS, which correlates closely to the level of urbanization. The entire country is relatively urbanized, but North and South Hamgyŏng and Yang-gang provinces are at or above the mean. The coastal cities in the Hamgyŏng provinces were the backbone of the country's heavy industrial base in sectors such as steel, chemicals, and fertilizer: Hamhŭng-Hŭngnam (1993 population, 701,000); Chŏngjin (520,000); Tanch'ŏn (284,000); Kimch'aek (179,000); Sinp'o (158,000) (City Population 2003). These cities were devastated by the collapse of foreign inputs and of the energy system but at the same time almost completely dependent on the PDS.

On the other hand, Yanggang and the western parts of North Hamgyŏng Province contain some of the most mountainous terrain in the country. Although much more sparsely populated, these areas are also highly dependent on the PDS. Moreover, they are not easily accessible for relief efforts even in the best of times, let alone when the transport infrastructure has been severely compromised.

At this critical juncture, the government took some fateful decisions. Grain rations to farmers had already been reduced, but the government took the further step of trying to recollect part of the grain that already been distrib-uted among farm households (Ahn 1996:251). This decision no doubt triggered

TABLE 3.4. Government Estimates of Population by Province and Food
Category (thousands)

	Population		Food Category %	
Province	Total	(% of Total)	Agricultural	PDS*
Pyongyang	3,044	13	8	92
S. P'yŏng'an	3,100	14	27	73
N. P'yŏng'an	2,625	12	40	60
Chagang	1,232	5	28	72
S. Hwanghae	2,290	10	49	51
N. Hwanghae	1,734	8	40	60
Kangwŏn	1,467	7	31	69
S. Hamgyŏng	2,932	13	31	69
N. Hamgyŏng	2,227	10	22	78
Y'anggang	703	3	21	79
Kaesŏng	386	2	35	65
Namp'o	814	4	18	82
Total	22,554	100	29	71

* Includes 767,000 service personnel
Source: FAO/WFP 1999b, table 6)

some of the behaviors that have been described above: hoarding, preharvesting,
diverting effort into private plots, and diverting yield to the market. Even more
important was the apparent decision to cut domestic grain shipments to the
northeast, a decision Natsios refers to as "triage" (2001:106).

The claim about triage has echoed through the literature on the North
Korean famine and, if true, would appear to constitute a damning indictment
of the regime. Nonetheless, the metaphor is unclear, and much of the evidence
cited for the claim is circumstantial.[16] Does triage imply that the government
was protecting stocks—perhaps on security grounds—that could have relieved
the distress? Was the government explicitly refusing to ship grain from provinces producing a surplus in order to protect politically favored jurisdictions?
Or had stocks been drawn down, and was the government struggling to procure adequate supplies and distribute them in the face of a general breakdown
in the transport system?[17] The ethical implications of these different possibilities are obviously not the same.

We do not know for sure which of these conditions pertained, but there is
one more direct source of evidence that the government was effectively limiting

food distribution to the east coast. That evidence stems from the government's posture toward the foreign aid that started to flow in late 1995. From the beginning of the relief effort, the government focused relief and monitoring efforts on the west coast and insisted that food be delivered through the main west coast port of Namp'o *despite the fact that the transportation system linking the west and east coasts had broken down.* Not until May 1997 was an agreement reached with the North Korean government that permitted direct shipments to the east coast through Ch'ŏngjin. Not until July was the first delivery to Ch'ŏngjin actually made, and even then the east coast received only one-third of a 25,000-ton shipment (WFP 1997). Natsios's analysis of shipping manifests comes to the conclusion that during all of 1997–98 only 18 percent of all WFP aid was shipped to eastern ports despite the fact that these provinces constituted approximately a third of the prefamine population and had a high overall dependence on the PDS (1999:108).

Nor is there any evidence that Chinese food shipments—the main source of food outside of the WFP—were targeted to the east coast. Although relatively small amounts of food no doubt leaked across the Tumen River, the major rail and shipping links between China and North Korea are along the west coast. Moreover, we know that the North Korean authorities denied that the east coast was facing particular problems, despite clear refugee evidence to the contrary. Either the government did not have information on the extent of the distress or it was willfully ignoring it.

The floods of July and August 1995 marked a new stage both in the famine and in the relationship with donors. In approaching the international community, the government quickly presented extraordinarily high estimates of the damage from the floods: 5.4 million people displaced—roughly a quarter of the population—330,000 hectares of agricultural land destroyed, 1.9 million tons of grain lost, and total damage of $15 billion. As can be seen from table 3.3, the North Koreans reported a dramatic decline in food production across all regions of the country in that year. Again, even if these numbers are exaggerated, the variation across provinces is notable. Early UN assessments found that the bulk of the crop damage (61 percent) and displaced persons (67 percent) came from the three northwestern provinces of North and South P'yŏng'an and Chagang (S. Lee 2003:238). This assessment was subsequently confirmed by detailed analysis using satellite imagery that suggested that as much as 42 percent of the total paddy area in the entire country was affected by the flooding, but with a high concentration of damage in the northwest (Okamoto, Yamakawa, and Kawashima 1997).

In responding to food emergencies, timing is crucial. Although the government had been making some belated efforts to secure commercial supplies and bilateral aid, the floods led the government to make an appeal for multilateral assistance through the UN on August 23. This got the wheels of the international humanitarian machinery moving, but initial commitments were modest: 20,250 tons of rice and 675 tons of vegetable oil, or enough to meet the consumption needs of 500,000 flood-affected people for three months. The second appeal—and the first of real substance—was not even issued until July 1, 1996, and the first shipment resulting from that appeal did not arrive until August, well past the shortages of the lean months that the flood damage would have severely exacerbated (WFP 1996).

The harvest of 1995 therefore once again presented the central government with a crucial dilemma. The government could seek to increase procurement from the farms in the face of an increasingly generalized shortfall but at the risk of generating the behaviors we have noted: preharvesting, hoarding, diversion of effort, and informal exchange. According to an assessment conducted by the WFP in the spring of 1996, the government chose to reduce farmers' rations at the time of the harvest quite dramatically: from 167 kilograms to 107 kilograms (Nathanail 1996:25). As figure 3.1 indicates, this is well below minimum human need. If farmers had not started their course of active and passive resistance to the government before this time, then the efforts to increase procurement in the wake of the floods would certainly have triggered it.

The most striking evidence we have for farmers' behavior comes from two sources. The first is the FAO/WFP crop assessment made in December 1996. This assessment estimates the losses from the floods at roughly 300,000 metric tons but notes—almost in passing—that fully half of the maize crop of 2.3 million metric tons was lost. The WFP's interpretation is that this grain was consumed in August and September because of hunger. Natsios is worth quoting at length on this point: "The weakness of [the FAO/WFP explanation for the disappearance of the maize crop] becomes more apparent when one calculates the population's consumption requirements. At a minimal ration, 15,000 MT of grain will feed one million people per month, which means that 345,000 MT of grain would feed the entire country for a month, and 1.3 million MT [somewhat more than the estimated losses] would feed the entire country for nearly four months" (1999:115). The magnitude of the loss of the corn harvest once again puts claims about the effects of the floods into perspective. The government claimed flood-related losses of 1.9 million MT. That amount is certainly higher than the sum of the WFP estimate of 300,000 MT of flood-related damage and 1.15 million MT of lost maize crop, or a total of 1.45 million MT of lost grain. One possible explanation for this discrepancy is that the government was including lost stocks that were in fact estimated in the 600,000 metric ton range.

But the implicit explanation for the shortfall is very different in the two cases: one emphasizes natural causes, while the other places more emphasis on the problems the government faced with farmers. Farmers were well informed about the extent of the flood—they were affected by the same weather systems—and motivated not only by hunger but also by the desire to hoard food in anticipation of still further cuts in their rations.

The second piece of evidence on farmers' behavior comes directly from the leadership itself. In Kim Jŏng-il's speech at Kim Il-sŏng University referred to above, he acknowledged that the food shortage was the most urgent problem facing the government. Curiously, he makes only passing reference to natural disasters. "Currently the farmers and miners are hiding food at every opportunity," he points out and acknowledges black market activities. The effect: "we cannot supply our military with rice." Kim Jŏng-il goes on to admonish the party both to undertake practical projects that will help solve the food problem—such as growing vegetables—and to raise the consciousness of farmers to the crisis and thus elicit higher contributions from them. "If we say you should eat only 450g a day and the remains should be sent to the army then they will agree" (1996).[18]

The final phases of the famine, from the 1996 harvest through the 1998 harvest, saw a more generalized spread of distress. Again, weather played a role, with floods in 1996 now affecting North and South Hwanghae provinces, Kangwŏn Province and Kaesŏng Municipality, which together produce some 60 percent of the country's food grain, principally rice. The FAO/WFP assessment team estimated losses as a result of these floods at 300,000 tons of grain. The 1997 growing season began auspiciously with good rains in May, but the country then experienced severe drought, a typhoon in August, and thus another severe challenge to the harvest in 1998 with a particular decline—perhaps as much as 50 percent—in the maize harvest.

Yet it is important to underscore that 1997 and 1998 also saw an increase in external supply as the aid effort ramped up. Thus, even if we accept the government's figures of a sharper decline in *production* in 1996 and 1997 than is suggested by other external estimates, *aggregate supply* did not change much in 1997–1998. What did change is that more grain was being consumed or distributed outside of official channels and the government abandoned even the pretense of consistent public supply. In June 1997, the WFP/FAO reported that the government admitted that rations since the first of the year had been as low as 100–200 grams and even went so far as to announce the precise dates, by province, on which supplies would be exhausted and PDS deliveries would cease altogether. These announcements were no doubt designed to influence the donors to accelerate shipments, but the truth remains that the PDS had effectively collapsed, leaving work units and households to depend entirely on their own efforts.

Tracking the Distribution of Misery

With the relatively strong harvest of 1998 and the upturn in foreign assistance, the worst of the famine was probably over by the end of the year. How was the misery of the famine distributed? Who had been most seriously affected?

One interpretation is that the famine was a classic food availability famine and that the government did all in its power to distribute food as equally as it could (S. Lee 2003, 2005; Woo-Cumings 2002). In such a setting, the command-and-control features of the socialist system might even have been an advantage because of the power of the state to command and reallocate resources. Under this interpretation, while a very small core elite might have been shielded altogether from the famine's effects, the rest of the population shared relatively equally in the declining food that was available.

Three types of data allow us to test this claim, at least for 1997–98: variation in provincial production of grain, variation in farmers' rations by province, and variation in provincial distribution through the PDS. These data show that while production varied enormously across provinces, the government maintained a relatively common target for farmers' rations in 1997. If we consider the problems that the government faced procuring grain following the 1994–96 harvests, then the effort to raise farmers' rations and to keep them constant across provinces was almost certainly a conscious effort to limit diversion.

A consideration of the PDS data in table 3.5, however, suggests anything but equality across provinces. Using data supplied by the government on the supply of food to the PDS population by provinces and the share of the population dependent on the PDS, we can calculate the per person allocation of grain across provinces during the last part of the famine, from September 1997 through April 1999.[19] The differences are striking. Pyongyang consistently comes out on top, sometimes receiving per person rations that are nearly twice those in less protected provinces. Chagang and the rice bowl of South Hwanghae also see higher allocations, while two cities—Namp'o and Kaesŏng—and the northwest and northeast provinces fare much less well. The government appears to do a quite remarkable job of allocating grain after the harvest of 1998; indeed, the uniformity of distribution is even suspicious. But by that point, the worst of the famine had passed.

TABLE 3.5. Monthly PDS Allocations, November 1997–April 1999 (kg per person)

	Nov. 97	Dec. 97	Jan. 98	Feb. 98	Mar. 98	Apr.–Aug. 98	Sep.-98	Oct. 98	Nov. 98	Dec. 98	Jan. 99	Feb. 99	Mar. 99	Apr. 99
Pyongyang	9.9	9.9	7.4	4.9	1.0	0.0	3.7	3.7	8.5	8.5	5.6	5.6	4.2	0.9
S. P'yŏng'an	6.6	6.6	4.9	3.3	0.7	0.0	2.5	2.5	8.6	8.6	0.6	0.6	4.3	0.9
N. P'yŏng'an	6.4	6.4	4.8	3.2	0.6	0.0	1.6	1.6	9.1	9.1	6.0	6.0	4.4	1.0
Chagang	10.5	10.5	7.9	5.2	1.0	0.0	2.6	2.6	8.7	8.7	5.7	5.7	4.3	0.9
S. Hwanghae	8.8	8.8	6.6	4.4	0.9	0.0	3.3	3.3	8.2	8.2	5.5	5.5	4.1	0.9
N. Hwanghae	8.8	8.8	5.3	3.6	0.7	0.0	2.3	2.3	8.0	8.0	5.3	5.3	3.9	0.8
Kangwŏn	5.6	5.6	4.1	2.8	0.5	0.0	1.4	1.4	7.9	7.9	5.3	5.3	4.0	0.9
S. Hamgyŏng	6.7	6.7	5.0	3.4	0.6	0.0	1.3	1.3	8.5	8.5	5.7	5.7	4.3	0.9
N. Hamgyŏng	7.5	7.5	5.8	3.9	0.7	0.0	1.5	1.5	8.5	8.5	5.6	5.6	4.2	0.9
Yanggang	9.5	9.5	7.0	4.7	0.9	0.0	1.9	1.9	8.3	8.3	5.6	5.6	4.1	0.9
Kaesŏng	8.2	8.2	6.0	4.0	0.8	0.0	1.8	1.8	7.2	7.2	4.8	4.8	3.6	0.8
Namp'o	6.8	6.8	5.1	3.4	0.6	0.0	1.7	1.7	8.2	8.2	5.5	5.5	4.0	0.9
Total	7.9	7.9	5.8	3.9	0.7	0.0	2.3	2.3	8.4	8.4	4.9	4.9	4.2	0.9

Note: Calculated as monthly PDS allocation to province as a share of the province's PDS-dependent population.

Sources: November 1997–October1998: FAO/WFP (1998b, table 6); November 1998–April 1999: FAO/WFP (1999a, table 3); Population by province: FAO/WFP (1999b, table 6)

Further insight into regional differences emerges from refugee interviews. Starting in September 1997 and continuing over a period of more than a year, the Korean Buddhist Sharing Movement (later Good Friends) researchers interviewed nearly two thousand North Korean refugees in the Chinese border area. These interviews combined more open-ended testimonials with structured questions designed to document the rise in mortality, the decline in birth rates, and the coping behavior of households (see, e.g., KBSM 1998; Good Friends 1998, 2004). As the Good Friends researchers freely admitted, the interviewees were not randomly selected and overrepresented both geographical regions close to the Chinese border, particularly the northeast, and households that were the most vulnerable relative to the nation as a whole. Nonetheless, with the appropriate cautions and adjustments, the Good Friends work tells us a tremendous amount about the famine.

An update of earlier research by Good Friends (1998) based on a sample of 1,694 refugees asks which areas they believe were the hardest hit. Sixty-two percent said South Hamgyŏng, 23 percent said North Hamgyŏng, and 22 percent said other provinces; only 9 percent said that provinces were experiencing equal levels of distress. These responses gain some credence because they do not simply mirror the residences of the refugees. Nearly 60 percent of respondents came from North Hamgyŏng and only 20 percent from South Hamgyŏng; nonetheless, a substantial majority saw the latter province as the more seriously affected. Information on mortality provides further confirmation of these regional differences. The average mortality of all respondents' families in the sample is 28.7 percent, but this ranges from a low of 16.7 percent for Pyongyang to 32.1 percent for South Hamgyŏng and 32.9 percent for Chagang.

A plausible reason for this difference between the two provinces is that it was somewhat easier for the residents of North Hamgyŏng to move across the border or to benefit from black-market exchanges and trade. These responses also provide more circumstantial support for Natsios's claim with respect to triage, particularly when we consider that food aid did not start to flow directly into the northeast until the second half of 1997. As we discuss in chapter 7, UN-sponsored nutritional surveys provide striking evidence of regional disparities in nutritional status and modest support for the notion that South Hamgyŏng was disadvantaged relative to North Hamgyŏng.

Both the nature of the PDS and the interview evidence suggest that the most severely affected were urban households in the disadvantaged provinces.[20] Without any direct claim on the harvest, with no access to private sources of supply, and with inadequate money wages to command food through the relatively limited market channels, urban workers and their families were completely at the mercy of a faltering PDS. This finding also gets support from refugee interviews. In the 1998 Good Friends study just cited, the overwhelming majority—88.7 percent of those answering—said that urban areas were more severely affected than rural ones. Only 9.5 percent said that urban and rural areas fared the same, and only a handful of respondents—1.8 percent—said that rural residents did worse.

The occupational data on mortality from the 1998 survey also provides a number of interesting clues about the breakdown of the urban industrial economy (table 3.6).[21] As we would expect, office workers, professionals, and soldiers—in descending order of vulnerability—were more protected than other occupational groups. Although manual laborers constitute the largest group of family members, they also show somewhat lower than average mortality rates.

What is striking is the large number of family members who are identified as jobless. While this could be capturing the elderly, refugee testimonials suggest that factories in the major industrial cities were effectively left idle by the absence of inputs and energy. New investment, and thus construction, had also ground to a complete halt. Despite the guarantee of employment that the socialist economy presumably provides, the industrial sector was almost certainly going through a process of informalization quite similar to that seen in other developing countries during economic crises. Some strata of more marginal workers—perhaps in sectors such as construction, in less favored cities and industries—were undoubtedly the very hardest hit.

TABLE 3.6. Mortality Rate by Occupation

Occupation	Family Members	Mortality	Mortality Rate
Manual labor	2,398	441	18.4
Office worker	633	75	11.8
Professional	43	3	7.0
Farmer	296	71	24.0
Student	1,951	336	17.2
Soldier	217	13	6.0
Housekeeper	284	95	33.5
Other	122	27	22.1
Jobless	1,769	807	45.6
Unknown	1,536	785	51.1
Total	9,249	2,653	28.7

Source: WFP 1998.

What about the rural sector? It is revealing that only a small share of the refugees interviewed—3.2 percent—were farmers, but whether this reflected tighter control at the village level and greater difficulty of movement or better material circumstances is difficult to say. Although the share of farmers in the Good Friends sample is small, the reported mortality rate among farm families is only slightly lower than the mean (24 percent vs. 28 percent). Even if in principle the allocation granted to farmers was relatively even across the country, the weather resulted in regional and more localized production shortfalls that pushed cooperative farm supplies near or below subsistence thresholds.

Thus, while farmers as a whole undoubtedly did better than urban dwellers, residence mattered: farmers living in areas strongly affected by the floods and drought depended largely on international largesse and the capacity of the central government to reallocate grain across provinces, counties, and villages. As we have seen, this capability was almost certainly impaired. Moreover, it must also be remembered that approximately 10 percent of farm households lived on state farms, and while these farmers had access to land and the ability to grow other crops, they, too, were dependent on the PDS for some part of the year and thus almost certainly experienced shortfalls as well.

In short, as the famine crested, the evidence emphasizing the crucial role of entitlements and distribution becomes more evident. The FAO/WFP assessment from November 1997 is worth citing at some length: "There is also mounting evidence that much greater polarity in food consumption exists in the population than perceived hitherto. Reasons why this is occurring include transport difficulties, geographical differences, where some provinces are better equipped to deal with shortages than others, greater access amongst rural communities than urban and differential access to assets and foreign remittances and the corresponding ability to purchase food from emerging, though relatively insignificant, 'private' markets." As we will argue in chapter 7, these comments are remarkably prescient. As early as 1997, the first signs were visible that the famine and food shortages were driven not only by the collapse of the PDS but also by the emergence of differential capacities to command resources to purchase needed grain on the market.

Mortality I: Who Died?

We have looked at the famine through the lens of how and to whom food was distributed in North Korea. Another cut on these questions is to consider who died and how. The growing work on famine has provided some general insights into this question that can be summarized quite succinctly (Devereux 2000). First, deaths occur not simply from starvation but from disease, as a result of either increased individual vulnerability or the simultaneous breakdown of public health systems and the unavailability of medicine. Second, the most vulnerable within the household are infants, children, and the elderly.[22]

These observations are borne out by the refugee interviews we have (particularly Robinson et al. 1999, 2001).[23] UN estimates for 1990–95 put infant mortality at 24.4 per 1,000 live births. The first Hopkins study finds under-four mortality to be nearly four times as high for the 1995–97 period (88.9 per 1,000). The second Hopkins study finds infant mortality of 57.4 per 1,000 and under-five mortality of 30.3. Both studies also find predictably high and elevated levels of mortality among the elderly as well. The 1998 Good Friends study, which asks about causes of death, underlines the significance not only of starvation but also of disease. Only 33 percent of respondents cited "starvation" as the cause of death; fully 51 percent ascribed death solely to disease and another 10 percent to starvation and disease.

In sum, the evidence we have on the distribution of mortality by age group confirms both prior research and the concerns of the donor community to focus on the children and elderly. This concern was compounded by an important institutional issue that became a point of conflict with the donors. Many of the most vulnerable populations were in institutions—orphanages and hospitals—that were less well positioned to defend their entitlements than were PDS centers or work units. Indeed, we have convincing evidence from the NGO community in particular that the government even sought to conceal the existence of these institutions.

Mortality II: How Many Excess Deaths?

Given the secrecy of the North Korean regime, it is unsurprising that contemporaneous estimates of the death toll from the famine vary enormously. Statements by North Korean officials in May 1999 and again in July 2001 offered an estimate of 220,000 famine-related deaths between 1995 and 1998, or roughly 1 percent of the population. Yet interviews with party defectors, including the highest-ranking official to leave the country, Hwang Chang-yŏp, suggest internal estimates ranging from 1 to 2.5 million deaths. Outside observers, by contrast, have offered estimates as high as 3.5 million famine-related deaths, a staggering 16 percent of the population.

What can we say about these efforts to quantify the famine's toll? The usual metric is "excess deaths": the elevation in the mortality rate as a result of premature death, inclusive of "births forgone," or the drop in fertility that accompanies a famine. Births forgone during famine are often at least partly offset by unusually high fertility once the famine has ended and normal conditions are reestablished; early or premature death is an obviously irreversible condition.

The first systematic attempt to quantify the demographic impact of the famine came from the Good Friends researchers; their work formed the basis of many subsequent statements about the famine's consequences. Extrapolating to the whole country, Good Friends and other commentators working from their survey produced estimates of famine-related deaths on the order 2.8 to 3.5 million (13 to 16 percent of the population).

Similar, though more methodologically rigorous work was subsequently conducted by a team from Johns Hopkins (Robinson et al. 1999). On the basis of 771 refugee interviews conducted in 1998 and 1999, this group reconstructed mortality rates for a single heavily affected province and concluded that between 1995 and 1997 nearly 12 percent of that province's population had died. Projected across the whole country, this would yield excess deaths of 2.64 million. That figure is consistent with a number of often-cited estimates. In 2003, for example, USAID administrator Andrew S. Natsios testified that "2.5 million people, or 10 percent of the population" had died in the famine (Natsios 2003), a number roughly consonant with South Korean estimates as of 1999 (KINU 2004). On the basis of defector accounts, Médicins sans Frontières offered a still higher estimate, of 3.5 million deaths (Terry 2001).[24]

The high end of these estimates is almost certainly exaggerated. The precrisis population of North Korea was approximately 22 million, but some share of that population in fact faced little or no risk of starvation, even if individuals may have experienced food shortages and even hunger. We do not know the size of this elite, and we have refugee evidence of malnutrition in the army as we have noted. But if we assume a privileged or protected share of the population of 4 million—roughly equal to but not coterminus with the populations of the armed forces (about 1 million) and Pyongyang (around 3 million)—this would leave a total nonprivileged or "exposed" population of around 18 million people.

The work of Robinson and his collaborators implies an excess mortality rate of roughly 12 percent for refugees coming from the most severely affected northeastern provinces, an estimate that the team then used to calculate excess mortality for North Hamgyŏng Province as a whole. Even applying this mortality rate to an entire province is questionable if we assume that refugees reflect a particularly affected part of the population. If we nonetheless apply the 12 percent figure to the total "exposed" population of 18 million, it yields a figure of just over two million excess deaths. In our view, this number has to be considered the absolute upper estimate. The reason is as follows: If one accepts the Robinson et al. estimate of 245,000 excess deaths for North Hamgyŏng Province out of a precrisis population of approximately 2 million, the Natsios statement implies that there must have been roughly 2.25 million deaths among the remaining 16 million "exposed" population, implying an excess mortality rate of 14 percent. Such a mortality rate would be higher for the country as a whole—fully 15 percent higher—than what Robinson et al. calculated for what was, by consensus, the worst affected province. This extrapolation is not plausible.

Two accounts that have attempted to take a somewhat more systematic approach to calculating excess deaths also come to somewhat lower estimates of total excess deaths. Taking 1994 as the base, Daniel Goodkind and Lorraine West (2001) use an age-specific death-rate model and official DPRK statistics on crude death rates to arrive at an estimate of excess deaths of 236,900 between 1995 and 2000. Using the same model with the much higher mortality rates implied by the Robinson et al. interviews generated an estimate of 2.6 million excess deaths over the same period—a figure more than ten times the estimate derived from the official statistics. Of all the alternative estimates reviewed by Goodkind and West, they prefer those based on data from the 1998 WFP nutritional survey and calibrated with crude death rates for the period of China's Great Leap Forward. This approach yields excess deaths for the period 1994–2000 of about 1 million based on the Chinese death rates, and 605,000 adjusted for nutritional status from the 1998 WFP survey.

A problem with the Goodkind and West study is that they date the start of the famine to 1995, using 1994 as a baseline for their calculations. Suk Lee's (2003) careful analysis of official statistics finds, however, that mortality was already elevated in 1994. Also using a gender- and age-specific model of death rates, Lee estimates that between January 1, 1994, and August 31, 1999, North Korea experienced 668,000 excess deaths. Lee ignores population loss stemming from refugee flows into China, and, as a consequence, his analysis may wrongly include these as famine-related deaths. But from what we know of the collapse of the economy, declining agricultural production, and anecdotal evidence from refugee interviews, Lee is almost certainly right that the famine started in 1994. If so, then the estimates by Goodkind and West probably underestimate its impact.

Both Goodkind and West, as well as Lee, assume that fertility rates remained unchanged and hence do not consider births forgone as part of the famine's demographic toll. This assumption is probably more defensible than it might appear at first glance. The Good Friends interviews document a decline in fertility, but the analysis of other famines has suggested that this drop in fertility is typically offset by a subsequent rise in fertility when the crisis passes.

There is still much we don't know about the demographic effects of the North Korean famine. Moreover, the excess deaths are just one summary measure of the famine's costs. Such statistics do not capture the long-run developmental effects of early childhood stunting, not to mention the wide-ranging social consequences of the food shortage, from the breakup of families to human trafficking, prostitution, and crime born of desperation. Nonetheless, in our view, the most sophisticated attempts to measure excess deaths put them in a range of roughly 600,000 to 1 million, or approximately 3 to 5 percent of the precrisis population.

Conclusion

In chapter 2, we took a broad approach to the famine by looking at overall food availability. In this chapter, we complemented that approach by considering in more detail the question of distribution and entitlements, including the question of who perished and how. We paid particular attention to the regional dimensions of the famine and its impact on the urban working classes in the industrial cities of the east coast. Yet perhaps the most important point to emerge from this overview is not the differences across groups—as important and fateful as those proved to be—but the systemic nature of the crisis. In the mid-1990s, the most fundamental component of the socialist social compact—the ability of the government to guarantee adequate food—broke down. This compact had been strained by food shortages and possibly by localized famine before. But the famine of the mid-1990s and the subsequent persistence of shortages were something altogether new: a chronic and generalized breakdown of the food distribution system. In chapter 7, we return to the long-run impact of this change. But before doing so we turn to a more detailed consideration of the aid effort, which after 1996 became a central pillar—arguably even the mainstay—of the ability of the government to provide food at all.

PART II

The Dilemmas of Humanitarian Assistance

CHAPTER FOUR

The Aid Regime

The Problem of Monitoring

Through the end of 1995, the availability of food in North Korea was over-whelmingly a function of domestic production, dwindling—and increasingly erratic—commercial imports, and stocks of unknown magnitude that the government was almost certainly drawing down.

After 1995, aid mattered. North Korea quietly negotiated some bilateral aid from South Korea and Japan in early 1995 that assisted the country in the spring of 1996 (see chapter 6). But it was not until the floods of July and August 1995 that the government made an unprecedented appeal for wider multilateral assistance. With a critical delay of almost a full year—caused in part by the North Korean government's misleading emphasis on the floods, in part by con-flicting assessments of the food situation within the donor community—aid finally began to flow into the country in large quantities.

We look at this decade-long aid experience through three related lenses. In this chapter, we consider the contentious relationship between North Korea and the humanitarian community over the issue of monitoring; in the next chapter, we address the related issue of diversion. In telling this story, we pay particular attention to the World Food Programme (WFP), which has managed the bulk of humanitarian assistance to the country. However, the WFP is an agent of governments; the organization secures all its food through an appeals process and is ultimately dependent on the largesse of the final donors. In chapter 6, we explore the conflicting humanitarian and political motives the donors have for extending aid, motives that have made coordination among them difficult.

From the very beginning of the aid effort, North Korean authorities made it clear that they did not ascribe to the most basic norms of the humanitarian community, which include access, transparency of the aid operation, non-discrimination in distribution, and a focus on the most vulnerable groups. As is true in any aid game, the North Korean government sought to maximize flows of aid while limiting the conditions attached to it. Among these restrictions were strict limits on the number of aid workers—multilateral, bilateral, and from the NGO community—and severe limits on movement and access.

In these circumstances—again, as in all aid relationships—the donor community faced a recurrent choice about whether to continue their efforts or to walk away. At various times, both individual governments and particular NGOs made the principled decision to halt their programs and in some cases to leave the country permanently. Yet for both humanitarian reasons and political ones that we detail in chapter 6, most donors acquiesced to North Korean exceptionalism and stayed. This continued commitment might have been morally appropriate. But it is also clear that once this commitment was made, the ability to exercise leverage over the terms of engagement was severely compromised.

This strategically compromised position did not imply a lack of effort to secure improved access; to the contrary. Because of both international and national norms of accountability, the donor community in general, and the WFP in particular, was under constant pressure to ensure that aid was going to its intended beneficiaries. As a result, the aid process can be viewed as a protracted negotiation centering on the two closely related issues we address here: monitoring and diversion.

We examine in some detail the efforts by the WFP to define appropriate target groups and the history of its efforts to monitor aid delivery to them; we also make these problems concrete by walking through the complex logistical difficulties of monitoring even a single food shipment. We conclude that monitoring became more sophisticated over time. Some NGOs probably slipped under the government's radar by building local-level programs that were not only effective in humanitarian terms but had other positive effects as well, such as building capacity and trust. We find a surprising degree of continuity, however, in the basic constraints on large-scale international assistance. Moreover, the gains made over time were reversible. We close this chapter by outlining the efforts by the North Korean regime to curtail significantly the activities of the WFP in late 2005 and early 2006, an episode that reveals very clearly the bargaining issues in the relationship.

Humanitarian Assistance to North Korea: An Overview

Food aid has constituted the dominant share of total assistance to North Korea from the onset of the relief effort and continues to dominate assistance to this day (see appendix 2, tables 1–3). Aid has passed through a variety of different channels, including multilateral institutions, bilateral aid agencies, and a diverse, active, and highly innovative NGO community.[1] The multiplicity of channels makes it difficult to track external assistance with complete confidence; in appendix 2, we provide a more detailed breakdown of total assistance by sector and agency. But this accounting exercise shows clearly the prominent role played by food aid.

From the opening of the country in 1995 through 2005, the world community poured over $2.3 billion of assistance into North Korea. Of that sum, 67 percent has taken the form of food aid, and another 9 percent has addressed food security or agricultural rehabilitation and development (appendix 2, tables 1 and 3).[2] Figure 4.1 looks at this wide-ranging international effort in the context of domestic production and two of the demand estimates that we constructed in chapter 2; Chinese food trade is included in these estimates, which are measured in millions of metric tons of basic grain equivalents. Several points are striking, the first of which is the continuing precariousness of North Korea's overall food supply. A second striking fact is the extent of aid dependence. The sluggish recovery of production since the collapse of the great famine and the government's continuing unwillingness to use foreign exchange for commercial imports have implied a steadily increasing reliance on humanitarian assistance.

The third point, however, is the declining willingness of the international community to continue to support North Korea. Even before the onset of the most recent nuclear crisis in the fall of 2002, total aid had begun to decline, reflecting a combination of severe pressures on the humanitarian system from other crises as well as donor fatigue with North Korea's uncooperative stance. WFP situation reports have always reflected concern about the timely flow of aid, even in years when international commitments appeared strong. In February 2002, however, the WFP experienced the first major break in the aid pipeline. WFP warnings became increasingly desperate in tone, and the organization was repeatedly forced to adjust food deliveries to targeted populations. In 2005 the position of the WFP became more precarious still as North Korea argued that it no longer needed international assistance and took steps to reduce its presence dramatically; we return to this episode in more detail in the conclusion to this chapter.

In any aid effort, coordination poses serious challenges to both donors and recipients. In 1991, following a problematic response to the plight of Iraqi Kurdish refugees, the United Nations General Assembly created the Consolidated

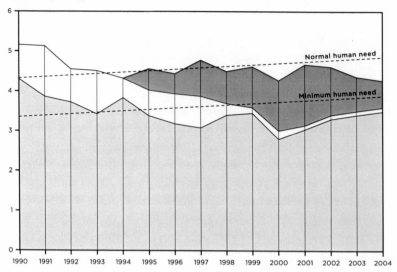

FIGURE 4.I. *Sources of Food Supply, 1990–2004*
Note: Figures are for November of year indicated to October of following year. *Source:* USDAFAS; PSD database, WFPINTERAIS 2004, 2005b, Noland 2000.

Appeals Process (CAP), led by the United Nations Office for the Coordination of Humanitarian Affairs (OCHA). The consolidated appeal rests on a planning cycle that includes consultations with the aid-receiving governments; independent assessments of needs; the formulation of an appeal; the tracking of international, bilateral, and NGO contributions; and the monitoring and assessment of subsequent aid delivery. The CAP was also designed to solve the coordination problems that can arise among the multilateral institutions and donor governments. As we will show, North Korea posed severe and ongoing challenges to this mandate.

The World Food Programme is the multilateral organization with primary responsibility for humanitarian food assistance.[3] Quite early, it was clear that the WFP would play a major role in the international community's response to North Korea's distress (appendix 2, table 2). Since 1995, $1.5 billion of aid has flowed through the consolidated appeals process; of that, the WFP is responsible for $1.3 billion, corresponding to roughly four million tons of food.

The dominance of food aid partly reflected the demands of the situation. The emphasis on food aid, however, has also reflected a reticence on the part of donors to lend to North Korea or extend any assistance that could be interpreted as balance-of-payments support. Table 4.1 tracks the appeal cycles from

TABLE 4.1. Results of UN Consolidated Appeals Process ($US millions)

Appeal	Target	WFP % of total target	Actual	WFP % of total income	% fulfilled
1995	n.a.	-	n.a.	-	n.a.
WFP	8.9	n.a.	6.7	n.a.	75.3
1996	43.6	-	34.4	-	78.8
WFP	26.8	61.5	26.2	76.2	97.8
1997	184.4	-	158.4	-	85.9
WFP	144.1	78.1	134.3	84.8	93.2
1998	383.2	-	215.9	-	56.3
WFP	345.8	90.2	202.7	93.9	58.6
1999	292.1	-	189.9	-	65.0
WFP	141.6	48.5	177.9	93.7	125.6
2000	313.8	-	153.1	-	48.8
WFP	222.5	70.9	145.6	95.1	65.4
2001	384.0	-	248.0	-	64.6
WFP	315.9	82.3	240.1	96.8	76.0
2002	246.8	-	220.0	-	89.1
WFP	216.7	87.8	206.1	93.7	95.1*
2003	229.4	-	133.1	-	58.0
WFP	202.7	88.4	117.8	88.5	58.1
2004	208.8	-	151.6	-	72.6
WFP	172.3	82.5	118.9	78.4	69.0
2005	n.a.	-	n.a.	n.a.	
WFP	202.3	-	29.7	-	14.7
TOTAL, 1996–2004	2,286.1	-	1,504.4	-	-
WFP (1996–2005)**	1,990.7	78.2	1,399.3	91.0	-

* Reported achievement rate reflects amount received during the appeal relative to the target and excludes $99.3 million carried over.

** Percentage only takes into consideration WFP contributions from 1995–2004

Notes: n.a. = not available. No consolidated appeal in 2005. Thus, for 2005, WFP data is not via consolidated appeals but its own appeal.

Sources: UN-OCHA n.d.a.; FAO/WFP 1995, 1996, 1997, 1998a, 1998b, 1999a, 1999b, 2003, 2004; WFP 2006b.

1995 through 2005, showing the role of the WFP in the consolidated appeal. The WFP share dominates in every cycle, accounting for between 48.5 percent of the appeal (1999) to just over 90 percent (1998). If we look at actual contributions, however, we see that the WFP always had greater success in securing support than did the other agencies included in the consolidated appeal. From 1998 through 2002, WFP requests constituted 76 percent of the appeal but nearly 95 percent of actual contributions. This changed beginning in 2003, but in the context of declining overall assistance and the faltering ability of both the consolidated appeal and the WFP to meet targets.

The reluctance of the donors to provide other forms of assistance can be seen most clearly in the fate of the Agricultural Recovery and Environmental Protection Plan (AREP) in North Korea (Kim 2001). At the behest of the North Korean government, the United Nations Development Program (UNDP) convened a thematic roundtable in 1998, the first international conference designed—at least from the perspective of the donors—to get at the root causes of North Korea's food and agricultural problems. The UNDP had been a party to the consolidated appeal from the outset, although by its own admission had met only limited success in securing support before the roundtable.

At the roundtable meeting—three years after the floods of 1995—the North Korean government continued to interpret the country's problems in terms of natural disasters and declining external trade rather than institutional and policy constraints. North Korean officials clearly viewed the roundtable process as a way to secure external support for rehabilitation projects, including not only rural infrastructure but also the modernization of plants producing fertilizer and farm equipment. The government initially sought $340 million through the roundtable process. Through April 2000, $128.4 million had been extended in support of the program. About $40 million of this came in the form of grants and loans from OPEC and the International Fund for Agricultural Development, approximately another third from the EU, and the remainder from bilateral donors—the Republic of Korea, China, Switzerland—and NGOs.

But contributions came overwhelmingly in the form of material supports, mainly fertilizer and commodity support for food-for-work programs. For example, large fertilizer contributions by the South Korean government were counted in AREP totals. No support was granted for the modernization and operation of fertilizer and agricultural machinery plants or for the foreign exchange costs of rural infrastructure rehabilitation (though private crop insurance payouts were available for this purpose). From 1996 through 2004, the UNDP and FAO together accounted for only $20 million of total consolidated appeal commitments, or just over 1 percent of total aid.

Although the bulk of total humanitarian assistance was provided through a multilateral process, a substantial amount of aid still flowed outside of the consolidated appeal (table 4.2). Of \$2.4 billion of total assistance (again excluding Chinese support), approximately 62 percent went through multilateral institutions, and another 26 percent through bilateral channels; European countries accounted for some of the bilateral aid, but South Korea and China accounted for the majority of it. The NGO community has accounted for the remaining 12 percent of total aid, although that share rose somewhat as government commitment began to flag in the early 2000s.

This share almost certainly undervalues the social contribution of private assistance. Dedication among the NGO community is extraordinarily high. Small projects are closely monitored, based on the development of trust at the local level and are no doubt relatively efficient as a result. Wages paid to NGO workers are also low compared to those of international civil servants. Nonetheless, it is clear that public aid dominates the total, and even these figures may overestimate the private share as measured in purely financial terms.

Humanitarian Norms

The forgoing sketch has established the centrality of multilateral food aid to the overall humanitarian effort but has said little about the operational nitty-gritty. In particular, we want to focus on two core questions: Whom was the aid designed to help? And how did the donors try to ensure that aid was getting to intended beneficiaries? Before turning to those questions, it is important to outline the principles on which the humanitarian community operates. During the postwar period, the public humanitarian relief system centered on the UN agencies, particularly the World Food Programme, has developed a well-articulated set of norms governing the implementation of relief operations. These principles received at least rhetorical support from most of the major national donors—with the exception of China—as well as the overwhelming majority of the NGO community.

The desire to articulate clear norms among the humanitarian community is not simply an exercise in idealism; it is also designed to solve a particular set of incentive problems that can emerge in any humanitarian operation. In the absence of normative constraints, differences among donors and competition among them can lead to a race to the bottom: a willingness to turn a blind eye to diversion, a tendency to exaggerate aid effectiveness, and even the empowerment of groups who bear responsibility for causing the humanitarian crisis

TABLE 4.2. Total Humanitarian Assistance, by Donor Organization
(millions of US$)

| | Within Appeal | | Outside Appeal | | | |
	Multilateral (through UN)	Bilateral	UN Agencies	NGOs (including Red Cross)	Other	TOTAL
1996/7	34.39	11.28	0.00	4.67	0.00	50.35
1997/8	158.38	105.79	1.80	26.49	0.00	292.46
1998	215.87	92.06	0.00	27.16	0.00	335.09
1999	189.89	41.64	0.00	4.32	0.00	235.85
2000	153.10	58.58	0.06	12.48	0.00	224.22
2001	247.97	61.16	1.51	66.80	0.15	377.59
2002	220.01*	79.24	2.98	58.60	0.00	360.83
2003	133.10	9.64	1.62	42.34	0.00	186.70
2004	151.51	121.39	2.20	24.76	0.63	300.49
2005**	0.00	61.09	0.68	1.80	0.00	63.56
TOTAL	1,504.23	641.87	10.85	269.43	0.78	2,427.16

* Includes $99.32 million carried over by the WFP

**2005: Bilateral data includes WFP data not listed in UN-OCHA.

in the first place.[4] These incentive problems can be exacerbated when private transnational groups act as subcontractors for the official donors, as has been the case in North Korea (see Cooley and Ron 2002).

The basic principles governing delivery of humanitarian aid are straightforward (Reed 2004:9). Aid should go to those in greatest need based on objective and systematic assessment. Access to aid should not be determined on the basis of age, gender, social status, ethnicity, and political beliefs (Ziegler 2002). Aid delivery should be transparent, enabling agencies to confirm that it is distributed to the target group. Donor agencies should also be allowed to assess the impact of aid, which requires direct and ongoing contact with the affected populations.

These basic norms, as well as principles of accountability within donor countries, drive the related insistence on thorough monitoring of aid. The WFP has a standard operating procedure embodying reciprocal obligations on the part of donors and recipients. The WFP's responsibility to the donor governments is to ensure that donations are used properly. Recipient governments are responsible for facilitating WFP oversight. Under the standard WFP agreement, the recipient government guarantees that commodities reach specified target beneficiaries and that improper diversion does not occur. Within a given time frame, the government agrees to account for all contributions by providing the WFP with an audited report containing specified information on the volume of food (and subsidies) received, the number of beneficiaries, location of distribution centers, losses incurred, their causes, and measures undertaken to limit those losses. Agreements also call for assessments that allow donors to gauge the impact of the aid effort on beneficiaries' nutritional status. Agreements specify in some detail the required monitoring, including repeat visits to all distributional units and the freedom to make spot checks, and further specify that recipient governments will facilitate the internal movement of WFP staff necessary to executing these duties (GAO 1999).

The NGO community is much more diverse than the public humanitarian aid machinery, and we do not pretend to treat its contribution thoroughly; other excellent accounts of their operations exist (most notably Flake and Snyder 2003). Although the NGO contribution is relatively small in financial terms, the private humanitarian community has had a substantial influence on the broader politics of aid to North Korea. On occasion, consortia of NGOs have been involved in the monitoring and even delivery of food. Moreover, the on-the-ground experience of the NGOs makes them an invaluable source of information on the country, and their conflicts with the North Korean government mirror closely the constraints facing the WFP.

Difficult ethical dilemmas in Bosnia and Central Africa in the 1990s pushed the NGO community to codify voluntary norms that overlapped at a number of points with those governing the multilateral aid effort.[5] Among these norms are prior understanding of basic conditions; evaluation of effectiveness; participation by recipients in the design management and monitoring of programs; distribution of aid through a transparent system that can be monitored and adequately audited; and impartiality, or the distribution of aid in a fair and equitable manner.

North Korea severely challenged the NGO commitment to these humanitarian norms, and the community has been deeply, even bitterly, divided on the propriety of staying; these debates are worth tracing in some detail. Beginning in mid-1998, the first of a series of highly publicized withdrawals by European and American NGOs took place, starting with Médicins du Monde in July 1998, Médicins sans Frontières (MSF) in September 1998, and Accion Contra la Faim in the spring of 2000 (Schloms 2003). These NGOs had several things in common, including a focus on medical issues, which of necessity required ongoing contact with patients, and a belief in the importance of training, which meant ongoing contact with doctors and nurses. These European NGOs also shared an approach to humanitarian assistance in which relief and concern for basic human rights and the empowerment of civil society were seen as closely linked. All issued strong justifications for their actions, and MSF quite explicitly criticized those who chose to stay and thus created tensions between the North Korean government and the entire NGO community (IFRC 2000:84). This first wave of departures was followed by still other withdrawals, including CARE and Oxfam (McCarthy 2000; Smith 2002; Schloms 2003; Flake 2003; Reed 2004).

In the wake of MSF's highly visible departure, the humanitarian agencies outlined a statement of humanitarian principles in November 1998; this was subsequently updated in April 1999 and March 2001.[6] A working group comprising all the resident humanitarian agencies established benchmarks for gauging progress on these norms, which is regularly recorded in reports by the OCHA. The humanitarian community also issued consensus statements, although these statements seem to have had the objective of reassuring the North Korean authorities following highly publicized departures as much as showing joint resolve. Before turning to the question of the extent to which WFP and NGO norms were met, it is first important to consider the question of whom food aid was intended to reach.

Principles in Practice I: Origins and Objectives of the Aid Program

From the outset, the multilateral agencies and NGOs in North Korea operated at a disadvantage because they did not have a presence in the country when the crisis broke and thus lacked accumulated, on-the-ground expertise. The United Nations Development Program had established an office in 1980 and helped to organize early humanitarian assistance (Smith 2002). But it took time for other organizations to establish even a rudimentary presence, and the North Korean government was far from cooperative. The WFP established an office in Pyongyang in November 1995, but early monitoring was limited to the west coast.[7] The NGOs faced the particular problem that the North Korean authorities were resistant even to granting residential status at all, forcing coordination both among the NGOs that did enjoy residential status and between those that were in-country and those that were not.[8]

The multilateral response was also affected by very different assessments of the nature and extent of the food problem among some of the principal actors, assessments that remain controversial and even divisive to this day. Information filtering out along the Chinese border provided evidence of severe food shortages and even famine conditions quite early, and a number of journalists, NGOs, and analysts jumped on these reports and reached conclusions that, with the benefit of hindsight, were largely justified (Becker 1996, 1998b; Snyder 1996; Lautze 1997; KBSM 1998). Certain analysts in the U.S., Japanese, and South Korean intelligence and foreign policy communities almost certainly had similar information, although they were in some cases constrained from speaking out (Natsios 1999:170–71).

But for some of those sitting in Pyongyang—or suspicious of North Korean motives, or reluctant to provide assistance—the evidence of famine was much less straightforward or altogether lacking.[9] Highly orchestrated visits to institutions housing the malnourished could be read as evidence of a much wider problem but could also be interpreted as a cynical play for sympathy—and more aid. With initial access limited entirely to the west coast and to tightly controlled visits, outsiders also lacked access to the types of information—the markers—that would allow them to gauge the extent and severity of the problem: information on food prices, which tend to rise sharply during famines; evidence of large-scale population movements and foraging; evidence on diet, such as the consumption of inferior foods; surveys on actual nutrition and health status or mortality. Not until the WFP pressed successfully for the opening of the northeastern provinces in May 1997 did the extent of the damage already incurred become fully apparent and was it possible to ramp up supplies to these highly distressed areas.

Whatever the differences among the early assessments, the first WFP/FAO teams were quite blunt in underscoring that the food crisis was not simply a result of the floods. Rather, structural and policy problems in the agricultural sector and in the economy more generally were to blame.[10]

From the outset, however, the North Korean government defined the issue as a humanitarian concern that centered on providing food aid to flood victims. The main interlocutor for both the WFP and NGOs was the FDRC, a committee of the Ministry of Foreign Affairs. The main objective of this committee was to maximize the flow of food aid to the country while stringently controlling the access of the multilateral agencies and NGOs. As one close observer put it, "The interaction between the FDRC and the international humanitarian aid community was adversarial from its inception, since the primary task of the FDRC was to watch the international food monitors and only secondarily to help ensure that assistance was delivered to end users" (Snyder 2003a:6). Indicative of this stance is the fact that through 2005 UN special rapporteur on the right to food Jean

Ziegler was denied entry to the DPRK five times, despite the fact that UN programs had been feeding nearly one-third of the population on an ongoing basis.

Despite the North Korean government's unwillingness to abandon its explanation that the floods were the driving cause of the food shortage, it quickly became apparent that the scope of the humanitarian disaster was much, much wider. In principle, the appropriate response to a geographically limited disaster would be to provide the victims with emergency financial support, enabling them to prioritize their needs and allocate resources accordingly. This approach was not possible in the North Korean case and frequently is not politically feasible from the perspective of donors. The donors surely did not trust the North Korean authorities to administer financial transfers. In any event, North Korea was not a market economy, and this first-best approach could not work. Instead, aid was provided in-kind and sourced outside the country. This approach was consistent with the politics of the main donor, the United States, where the farm lobby supports US-sourced food as the primary modality of relief. But it also accorded with the political interests of the North Korean government, which insisted that the PDS serve as the conduit of this externally sourced aid.

Given donor concerns about North Korean reticence with respect to access, the WFP had to define the target groups it sought to reach and construct an elaborate mechanism to ensure that externally sourced aid was actually reaching the intended beneficiaries. Each WFP appeal was thus accompanied by a relatively detailed outline of target groups (appendix 2, table 4).

This targeting went through several phases. In the first appeal cycle in 1995, food was targeted at flood victims. In subsequent appeals, the pretense that humanitarian relief was going to immediate victims of the floods or other natural disasters was dropped. As the numbers fed through the WFP rose dramatically, from 500,000 in 1995 to nearly 7.5 million in 1998, the WFP identified two basic target groups (figure 4.2; appendix 2, table 4). The first was a set of groups that were vulnerable because of their particular food needs, age, or position within the household, such as children, pregnant and nursing women, and the elderly. These groups dominated the highly elaborated—and spuriously precise—language of the appeals ("297,955 pregnant/nursing women" [FAO/WFP 2003]). After 1998 these groups were also the target of WFP-sponsored factories that began to produce fortified biscuits and noodles. A second target group comprised the beneficiaries of a food-for-work program. This program combined distribution of food to rural reconstruction projects that fed as many as 1 million people (including direct participants and dependents) each year. The total targeted populations peaked at more than 8 million in 1999 and 2000, amounting to well over one-third of the population, and remained in excess of 6 million through 2005. This policy of casting relief in terms of narrowly

Number of beneficiaries (in millions)

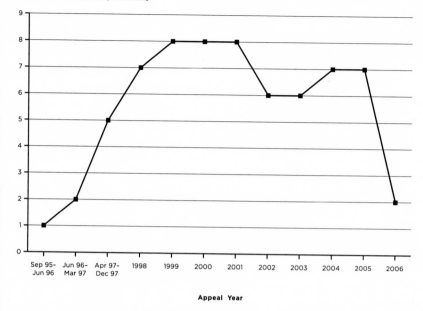

Appeal Year

FIGURE 4.2. WFP Targets by Appeal
Sources: FAO/WFP 1995, 1996, 1997, 1998a, 1998b, 1999a, 1999b, 2003, 2004; UN-OCHA n.d.b.

targeted groups was almost certainly suboptimal in principle but arose out of the specific political constraints embodied in the North Korean case.

In the period since the 2002 reforms, the WFP began to collect survey and focus group information suggesting the particular vulnerability of PDS-dependent urban households and to develop a quite nuanced understanding of the identity of the most seriously affected groups (FAO/WFP 2003, 2004). The target groups did not change in composition, but WFP statements suggest an effort to shift resources toward urban households in the northeast in particular and to extend the food-for-work effort into the cities.

A crucial feature of the North Korean setting was that the multilateral agencies had no independent channels for delivering food to these targeted groups and were not allowed to develop them. A number of vulnerable groups, however, were either institutionalized or had daily contact with institutions, namely, hospitals, orphanages, kindergartens, and schools.[11] By targeting these groups, the WFP could sidestep the charge that it was supporting a public distribution system used to control the population and channel food to privileged groups.

Whatever the political merits of focusing on such vulnerable groups, the substantive merits are somewhat less clear. First, it is not obvious that this particular definition of the vulnerable was appropriate given the setting. These groups were certainly among the hardest hit in any community that faced serious shortages, and feeding children frees up food that can be consumed by other household members.

But distress had a strong regional dimension, and some members of the groups targeted were in fact protected. Attempting to feed all the children in the country almost certainly channeled food to less deserving households. This targeting strategy would also have done little for an urban family with no school-age children.

Although these criticisms have some merit, it is probably misguided to over-target in a setting in which distress is broad. The larger problem was institutional. The North Korean food system does not have a distinct channel for distribution to schools, hospitals, and orphanages or to pregnant and nursing mothers. Even if it did, the WFP would not have controlled it. Food going to these institutions and individuals passed through the county-level warehouses and thus the county-level People's Committees, as did processed food coming from the factories that the WFP set up after 1998.[12]

These crucial decision makers do not have an interest in seeing the people in their jurisdictions starve. They are closer to their constituents than the government in Pyongyang. Many aid workers have remarked on the fact that local officials were generally more engaging and responsive than their political superiors. County-level officials may also be influenced at the margin by checks on their behavior through monitoring, an issue we take up in more detail below.

But these party and administrative leaders had to deal with a number of competing demands on any food they received: from local military and important work units, to the "retail" distribution centers (PDCs), to the lures of corruption and diversion to the market. Whatever the target groups designated by the WFP were, multilateral food assistance passed through the same basic distribution channels that supported the PDS and was ultimately commingled with other sources of supply. Food-for-work beneficiaries were essentially supplied through the same distribution channels. On this point, the critics are undoubtedly right: food aid passed through and supported the PDS.

An important question, therefore, is whether dependence on state distribution channels, and effectively the PDS, affected the extent to which food reached intended beneficiaries. We argue that this debate is to some extent misguided. The problem was not the reliance on state distribution channels per se but the cooperativeness of the government in using them. Such cooperation was limited, to say the least.

Principles in Practice II: The Monitoring Regime

For nearly a decade, the North Korean government has consistently violated its fundamental obligation to facilitate WFP operations within the country.[13] When shortages have been acute, North Korean officials have made tactical concessions. The converse is also true. When supply constraints have relaxed, as they did in 2005 as a result of increased aid and an improved harvest, the government has tightened access and threatened to evict the WFP and NGOs altogether. As a result, the evolution of the aid regime has had a grudging, "two-steps-forward, one-step-back" quality.

One of the most contentious constraints has been a very basic geographical one: the WFP and other groups have been denied access to parts of the country—and parts of the country believed to be particularly vulnerable. North Korean behavior with respect to the geographic scope of monitoring can be seen in figures 4.3 through 4.5. At the outset, whole provinces were simply ruled off limits, and monitoring visits were tightly circumscribed even within those provinces that were accessible.[14] By the end of 2000, the WFP had gained access to approximately 167 of 201 counties. But this changed very little between 2000 and 2005: large parts of the country remained off limits, and marginal increases in access were offset by the exclusion of some new counties. For example, in January 2003, part of Kaesŏng Municipality was placed off limits because an industrial complex was being developed in conjunction with a South Korean company!

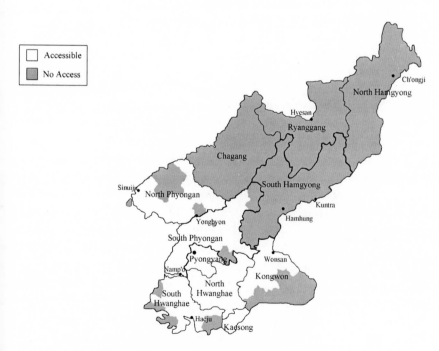

FIGURE 4.3. Accessible and Restricted Counties, 1995–96
Source: WFP Asia Regional Bureau, personal communication 2005.

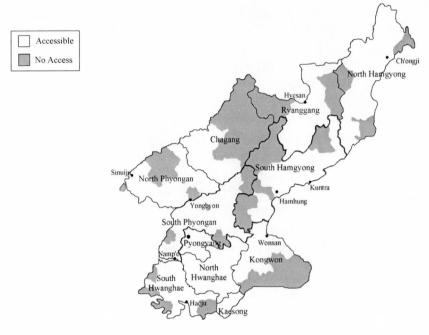

FIGURE 4.4. Accessible and Restricted Counties, February 2000
Source: WFP Asia Regional Bureau, personal communication 2005.

A number of direct conflicts over these issues provide insights about North Korean behavior in the face of external pressure; these cases also buttress our conclusions about triage in chapter 2.[15] The first had to do with the opening of the east coast. According to Natsios (1999:174), each of the first three WFP directors (serving between August 1995 and May 1997) had been directly rebuffed when they sought to make arrangements to visit the northeast and Chagang Province. Initial monitoring visits were limited to the west coast. In March 1997 WFP executive director Catherine Bertini visited North Korea and appeared to extract a promise to allow a WFP tour of conditions in the northeast. Bertini sent Tun Myat, a Burmese international civil servant, to North Korea to undertake this mission in May. Again according to Natsios, Myat threatened that the WFP would undertake no more appeals unless he were permitted to visit, and the North Korean government relented, opening up the east coast. This pressure was applied in the lean months at the very peak of the famine, and by the end of 1997 the WFP in principle had access to 159 counties, although it had only visited 110 (Bennett 1999:15).

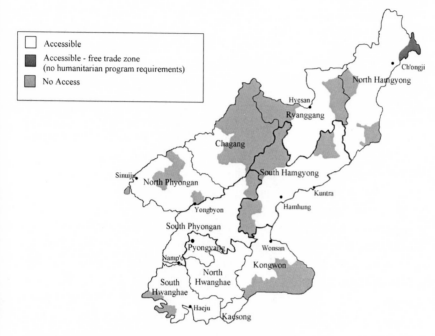

FIGURE 4.5. Accessible and Restricted Counties, October 2005
Source: WFP Asia Regional Bureau, personal communication 2005.

The ongoing conflict over access next came to a head in April 1998, when Bertini visited North Korea and warned the government that the WFP would suspend operations in 50 of the country's 210 counties if the agency could not monitor food distribution. The timing presents a close parallel to events of the previous year: this, too, was during the lean months. The government subsequently opened 11 more counties, but 39 were left inaccessible, and many of those remain inaccessible to this day. The WFP followed through on its threat by scaling back its proposed operations by 55,000 metric tons, or about the amount of food that would have been allocated to these counties. In this case, the outcome is ambiguous. Pressure did open some new counties, but the government also held firm on those about which it felt strongly, most probably counties with either military facilities, prison camps, particularly bad conditions, or all three.

In addition to the question of geographic access, the WFP has faced constant North Korean opposition to its desired number of outside monitors. The number of international WFP staff peaked at approximately fifty in 2001, despite a program delivering hundreds of millions of dollars in food annually to a country the size of the state of New York or Louisiana. The North Korean authorities have also consistently stuck to the principle that agency staffing levels are contingent on the dollar value of aid. Operational protocols specifically reflect this, and if donations drop, staff are asked to leave. By the time of the standoff of 2005, when North Korea first threatened to evict the WFP altogether, the number of international staff had fallen to approximately forty.

An additional barrier to humanitarian operations is that official relief agencies are not permitted to use Korean speakers or ethnic Korean staff. Not until 2004 did the North Korean government allow resident WFP staff even to take Korean language lessons. The North Korean practice of seconding to relief operations only people with training as English-language translators also has a number of implications, the most obvious of which concerns the loyalty of staff. Without outside Korean speakers, the WFP and other organizations are reliant on government-supplied interpreters who owe their primary allegiance to the FDRC, not the relief agency that pays their salary. As one observer put it, "Their reporting loyalties are almost always toward the government" (Bennett 1999:16). A current aid worker put it less diplomatically: "In other countries, local nationals are on our side. In the DPRK even your driver tries to cheat you." In a private interview, one aid worker described a situation that would be amusing if not for the stakes. Unable to speak Korean or read Korean-language signs, aid workers had no idea if they were being shown the institutions that they had requested to visit and in multiple instances strongly suspected that they had been taken to the same institution twice.

The restrictions on staff not only severely limit the overall supply and their loyalty but affect quality as well. With aid workers trained primarily in English rather than a substantive field, local staff are unlikely to have the specific technical abilities to manage an aid effort, such as background in logistics, nutrition, and health. Dammers, Fox, and Jimenez observed in 2005 that of UNICEF's ten North Korean counterparts, none had specific technical or sectoral skills.

The exception to the use of Korean speakers is the growing involvement of South Korean agencies in humanitarian efforts. Interviews with South Korean government officials indicate that as of mid-2005 the country had sixty people at twelve distribution centers in six major cities involved in their monitoring efforts. But the South Korean Red Cross is constrained to work with its North Korean counterpart and has avoided confrontation over monitoring (Becker 1998b). South Korean NGOs are also highly restricted in interactions with their North Korean counterparts.

The constraints associated with these personnel practices are reinforced by North Korean laws prohibiting unauthorized contact with foreigners; these laws constitute a substantial disincentive for North Koreans to interact with foreign aid workers at all, let alone to provide information that might appear unflattering to the regime. When making monitoring visits, WFP staff are accompanied not only by local officials—who may be quite sympathetic to WFP concerns—but by FDRC staff as well. Given the rigidly authoritarian nature of the political system, the presence of representatives of the central government stifles the creation of alliances and networks with local officials or the revelation of any information that may be unflattering to the government. Reputedly, local officials who get too close to donors have been removed.

Leaving little to chance, the government also seeks to restrict the possibility of unauthorized contacts through pervasive controls and surveillance of foreign personnel as well. Not until April 2000 were WFP suboffice employees outside Pyongyang permitted to walk outside their hotels without being accompanied. We now have a handful of personal accounts of life in North Korea written from the perspective of diplomats and other foreigners working in the country (Cornell 2002; Harrold 2004). All contain descriptions of incidents—sometimes humorous, sometimes maddening—where personal belongings were rifled and searched without consent, phones tapped, and personal movements and contacts subjected to surveillance.

Beyond geographic restrictions, personnel practices, and the barriers discouraging unauthorized contacts, the North Korean government imposes a variety of restrictions on aid operations that make satisfactory monitoring difficult. The key instrument the WFP uses to ensure the integrity of its aid effort is the site visit. In principle, such visits should include the institutions that are final recipients of aid, such as schools, hospitals, public distribution centers, and food-for-work sites. These visits should include a random and even surprise component, allowing monitors to observe everyday rather than staged practices. Given the growing importance of the market in overall food consumption, it is also important for aid workers to be aware of market trends by being able to monitor food prices in farmers' and other markets. Finally, monitors should be able to collect systematic statistical information—for example, on nutritional status—in order to guarantee and improve the effectiveness of aid.

There is some evidence of progress on these fronts after 2000. Figure 4.6 provides some sense of the sheer number of monitoring visits conducted by the WFP staff over time by tracking the monthly number of visits from mid-1999 through early 2005. The number of contacts is large and shows a steady upward trend.[16] Outside of special travel restrictions imposed around the time of the 2000 summit, variation across months during the time periods was largely a function of weather and staff availability rather than fluctuations in access.

Number of visits

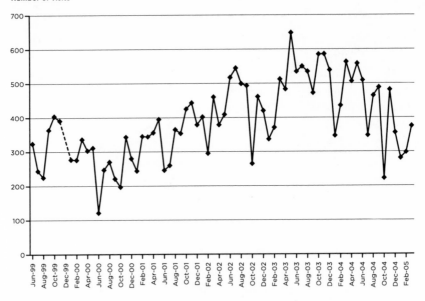

FIGURE 4.6. Number of Monthly Monitoring Visits, June 1999–March 2005
Note: Figure for March 2005 is preliminary. *Source:* WFP Monthly Updates (various issues), www.wfp.org/DPRK; USAID 2005.

These visits included a variety of institutional locations. PDS centers and targeted institutions typically dominated the number of visits, and ports were also covered. Prenotification is required, and visits to specific sites may in principle be denied. The standard procedure is for the WFP to make weekly requests to visit facilities in particular regions, which DPRK authorities then review. In 2002 about 8 percent of requests were denied. By 2003 this had fallen to 1 percent, and by the end of 2004 virtually all requests were met (Takahara 2004).

Table 4.3 moves beyond itemizing the sheer number of contacts by providing an overview of qualitative developments in the monitoring regime. Although a number of NGOs chose to leave, as we have mentioned, others reported marginal improvements in the operational climate (Smith 2002). Not only did the number of WFP visits increase, but the program also made a number of substantive gains beginning in 2002. One important new source of information came from focus groups that allowed WFP officials to discuss sources of income and food with target groups. These expanded over subsequent years, allowing the WFP to shift its focus from overall, national-level food security to household-level food security and a more nuanced understanding of who was vulnerable. The government also agreed to new nutritional surveys, one in 2002 and a second in 2004, that provided new information (see chapter 7).

TABLE 4.3. Developments in the Monitoring Regime

Appeal	Policy Developments	International WFP Staff (end of year)
Sept. 1995-June 1996	All early monitoring visits limited to west coast: North and South Hwanghae, North and South P'yŏng'an, Pyongyang and Nampo	WFP has four international staff
June 1996-Mar. 1997	June: USAID monitoring report argues against use of PDS, reports evidence of preferential distribution of food	WFP has five international staff
April 1997-Dec. 1997	The WFP negotiates the opening of the northeast provinces to direct shipments and some monitoring, but parts of the provinces of Chagang and all of Yanggang were basically inaccessible. At beginning of appeal, WFP has access to 159 of 211 counties.	WFP has 24 international staff
	WFP suboffices opened in Ch'ŏngjin, Hamhŭng, and Sinŭiju	
1998	WFP threatens to suspend planned operations in 50 of 210 counties if not allowed to monitor. DPRK responds by opening 11 counties where 2 percent of population live, bringing total in May 1998 to 171 counties. WFP scales back assistance accordingly, reducing proposed operations by 55,000 tons ($33 million)	WFP has 35 international staff
	May: WFP suboffice opened in Wonsan	
	September—October: EU, UNICEF, and WFP, in collaboration with the DPRK government, conduct nutritional survey	
	October: WFP suboffice opened in Hyesan	
	November: Humanitarian principles outlined by NGOs participating in the 1999 appeal and first Consensus Statement of all UN agencies, NGOs, and donors operating in the DPRK, expressing commitment both to relief and to the humanitarian principles, including effective monitoring	
1999	April. Update of humanitarian principles to reflect new donors	WFP has 41 international staff
2000	Regional Programming Monitoring Teams established to decentralize monitoring.	WFP has 37 international staff

TABLE 4.3. Developments in the Monitoring Regime, *continued*

Appeal	Policy Developments	International WFP Staff (end of year)
2001	Four new counties opened to monitoring (three in South Hwanghae and one in P'yŏng'an)	WFP has 51 international staff
	March: Update of humanitarian principles to reflect new donors and third consensus statement	
	August: Government commits to providing WFP with full list of beneficiary institutions	
2002	Authorities allow double teaming; simultaneous monitoring by two WFP teams in the same province on the same day.	WFP has 39 international staff
	The WFP is allowed to use focus groups to gather information on sources of food and income	
	Satellite agreement reached allowing satellite communications facilities in Pyongyang and five field stations	
	Government honors its commitment to conduct a nutritional survey	
	Substantial personnel allowed to walk unaccompanied outside their hotels	
	August: DPRK and WFP sign protocol on conduct of a nutrition survey	
2003	January: A county in Kaesŏng is closed to monitoring because of the establishment of an industrial complex in conjunction with a South Korean firm.	WFP has 45 international staff
	May: Internal travel restrictions associated with SARS impede monitoring in North Hamgyŏng province and Sinŭiju	
	October: A new county in South P'yŏng'an is made accessible	
2004	Discussions with government over apparent sale and purchase of grain by county level officials at market prices.	WFP has 42 international staff

TABLE 4.3. Developments in the Monitoring Regime, *continued*

Appeal	Policy Developments	International WFP Staff (end of year)
2004, *cont'd*	From fall, increasing conflict over monitoring as government authorities review humanitarian operations and limit access to seven counties in Chagang province, seek to reduce the overall number of site visits, and limit the nature of questions posed through focus groups and surveys.	
	December: WFP suspends operations in Chagang on "no access, no food" principle	
2005	March: WFP regional director for Asia Tony Banbury outlines elements of a new monitoring regime under negotiation with North Korean authorities, including more visits to PDCs, more extensive baseline surveys, expanded survey groups and electronic tracking of shipments.	WFP has 43 international staff (as of the end of January)
	This regime is never implemented. At the end of the year regional offices, food factories, and food-for-work programs are closed.	
2006	March: WFP and North Korea negotiate over a greatly circumscribed program, involving a dramatic reduction in staff and restricted (quarterly) opportunities to monitor projects outside Pyongyang.	WFP has prospectively 10 or fewer staff

Sources: FAO/WFP 1995, 1996, 1997, 1998a, 1998b, 1999a, 1999b, 2003, 2004; UN-OCHA n.d.a.

It is important to underline, however, that these marginal changes have taken place in the context of quite substantial limitations on the freedom of movement of monitors, as well as clear evidence of the reversibility of any gains that the WFP has been able to make. In large humanitarian operations, it is impossible to monitor every transaction. Random, unannounced inspections are thus critical to maintaining the integrity of the relief effort, but in North Korea they are not allowed. WFP officials claim they can increase the effective randomness in the context of a system that requires prenotification, for example, by proposing to visit an orphanage in a particular county (of which there are, say, seven) and on visitation day demanding to be taken to a particular orphanage of the seven possible. Yet even these techniques are imperfect since interviewees at any given site cannot be chosen at random. Moreover, as of late 2005, the North Korean government had still not provided the WFP with a comprehensive list of institutions that benefit from foreign support despite repeated requests over a period of years.

A Typical WFP Shipment

To see how these various constraints work in practice, it is useful to consider a typical WFP delivery.[17] Following the appeal and commitments from donor governments, the WFP works with donors to orchestrate shipments, which land at North Korean ports. The WFP and FDRC agree on a delivery plan for each shipment, specifying the final distribution of aid by local jurisdiction and targeted group.

The WFP and FDRC meet the food at the port. The logistics of distribution within North Korea, however, are handled not by the FDRC but by the Ministry of Food Administration, and the food ultimately passes through the public distribution system (Bennett 1999). As early as 1997, it became clear that limited trucking capacity and fuel shortages were a major constraint on effective delivery of food. The WFP offered the North Korean government fuel subsidies, but to keep track of food trucked to the county-level warehouses and to justify the subsidies, the WFP and the North Korean authorities developed a "consignment note system" to monitor shipments. The system used waybills in English and Korean that identified the contents of the shipment and its destination (Bennett 1999:12; GAO 1999:11–12). The North Korean authorities compile the waybills for a particular shipment. When delivery is complete, the waybills are returned to the WFP for the fuel reimbursement. The WFP in turn maintains a database of shipments.

The opportunities for leakage in such a system are multiple. Major diversion at the port is unlikely, but much food does not go from port to truck but rather to trains and barges before it is transferred to trucks; these shipments are not tracked. The staff in the WFP suboffices receive copies of the distribution plans. In principle, warehouse managers are supposed to receive copies of these as well. WFP staff have reported on a number of occasions their suspicions that much of the paperwork required by the WFP was fabricated ex post (Kirk and Hochstein 1997; Bennett 1999; Kirk, Brookes, and Pica 1998), although whether this was to hide diversion or simply reflected lack of administrative capacity is impossible to say. The WFP field offices attempt to check as many county warehouses as they have access to, and although access has been limited, Bennett claims that through the peak of the famine there were "only very few occasions when consignments were not received as stated in the counties visited" (1999:12).

Nonetheless, there is at least anecdotal evidence of problems at this stage in the distribution chain. Kirk, Brookes, and Pica (1998), for example, report observing food donated by the European Union (EU) loaded onto a military truck with military personnel and headed toward a province not covered by the EU assistance program. Another example is recounted by Chin Yong-gyu, a former sergeant in the Korean People's Army and driver (1998–2002), who described in detail how the military diverted foreign relief supplies and fooled UN monitors (International Federation for Human Rights 2003). Yet more recent incidents of this sort are provided by Good Friends (2005).

Once food reaches the county warehouse, the only check on delivery to the final institutional destinations—whether public distribution centers (PDCs) or targeted institutions—and on the use made of the food by those final destinations is through spot checks by WFP suboffices. Although large-scale diversion at higher stages in the distribution chain is possible, it is at this lower level of the chain that monitoring is the weakest and diversion thus most likely to occur. The task of tracking supplies across tens of thousands end-user institutions under difficult working conditions is vast. Ironically, some NGOs operating on a smaller scale may have a more accurate grasp of where their contributions are ending up, despite what appears to be less rigorous monitoring.

With approximately 43,000 ultimate destinations and the multiple restrictions on monitoring, it is extremely difficult for the WFP and NGO leadership to say with certainty where food is going. We take up the issue of diversion in more detail in the following chapter, but a fascinating example is documented by Dammers, Fox, and Jimenez (2005). UNICEF maintains an EU-funded program to distribute therapeutic milk, which can be fatal if administered incorrectly. According to the 2003/2004 agreement, this milk was to be provided to three provincial hospitals with properly trained staff. During a monitoring visit in November 2003, however, the EU's technical assistant discovered that the supplies were being distributed to baby homes in the cities of Hyesan and Ch'ŏngjin. The DPRK then proposed for the 2004/2005 aid cycle that the product be distributed to 157 rehabilitation centers of various sorts, an alteration in terms of reference that Dammers, Fox, and Jimenez describe as without justification, cost-ineffective, and potentially dangerous.

Centrally directed conspiracies to divert aid may well exist,[18] but our reconstruction of an aid shipment suggests that local politics are likely to play a more important role in the final distribution of food than are central government authorities. County-level administrators have substantial influence over the disposition of aid supplies and face a host of motivations ranging from genuine and sincere differences with donors over priorities, to the universal local politics phenomenon of back-scratching, to personal pecuniary gain. The latter may be particularly important if we consider that these midlevel government and party officials are living on rapidly eroding won-denominated salaries, as we discuss in more detail in chapter 7.

According to interviews with WFP officials, staff members occasionally go to the PDCs and observe distribution to final aid recipients. Yet as one UN official put it, "We are not naïve. We have 300 monitoring visits a month. They don't mean anything, because there are no random visits" (quoted in Flake 2003:37). Both U.S. and EU official monitors indicated "staging" and significant discrepancies between reported numbers of beneficiaries at particular institutions and those actually observed during the 1997–98 period. More important, refugee interviews suggest that there is diversion from the warehouse level to the army and privileged party personnel.

Conclusion: The Stand-Off of 2005–6

In this chapter, we have outlined the principles governing the monitoring of food aid and the evolution of those principles in practice. We argued that these principles were in effect the subject of an ongoing negotiation between the donor community and the government, with some signs of progress—albeit from a low base—after 2000. But these gains were by no means irreversible, and 2004 witnessed a backlash against foreign monitoring that ended with the WFP narrowly managing to maintain its operations in the country.[19]

This backlash began in the summer, when the North Korean authorities indicated that they would not participate in the UN's annual consolidated appeal, were requesting the dissolution of the UN's Office for the Coordination of Humanitarian Affairs in Pyongyang after August 2005, and were threatening to expel NGOs that did not bring in sufficient volumes of aid. In September 2004, the government began to take a number of restrictive measures: limiting the overall number of visits (from over five hundred a month to around three hundred a month; see figure 4.6), closing a number of counties and the whole province of Chagang (although some counties were subsequently reopened); and limiting household survey questions not directly related to food.

Observers ascribed a variety of motivations to these developments. One line of reasoning was that with the worst of the food emergency easing and with South Korean aid beginning to flow in large quantities, the DPRK did not need other, more intrusive assistance as badly and was less willing to make political concessions to secure it. The DPRK was receiving enough food aid, if all sources were considered, and would prefer development assistance because it was more fungible. Moreover, North Korean authorities were tired of WFP requests to visit PDCs, follow trucks carrying supplies, and do more interviews with recipients and focus groups. In short, in the words of one WFP official, the North Koreans were getting fed up with having forty WFP monitors "traipsing around their country."

Yet another possible explanation is that the government's fears were in fact warranted. The period after 2000 had seen an increasing penetration of information originating from outside the country through increased access to mobile phones, videotapes, and other sources of information such as travel to China (Lankov 2006a). The North's harder line might therefore have been a reflection of a government increasingly concerned about losing internal political control and the impact of a visible foreign presence on this process. And, of course, there is yet another, and perhaps simpler, explanation: monitoring did in fact constitute a partial check on behavior, and, as we will discuss below, members of the North Korean government who were involved in diversion might have simply preferred a less rigorous monitoring regime.

These conflicts gave rise to intense negotiations between the North Korean authorities and the WFP over monitoring questions. In a press conference in March 2005 that received wide distribution, WFP regional director Anthony Banbury suggested that the government and the WFP had reached an agreement "in principle" to a shift in the monitoring regime.[20] In return for a reduction in the overall number of visits, the WFP proposed four changes to the monitoring system:

- Household food information. Every four months the WFP would under-take baseline household surveys, interview local officials and others (e.g., farmers, factory officials), hold focus group discussions, and take observational walks. The first household survey was conducted in June 2005.
- Distribution monitoring. The WFP would shift at the margin to monitoring distribution centers and food-for-work projects, interview those receiving food aid there, and increase monitoring visits to nonhousehold sites (e.g., county warehouses, factories producing food products with WFP commodities, institutions receiving food aid).
- Ration cards. All WFP beneficiaries would be given a WFP-designed and -printed ration card that would be checked by the WFP at distributions. As of August 2005, the distribution of these cards was nearly complete.
- Commodity tracking. WFP staff would be allowed to follow food aid physically from the port of entry, to county warehouses, to three to six public distribution centers per county, as well as implementing a more uniform and consistent system to track commodities by waybill number, with the ultimate goal of eventually introducing an electronic system that would allow tracking of individual bags from port to final point of delivery. The first visits to PDCs began in June 2005.

These developments were promising; fully implemented and sustained, the changes would have marked an important advance in monitoring. Subsequent events, however, revealed that the North Koreans had no intention of subjecting themselves to greater scrutiny; to the contrary, increased aid and an improved harvest provided them with the leverage to squeeze the WFP.

In the fall of 2005, North Korea experienced its best harvest in a decade, and South Korea increased its aid. The North Koreans responded to these eased supply conditions by demanding that the WFP switch from food aid to development assistance and that all foreign personnel from private aid groups leave the country by year's end. They also banned private trade in grain, announced a revival of the PDS, and confiscated grain from North Korean farmers, policy developments we take up in greater detail in the conclusion to chapter 7. According to the WFP's resident representative in Pyongyang, Richard Ragan, the monitoring regime constituted a major motive for these actions. According to Ragan, the North Koreans "repeatedly stressed that our monitoring is too excessive" (Agence France Press 2005). (This claim was paradoxical insofar as development assistance would require even greater contact with foreigners and transparency in financial operations.)[21] A North Korean diplomat similarly cited the passage of the North Korean Human Rights Act in the United States, which linked continuing support for humanitarian activities to improvements in transparency (Brooke 2005).

The United Nations' immediate response was to underline the continued precariousness of the situation in North Korea and the indispensability of its presence. Whatever the humanitarian merits of this position, it effectively signaled that the WFP was unwilling to walk away and consequently reduced negotiating leverage with the North Koreans over the terms of engagement.[22] What followed was a diplomatic dance that ultimately resulted in the suspension of WFP operations in North Korea at the end of 2005, followed by the approval in February 2006 by the WFP executive board of a proposal for a greatly scaled-down program. The proposed program would feed roughly 1.9 million beneficiaries, less than one-third of the previously targeted population, requiring 150,000 metric tons of commodities at a cost of approximately $102 million (WFP 2006a). Confirming our emphasis on the government's concerns about monitoring, the North Koreans demanded a reduction in staff to ten or fewer, closure of the regional offices outside Pyongyang, and confinement of this staff to Pyongyang with only quarterly opportunities to visit project sites in the field, a stunning concession that the WFP incorporated into its proposal.

As of this writing, critical aspects of the terms of engagement remained to be negotiated with the North Korean government, and the United States remained noncommittal pending the outcome of these negotiations. But the negotiations underscore the basic points we have made here about the strategic nature of negotiations over transparency and monitoring issues with North Korea. When times are good, the government moves to limit access; when times are tough, they make the concessions necessary to secure at least adequate assistance.

The importance of transparency and monitoring for donors is not simply a humanitarian issue; it relates to the politically sensitive question of whether assistance is being diverted into unauthorized uses. It is to this contentious issue of diversion that we now turn.

CHAPTER FIVE

Diversion

Allegations of diversion and the corruption of the aid effort have dogged relief efforts in North Korea from their start in 1995. There are three reasons to be concerned with the diversion of food aid. The first is the obvious, humanitarian one: aid is intended to relieve the suffering of the most vulnerable, and having it reach its intended beneficiaries is a better outcome than having it consumed by those who are less vulnerable or altogether undeserving. A second reason for concern has to do not with the deserving but with the undeserving. Most forms of diversion involve corruption: not only do targeted beneficiaries go without allotted food while the less deserving are fed, but corrupt officials and others enrich themselves in the process.

But beyond these direct welfare considerations lies a third concern: that diversion could destroy political support for relief programs in donor countries. In February 2001, the UN special rapporteur for food rights, Jean Ziegler, wrote, "Most of the international food aid was being diverted by the army, the secret services, and the Government" (United Nations Commission on Human Rights 2001:11). In asking that this assessment be retracted, the executive director of the WFP, Catherine Bertini, admitted that her "gravest concern is that this erroneous information will undermine the political will of our donors" (*NAPSnet Daily Report* 2001).

The question of diversion is both contentious and poorly understood, and we therefore begin with the microeconomics of the process. Diversion is a distributional issue. Diverted aid does not vanish into the ether; someone consumes it. The incidence of the gains and losses across different social groups therefore requires careful analysis. In the case of North Korea, where markets had historically been suppressed, we argue that aid diversion contributed to their development. This change in the institutional environment in turn altered the distribution of gains and losses from diversion and the nature of food vulnerability more generally as an increasing share of total demand was met through the market.

In such a system, the incentives to divert aid from its intended recipients are clear and strong. Moreover, the weakness of the monitoring regime undoubtedly provided ample opportunity to do so. Assessing the actual magnitude of any illicit activity is difficult, however. In making our evaluation, we appeal to a variety of sources of evidence: eyewitness and participant accounts, interviews with humanitarian aid workers, refugee surveys, and documentary evidence such as photographs and video footage. Finally, we present a balance sheet exercise that demonstrates that the estimates derived from these various sources are consistent—in a quantitative, accounting sense—with information about other aspects of the North Korean food economy in which we have at least somewhat greater confidence. Taken together, this evidence suggests that the magnitude of diversion is probably large, perhaps 30 percent or more of total aid.

Before considering evidence on the magnitude of diversion, it is important to distinguish between the common image of large-scale centralized diversion by state officials and the military, as implied by Ziegler, and what we call decentralized diversion by lower level officials. It is also important to note that, in the context of the state-controlled Public Distribution System, food can be diverted not only from aid sources but also from domestic production and the PDS. Moreover, aid can be diverted directly to consumption by the undeserving but also into the market. The end recipients of diverted food purchased in the market might include the military and political elite and nontargeted groups. But purchasers of diverted aid also include targeted groups, who pay for the food instead of receiving it gratis.

We begin with the standard image of diversion as a centralized, large-scale process directed by the party and military for its own benefit. Certainly, the North Korean military has the ability to divert aid in this fashion if it wishes to, in part because of its political power, in part because of its logistic capabilities, in part because of the general weakness of the monitoring system and the specific exclusion of militarily sensitive areas. Anecdotal evidence has certainly confirmed that at least some donated food finds its way to the military and party cadre; often-repeated stories of this sort include the discovery of cans of food from a private NGO on a North Korean submarine that ran aground in

1997 and eyewitness accounts by a U.S. House of Representatives staff delegation that visited the country in 1998 (U.S. House of Representatives 1999:23).

There are several reasons, however, to doubt centrally directed, large-scale diversion of humanitarian assistance to the military for its own consumption. As the WFP's John Powell testified with admirable frankness before the U.S. Congress, "The army takes what it wants from the national harvest upfront, in full. And it takes it in the form that Koreans prefer: Korean rice" (Powell 2002:52). The form that most WFP aid takes—wheat, corn, protein biscuits— is less appealing to an elite that has access to more desirable foods. In addition, there are other international sources of aid besides those channeled through the WFP that are not subject to monitoring at all. One WFP official, speaking from firsthand experience but on the condition of anonymity, described a bargain under which the DPRK military has access to aid donated by China, thus preserving the WFP's claim that its food does not go directly to the military.

There is, however, a second and more plausible process that we call "decentralized diversion": a variety of actions taken by lower-level party, administrative, and military personnel that divert food from intended beneficiaries to other consumers. The military no doubt undertook some of these actions during the famine and acute shortages, but not at the direction of central command. Indeed, almost exactly the opposite was the case: incentives for diversion at the unit level arose because of the inability of the central military command structure to orchestrate supplies. Defectors have reported at various times that lower-ranking military personnel and those stationed in certain regions were not protected from food shortages. As early as 1993, a military defector reporting malnutrition—and discontent—in the army stated that "soldiers are sometimes selected to raid government food supplies meant for the people" (Associated Press 1993; Becker 1996). Refugee interviews conducted in 1997 just as the famine was cresting go further, suggesting a partial breakdown in military authority, with units in some areas of the country even having been broken up and soldiers told return to their villages (Becker 1997c).

These reports are by no means inconsistent with refugee interviews claiming that the military and party were shown preference in the distribution of food (Becker 1997b; 1998a).[1] These interviews, reflecting on the high famine period, suggest that diversion from the PDS was occurring even before humanitarian aid arrived. Other reports suggest that soldiers in the northern part of the country were not simply diverting food from official channels but extorting food and money from households with Chinese relatives. One defector's account is worth citing in full: "Soldiers received daily rations, but those were not enough to live on. So the chief of my son's unit ordered them to forage in the countryside. Small companies were sent out to steal village stocks and if they found nothing in the granaries, they robbed people's homes. One day my son protested and said he was not in the army to steal from people. He was immediately shot" (Becker 1997a). As succinct as this testimony is, it contains a wealth of information as well as drama: the breakdown of the military's capacity to feed its troops; the organized pursuit of coping strategies through foraging; the ultimate and no doubt desperate turn to violence; the fate of those who protested.

A related source of decentralized diversion to military consumption arose from what Natsios calls the "militarization of agriculture" (1999:117). Partly to increase able-bodied labor, partly to prevent hoarding, the military established a greater presence on the state farms and collectives from 1996 on. So-called corn guards were deployed to stop preharvesting and diversion by farmers and had orders to kill "thieves." The corn guards were themselves ill fed, however, and farmers were able to bribe them with food.

The political and ethical implications of decentralized diversion to consumption by the military or other less-deserving groups are more ambiguous than is commonly recognized. Certainly, the extortion of food at the barrel of a gun is hard to condone. But the North Korean army is made up of forced conscripts who serve for long periods in Spartan conditions. Decentralized diversion occurred not only to the military elite, and not because of the overwhelming power of the state, but to low-level conscripts and because of the inability of the military machine to feed itself. Indeed, as we have seen from Kim Jŏng-il's speech, cited in chapter 3, a plausible explanation for the government's reluctance to reveal the extent of its food problems was to conceal the deterioration of the military's most basic capabilities.

To this point, we have focused largely on the politically contentious issue of diversion to the military. Yet this overlooks other channels through which food might be diverted and other sets of beneficiaries, including diversion to other undeserving groups and to the market. As we have seen, outside donors prioritized vulnerable segments of the population: children, pregnant and nursing mothers, the destitute, the infirm, and the elderly. The repeated experience of the aid community is that the North Korean regime did not fully share these priorities and was also seeking to protect key constituencies: not simply the military and senior party officials but also the capital city of Pyongyang and productive workers in key sectors. This struggle for political survival was being replayed at the local level, where county-level committees similarly had to choose between allocating food to vulnerable groups with little political influence and productive workers and farmers. A report from a South Korean NGO that we outline in more detail below claims to find evidence of exactly such priorities: government instructions that aid be channeled not just to the military but to workers in state-owned enterprises and administrative functions. Conversely, a recent report from an NGO worker with substantial experience in-country found an increase in overall access by 2005 and a willingness to let her drive across the countryside but continued resistance to meeting with the disabled who constituted one of the organization's target groups (Caritas—Hong Kong 2005b).

Aid and Marketization

A more complex problem has to do with diversion not for consumption or stockpiling but for sale in the market;[2] again it is important to underline that such diversion can come out of domestic supply as well as aid. We are skeptical that the military diverts aid in order to gorge itself on low-quality foods such as protein biscuits. However, organization, logistical capabilities, and ability to compel compliance make it certain that party, state, and military officials are involved in diverting aid to the market for the purposes of self-enrichment. We devote somewhat more attention to this issue because it is highly consequential for the more general question of reform and transition to a more market-oriented system in North Korea that we take up in chapter 6.

The incentive for this type of diversion depends on three key variables: the price of food, the existence of markets, and the ability of public-spirited authorities or donors to limit it. The economic incentives have undoubtedly varied over time with the degree of scarcity and the extent of marketization, and we return to them in more detail below.[3] Under conditions of food scarcity, however, the returns on this type of activity can be astronomical; there can be little doubt that the incentives for diversion are extraordinarily strong.

As the institutional environment changes, so does the likely impact of diversion away from its intended recipients. These effects are not well understood and as a result have given rise to misleading assumptions about the effects of diversion; it is worth spelling them out in some detail.

Take the simplest case, in which food cannot be stored—perhaps because of the insecurity of attempting to do so—but there are functioning markets. If aid goes only to individuals who have no command over resources—orphaned children, the destitute, or those wholly dependent on institutions—it will not have any effect on the market price of food. These individuals do not have the resources to purchase food in any case. Aid is purely *additional*. In this limiting case, the recipients capture the benefits of aid wholly, and any diversion of aid away from them is a zero-sum game. Diversion represents a direct reduction in the welfare of the targeted group. The benefits of such diversion are shared between the sellers and buyers.

In the North Korean case, however, aid went not only to these vulnerable groups but to households and individuals who were also purchasing some of their food on the market in any case; as we have seen above, dependence on the PDS was declining over time, and more and more individuals relied on the market (and other means) to secure food. In this case, the consequences of food aid are more complex. First, aid directly satisfies some portion of the recipients' demand, its traditional purpose. But it also has a second, indirect effect of reducing overall demand in the market and thus leading to a fall in the price of food (figure 5.1).

Put differently, the benefits of aid include not only the direct transfer but also the more general benefit to consumers from a reduction in the prices paid for the portion of consumption that comes from purchases on the market.

Cultivators, on the other hand, will suffer because the price of their product has fallen. The effect on cultivators cannot be dismissed. As a matter of equity, farmers typically have lower incomes than urban residents. The provision of aid can thus have a regressive distributional impact. Equally if not more important is the fact that maintaining low producer prices results in adverse incentives, discouraging production and thus the eventual resolution of the chronic food

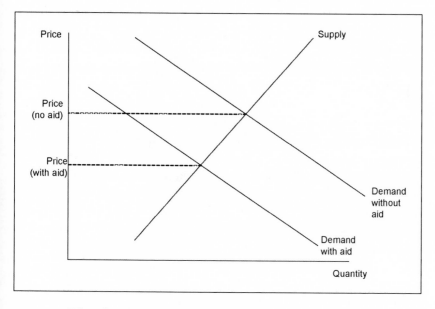

FIGURE 5.1. Effect of Food Aid on the Market Price of Food

emergency. It is noteworthy that domestic production in North Korea has never recovered to its precrisis level, and the absence of strong incentives to farmers is certainly one cause.

What is the effect of diversion in these more realistic circumstances where some share of demand is being supplied by the market? As under our first set of assumptions, diversion directly reduces the welfare of those who would have received the food for free and increases the welfare of the diverters. But the effect on the rest of the population is mixed. If the aid is diverted to groups that would have purchased food, diversion contributes to a fall in the price of food, conveying benefits to consumers and losses to producers.[4]

Additional difficulties in assessing the effects of diversion arise when we add in two additional institutional complications: the existence of PDS entitlements and the fragmentation of markets. North Korean officials have continued to insist that the PDS provides a subsidy to urban consumers, although, as we will discuss in chapter 7, the size of that subsidy has diminished over time as the PDS has moved toward more market-based pricing. The system of entitlements in such a system might be thought of as a kind of cascade. The privileged get the first draw on PDS rations and enjoy the subsidy associated with access to the rationing system. After their need is satisfied, PDS supplies go to less-favored groups, including the vulnerable. Diversion from the PDS therefore does not affect all equally but is more likely to reduce the consumption of those at the bottom of the hierarchy of food entitlements.

Finally, the analysis of diversion must take into account the fact that markets in North Korea are not fully integrated. We provide some evidence of wholesale networks operating over long distances, but difficulties in transport and the absence of middlemen who can openly profit from arbitrage suggest that market fragmentation is a plausible assumption. The effects of the cascade we have described are therefore highly localized and thus subject to substantial variation across the country. Any additional supply to one region is likely to pool there, benefiting consumers (and hurting producers) in those locales but not necessarily having wider effects. Evidence we provide in chapter 7 on price differentials across the country provides strong support for the segmented nature of markets in North Korea.

The Magnitude of Diversion

Firm evidence of diversion is, of course, difficult to come by because it reflects illicit behavior, at least in the eyes of the international donor community. As

a consequence, prior expectations are likely to play a strong role in any evaluation of the imprecise and fragmentary evidence that exists. Before turning to
that evidence, however, it is important to restate the context. North Koreans
have a multiplicity of motivations for diversion. In discussing diversion to consumption, we have already noted how the government has different priorities
with respect to distribution than donors do. But we should not rule out simple
greed. We will provide a more detailed discussion on the evolution of prices in
chapter 7, but we begin here by considering briefly information on the wedge
between official and market prices.

Table 5.1 reports such differentials for rice and corn both before and after
the introduction of price reforms in July 2002. The table makes a very simple
point: before the reforms, the differences between the official and market
prices for staple foods such as rice and corn were gigantic and widened as
the country entered the famine and the real price of food increased. During
the peak famine years, a farm household could make roughly one hundred
times as much money by selling rice in the market as it could receive by
selling it to the state. This constituted a powerful incentive to funnel output
through unofficial rather than state-sanctioned channels. These differentials
narrowed dramatically after the July 2002 reforms, although they widened
somewhat thereafter as the official price remained fixed and inflation surged.
But even after the reforms, market prices remained multiples of official procurement prices.

While the economic incentives for farmers to redirect supply were enormous, the incentives for public officials to divert food, including food aid,
were even greater still. As table 5.1 makes clear, the wedge between PDS and
market prices was even larger than the wedge between procurement and market
prices. Given the high real price of food in North Korea, the opportunity to
steer donated grain into the market was virtually a guarantee of riches, and in
an environment in which the economy was collapsing and the ability to secure
the necessities of life was increasingly tenuous.

Of course, temptations of this magnitude carried corresponding risks. As
theories of corruption routinely note, the incentives for corrupt behavior are
affected not only by the size of the rents that can be earned but by the certainty and severity of punishment for getting caught. The severity and swiftness
of punishment surely constituted a deterrent for some groups, although in a
context in which the state was losing its ability to provide food and playing by
the rules could risk a slow death. For the politically connected, however, it is
not clear that punishment was either certain or severe. Higher-level authorities
faced problems of monitoring their subordinates similar to those outlined in

TABLE 5.1. Price Wedges

	Official Procurement Price	PDS Price	Market Price	Market Price as Multiple of Procurement Price	Market Price as Multiple of PDS Price
Rice					
1990	0.8	0.08	20.0	25.0	250.0
1992	0.8	0.08	25.0	31.3	312.5
1996	0.8	0.08	100.0	125.0	1250.0
1997	0.8	0.08	102.5	128.1	1281.3
1998	0.8	0.08	77.0	96.3	962.5
1999	0.8	0.08	64.0	80.0	800.0
2000	0.8	0.08	46.6	58.3	582.5
2001	0.8	0.08	49.5	61.9	618.8
2002	17.1	18.40	52.5	3.1	2.9
2003	40.0	44.00	156.6	3.9	3.6
Corn					
1998	0.5	0.06	39.6	80.8	660.0
1999	0.5	0.06	32.6	66.5	543.3
2000	0.5	0.06	27.2	55.5	453.3
2001	0.5	0.06	31.8	64.9	530.0
2002	8.6	10.00	35.0	4.1	3.5
2003	20.0	24.00	115.6	5.8	4.8

Notes: Prices are won per kilo. The price series for 1990–1997 and 1998–2003 are from different sources and not directly comparable.

Sources: 1990–1997: S. Lee, 2003; 1998–2003: Lim 2005.

chapter 5, while the absence of any system of accountability made it impossible for the victims of diversion to bring those responsible to justice.

We have already shown that the weakness of the monitoring system provides ample opportunity for diversion along the entirety of the supply chain, from port of entry to end user. The pilferage rate for major multinational retailers like Walmart, equipped with the world's most advanced electronic inventory control and security systems, is roughly 2 percent (Hollinger and Davis 2003). We would find it astonishing if forty non-Korean-speaking foreigners operating under highly constrained circumstances and responsible for forty thousand retail outlets in a country the size of Louisiana or New York could meet this standard.

Yet an additional shortcoming of the monitoring system that deserves mention here concerns the markets themselves. During the famine and its aftermath, markets grew in importance as a point of distributing food. The monitoring of markets is considered a crucial tool for humanitarian aid workers since it provides clear evidence of the extent of scarcities. But foreign observers have consistently been kept away from markets where illicit transactions might occur.

We thus begin with an appeal to plausibility: at the most basic level, the diversion story makes sense. WFP officials have admitted as much publicly (Fairclough 2005; Reuters 2005). Adherence to an alternative story—that the diversion of aid is absent or minor—contradicts both our understanding of human behavior and a variety of evidence: it demands a willful suspension of disbelief. Having established the underlying plausibility of diversion, it is nonetheless incumbent on us to consider the types of evidence that might shed light on its nature and magnitude. We consider briefly the evidence coming from aid workers, from documentary sources, and from refugee interviews before attempting our own estimate of the size of the market.

Probably the most reliable source of information on this issue is interviews with humanitarian aid workers themselves. For quite obvious reasons, neither the WFP nor any NGO has made a public effort to determine the size of diversion, although, as we have mentioned, some organizations left the country precisely because they believed that aid was not reaching its intended beneficiaries.[5] Nonetheless, these workers have extensive in-country experience and know the institutions with which they are working and the limitations of the monitoring regime. Several have attempted overall estimates of diversion from their own organization's programs in private background conversations, and these estimates range from 10 to 30 percent. If one accepts the notion that there have been improvements in monitoring in recent years, then it could well be the case that losses were even higher in the past.

A somewhat harder bit of evidence from an NGO source is contained in a 2005 report from the South Korean organization Good Friends (H. J. Lee 2005). Good Friends has been at the forefront of publicizing the food problem in North Korea since the mid-1990s; however, it is also important to underline that the group has been openly skeptical of the South Korean government's aid efforts. Nonetheless, the 2005 report from the organization claims to have secured an internal North Korean document or information from such a document that actually outlines the principle for allocating South Korean food aid. This document states that the first allotment was to the Department of People's Armed Forces (30 percent), the second allotment was to Special Government Offices (10 percent), the third went to factories manufacturing military goods and other state-owned enterprises (10 percent), and the remainder to the municipal and district food administration centers of the PDS (approximately 50 percent). This allocation is arguably not diversion in the technical sense since, as we will show in chapter 6 in more detail, the South Koreans place only minimal demands on their North Korean counterparts. Moreover, we have been unable to vouch for the authenticity of the evidence behind Good Friends' claim. Nonetheless, the priorities reflected in the document are certainly plausible given the larger context we have sketched and suggest a level of diversion that is even higher than our estimates.

The experience of the NGO Médecins sans Frontières is instructive in this context, as it suggests more precisely the problem of assessing the extent of diversion (the following is based on Schloms 2003). MSF was one of the first NGOs to gain entry into the country. One of its major efforts targeted severely malnourished children under the age of five by setting up feeding centers in the pediatric wards of county and provincial hospitals. At the beginning of the program, the FDRC provided the MSF with a list of all health facilities in each county in which it sought to operate. On site visits, MSF personnel saw institutions that were not on the provided lists and found evidence of children who were denied access to the program. MSF—and other European NGOs—gradually came to the recognition that the demographic information provided by the government was implausible. MSF estimated that as many as 25 percent of the children in South P'yŏng'an Province were orphaned or abandoned, housed in institutions that North Korean authorities initially denied existed and subsequently failed to open to relief efforts. MSF found evidence that provision of aid within these institutions was systematically conditioned on the political status of the parents, and, as a result, large numbers of the target population were in fact not being reached. Other NGOs reached similar conclusions with respect to areas under their jurisdiction (Bennett 1999; Schloms 2004).

The problems facing MSF and the other European NGOs do not denote diversion per se but rather concealment to further discrimination in the provision of relief. The government was effectively denying access to a particular target population, namely, vulnerable children and particularly the many orphaned and abandoned ones that the famine spawned. The case is instructive, however, because it plausibly mirrors the process of diversion in which some target population is effectively denied access to food in favor of a privileged group.

A second form of substantiation takes the form of a small but revealing body of direct documentary evidence of diversion. Although this corroboratory evidence cannot speak to the question of magnitude, it reveals important institutional details. The most important source of such evidence is a network associated with a Japanese NGO called Rescue the North Korean People Urgent Action Network (RENK). RENK has supported North Koreans who, for ideological or pecuniary motives or both, have surreptitiously taken extensive video footage of market activity in North Korea by concealing cameras in bags. The video footage has then been smuggled out along the Chinese border. The first tape of this sort was made in 1998. The first suggesting diversion was shot in August 2003 and contains scenes of food aid from South Korea, the United States, and the WFP in marked bags being sold in a market in Hyesan City, Yanggang Province. This video was strongly contested by the aid agencies at the time. In particular, it was argued that in an economy of such pervasive shortages, the bags in which humanitarian rice are shipped have value and are reused. WFP Asia bureau director Anthony Banbury has cited an amusing example of WFP bag material being recycled as tablecloths (Banbury 2005). The rice pictured in bags marked as aid could in fact be North Korean.

A second video made in July 2004 and viewed by the authors shows scenes of the Sunam market in Ch'ŏngjin, North Hamkyung Province. Several features of this video are interesting (Y. H. Lee 2005). The video shows unopened bags of rice from a variety of aid agencies, including South Korea, USAID, the WFP, and the Red Cross, as well as several NGOs, and documents that the particular foodstuffs sold in open bags correspond to the contents marked on the bags. The bags could have been resealed, and the sellers could be compulsive types who only store beans in bags labeled "beans." But the videos at least call into question the interpretation that bags are being reused. Moreover, the video contains conversations with sellers who testify openly that the food—as well as medicine—came from foreign sources and was associated with an additional humanitarian response that followed a devastating train explosion near the Chinese border at Yongch'ŏn. Given the distance from Yongch'ŏn to Ch'ŏngjin and the ongoing difficulties in the internal transportation system, it is utterly implausible that such food shipments could have occurred without relatively high level military or official involvement. The prices of the rice are clearly market prices (430 won per kilo, or approximately ten times the official price); there is no doubt that the food is being sold. A third video—which aroused particularly controversy in Japan—was released by RENK in June 2005 and showed aid from Japan that had been given in conjunction with Prime Minister Koizumi's visit in 2004 (and rice purchased by Japan from Pakistan) being sold in the Namhŭng market in Anju (E. J. Lee 2005).

This video evidence should be approached with appropriate caution; most important, it cannot speak to the issue of magnitude. It is nonetheless revealing of an emerging practice before the crackdown on markets in late 2005. The existence of private traders openly selling donated rice in markets reveals important institutional details, at least for the time it was taken. First, the location of these markets and the reference to the fact that aid was coming from Yongch'ŏn suggests that it was transported over long distances, implying the involvement of those in control of transport capabilities and an illicit wholesale system operating over large distances. This is consistent with other information of the gradual emergence of trading networks extending over somewhat larger areas. The WFP, for example, has reported that provincial and local PDS officials have engaged in trading food among themselves as a way of balancing supply and demand across jurisdictions. The case of the EU-donated baby formula cited in the last chapter also shows that donated materials had traveled significant distances beyond the intended recipient hospitals.

Second, the fact that this aid was sold openly suggests the effective complicity of local officials and market managers; these sales were not conducted on the quiet but in plain view. Finally, the video reinforces our core point that diversion does not take place only to serve direct consumption but also to stock the market.

A final, more indirect source of evidence is refugee surveys. The testimony of refugees about their individual access to food does not constitute firm evidence of diversion, since many other factors might account for shortages.[6] Nonetheless, they do provide revealing information on the nature of the distribution system. As we indicated in chapter 2, refugee interviews from the late 1990s attested to the breakdown of the PDS even after large-scale aid operations designed to serve as much as one-third of the population had begun; these earlier studies have been confirmed by a more recent survey conducted by Chang (2006). As with all such samples, the respondents are not representative of the country as a whole. Nonetheless, the results are astonishing. Only 57 percent of the respondents reported knowing of the existence of aid at all; ten years into the humanitarian effort, more than 40 percent of the population remained unaware of it. Of those who knew of the existence of food aid, only 3.4 percent reported having received any (or less than 2 percent of the total sample, including those who were unaware of aid deliveries). These numbers do not imply that only 3 percent of the population received aid, nor do they constitute proof of diversion; respondents might have received donated food without knowing it. The responses do, however, testify to the extraordinary power of the government to control information. Despite the fact that aid constituted a major component of total PDS supplies as we show below, many were unaware that these supplies came from foreign donors. When asked who the recipients of aid were, fully 94 percent responded "the military."

Again, these responses do not prove that the military has been the primary recipient of food aid, but they do attest to perceptions of the privileges accruing to the military, many no doubt observed firsthand.

The Scope of the Market

Is there any additional way to evaluate the competing claims about diversion? Although not precise, one way is to go back to the basics. In an economic exchange, every purchase is also a sale, and regardless of the channels through which they flow, the quantities bought and sold have to match up. As a plausibility check, we use a simple balance sheet calculation to stack these diversion estimates up against what we know about the North Korean food economy. By comparing data on production, aid, and imports against estimates of the food passing through the PDS, we can get some broad order-of-magnitude estimates of the share of total supply passing through the market. As we will show, these estimates are highly germane for understanding the extent of diversion. Moreover, they can be triangulated using sources of information such as household surveys done by the WFP. We conclude that the numbers add up: the estimates of significant diversion are consistent with these other sources of information about the North Korean food economy.

As the external aid effort ramped up, the WFP targeted roughly 30 percent of the population through its feeding programs. The size of the targeted group had to be adjusted after 2003 as donations fell. But if we combine the WFP targets with the estimates of diversion cited above—taking 10 percent as the lower bound and the 50 percent cited in the Good Friends report as the upper bound—it suggests that enough food to feed 3 to 15 percent of the population has been diverted. What do we make of such an amount? First, it is not trivial. It is not massive in terms of overall demand but clearly large enough to divert substantial amounts of food aid from intended beneficiaries and to provide substantial rents to those who manage to gain control over it.

At the same time, the diversion is large enough to have had an effect on the broader process of marketization. By acting as an additional source of supply outside government control, the diversion of aid probably contributed to the development and scope of markets as institutions for intermediating the allocation of supply. Diversion probably contributed to the downward trend in market prices at least as the worst of the famine started to ease, before the post-2002 surge in inflation (table 5.1). If true, diversion helped those consumers who were obtaining food through the market, and disadvantaged producers.

How far has the process of marketization gone, and how do aid and its possible diversion fit into it? We have information on the allocation of grain to farmers, average PDS rations, and the share of the population dependent on the PDS (in effect, the nonfarm population). If we make some simple, but we believe reasonable, assumptions about the share of the population that is working and the rations allocated to workers as opposed to dependents, it is possible to make some very rough estimates of the share of total food supply from all sources that was moving through the PDS. The remainder constitutes the share of total supply that was being channeled in one form or another to the market or non-PDS forms of exchange.

As we have seen, rural North Koreans on cooperative farms receive grain at the time of the harvest, which they can supplement with other own-grown sources. The urban story is more complex, as there are four channels through which urban households obtain food: PDS monthly rations, WFP support to institutions such as schools and hospitals, the WFP's food-for-work (FFW) programs, and the market. For the purposes of these calculations, we assume that non-WFP aid, primarily from China and South Korea, goes directly into the PDS to support monthly rations (we include the military as part of urban North Korea and thus do not count Chinese aid as being diverted to the military). For the purposes of these calculations, we assume that the food-for-work program, which is small in relative terms, is effectively outside the PDS and not subject to diversion. Non-FFW distribution is assumed vulnerable to diversion to the market at rates ranging from 10 to 50 percent per the estimates we have culled from the humanitarian community.

We further assume that WFP aid either goes exclusively to the PDS monthly ration channel or, if it goes to institutions such as schools and hospitals, that aid is offset by corresponding reductions in the monthly rations of families receiving support through the institutional channel, as has been confirmed by WFP staff. For example, if a family is entitled to a certain PDS ration but includes a child who is also fed at school, then the household sees a reduction in its PDS ration. The implication of this assumption is that, on net, WFP aid does not expand the coverage of the PDS system. These assumptions are detailed in algebraic terms in appendix 3.

Finally, we have to consider the impact of diversion. We assume that once food is diverted into the market, it is lost to the PDS, and the system delivers to consumers less than it was supposed to on paper—that is, the state does not subsequently extract more food out of the cultivators to compensate for pilferage.[7] In this balance sheet calculation, diversion will increase marketization from the standpoint of consumers by forcing them into the market, but from the standpoint of producers it does not make any difference. Once the state has collected its share of cooperative output, its final disposition does not matter. We also assume that food obtained from domestic production is not subject to diversion; only aid is.[8]

Food is fungible to a large degree, and it is therefore impossible to say which sources of food are going where: food might find its way to the market as a result of the behavior of farmers or because of the diversion of aid. Nonetheless, we think of marketization in at least three ways: the share of total domestic production (minus the allocation to farmers; this is important) going to the market, the share of food consumption sourced through markets, and, an inverse indicator, the value of aid as a share of food passing through nonmarket channels. The results of these calculations for the period 1999–2003 are striking: 84 percent of output is either consumed on the farm or goes into the market. This means that the state is unable to procure very much domestic production for the purpose of supplying the PDS. Under the assumption that between 10 percent and 50 percent of aid is diverted, consumers rely on the market for roughly half of their consumption (42 percent under the lower diversion assumption; 52 percent under the higher diversion assumption). This implication is consistent with recent WFP survey results that are discussed in chapter 7 and is also consonant with refugee interviews and defector surveys that indicate that the market, not the PDS system, is the primary source of food for a significant share of the population.

Last, we can express the value of aid as a share of what passes through the PDS system. In essence, this is the flip side of the marketization estimate from the cultivator perspective. Since the state procures little local production for the PDS, these calculations suggest that the PDS system has largely become a mechanism for distributing aid. Aid accounts for 78 percent—nearly four-fifths—of what is reputedly distributed through the PDS system.

This exercise is subject to a number of possible risks. One has to do with our assumptions about the demographics. Farmers may also choose to consume some of their surplus rather than selling it on the market, managing to secure larger allocations than the ones formally given them. This may seem almost self-evidently true, but in fact it is not obvious. Farmers have access to other sources of food grown on either legal or illegal private plots, and this diversion of effort may have some effect on overall output. But we are doubtful that cooperative farms are able to divert large quantities of the main food grains. At least until the 2005 harvest, allotments had increased quite clearly, in part to avoid this very problem. Moreover, the government had become harshly vigilant in trying to check the hoarding behavior of the high famine period even before the effort to increase grain procurement and revive the PDS in late 2005. A third possibility is that some portion of the population—a protected elite—is getting higher rations and consuming very much more than these numbers suggest. Again, this is possible, but, as we have seen, the protected elite—at least during the famine—was not large, and in any case there are limits to how much grain an individual can consume. Those privileged enough to have access to larger rations of food would also be in a position to supplement those rations on the market and through consumption of a more varied diet. We are therefore skeptical of the idea that diversion to elite consumption would account for a large share of what we observe.

Instead, these results are consistent with the notion that diversion of aid away from state-controlled channels has contributed to the broader process of marketization. North Korea's own statistics suggest—no doubt unwittingly—that the PDS is increasingly a mechanism for distributing international aid in the context of an economy in which food is increasingly distributed through the market.

Conclusion

As we are learning from a growing literature on the political economy of aid, the donor-recipient relationship must be seen as a bargaining game. Donors seek to advance their objectives—both humanitarian and political—and recipients seek to maximize aid while limiting the conditions to which this aid is subjected. Aid to North Korea is dominated by food assistance through the WFP, as we have seen, but in other aspects it shares this basic structure. What is distinctive is that the nature of the North Korean political system—its overweening control and willingness to allow its citizens to experience extreme deprivation—actually gives it surprising leverage over the aid community. Because the international humanitarian community, humanitarian interests within the major donors, and the NGOs place such strong weight on the plight of the North Korean people, they have little bargaining power vis-à-vis the government. As a result, the outside community has largely been forced to accept what we call North Korean exceptionalism: an aid regime that is subject to much more substantial constraints than those typical of most aid settings. Until 2005, we saw incremental changes in this regime over time, and some signs of marginally greater access than in the past. But the events of late 2005 and early 2006 described at the end of chapter 4 show how reversible these developments are.

The flip side of the weak monitoring regime in the country is the problem of diversion that we have taken up in this chapter. We analyzed a variety of sources of evidence on diversion and its potential welfare impact across different social groups. Our conclusion is that something on the order of 30 percent of aid was probably being diverted by 2005. The plausibility of this estimate is supported by a simple balance sheet exercise that suggests that diversion on this scale appears to be consistent with what we can observe about the extent of marketization of local grain production and the increasing primacy of the market as the institution through which households secure food.

The next two chapters extend and elaborate these two themes. In chapter 6, we look in more detail at the sometimes conflicting interests of the donors and the problem of coordination these differences pose. In chapter 7, we return to the issue of marketization and examine how economic reforms and ongoing institutional changes within North Korea affect the severity and incidence of food insecurity.

CHAPTER SIX

The Political Economy of Aid

In our discussion of the origins of the great famine in chapter 2, we placed particular emphasis on the failure of the North Korean government to respond in a timely way to evidence of food shortages. An aggressive promotion of exports and foreign investment, the maintenance of even a minimal capacity to borrow, or an earlier appeal for humanitarian assistance all would have mitigated the severe distress the country experienced in the mid-1990s. As the extent of the country's economic problems became more apparent, the North Korean leadership did belatedly place greater emphasis on generating or economizing on foreign exchange, for example, by seeking to revive export-processing zones, increase remittances from Japan, and expand illicit export activities.

Aid seeking was a critical component of this new strategy. As we indicated in chapter 4, North Korea's quest for aid faced the dilemma that confronts all aid relationships. The political leadership sought to maximize aid flows, and on highly concessional terms, while maintaining its political autonomy and control over resources to the greatest extent possible. Donors, by contrast, sought to ensure that aid went to intended beneficiaries, was not diverted, and adhered to the principles outlined in the preceding chapter: transparency, access, effective monitoring, assessment, and even empowerment and organization of final recipients, in short objectives that were largely anathema to the North Korean regime.

Even were aid motivated solely by humanitarian considerations, this game would be complex. But donors faced two additional problems. First, aid and politics were not, and could not, be held on altogether separate tracks; indeed, it is largely in the United States that this fiction is continuously repeated. Aid is used for diplomatic purposes. Moreover, in democratic societies, it is also subject to the pull of domestic political forces. Across the major donors, some groups sought an expansion of aid for various ends (engagement), and others wanted to see it curtailed (pressure, sanctions). Initially, these pressures contributed to crucial delays in getting aid into North Korea in the immediate aftermath of the flood announcement; the international community cannot be held completely blameless. South Korean pique at North Korean behavior following some early and very large food shipments was particularly important in this regard, influencing both the United States and Japan. But U.S. and Japanese policy also sought to limit aid for political ends.

Over time, political calculations lead to oscillations in aid flows across all the major donors. Figure 6.1 shows the volatile pattern of aid by focusing on the five major donors that are the subject of this chapter: the United States, Japan, the EU, South Korea, and China. U.S. aid rose sharply in 1998–99 but then fell dramatically in 2000, exhibiting a steady decline through the remainder of the first administration of George W. Bush. South Korean aid moved in nearly the opposite direction, largely offsetting the decline in U.S. aid until 2004. Chinese aid rose steadily through 2001 but then declined thereafter. EU assistance has been somewhat changeable, rising slightly as U.S. aid has fallen in recent years. Japanese aid flows, finally, spike, fall, and are terminated completely on several occasions.

It could be argued that this volatility reflected changing needs in North Korea, but as we have reported, the dependence of the country on aid—in terms of material need—has been surprisingly constant. Rather, this volatility reflects political and policy cycles in the donors themselves.

A second dilemma was that these divergent political calculations at the national level created coordination problems among the donors. Once aid began to flow, North Korean diplomacy sought to exploit this coordination problem, sometimes adroitly, sometimes less so. While the United States showed a declining willingness to extend humanitarian assistance, and Japan has oscillated between engagement and the imposition of outright sanctions, the EU and particularly South Korea have shown a growing willingness to expand assistance to the country. Moreover, South Korea's foreign assistance is but one component of a much broader strategy of economic engagement with the North that has created a variety of other channels for effective transfers to the country, from private (and in some cases subsidized) investment to cooperative projects of various sorts. North Korea has also managed to maintain its

Thousands of metric tons

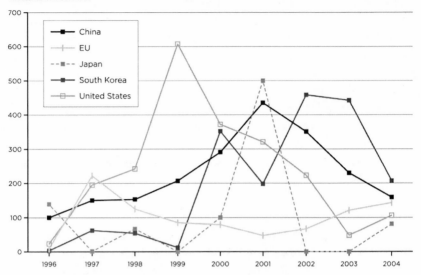

FIGURE 6.1. Total Food Aid by Major Donors, 1996–2004

Note: EU includes contributions by the European Commission and EU member countries. *Source:* WFPINTERFAIS 2005.

economic relationship with China. Although political relations between the two socialist countries have seen ups and downs, the informal Chinese penetration of the North Korean economy is proving to be one of the most important external factors in its transformation.

This fundamental inability to coordinate aid policy has crucial implications for the debate over engagement. Hawks and critics of the current aid effort have consistently argued for a policy of containment, isolation, or the use of sanctions against North Korea.[1] Conversely, even those more favorably inclined to engage North Korea have argued that such engagement should be done selectively, using incentives in order to modify North Korean behavior. Yet both these approaches would require careful calibration not only of aid flows but of the entirety of North Korea's foreign economic relations. In particular, the calls for tougher sanctions against North Korea that tend to emanate from hawks in the United States and Japan face the problem that both Chinese and South Korean foreign policy are not only resistant to such a strategy but at times exhibit a pattern of explicitly offsetting efforts to isolate North Korea by increasing their own contributions.

By carefully calibrating its aid-seeking diplomacy, the North Korean government managed to maintain a surprisingly constant level of assistance in the decade after 1995. By 2004 this strategy hit some limits. The onset of the second nuclear crisis in 2002 was an important event in this regard. In October of that year, the United States accused North Korea of seeking to enrich uranium for the purpose of making nuclear weapons. When the United States responded by cutting off heavy fuel oil shipments promised under the Framework Agreement of 1994, North Korea began a calibrated escalation of the crisis by kicking out inspectors, withdrawing from the Nuclear Non-Proliferation Treaty, restarting the 5MW(e) nuclear reactor in Yŏngbyŏn, reprocessing spent fuel into plutonium, and ultimately declaring in February 2005 that the country possessed nuclear weapons. During this same period, the regime ran afoul of the Japanese over the abduction of a number of Japanese citizens.

Needless to say, these and other political issues—such as mounting evidence of North Korean involvement in illicit trade, counterfeiting, and missile exports—had the result of sharpening disagreements over the utility of engagement. Hawks in the United States, Japan, and South Korea once again argued that economic pressure should be used more aggressively to secure North Korean compliance with its international obligations; the European Union pulled back at the margins as well. Through 2005, these calls largely proved ineffectual as China and particularly South Korea not only maintained existing economic relations but, in South Korea's case, also promised even wider economic cooperation. Not until 2006 did a set of financial sanctions appear to have a substantial, and largely unanticipated, effect on North Korea's trade relations. But even these had not—by mid-2006—forced North Korea back to the bargaining table.

In addition to the constraints on aid posed by these political issues, aid to North Korea faced rising resistance within the humanitarian community itself. Aid hawks were by no means limited to those preoccupied with the nuclear question. As we noted in chapter 4, a number of NGOs walked away from North Korea, human rights groups pressed for a tougher stance, and prominent refugees argued forcefully that the regime should be cut off (for example, C. Kang 2005). In addition, donors have faced strong demands on aid resources from other quarters, including ongoing crises in the Middle East and Africa and the South and Southeast Asian tsunami of 2005. As a result, supporters of humanitarian assistance faced increasing skepticism about the prolonged and seemingly open-ended nature of aid to North Korea.

In this chapter, we explore these issues by focusing on the five major donors beginning with the hawks—the United States and Japan—before turning to the doves: the EU, South Korea, and China. In each case, we outline the development of the aid program over time and provide some sense of the overall economic relationship of which it is a part. We then discuss the ways in which both international and domestic political concerns have influenced the magnitude and nature of aid flows. Throughout, we concentrate on the problems of coordination that have resulted from shifting patterns of support for aid and engagement and the surprising ability of North Korea to maintain its external economic lifeline even while once again pursuing a high-risk nuclear diplomacy.

The United States

The United States was not the first country to come to North Korea's aid after the famine, and neither did it move with particular speed. Moreover, private investment and trade have been limited because of both the political tensions between the two countries and the fact that North Korea does not enjoy normal trade relations status.[2] But, ironically, the United States has been North Korea's largest benefactor (table 6.1 outlines the U.S. contribution). Between 1995 and 2005, the United States provided over $1 billion in aid to North Korea. Fully 40 percent of that aid was the result of U.S. commitments under the Agreed Framework of 1994 through the Korean Peninsula Energy Development Organization (KEDO).[3] As we have indicated, this channel ended with the U.S. decision in December 2002 to terminate heavy oil shipments, and by the end of 2005 KEDO itself had been wound down. The remainder of the aid, over $600 million, has been channeled through the WFP, with some of the aid monitored by a consortium of NGOs, the Private Volunteer Organization Consortium.

As evidence of the famine continued to mount in the second half of 1995 and first half of 1996, a number of NGOs played an important role in mobilizing support for U.S. assistance. In Congress, Representative Tony Hall (D-Ohio) and Senator Paul Simon (D-Illinois) argued strongly that aid and politics should be separated, and a bipartisan group signaled to the administration that Congress could support aid if certain monitoring conditions were met.[4]

From the beginning, however, aid was also closely tied up with the effort of the Clinton administration to engage North Korea (table 6.2 traces the diplomatic context of various aid initiatives). The initial strategy of the United States in 1996, taken in consultation with South Korea and Japan, was actually to withhold aid altogether and subsequently to use it only to reward North Korean cooperation, a position vigorously opposed by most of the NGO community. In June 1996—nearly a year after the flood appeal—Secretary of State Warren Christopher finally announced that the United States would make a small

TABLE 6.1. U.S. Assistance to North Korea, 1995–2005

Calendar or Fiscal Year (FY)	Food aid (per FY)		KEDO assistance (per calendar yr; $US million)	Medical supplies and Other (per FY; $US million)	Total ($US million)
	Metric tons	Commodity value ($US million)			
1995	0	0.0	9.5	0.2	9.7
1996	19,500	8.3	22.0	0.0	30.3
1997	177,000	52.4	25.0	5.0	82.4
1998	200,000	72.9	50.0	0.0	122.9
1999	695,194	222.1	65.1	0.0	287.2
2000	265,000	74.3	64.4	0.0	138.7
2001	350,000	58.1	74.9	0.0	133.0
2002	207,000	50.4	90.5	0.0	140.9
2003	40,200	25.5	3.7	0.0	29.2
2004	110,000	36.3	0.0	0.1	36.4
2005	25,000	5.7	-	-	5.7
TOTAL	2,088,894	606.0	405.1	5.3	1,010.7

Souces: Manyin 2005; USDAFAS: Food Aid Reports.

additional contribution to the WFP appeal, an extraordinarily modest contribution given the projected shortfall. This move was interpreted at the time as an attempt to induce North Korean participation in a preparatory briefing for the Four-Party Talks as well as adherence to the terms of the Agreed Framework.

With tensions over the implementation of the Agreed Framework continuing into 1997, the United States made another, larger $25 million donation to the WFP in the spring. In July 1997 former senator Sam Nunn (D-Georgia) and former U.S. ambassador James Laney visited Pyongyang to pave the way for the anticipated August start of preliminary discussions to set the agenda for the Four-Party talks. These negotiations between the United States, China, and South and North Korea were designed to follow up on the Agreed Framework and address longer-term issues such as replacing the armistice with a final settlement to the Korean War. After the Nunn-Laney trip, the United States announced a $27 million (100,000 MT) donation of grain. Aid did not flow in substantial quantities until 1998, but when it did, it inaugurated a virtual policy of "food for meetings" (table 6.2) that continued through 1999, the year when U.S. aid to North Korea peaked.

TABLE 6.2. U.S. Food for Talks, 1995–2005

Date	Value	Form	Channel	Diplomatic Objective
February 1996	$2 million	Food	WFP	Encourage North Korean adherence to the Agreed Framework during a period of increasing tension between the two Koreas.
June 1996	$6.2 million	Food	WFP	Encourage North Korean flexibility with respect to a secret proposal for four-way talks among the US, North Korea, South Korea, and China.
February 1997	$10 million	Food	WFP	Quid pro quo for North Korean agreement to participate in joint US-South Korea briefing on Four-Party talks proposal.
April 1997	$15 million	50,000 MT of food	WFP	Quid pro quo for North Korean agreement to participate in missile proliferation negotiations.
July 1997	$27 million	100,000 MT of food	WFP	Quid pro quo for North Korean agreement to participate in Four-Party Talks.
October 1997	$5 million	Grant	UNICEF	Quid pro quo for North Korean acceptance of 10 additional food relief monitors.
February 1998	n.a.	200,000 MT of food	WFP	Quid pro quo for North Korean agreement to participate in ad hoc committee meeting associated with the Four-Party Talks.
September 1998	n.a.	300,000 MT of food	WFP	Quid pro quo for North Korean agreement to resume missile talks, attend the third plenary session of the Four-PartyTalks, enter into negotiations over the second suspected nuclear site, and resume talks aimed at removing North Korea from the list of states sponsoring terrorism.
April-May 1999	n.a.	600,000 MT of food, 1,000 tons of potato seed	WFP	Quid pro quo for agreement on access to North Korea's underground construction site and participation in Four Party and missile talks; 400,000 MT of this commitment announced one day before U.S. mission to Pyongyang.
September 1999	n.a.	Sanctions eased		Quid pro quo. Agreement in principle on missiles.
September - October 2000	Unspecified			Prospective quid pro quo. North Korea agrees to drop demand for cash compensation for ending missile program, but seeks equivalent in in-kind aid including food. In subsequent talks, U.S. promises unspecified aid but talks do not reach conclusion.

TABLE 6.2. U.S. Food for Talks, 1995-2005, (continued)

Date	Value	Form	Channel	Diplomatic Objective
June 2002	Unspecified			Prospective quid pro quo. Bush administration announces a baseline approach: additional aid over 155,000 metric tons conditional on improvements in access and monitoring.
January 2003	Unspecified			Prospective quid pro quo. Bush administration offers a "bold approach" including food aid in return for North Korea dismantling its weapons program.
June 2004	Unspecified			Prospective quid pro quo. Bush administration offers a package of measures including unspecified assistance in return for complete, verifiable, irreversible dismantlement of North Korea's nuclear program.
July - August 2005	Unspecified			Prospective quid pro quo. Bush Administration continues to provide commitments of 50,000 MT per year in 2003, 2004 and 2005, but claims they are unrelated to talks. In 2005, it reiterates its commitments to unspecified assistance in return for resolution of the nuclear issue; supports South Korean promise to supply energy.
December 2005	n.a.			US suspends aid following WFP expulsion

Source: Adapted from Noland, 2000), table 5.3

The Clinton administration faced recurrent criticism of its North Korea policy in general and of the apparent use of food aid as an inducement to talks in particular. In the early period, this criticism came from NGOs concerned about the linkage of humanitarian assistance to political cooperation. As aid began to flow, the criticism increasingly came from the other direction: those who felt that the United States was being too generous and was getting little in return. Moreover, charges were repeatedly leveled at the administration of ignoring evidence of aid diversion.[5] Secretary of Defense William Cohen even said openly that he had "no doubt" that the North Korean regime had diverted food aid to the military.[6] In 2000 U.S. food aid dropped sharply from its 1999 high, and the administration became more circumspect in its aid policy. Yet despite congressional protests and concerns within the humanitarian community itself, a major House report on the issue contained no recommendations, and the Republican majority never acted directly to curtail U.S. aid. Although Clinton's secretary of state, Madeline Albright, denies in her memoirs that economic compensation was explicitly used to negotiate a last-minute agreement over the country's missile program, she is equally clear that she understood that normalization and economic assistance were the crucial quid pro quo (2003:593).

From the outset, the Bush administration pulled back from the engagement strategy pursued by its predecessor. Humanitarian aid continued, but, in the words of Manyin and Jun, the administration "gave conflicting signals about whether it would continue donating food aid to North Korea, and if so, how much and whether aid should be conditioned on North Korean actions in the humanitarian and/or security areas" (2003:17). In June 2002, USAID outlined a new approach under which the United States would provide a baseline amount of food aid of 155,000 metric tons. Consideration of further assistance would be conditional on verifiable progress on monitoring. Rather than aid constituting a quid pro quo for some specific North Korean commitment, the Bush administration made additional aid contingent on North Korea moving first (table 6.2).

In October 2002, the nuclear crisis broke over U.S. intelligence that North Korea was seeking to enrich uranium. In December, KEDO funding was cut in response, and in the ensuing period there was open discussion of economic sanctions. U.S. officials claimed that North Korea had not responded to offers and hinted that humanitarian assistance might not be extended, at least at the same level. The administration appeared to be linking humanitarian aid to the nuclear crisis, despite protestations that the delay was a function of monitoring concerns and the budget cycle. Moreover, this delay occurred just as the WFP was experiencing shortfalls in the pipeline and thus generated concern that the United States was backtracking on its commitment to separate humanitarian considerations from political ones.

It would be a mistake to attribute the decline in aid purely to the political preferences of the Bush administration alone. Aid had begun falling in the final year of the Clinton administration, as we have seen, and increased demands elsewhere in the world meant that aid to North Korea would have probably declined under any administration. Nonetheless, the nuclear crisis coincided with a further reduction of aid. In February 2003, the administration gave in to its critics by promising 40,000 MT of food, with another 60,000 MT made conditional on further progress with respect to monitoring. In December 2003 and again in July 2004, the State Department announced contributions to the WFP (the proposed 60,000 MT and a 50,000 MT contribution to the 2004 appeal, respectively), but they were clearly more modest than U.S. commitments had been in the past; as can be seen from table 6.1, U.S. aid fell in both 2003 and 2004.[7]

In the fall of 2004—just as the WFP and North Korean authorities were entering their standoff over monitoring—the 108th Congress passed and President Bush signed the North Korean Human Rights Act.[8] The bill stipulated that human rights be on the agenda of any negotiations either with North Korea or "other concerned parties in Northeast Asia." The bill had a number of other implications for U.S. policy, both with respect to aid in general and food aid in particular. The bill:

- required that U.S. nonhumanitarian assistance be contingent on North Korea making "substantial progress" on a number of specific human rights issues;
- required USAID to issue a report to Congress on humanitarian assistance to North Korea and North Koreans in China and to report any changes in the transparency, monitoring, and access of food aid and other humanitarian activities; and
- included hortatory language stipulating that any "significant increases" in humanitarian assistance be conditioned on "substantial improvements" in transparency, monitoring, and access.

In addition to these stipulations, the United States had also developed a policy that 75 percent of its food would be shipped to east coast ports for delivery in these more severely affected areas (USAID 2005). In June 2005, the administration announced another 50,000 MT contribution, the same level that had been offered in 2003 and 2004. Although testimony to the continuing weight of humanitarian interests despite the ongoing nuclear crisis, the donation also implicitly confirmed the policy that no additional aid would be offered in the absence of meaningful improvements in monitoring. In late 2005, with North Korea threatening to expel the WFP, the administration finally suspended further aid commitments altogether pending the outcome of negotiations between the WFP and North Korea over continuing operations (see chapter 4); total assistance for 2005 was less than $6 million.

In sum, U.S. policy has undergone an important evolution. Immediately following the groundbreaking flood appeal, the humanitarian community was divided over the extent of the problem, and the administration delayed food aid in support of South Korean preferences at the time. Aid subsequently began to flow in large quantities, but even before the inauguration of President Bush in 2001, aid had begun to fall. The Clinton administration shifted from a policy of "aid for meetings" to an approach in which humanitarian aid continued but any increased food aid would be contingent on substantive progress in negotiations and improved access and monitoring. Under the Bush administration, this policy became more explicit, and U.S. aid commitments continued to decline to relatively low levels before being suspended altogether in late 2005. The North Korean Human Rights Act placed new constraints on aid, such as requiring that any increase be preceded by improvements in the monitoring regime, and the United States suspended aid to the country altogether in late 2005. Moreover, a variety of other initiatives that we take up in more detail in the conclusion to this book suggested a continuing attraction to a broader policy of controls and sanctions.[9]

Japan

The history of Japanese assistance to North Korea is more tumultuous than that of the United States, a function of both the high politics of diplomatic relations between the two countries and a variety of domestic political constraints, from a large pro-Pyongyang community of North Koreans in Japan to public outrage over the 1998 North Korean missile launch and revelation of the abductions of Japanese citizens.[10]

Japan–North Korean relations had gone through periods of promise and disappointment in the 1970s and 1980s. Democratization in South Korea and President No T'ae-u's *Nordpolitik*, announced in his inaugural speech in 1988, appeared to open the way toward a normalization of relations.[11] This promise was forestalled by the onset of the first nuclear crisis, but the Agreed Framework once again opened up the opportunity for rapprochement, and Japan was a major financial backer of the KEDO process. Moreover, Japan has maintained more extensive trade relations with North Korea over time than has the United States, as well as large remittances from the Korean-Japanese community that have been tapped directly by the regime.[12] These trade and financial ties were particularly important during the peak famine years (figure 6.2). More important than trade was the promise of aid. Japan's normalization of relations with South Korea in 1965 had been accompanied by a large package of assistance to the country, and the North Korean government was clear that it expected a similar resolution of postcolonial claims.[13]

In contrast to the United States, Japan's aid has been characterized by large, discrete initiatives, either connected with efforts to start talks or in recognition of a diplomatic breakthrough; table 6.3 traces the major initiatives in this history. These initiatives, however, have been followed by complete cessations of aid as a result of diplomatic strategy or public pressure to curtail assistance.

Even before its appeal to the multilateral institutions in August 1995, the North Korean government had approached Japan about the possibility of aid in the fall of 1994, a request that was refused. In January 1995, Pyongyang repeated the appeal. The Kim Yŏng-sam administration signaled that it would look unfavorably on any unilateral action by Tokyo, and over the next several

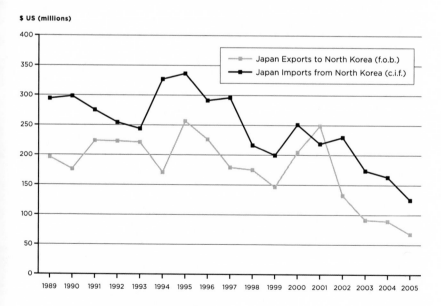

FIGURE 6.2. Japan's Trade with North Korea

Note: 2005 data annualized based on January–September 2005. Sources: IMF 2005, 2006; KIEP 2004.

TABLE 6.3. Japanese Food Aid to North Korea, 1994–2005

Date	Action and Context	Amount
Fall 1994	North Korea solicits aid; Japan denies request	
January 1995	North Korea solicits aid; Japan denies request	
June 1995	Japan agrees to supply rice in context of agreement with South Korea; Japan seeks resumption of normalization talks	150,000 MT gratis; 150,000 MT on concessional terms
October 1995	Japan agrees to an additional 200,000 MT food shipment, but South Korea objects	
January 1996	North Korea solicits aid; Japan denies request	
November 1997	Following LDP delegation visit to North Korea, the two countries state intention to restart normalization talks; Japan announces intention to provide aid	
August 1998	North Korean missile launch; Japan suspends normalization talks, food aid, and support for KEDO; subsequently returns to KEDO	
December 1999	LDP delegation visits North Korea and announces intention to restart normalization talks and food aid	
March 2000	Prior to 9th round of normalization talks, Japan announces intention to provide food aid	100,000 MT through the WFP
October 2000	Food aid promised in context of normalization talks; 2001 marks highpoint of aid, but subsequently it is not renewed as a result of conflict over abductee issue	500,000 MT through the WFP
September 2002	Koizumi visits North Korea, announces intention to restart normalization talks. Joint declaration outlines prospective aid and economic cooperation. Resumption of talks blocked by revelations about abductees	
May 2004	Koizumi visits North Korea, announces food aid in context of effort to restart normalization talks, but full commitment not delivered because of ongoing conflict on abductees	250,000 MT, only 80,000 delivered through the WFP

years South Korea effectively vetoed several Japanese aid initiatives. But in June 1995 an agreement was reached that the two countries would act jointly (Snyder 1999). South Korea would provide 150,000 MT of grain in unmarked bags, and Japan would provide 150,000 MT gratis and another 150,000 MT on concessional terms. In October 1995 and January 1996, North Korea again approached Japan for assistance. On these two occasions, which came at a crucial moment in the evolution of the famine, opposition from both South Korea and domestic political sources quashed the deals.

In 1997 new evidence surfaced that Japanese citizens had been abducted by North Korean intelligence agents as had been long alleged. North Korea's launch of a multistage rocket that flew over Japan in August 1998 was also a more immediately threatening event for Japan than it was for either South Korea—which had long fallen within the range of North Korean artillery and short- and intermediate-range missiles—or the United States.[14] Japan had engaged in both party- and government-level discussions aimed at restarting normalization talks during this period, but the missile launch led to their cancellation. Food aid was again dropped from consideration, and Japan even had to be persuaded by the United States and South Korea to resume support for KEDO.

In August 1999, the cycle began again with a North Korean statement that it intended to improve its relations with Japan. In conjunction with the reopening of normalization talks in 2000, the Mori government announced a large food aid package that accounted for over half of the entire WFP appeal that year and constituted an important offset to the decline of American assistance. The Mori cabinet proved too weak to capitalize on this initiative, however, and it was left to the Koizumi government (taking office in April 2001) to initiate a new phase of political negotiations.

Koizumi was quite open in stating that he sought normalization of relations, a position that periodically put him at odds with the Bush administration. A crucial step in this process was his summit with Kim Jŏng-il in September 2002. The Japanese government did not extend aid either in anticipation of the summit or in conjunction with it, but the joint declaration held out the promise of wide-ranging economic support in the context of normalization talks, including humanitarian assistance. The promise of these talks was overshadowed at the summit, however, by North Korea's admission that the abductions had occurred and a number of abductees had died; between these revelations and the onset of the nuclear crisis, Japanese policy and public opinion once again hardened, and food aid was suspended as of December 2003.

In May 2004, Koizumi again visited North Korea and reconfirmed the 2002 declaration; this time, he announced his intention to provide 250,000 MT of food aid and $10 million in pharmaceutical supplies through the multilateral institutions. This aid was interpreted not only in the context of both the stalled Six-Party and normalization talks but as payment for the release of five family members of the abductees, who accompanied Koizumi on his return to Tokyo. As in 2000, this aid was timely, as the WFP was continuing to experience pressure on supplies.

The decision to release the first half of the promised assistance was taken in August, just before the first round of working-level meetings on normalization. At the third meeting in November, North Korea provided Japan with a photograph and the remains of one of the abductees, Yokota Megumi, whom the North Koreans claimed had passed away. After the delegation returned to Japan, the photo and remains became a point of intense national interest and controversy as both appeared to be fake (International Crisis Group 2005:12–14). The Koizumi government not only froze the second shipment of food aid but also faced a growing tide of sentiment—including from Liberal Democratic Party (LDP) Diet members—that Japan should impose wider sanctions. Since that time, the Japanese government has taken a number of piecemeal actions that—when viewed together—constitute a substantial set of restrictions on Japan-DPRK economic relations, in effect a virtual sanctions regime.[15] Through 2005 Japan continued to raise the issue of abductees within the context of the Six-Party Talks despite resistance not only from North Korea but from other parties as well for linking the issue to the nuclear question.

From North Korea's perspective, the approach to Japan not only constituted a political counterweight to the United States but an alternative source of assistance. But the link between high politics and food aid proved even stronger in Japan than in the United States. Despite political economy and factional pressures within the LDP to extend assistance, Japanese governments have proven more willing than the United States to cut aid to North Korea altogether, and the Koizumi government has drifted toward a piecemeal sanctions regime that has had unambiguous consequences for bilateral trade and financial relations (figure 6.2).

South Korea

Like Japan, South Korea's food aid to the North has gone through important political ups and downs, and because of its significance and complexity we devote somewhat more detailed attention to it.[16] The debate over aid has been embedded in a much larger transformation of South Korea's foreign policy, from a policy of deterrence and containment to one of engagement. Aid has been subjected to vigorous domestic debate, but in contrast to the United States and Japan, the general trend in South Korean aid policy since 1998 has been in the direction of greater generosity. Moreover, aid has been embedded in a larger strategic vision of engagement that has resulted in increased trade (figure 6.3), investment, and even illicit transfers.[17]

This dramatic change in foreign policy has roots in the No T'ae-u initiative of 1988 noted above and in the Kim Yŏng-sam administration. But its full articulation is not to be found until the so-called Sunshine Policy of President Kim Dae-jung (1998–2003) and the subtle but important amendments to this approach under his successor, President No Mu-hyŏn (elected in December 2002 and inaugurated in February 2003). The No administration has not only been more willing to engage North Korea at all levels but has even sent explicit signals that its policy has been designed as a counterweight to the United States.

South Korean aid to North Korea is much more complex in its structure than that of the United States, which was basically limited to food and oil shipments, and Japan's, which was confined to a limited number of large food shipments. Table 6.4 outlines the various channels that have been used, which include multilateral, bilateral, and a large NGO sector that has in the past been quasi-official and continues to receive direct government subvention.[18]

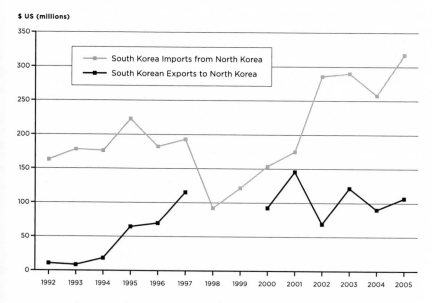

$ US (millions)

FIGURE 6.3. Commercial Trade Between North and South Korea
Source: Korean Ministry of Unification: Inter-Korean Cooperation, www.unikorea.go.kr/index.jsp.

TABLE 6.4. South Korean Humanitarian Assistance, 1995–2005 (in $US millions except where noted)

	1995	1996	1997	1998	1999	2000	2001	2002	2003	2004	2005	Total
Total public of which:	232.0	3.1	26.7	11.0	28.3	78.6	53.3	83.8	87.0	115.1	123.9	720.6
Multilateral	0.0	3.1	26.7	11.0	0.0	0.0	0.6	18.0	17.4	25.9	1.8	104.3
(% of public)	0.0	100.0	100.0	100.0	0.0	0.0	1.1	21.5	19.9	22.5	1.5	14.5
WFP	0.0	2.0	20.5	11.0	0.0	0.0	0.1	17.4	16.2	24.0	0.0	91.2
(form)	-	CSB	CSB, maize, powdered milk	Maize, flour	-	-	Maize	Maize	Maize	Maize	-	
Non-WFP	0.0	1.1	6.1	0.0	0.0	0.0	0.5	0.6	1.2	1.9	1.8	13.1
(channels)	-	UNICEF; WMO	UNICEF; WHO, UNDP; FAO	-	-	-	WHO	WHO	WHO, UNICEF	WHO, UNICEF	WHO, UNICEF	-
Bilateral	232.0	0.0	0.0	0.0	28.3	78.6	52.7	65.8	69.7	89.3	122.1	616.3
(% of public)	100.0	0.0	0.0	0.0	100.0	100.0	98.9	78.5	80.1	77.5	98.5	85.5
(form)	Rice	-	-	-	Fertilizer	Fertilizer	Clothing, fertilizer	Fertilizer	Fertilizer	Relief supplies, fertilizer	-	-

TABLE 6.4. South Korean Humanitarian Assistance, 1995–2005 (in $US millions except where noted), (*continued*)

	22.4 (1995—1997)	20.9	18.6	35.1	64.9	51.2	70.6	141.1	88.7	424.8
Total NGOs of which										
Korea National Red Cross	22.4	20.9	13.1	9.4	22.0	6.9	5.9	37.0		137.5
(% of NGOs)	100.0	100.0	70.1	26.8	33.9	13.5	8.3	26.2		32.4
Other NGOs	0.0	0.0	5.6	25.7	42.9	44.2	64.8	104.1		287.3
(% of NGOs)	0.0	0.0	29.9	73.2	66.1	86.5	91.7	73.8		67.6
Number of other NGOs	0	0	10	12	19	25	29	33		

Sources: 1995—2004: Korean Ministry of Unification 2005a; 2005 non-WFP data: Korean Ministry of Unification 2005b, 2006; 2005 WFP data: WFP 2006b.

Several features of South Korean aid are worth noting. The first is that while the government has made modest contributions through the WFP, the over-whelming majority of public assistance has passed through bilateral channels in the form of concessional loans, a useful fiction for both sides, as we will discuss. Over time, a large and growing share of this aid has been in the form of fertilizer, but food aid remains an important element both through govern-ment and NGO channels. Since public bilateral aid does not pass through the WFP—and indeed is not technically aid at all but loans—it is not subject to any of the WFP's protocols with respect to targeting, access, monitoring, or assessment. Through 2004 South Korean aid was not monitored at all. In July 2004, North Korea finally agreed to establish a monitoring regime for South Korean food assistance, but it is substantially weaker than the WFP regime and makes no pretense of population targeting.[19] Food aid goes directly into the PDS for delivery to the PDCs; as a small number of dissident South Korean NGOs have noted, the direct use of the PDS, the absence of targeting, and the relatively weak monitoring regime makes it even more difficult to guarantee that rice is not being diverted to elite consumption, other undeserving groups, or the market (see chapter 5). South Korean assistance is also provided in the form of rice, which is the preferred staple of the elite rather than less desirable grains such as barley or millet, which would be less prone to diversion and therefore more likely to reach vulnerable portions of the population.

The minimalist nature of the monitoring regime reflects differences with the United States and Japan in underlying strategy and objectives. Aid policy is clearly motivated by a broader political strategy of engagement and strong inter-est in forestalling a collapse of the North Korean state, which successive govern-ments have believed would impose unacceptable financial costs on the South.

The second characteristic of South Korean aid is that a large share passes through NGO channels, fully 37 percent. This is misleading in several important respects, however (O. Chung 2003). Until 1999, the South Korean Red Cross was the main channel for both government and private aid to North Korea, working directly with its North Korean counterpart (which appeared to be used almost exclusively for this purpose). With the coming of the Sunshine Policy, the government established more direct ministerial contacts and the Ministry of Unification developed protocols for private inter-Korean exchanges. NGOs that managed to establish a consistent record of raising funds and conducting humanitarian operations for a year were entitled to apply for a license that desig-nated them as North Korea support groups. These organizations are diverse and involved in a variety of projects that go far beyond food aid and food security. But as Oknim Chung summarizes, "They put more emphasis on confidence-building through frequent contacts than on hewing closely to humanitarian principles" (2003:82), and while U.S. and European NGOs have reduced their activities in North Korea, South Korean groups have expanded theirs quite dramatically. Moreover, a share of the aid passing through these organizations is ultimately public, funded through the Inter-Korean Cooperation Fund. In addition to financing humanitarian efforts and activities such as family reunions, the fund has also been used to finance North-South infrastructure projects—the road and rail links, the Kaesŏng industrial park—and to provide loans to private companies engaged in trade and investment with the North.

The final point is that, as in the United States and Japan, aid has also followed political cycles. The very large 1995 contribution was seen by the Kim Yŏng-sam administration as a gesture that would contribute to a political breakthrough, but these hopes were quickly disappointed. In contravention to the agreement, the North Korean authorities forced the first ship carrying grain to fly a North Korean flag and later detained the crew of another relief vessel (Noland 2000:185). The government was predictably outraged and not only ruled out the possibility of further assistance but actively lobbied other countries to condition their aid on improvement in North-South ties; as we indicated above, both the United States and Japan pulled back their assistance to North Korea at a critical juncture—early 1996—in response to South Korea's wishes (Natsios 1999:185).

In the last year of his administration (1997), however, Kim Yŏng-sam revised this policy as evidence continued to accumulate that famine conditions were worsening and political support for assistance grew.[20] South Korean researchers had devoted substantial effort to estimating North Korean food supplies, going so far as establishing test plots near the DMZ that mirrored North Korean conditions and even using North Korean agricultural techniques to cultivate them. These exercises noted substantial shortfalls between estimated supply and demand. They assumed, however, that the differences were being made up—or could be—by drawing down ample military stocks. Other analysts outlined conflicting evidence that pointed to serious shortages (most notably Lim 1997). The Korean Buddhist Sharing Movement (KBSM; subsequently Good Friends) reports that we have cited above began to get public attention as well. In May 1997, the first Red Cross agreement was struck, establishing the Red Cross as the window through which private contributions could flow to the North. From June, the Red Cross sent 53,800 MT of food to Sinŭiju, Namp'o and Namyang through the ports of Namp'o and Hŭngnam.

With the coming of the Kim Dae-jung administration in 1998 and the initiation of the Sunshine Policy, the stage was set for broader and more consistent assistance. In the first year of this administration, however, the new government was hamstrung both by the regional financial crisis and a recalcitrant legislature dominated by the opposition party.[21] As a result, the administration had to make concessions to conservatives in Kim Dae-jung's coalition, including important cabinet positions and the promise that engagement would only be pursued on the basis of strict reciprocity (Levin and Han 2002:91).

Nonetheless, the administration took a number of steps that established the institutions and policies of deeper engagement with the North. Among them was the early announcement of the principle that economics and politics should be separated, including an announcement in April 1998 that the legal foundation would be set for private investment in the North. Another early change was to allow agencies other than the Red Cross to operate; as can be seen in table 6.4, the Red Cross share of total NGO aid began to decline from this point as the Inter-Korean Cooperation Fund grew and a wide array of NGOs began working in North Korea on issues from agriculture to health, nutrition, and education.[22]

On January 4, 1999, the administration held a National Security Council (NSC) meeting that reached a number of important decisions on the overall direction of aid policy. The government decided to continue emergency food aid but would also focus on agricultural development by providing fertilizer, seeds, and pesticide as well; as can be seen from table 6.4, the fertilizer share of total aid has consistently been high. South Korea provided 200,000 tons of fertilizer aid to the North in 1999, 300,000 tons in 2000, 200,000 tons in 2001, and 300,000 tons in 2002, the final year of the Kim Dae-jung administration.

A second decision had to do with South Korea's participation in the multilateral appeals process. The provision of fertilizer was motivated at least in part by ongoing concerns about transparency in the distribution of aid; diversion of fertilizer seemed less of a threat to the integrity of the aid program than was diversion of food. Nonetheless, the decision was taken that South Korea would also supply its growing food aid largely on a bilateral basis and technically in the form of loans rather than grants. The government has made contributions through the WFP, but they constitute a small share of total assistance.

As the administration stepped up its multifaceted push to orchestrate a summit meeting between Kim Dae-jung and Kim Jŏng-il in the spring of 2000, bilateral food and fertilizer aid increased dramatically. As we have subsequently learned, a complex set of public and private payments also accompanied the more open aid offer.[23] In the wake of the summit, the two governments not only reached broad agreements on principles but also established the Inter-Korean Economic Cooperation Promotion Committee, which served as the locus for discussions on normalizing commercial relations and cooperative infrastructure projects as well as humanitarian assistance.[24]

Conservatives had expressed doubts about the outcome of the summit from the beginning, and as the euphoria of the June 2000 summit faded and North Korea offered little in return, domestic opposition to the Sunshine Policy mounted (Levin and Han 2002:chap. 6). Kim Dae-jung's diplomacy was complicated not only by the lack of North Korean reciprocity and growing conservative opposition but by the transition from the Clinton to Bush administrations in the United States and the new president's open skepticism about the Sunshine Policy and hostility toward the North Korean regime. Yet despite the dramatic slowdown in policy initiatives in the late Kim Dae-jung years, the separation of the political and economic tracks remained a cornerstone of the administration's approach to the end. As can be seen in table 6.4, despite growing domestic opposition to the Sunshine Policy, total aid continued at levels roughly equal to those during 2000, and for the five years of his administration, total aid through public and NGO channels totaled over $450 million.[25]

The election of No Mu-hyŏn occurred just as the second nuclear crisis was breaking in late 2002; by the end of the election campaign, the U.S. management of the crisis had become a potent issue, and No signaled his intention to distance South Korea from the American approach. No's election also seemed to signal continuity with the Sunshine Policy, but in fact the new administration placed even greater faith on using economic ties as a means of advancing broader political reconciliation. The administration's Policy for Peace and Prosperity included aid, commercial relations, investment, and cooperative projects as components of a larger project of regional integration that included not only the Korean peninsula but Northeast Asia more generally (Ministry of Unification 2003; Moon 2004).

On coming to office, the No administration quickly made a contribution through the WFP (100,000 MT of maize), but aid policy reverted to the bilateral format that developed since the 2000 summit. The bilateral Inter-Korean Economic Cooperation Promotion Committee became the venue for the discussion of aid commitments. In May 2003—while the nuclear standoff with the United States was continuing—the North Koreans requested 200,000 tons of fertilizer, which the South Koreans delivered, and a total of 500,000 MT of grain. This amount proved somewhat higher than the approximately 400,000 MT South Korea ultimately supplied for the year, which was equal to nearly half the country's uncovered food deficit for the year (that is, the shortfall between WFP estimates of domestic production and commercial imports and total demand). Requests to maintain these levels of support were subsequently made in the June 2004 meetings of the bilateral economic cooperation committee and approved by the South Korean side

Several things are noteworthy about these commitments. First, they are quite large when scaled either to the total uncovered food deficit or the total WFP appeal. Second, this commitment was initially made in the absence of any monitoring system, in part because of the aid-as-loan fiction. Monitoring was only put in place and became operational in the following year as pressures mounted for greater accountability. Third, the aid extended by South Korea was unconditional on progress on the nuclear issue or even in bilateral relations; after June 2004, bilateral relations fell into a freeze that would not thaw until June, when a high-level South Korean envoy met directly with Kim Jŏng-il in an effort to restart both North-South talks and the broader Six-Party effort. As during the Kim Dae-jung administration, the engagement policy explicitly sought to separate the political and economic tracks, including not only humanitarian assistance but commercial relations as well.

This commitment was severely tested by the February 10, 2005, announcement that North Korea was suspending its participation in the Six-Party Talks and had nuclear weapons; only a month before this announcement, the North Korean government had placed its largest aid request to the South Korean government ever: 500,000 tons of fertilizer. The government was divided over how to respond to the February 10 statement and was pressured by the United States not to grant the aid request. South Korean public opinion was by no means altogether unified on this issue. The opposition Grand National Party has argued for more stringent monitoring, and a minority voice within the South Korean humanitarian community has argued strenuously that large amounts of aid are diverted to the military and that food aid should be cut sharply.[26] But as table 6.5 shows, Korean public opinion has changed dramatically in recent years, despite the onset of the second nuclear crisis; opposition to aid has fallen to new lows and even support for conditional aid has been replaced by sentiment that South Korea should extend assistance without strings attached.

Despite statements by President No that additional aid should await progress in the talks, humanitarian assistance—in which the government counted both its fertilizer and food aid shipments—was not so conditioned. Moreover, as was subsequently made clear, the June breakthrough and the resumption of both the bilateral and Six-Party Talks in mid-2005 had been facilitated by promises of generous economic assistance, including not only humanitarian assistance but also massive commitments to provide energy in the form of electric power, deepen commercial relations, and expand government-to-government projects.[27] In early 2006, as the United States was cutting aid and tighten-

TABLE 6.5. South Koreans' Opinions on the Nature of North Korea (2003, percentage)

Question:		2003		
In your opinion, North Korea is a country . . .	1996	All ages	20s	50s and older
In need of our assistance	22.3	11.8	6.4	14.4
To cooperate with	45.7	46.1	63.1	28.4
In bona fide competition	4.0	2.7	3.1	2.3
Impeding South Korea's advancement	6.3	31.4	25.1	40.2
Threatening national security	19.2	7.8	2.4	14.4

Source: Bong 2003, table 6.

ing sanctions, South Korea announced it was doubling its budget for economic cooperation with the North despite the fact that Pyongyang was continuing to boycott the Six-Party Talks (Agence France Press 2006).

The statements of President No and South Korean officials have remained consistent on the principle that humanitarian assistance (and even broader economic cooperation) should not be linked to political progress on other issues. Decisions concerning aid were to be taken by South Korea in consultation with the North and were not subject to either multilateral cooperation or coordination with the United States and other parties to the Six-Party Talks. South Korean officials consistently expressed their reservations concerning the use of sanctions, which would require a substantial adjustment of an increasingly well-entrenched aid strategy. Moreover, the South Korean government supported liberal use of both current and prospective economic assistance as a means of facilitating political cooperation.

The Tangle of European Assistance

The coordination problems that we have underlined for the aid effort as a whole are reproduced within the European Union itself, which exhibits both a diversity of approaches across countries and changing views over time of how to engage North Korea most effectively.[28] Table 6.6 tracks European assistance to the DPRK from the onset of the famine through 2005.[29] Viewed as a whole, the European countries responded quickly to the famine. Following years saw a brief pause as the humanitarian imperative appeared to wane and a number

of major countries remained unclear about how to structure their political relations with North Korea. Kim Dae-jung's Sunshine Policy provided an opening
for engagement and wider normalization of relations; Pyongyang also began to
reach out at this juncture. Overall aid commitments saw a strong revival following the 2000 North-South summit and a more subtle shift in composition away
from the consolidated appeal toward programs outside it, including a focus on
technical assistance.[30] But engagement, and the hope in some quarters that
Europe might even play an independent political role in Northeast Asia, fell
afoul of continuing concerns about human rights, the integrity of the aid effort,
and the onset of the second nuclear crisis. By 2005 aid had fallen sharply.

Even to talk about European aid is arguably misleading given that individual
countries, both inside and outside the EU, maintain their own aid policies
and the extent and timing of their involvement has varied. The Scandinavian
countries were large and consistent supporters of the Consolidated Appeals
Process from the outset, and each ran programs or made contributions outside
the appeal process as well; Sweden's total aid in 2004 was more than $10 mil-
lion. The Scandinavian countries were among a group that normalized relations
early and also included Portugal, Austria, and Switzerland.

A second group of countries, including most notably Italy and Germany,
responded to the early humanitarian demand in 1997–98 and subsequently
became more forthcoming as North Korea aggressively reached out to them
as a political and economic counterweight to the United States. This group of
countries—Germany in particular—had expressed a variety of concerns about
normalization of relations with North Korea, but Italy normalized relations
in early 2000, citing South Korea's Sunshine Policy, and was followed, after a
lag, by Germany (as well as the United Kingdom and Spain) later in the year;
a number of other countries quickly followed suit. A third group of countries
has chosen to provide only minimal assistance (in Britain's case) or virtually
none at all (Belgium, Austria, Spain, and France). France, in particular, stood
on the principle that aid should not be extended to North Korea until underlying political issues—including both the nuclear weapons question and human
rights concerns—were addressed and steadfastly refused to provide any assistance to North Korea whatsoever.[31]

In another sense, however, we can speak of European assistance because of
the European Commission's aid programs. The commission provided over 320
million euros from 1995 to 2004 from the European Commision Humanitarian Aid Office (ECHO) and Food Aid/Food Security budget lines, roughly
half of it through the consolidated appeal, the rest outside it. After the floods,
the commission's Food Aid/Food Security budget line accommodated the

TABLE 6.6. European Humanitarian Assistance by Donor Organization, 1996–2005 ($US millions)

	1996/7	1997/8	1998	1999	2000	2001	2002	2003	2004	2005
Inside UN Consolidated Appeal										
Donor governments										
European Commission	8.6	27.5	9.5	8.0	4.8	0.0	9.5	16.0	15.6	n.a.
EU member countries	2.5	12.4	6.8	7.2	8.9	14.8	7.7	19.2	25.6	n.a.
Other European countries	2.7	3.7	4.1	2.3	3.2	4.3	1.4	13.2	3.8	n.a.
European NGOs	0.0	0.3	0.0	0.0	0.1	0.1	0.0	0.2	0.7	n.a.
UNICEF national committees										
EU member countries	0.0	0.9	1.2	0.1	0.7	0.0	0.0	0.0	0.0	0.7
Other European countries	0.0	0.1	1.7	0.1	0.0	0.0	0.0	0.0	0.0	0.0
Sub-total	13.9	45.0	23.4	17.8	17.7	19.2	18.7	48.7	45.7	0.7
Outside UN Consolidated Appeal										
Donor governments										
European Commission	0.5	36.2	36.0	0.3	0.2	0.0	6.1	4.1	15.3	13.4
EU member countries	1.4	5.7	3.1	2.5	2.4	3.2	5.3	4.3	10.2	17.8
Other European countries	0.7	9.9	6.2	0.3	0.2	3.5	1.3	0.6	1.6	4.0
European NGOs	0.0	8.0	5.7	0.0	0.0	1.5	3.4	1.3	1.6	0.0

(continued)

TABLE 6.6. European Humanitarian Assistance by Donor Organization, 1996–2005 ($US millions), (*continued*)

	1996/7	1997/8	1998	1999	2000	2001	2002	2003	2004	2005
Red Cross national committees										
EU member countries	1.2	1.3	0.7	0.4	1.7	0.0	0.0	0.0	1.7	1.6
Other European countries	0.2	2.2	1.0	1.1	0.6	0.0	0.0	0.0	0.0	0.0
Private	0.0	0.0	0.1	0.0	0.0	0.0	0.0	0.0	0.0	0.0
Subtotal	4.1	63.3	52.8	4.6	5.0	8.1	16.0	10.4	30.5	36.9
Grand total	18.0	108.3	76.1	22.3	22.7	27.4	34.7	59.0	76.2	37.6

Note: No consolidated appeal for 2005. Numbers for UNICEF National Committees are not within a consolidated appeal process. Data reflect only European contributions explicitly documented as such in the UN-OCHA FTS. Other European countries include contributions from: Czech Republic, Iceland, Liechtenstein, Monaco, Norway, Poland, Russia, Slovakia, Switzerland, and Turkey.

Source: UN-OCHA.

basic provision of substantial humanitarian aid including food aid, fertilizer, and agricultural rehabilitation projects (59 million euros in 1997, 55 million euros in 1998). Currently, it is again through ECHO funds that most of the aid is provided.

The coming of the Sunshine Policy, and the 2000 summit in particular, led to the formulation of a wide-ranging approach that combined political and economic objectives; some analysts even proposed that Europe develop an independent role in the security process in Northeast Asia.[32] Humanitarian aid was funded through the food security budget line, but to it were added operations through ECHO.

The European guidelines and commission documents are cautious. The 2001–4 country strategy paper (European Commission 2001) says that aid should be extended in a measured way and that the extension of aid should be made contingent on accommodating EU concerns. The 2000 humanitarian strategy extended aid on an ad hoc basis and required the North Korean government to sign letters of understanding for each project; these contained an EC clause where minimum humanitarian standards are clearly laid out. Moreover, the commission also consistently emphasized the risks of long-run humanitarian assistance and argued for a shift in the focus of aid away from food toward rehabilitation and longer-run development issues through the provision of technical assistance.[33] A number of discrete EU projects were to move in that direction before the second nuclear crisis in a variety of functional fields, from agriculture to health and nutrition. But these were not implemented because of the crisis, and the EU refocused primarily on humanitarian projects in these areas.

Despite these cautions, commission assessments were hopeful about the benefits of engagement and the particular niche Europe had carved out as a provider of technical assistance. The 2001–04 country strategy paper, reflecting on the experience of the previous five years, noted important improvements in access and the leading role played by NGOs financed in part through the commission:[34] "The presence of European NGOs in the country, besides helping to address important humanitarian needs, is also acting as an ice-breaker in the opening process of the country. The relation with the European NGOs, even with its important limitations, is in most places the only access to the outside world for the North Korean population in the areas where these operate" (European Commission 2001:14). In their assessment of the overall aid effort, Dammers, Fox, and Jimenez (2005) are similarly hopeful. The report argues for the benefits of channeling aid through the WFP from Europe's perspective but comes to somewhat uncritical conclusions regarding the effectiveness of such aid and of the PDS in particular.[35]

With the onset of the second nuclear crisis, the European Union's General Affairs and External Relations Council drafted a toughly worded conclusion calling on North Korea to abide by its international commitments (2002). The conclusion reaffirmed humanitarian aid but also contained a request that the commission and member states review their activities regarding North Korea, including technical assistance and trade measures. Moreover, European countries shared a common concern about human rights abuses in North Korea, and the EU was the chief sponsor of the first resolution of the UN Commission on Human Rights ever to address the country, a hard-hitting overview that passed again in 2004 and 2005 (with South Korea abstaining). The nuclear issue and human rights concerns put a pause on the move toward deeper economic engagement and development assistance. But as the data in table 6.6 show, this did not have an immediate effect on overall assistance, in part because some technical assistance projects could no doubt be reclassified as humanitarian. But Europe's collective engagement has clearly been conditional, reflecting a continuing divergence of views. Some countries have been more forthcoming and argued for more open-ended engagement that would represent an independent European stance. Other countries—most notably France and Great Britain, Europe's duo nuclear powers—made policy decisions not to extend assistance to North Korea except indirectly through the commission's efforts and after 2002 pushed for a slowdown in engagement.

China

China's relations with North Korea are shrouded in patron-client privilege. Information on such basic issues as the prices that North Korea pays for imports from China are unavailable, and as a result it is difficult to distinguish among commercial imports, barter, and outright grants.[36] The data we have on trade are subject to a fairly wide range of estimates, compounded by a border trade that exploded in the early 2000s. Furthermore, we have only indirect evidence of China's political motives with respect to North Korea and of the extent—if any—to which Beijing might have sought to exercise leverage over Pyongyang by economic means. The centralized nature of the Chinese system leads us to believe that large fluctuations in trade almost certainly reflected political decisions by the top leadership, and that is no doubt true for core commodities such as food and fuel. But decentralized interactions between the two countries have grown dramatically in recent years as trade restrictions have been lifted in China and North Korea has tolerated a much denser bilateral relationship. By our estimate, such decentralized trade accounted for fully 80 percent of all Chinese exports by 2005, providing critical impetus to the marketization process we describe in the next chapter.

It is possible to get some sense of the evolution of the relationship by triangulating trade, aid, and the high-level political exchanges and statements that are in the public record. Several points are relevant for our purposes here. First, despite the shock of normalizing relations with South Korea in 1992, China emerged as North Korea's primary benefactor following the collapse of the Soviet Union. In 1993–94, however, particularly following the death of Kim Il-sŏng, bilateral relations became increasingly strained. Trade fell sharply at this time, contributing to the famine that subsequently developed.

After the devastating loss of food imports from China in 1994, bilateral trade relations rebounded, and China became a mainstay of economic support. China lifted some restrictions on small border trade in 1996, and North Korean companies even enjoyed selective tariff exemptions. North Korea apparently even benefited from tariff reductions undertaken when China joined the World Trade Organization, even though China had no obligation to extend its concessions to North Korea, which is not a member of the WTO. As relations improved, China was willing to maintain trade relations with North Korea in critical commodities, including not only food but also oil delivered by pipeline from the Daqing field in the northeast. These core commodities were almost certainly shipped at "friendship prices" or on deferred payment terms and were quite possibly altogether gratis. Whatever food North Korea did import from China was also not subject to any of the monitoring and targeting requirements, however porous, that characterized aid channeled through the WFP or from South Korea. We can only speculate on the end use of these grain shipments, but there would appear to be no constraint on the North Korean leadership using them to supply core groups, including the military.

China's overall economic support for North Korea can be demonstrated by examining the two countries' bilateral trade since 1981 (figure 6.4). Through 1986 trade was roughly balanced (again, with the caveat about friendship prices and North Korean exports of dubious value). But what is striking is the sharp divergence that takes place thereafter. In the absence of international capital flows to finance trade, China's willingness to allow North Korea to run chronic bilateral deficits and accumulate large arrears in its trade account must be seen as a form of foreign aid or subsidy. We estimate that the value of this implicit aid cumulatively reached nearly $6 billion by 2002, which would make China by far Korea's most significant supporter over the last decade. Around that time, however, North Korean exports to China start to take off and while the bilateral deficit widened in 2004 and 2005, it did so in the context of greatly expanded

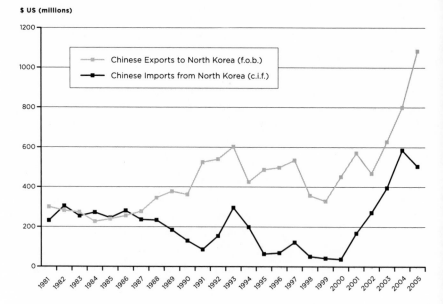

FIGURE 6.4. China's trade with North Korea
Note: 2005 is based on annualized January to September data. *Source:* IMF 2006.

North Korean exports to China. We interpret this pattern as reflecting the fact that China was no longer willing to conduct bilateral trade on an unrequited basis and at least some share of bilateral trade was increasingly conducted on commercial terms.

With respect to food trade in particular, the data we have on cereal imports come from two sources: Eberstadt 2003—using Chinese export data—provides a volume estimate in million metric tons of grain equivalent, while the UN provides value data denominated in dollars (figures 6.5 and 6.6). China promised to enlarge its supply of grain and petroleum to North Korea as early as 1994 in the wake of Kim Il-sŏng's death and made modest promises of assistance in 1995. But these early North Korean appeals and Chinese promises did not translate immediately into increased grain exports (*BBC Summary of World Broadcasts* 1994; *Donga Ilbo* 1994).[37] As the depth of the situation became apparent, however, and perhaps motivated by the growing movement of refugees across the border, Chinese premier Li Peng and North Korean vice premier Hong Song-nam signed an agreement on May 22, 1996, that reestablished high-level contacts, promised a widening of economic cooperation, and included large commitments of food aid. China also explicitly reverted to friendship prices for its commercial transactions (Agence France Presse 1996). Both estimates of grain trade that we have show sharp increases in 1996–97, with the UN data appearing to confirm Eberstadt's estimate of as much as 1 million metric tons.

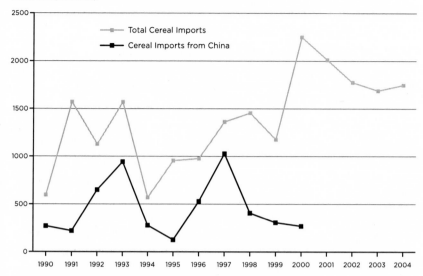

Metric tons (thousands)

FIGURE 6.5. Volume of Cereal Shipments to North Korea, Total and from China, 1990–2004
Sources: Total: FAOSTAT; Cereal imports from China: Eberstadt 2003.

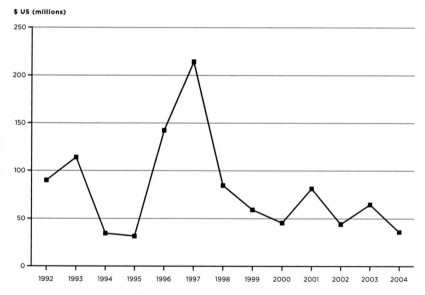

$ US (millions)

FIGURE 6.6. Value of Cereal Imports from China, 1992–2004
Notes: Original data reported by China. 10% c.i.f./f.o.b. adjustment made. Based on SITC (Rev. 3) Chapter 04 commodities. *Source:* UN-COMTRADE 2005.

China's grain shipments continued throughout the remainder of the decade, albeit at reduced levels, and China even appealed to the international community for more aid on behalf of North Korea (Japan Economic News Wire 1997). Beginning in 1999, relations between the two countries began to show signs of a higher-level political rapprochement (Kim and Lee 2002). Chairman Kim Young Nam of the Workers' Party visited Beijing and in a meeting with Premier Zhu Rongji obtained more aid from China (Kyodo News Service 1999). This was followed by three visits from Kim Jŏng-il himself in 2000, 2001, and 2004 (when he met with the entire standing committee of the Politburo of the Communist Party) and again in 2006, when he visited Guangzhou on a trip that was likened to Deng Xiaoping's famous southern tour of 1992 when the Chinese leader strongly affirmed the reformist path.

The nature of Chinese influence over North Korea during this period, and particularly since the onset of the nuclear crisis in 2002, has become a virtual cottage industry because of U.S. hopes that China would bring its influence to bear on North Korean behavior (Mansourov 2003; Scobell 2004; Wu 2005; International Crisis Group 2006). The result is a divide among China scholars on the extent to which China is either capable or willing to influence North Korea in general and through the manipulation of economic assistance in particular.

On the one hand, Chinese officials and scholars have become more open in their calls for economic reform in North Korea. China has as a matter of policy also consistently held to the view that the Korean peninsula should be nonnuclear; Bejing played a pivotal role in orchestrating the Six-Party Talks. In August 2003, for example, President Hu Jintao publicly suggested that North Korea stop its "constant war-preparation" and pursue economic reforms (Lam 2003). Hu also stated that a continued North Korean effort to develop a nuclear program would impede China's ability and willingness to aid North Korea. Analysts have also seized on particular episodes, such as reports of interrupted fuel supplies, as well as the size of the overall economic relationship and its significance for North Korea, to suggest that China has the power to influence the course of the negotiations if it chooses.

Nongovernmental sources are even more openly critical, although they have at times run afoul of stated government policy. In September 2004, the Chinese-language journal *Zhanlue yu guanli* (Strategy and Management) published an article that criticized North Korea's domestic and foreign politics and was subsequently shut down as a result. But a variety of reports and discussions with Chinese academics suggest more-or-less open disaffection with North Korea, including from economic actors who have been burned in their economic dealings with the country (Mansourov 2003; Kim 2005; International Crisis Group 2006).

On the other hand, the idea that such disaffection would translate into the use of sanctions reflected wishful thinking, as China also repeatedly sent signals that it was unable or unwilling to bring economic leverage to bear on North Korea or participate in any exercise that did. With respect to Chinese capabilities, Beijing claims that its importance to North Korea is less than thought because of the closed nature of the economy and the vacillating nature of the economic relationship. In fact, North Korea's economic relationship with China has become more important over time. Food imports dropped as the agricultural economy revived, but fuel is the most critical item, since North Korea could almost certainly not secure fuel imports on similar terms (figure 6.7).

A final variant of the capability argument—that China has limited leverage—strikes us as more plausible and lies with the increasingly decentralized nature of trade. The common assumption is that Chinese exports are tightly controlled from Beijing, and in one sense this is true. The central government controls large-scale food and fuel shipments and has the power to affect exchange through tightening or loosening border controls. But disaggregated data on the sources of Chinese exports by the level of the firm (central government, provincial, municipal) shows that an increasing share of Chinese trade and investment is decentralized, the result of provincial and lower level entities and purely private traders. In the long run, these Chinese economic networks are likely

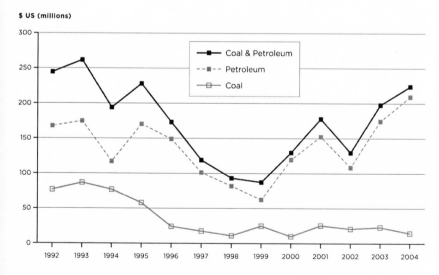

FIGURE 6.7. Fuel Imports from China, 1992–2004
Note: Original data reported as exports from China. Based on SITC (Rev. 3) Chapter 3 (total), 32 (coal), and 33 (petroleum) commodities. *Source: UN*-COMTRADE 2005.

to be the most important source of economic transformation in North Korea, more important than the tightly controlled interactions with South Korea. At the same time, however, their depth may limit Beijing's ability to control trade ties or at least raise the cost of doing so.

The second line of argument about Chinese influence goes not to capability but to intent. To the extent that China has used its economic leverage with respect to North Korea, it appears to take the form of inducements to participate in talks rather than constraints for failing to do so (see, e.g., Kyodo News Service 2004). China also has a number of other concerns with North Korea, including the growth of the refugee problem (Lankov 2004). But the refugee problem is just the tip of a much larger iceberg of concerns. Although China has continued reservations about North Korea's economic strategy and nuclear ambitions, it has equally significant concerns about economic pressure that would lead to political upheaval, a second economic collapse, and a flood of refugees. This very risk increases North Korean leverage vis-à-vis its patron. The evidence to date suggests that China has been willing to step in as a lender of last resort in crises—albeit it with a lag—and is likely to continue to provide crucial support if needed.

The Coordination Problem: A Reprise

In the early 1990s, North Korea faced an extremely difficult international environment. Soviet foreign policy was transformed under Mikhail Gorbachev, leading to the normalization of relations with South Korea. The subsequent collapse of the Soviet Union meant the end of North Korea's main patron. China stepped into the breach but not smoothly. The dictates of the famine required North Korea to develop these existing relationships while aggressively cultivating new ones, for example, with Japan, the EU and its member countries, and, perhaps most important, South Korea.

North Korea found itself caught in the terrible downdraft of the 1993–94 crisis. Slow to adjust and seek support and pursuing a reckless bargaining game with the United States, the country initially found it hard to secure the assistance it needed at a very crucial moment in the evolution of the famine.

Over time, the plethora of relationships North Korea was able to develop generated a quite different problem for the donors: the coordination of aid became increasingly difficult, including with respect to the basic issues of targeting, monitoring, and assessment that we took up in chapter 4. This point can be made by reproducing figures from Manyin's thorough 2005 study of

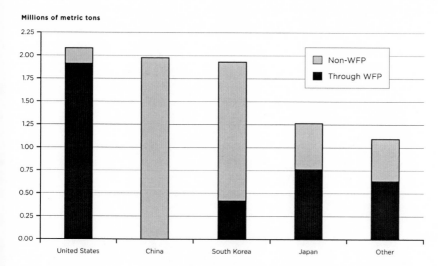

Millions of metric tons

FIGURE 6.8. Food Aid to North Korea, 1996–2004
Source: Manyin 2005.

U.S. aid policy (figure 6.8). The graph shows the share of food that has passed through the WFP and that which is entirely outside it.[38] The data refer only to food aid. As can be seen, Japan and the United States are the most multilateral on this simple measure, channeling the bulk of their contributions through the WFP; even the residual non-WFP contribution from the United States was in fact undertaken with close collaboration with WFP officials. When we turn to Europe, Korea, and China, however, we find that large shares of food aid passed to North Korea outside WFP channels. In principle, this aid could also be well targeted and monitored, although this would in any case involve an inefficiency given the accumulated expertise of the WFP on this score. But we are skeptical.[39] As we will argue in more detail in the conclusion to this book, the coordination of assistance and the integrity of the monitoring regime are closely related. Before getting to those issues, however, we must first understand the marketization that occurred in the wake of the famine and the subsequent efforts at economic reform.

PART III

Dealing with a Changing North Korea

Coping, Marketization, and Reform

New Sources of Vulnerability

Famines have long half-lives. The consequences of acute food shortages are not only felt in the short run but also reverberate for generations through the polities and societies they strike. In the first instance, households are forced into a variety of coping behaviors—migrating, foraging for food, selling assets, and engaging in barter and market exchanges—that can fundamentally alter the economic landscape. In this chapter, we argue that the famine and these coping behaviors contained the seeds of an increasing marketization of the North Korean economy. This was a bottom-up process resulting from the very coping behaviors we have just noted. Over time, de facto marketization also placed pressures on the government, which initiated a variety of economic reforms in the postfamine period, most notably a major package of policies introduced in the summer of 2002 that we analyze in some detail.

Marketization has had profound social impact in North Korea. Before the famine, the socialist system of entitlements rested on a particular pattern of social stratification based first on political status (loyal/wavering/suspect; party/ nonparty) and then on occupation (see table 3.1 on PDS rations). In this chapter, we show that entitlements to food have become increasingly dependent on the capacity to purchase food in the market.

Yet the government's commitment to marketization and reform was tentative at best, and the initial response was to crack down on activities deemed threatening to political and social stability. An almost primal impulse of the regime was toward the imposition of even tighter controls. As we will argue, even the reforms of 2002, particularly the major reform of prices, can be seen as a desperate effort by the state to gain access to resources and reassert control over markets that threatened to operate both outside state control and at the government's expense.

The result of these reform efforts is a hybrid transition that varies in important respects from those in other socialist countries. As in China and Vietnam and unlike what took place in Russia and Eastern Europe, the reforms in North Korea were undertaken by an incumbent Communist Party that exhibited a primary concern with the maintenance of political control and extreme caution toward any policy measures that might loosen it; North Korea is certainly not a case of a dual economic and political transition.[1] Rather, North Korean reforms should be interpreted as a ratification under duress of a bottom-up process of marketization that the regime has subsequently struggled to control.

A second distinctive feature of the transition lies in the composition of output at the beginning of the process. North Korea is relatively industrialized and looks more like Eastern Europe or parts of the former Soviet Union than it does the more agrarian China or Vietnam. These two countries both had more than 70 percent of their labor forces employed in agriculture when they initiated reforms (Noland 2000:table 3.7) and saw high returns from early policy changes relating to agriculture. North Korea, by contrast, has had to deal with an industrial sector that shows signs of virtual collapse (figure 7.1).[2] Given these political and economic circumstances, it is not surprising that the result of reform efforts to date have proven mixed at best and that the transformation of the North Korean economy has taken place in spite of the stance of the government rather than because of it.

We begin our analysis by looking at the political aftermath of the famine: the emergence of "military first" politics and the efforts to maintain control. We then consider in more detail the underlying process of marketization that we have already noted in chapter 3 before turning to the policy reforms and their consequences for access to food. We begin with the agricultural reforms, which predate the 2002 package, before turning to crucial developments in the industrial sector and macroeconomic policy that have had profound implications for access to food.

We closed our consideration of the famine with a review of the death toll. We evaluate this more recent period with an overview of a succession of nutritional surveys of children that have been done since the mid-1990s. Children are of particular interest to the humanitarian relief effort because of their intrinsic vulnerability to both shortages and entitlement failures, including those within the household itself. The portrait these data paint is grim. Ten years

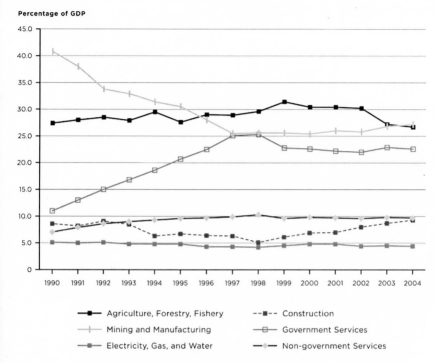

FIGURE 7.1. North Korea's Composition of Output
Source: Bank of Korea 2005.

after the famine, we still find classic signs of chronic malnutrition, with all the long-range developmental implications they carry. In this way, too, the results of the famine and ensuing shortages are proving to be enduring.

We close the chapter with a consideration of events in 2005 and early 2006, including the effort to revive the PDS. It is too soon to reach a firm conclusion about the longer-term meaning of these developments. But they show very clearly the ongoing ambivalence of the regime toward the de facto decentralization and marketization that has occurred in the country in the decade after the famine.

The Government Responds: The Quest for Control

The onset of the famine coincided with the first nuclear crisis, the death of Kim Il-sŏng, and the final transition to the political leadership of his son. As he came to power, Kim Jŏng-il faced the virtual collapse of the economy and, as the famine broke, social disintegration on a massive scale. The emergence of "military first" politics (*sŏn'gun chŏngch'i*) must be understood in this context. The military had long held a privileged position in North Korea; a primary source of Kim Il-sŏng's legitimacy was his role as an anti-Japanese guerilla fighter. Yet "military first" politics refers to an important shift in the political, organizational, and ideological base of the North Korean regime that took place following the death of Kim Il-sŏng, if not before. A renewed emphasis on the military emerged quite clearly during the period of the "arduous march"—the leadership's euphemism for the deprivations of the famine—that began in 1995. The term " 'military first' politics" (*sŏn'gun chŏngch'i*) was first officially unveiled in 1997 and appeared to become the ideological cornerstone of political rule in 1998 following the end of the official three-year mourning period after the death of Kim Il-sŏng.

The "military first" credo reflected two main political imperatives, one external, the other internal (Suh 2002; Koh 2005; I. Kim 2006). The first was a renewed emphasis on national security during the standoff with the United States over the nuclear issue in 1992–94. During periods of external threat, it is not surprising that the military would gain in stature and significance. The primary role of the military was reiterated strongly in official speeches after the onset of the second nuclear crisis in October 2002 as well.

But the timing of the ultimate announcement of the "military first" politics suggests that external circumstances were not primary. Rather, this shift reflected a complex set of internal political calculations associated with the succession as well. Kim Jŏng-il did not have a military background, which had been a key component of Kim Il-sŏng's political legitimacy. Kim senior was no doubt concerned that Kim Jŏng-il gain control over the military before the succession. Once Kim junior assumed key military-related posts beginning in 1990, he was able to use his position on the National Defense Commission (NDC) and power over appointments and spending to shore up this crucial base of support.[3] We see evidence of this before the succession and even more clearly in the wake of Kim Il-sŏng's death in July 1994. In constitutional amendments engineered in 1998, the National Defense Commission was effectively elevated above the Central Committee of the Korean Workers' Party as the central organ of political power. Since that time, Kim Jŏng-il has ruled the country from his position as chairman of the NDC rather than through either party or other government positions; the position of president was granted to Kim Il-sŏng in perpetuity.

To this, however, must be added a third motivation that we believe has received inadequate attention: the increasing use of the military, including paramilitary and reserve forces, both as a model of social discipline and hierarchy and as an additional instrument of control in the face of the widespread social disruption arising from the famine.[4] In his speech at Kim Il-sŏng University, Kim Jŏng-il (1996) derided the party for its lack of dynamism and hinted at increasing corruption in its ranks. The military, by contrast, was lauded for its discipline and revolutionary purpose (I. Kim 2006:65–66).

The problems were also short run in nature. It is standard during food shortages and famines for people to seek to move in search of food. However, all travel within North Korea is controlled and requires permits. As early as 1992, the government began to relax internal travel for the purpose of securing food (Ahn 1996); such movement undoubtedly accelerated thereafter and was even noted by Kim Jŏng-il in his December 1996 speech, cited earlier. Undocumented movement remained illegal, however, and thus vulnerable to low-level extortion and corruption. Good Friends interviews conducted in 2000 found that roughly half of 512 refugees interviewed had faced punishment for traveling without permits and that 70 percent either paid a fine or bribed officials (Good Friends 2004). Not only are internal migrants vulnerable to harassment by the security forces, but they are also effectively denied protection. Of the 512 refugees interviewed, 42 percent reported that they had been robbed, and 98 percent believed that public security was a problem. In short, the government had criminalized key coping behaviors, including internal migration and various forms of exchange.

The government also moved to crack down on cross-border movement. The right to leave one's country is enshrined in both the Universal Declaration of Human Rights and the International Covenant on Civil and Political Rights to which the government of the DPRK is a state party. Nonetheless, the North Korean penal code prescribes sentencing of up to three years in a prison camp for unauthorized departure. Detention in these camps is characterized by extreme deprivation, torture, and high rates of death (Hawk 2003). As the food situation worsened in the mid-1990s, the number of refugees fleeing into China's border provinces rose dramatically. This population has received increasing attention in recent years because of its size—estimates vary from the tens of thousands up to half a million—and the increasing vulnerability to forced repatriation of North Korean refugees in China.[5] Interviews reveal not only that the overwhelming majority of refugees moved for food or economic reasons but that some either moved back and forth between North Korea and China or sought to do so, bringing small amounts of money or food with them (Good Friends 1999, 2004).

As the ranks of the internal migrants and cross-border refugees expanded, the North Korean government responded in a variety of ways, including establishing

a network of ad hoc detention facilities, again characterized by extreme deprivation, torture, and, in the case of pregnant women repatriated from China, forced
abortions and infanticide (Hawk 2003). Adults engaged in illegal internal movement and famine-orphaned children (the *kotchebi*, or "wandering sparrows")
were subject to detention in so-called "9-27 camps" named after the date (September 27, 1995) when Kim Jŏng-il issued the edict authorizing their establishment. Males over sixteen who had crossed the border were vulnerable, however,
to incarceration in prison camps, and those suspected of more extensive engagement—frequent trips, trade, trafficking, marriage to a Chinese, contacts with
South Koreans or Christians who were active in sheltering refugees—faced more
extended incarceration in the long-term political prison camps that constitute
the North Korean gulag.[6]

In addition to controls on movement, a second aspect of the command-
and-control response to the famine and its aftermath was the use of the military to reassert authority over both the cooperative farms and the industrial
workplace. One element of the new order was what Andrew Natsios calls the
"militarization of agriculture," described in chapter 5 (1999:117): the mobilization of military reserve units (the Workers'-Peasants' Red Guard) not only for
planting and harvesting but also for security purposes. Refugee interviews make
reference to corn guards sent to protect against preharvesting or diversion in
1997. They also report the growth of a phenomenon that is virtually inevitable
given the combination of rationing, extreme shortages, and very high market
prices for food: bribery and corruption between farmers and the military. In
August 1997, the Public Security Ministry issued a decree on hoarding and theft
of food that stipulated the execution of individuals involved in either stealing
grain or trading in it.

The internal security forces were also called upon to address similar problems that were emerging in the industrial workplace. The general breakdown
of the industrial economy forced enterprise managers to engage in a variety
of coping behaviors to secure the inputs required to maintain production and
food to feed workers. State-owned enterprises with access to land or other
resources sought to grow food or to harvest resources that could be traded
for food; the deforestation along the Chinese border attests to the fact that
these coping strategies were not just employed by individuals but involved
well-organized efforts coordinated by either military units or enterprises in
the region. This process of adaptation and spontaneous privatization from
below was ultimately sanctioned by the government and institutionalized.
There is also evidence, however, that firms engaged in asset stripping and
theft as well.

Scott Snyder's early reports (1997) from the border region provide insight into these coping strategies. He found that in addition to the representatives of the central government, hundreds of trading interests representing local and provincial authorities appeared in Dandong and other Chinese cities near the border during the famine. He estimates that as many as eight hundred firms were engaged in such activity at the peak, although this number declined as their trading efforts proved less successful over time. These groups were authorized to conduct barter trade deals and to procure other resources on behalf of local authorities or even individual work units. For example, Snyder reports that a representative of the Hwanghae provincial government was authorized to sell scrap metal or timber resources in return for wheat flour, which was delivered to provincial authorities for local distribution.

But some of this illicit trade came from the dismantling of factories and/or involved personal enrichment. Becker (2005:190–93) relates the story from two refugees of public executions at the Hwanghae Iron and Steel Works in February 1998 for theft of state property; this episode was confirmed by Kim Jŏng-il himself in an interview with a delegation of North Koreans from Japan (Martin 2004:573–74). Bradley Martin (2004:551–78) presents a number of refugee accounts of work unit efforts to secure grain but also of widespread corruption and bribery in managers' efforts to secure inputs and periodic efforts to punish such behavior. Again, one of the most revealing sources of evidence on this point is the Kim Jŏng-il speech of December 1996, which recognizes the risks of "letting the people solve the food problem for themselves." The North Korean leader derided the party for maintaining inadequate control over work units and relying on "legal measures imposed by the police and other law enforcement agencies" as opposed to adequate political and ideological work that would guarantee appropriate work effort and protection of state assets.

Coping and Marketization

Yet as the government attempted to crack down on illicit activities and regain social control, it was at the same time forced to tolerate, if not sanction, a variety of behaviors that it had not tolerated before. Some of these coping strategies constitute the grisly survival mechanisms evident in all famine settings: purchasing or foraging for inferior foods, such as grasses and tree bark; begging; criminal activity; and even cannibalism (see, e.g., Becker 1997c, 1998b; Associated Press 1998; Struck 2003). Yet an important component of these coping strategies involved some form of trade: barter, sale of assets in order to purchase

food, prostitution, or foraging for foods that were then sold in order to purchase grain. Many of these activities implied the diversion to emerging markets
of grain and other foods not only from aid (chapter 5) but either from farm
households or the PDS. As a result, access to food was increasingly determined
by the position of the individual or household vis-à-vis these markets. These factors included geographic location (food-surplus or -deficit region), occupation
(urban or rural), and, increasingly, access to foreign exchange (either through
official employment or nonofficial economic activities or through remittances,
principally from relatives in Japan or China).

To some extent, this process of marketization reflected piecemeal policy
changes that occurred well before the reforms of 2002 discussed in the next section and even before the famine (the following draws on S. Lee 2003:298–303).
These can be classified into two basic sorts: those that regularized the use of
private plots and thus affected the supply side of the equation and those that
regularized markets and thus provided new distribution channels for food. One
innovation was to allow PDS populations, most notably those on state farms, to
grow grains other than maize and rice as well as other foodstuffs. These private
plots were officially incorporated into the supplementary channels of supply in
1987. At that time, the government ordered all state farms to allocate a certain
amount of land and work time to these activities and allowed the cultivation of
maize, clearly in compensation for the declining ability to provide PDS rations.
(In 1995 the right to cultivate private plots was also granted to military personnel, although it is interesting that these grants to the state farms and military
were not formally approved by the government until the constitution of 1998.)
In 1987 the government also allowed cooperative farm households to grow any
crops they chose on private plots, which supplemented overall supply but generated the incentive problems we highlighted in chapter 2.

In addition to these formal grants, the government tolerated to varying
degrees illegal private plots (*t'uigibat*). These plots included urban gardens near
residences or workplaces but primarily illicit holdings by cooperative and state
farmers on marginal lands such as steep hillsides. This tolerance was not sanctioned, however, and thus was subject to classic credibility problems about
future policy reversal. In 1989 the government announced that such plots were
illegal, and in 1992 groups aimed at breaking up such nonsocialist activities
were sent down to the countryside to eliminate them. Thus while local officials
may have tolerated these sources of supply, they, too, were undoubtedly sur-
rounded by corruption and bribery.

Finally, the government did allow farmers' markets to function to a greater
extent than in the past. From the banning of private grain trade in the late

1940s until the revival of private plots in the 1980s, farmers' markets played a minimal role in the overall distribution system, confined largely to supplementary foodstuffs. In 1982 markets were allowed to operate on a more regular basis: daily instead of every ten days. In May 1984, additional markets were allowed to operate, with the total number rising to three or four per county. In the early 1990s, as the capacity of the PDS began to falter, such markets were allowed to trade in grain, although this was not formally institutionalized.

As the PDS went into decline, these markets spread and, according to a study by the South Korea's Ministry of Unification, totaled between 300 and 350 as early as 1998, covering all counties in the country (Lintner 2005). The scope of goods traded also increased from supplementary food and grains to industrial products and came to include not only farm households but also professional merchants, even Chinese-Korean ones granted permission to enter the country and trade. Trade in these markets remained a precarious undertaking, however. In his December 1996 speech, Kim Jŏng-il expressed his antipathy to these activities, underlining that "the party and the government have full responsibility for the care and well-being of the lives of the people" and that "if the party lets the people solve the food problem themselves, then only the farmers and merchants will prosper, giving rise to egotism and collapsing the social order of a classless society. The party will then lose its popular base and will experience meltdown as in Poland and Czechoslovakia." In January 1999, Kim Jŏng-il ordered the government to reinforce state control over farmers' markets and prevent labor from being diverted to them.

In sum, the course of policy before the 2002 reforms suggests a tolerance but not institutionalization of market means of allocating food. But precisely what role did market-based activities play? Again, we start with the evidence from refugee interviews. Although the questions were not addressed in every interview, putting the results of these surveys together in sequence suggests a process of increasing marketization over time.

The Johns Hopkins studies (Robinson et. al. 1999, 2001) ask respondents what their principal source of food was from 1994 to 1997; we reproduce their results in tables 7.1 and 7.2. As the famine deepened, the share of respondents in the first sample depending primarily on foraging increased dramatically, reaching 40 percent by 1997. But fully 16 percent of respondents claimed that purchases were their main source of food in 1994, and another 4 percent said they relied on barter. By 1997, 39 percent relied primarily on food purchases (26 percent) and barter (13 percent). When this question was posed again in the second, larger set of interviews in 1998, a marginally larger share of respondents—31 percent—said that they had come to rely primarily on food purchases, but a

TABLE 7.1. Johns Hopkins 1999 Survey Results on Principal Source of Food, 1994–97

	Government Ration*		Buy		Barter		Forage		Grow		Other		Total	
	n	%	n	%	n	%	n	%	n	%	n	%	n	%
1994	260	60.6	70	16.3	16	3.7	51	11.9	18	4.2	14	3.3	429	100.0
1995	122	28.4	99	23.1	60	14.0	98	22.8	29	6.8	21	4.9	429	100.0
1996	42	9.8	117	27.4	67	15.7	148	34.7	31	7.2	22	5.2	427	100.0
1997	24	5.7	108	25.8	54	12.9	168	40.2	36	8.6	28	6.7	418	99.9**

*Includes public distribution system as well as government allocations to farmers and the military.

**Total does not sum to 100 because of rounding

Source: Robinson et al., 1999.

TABLE 7.2. Johns Hopkins 2001 Survey Results on Principal Source of Food, 1995–98

	Government Ration		Buy		Barter		Forage		Gift		Grow		Other		Total	
	n	%	n	%	n	%	n	%	n	%	n	%	n	%	n	%
1995	802	30.1	651	24.4	479	18.0	339	12.7	34	1.3	269	10.1	93	3.5	2,667	100.1*
1996	242	9.1	756	28.4	696	26.1	416	15.6	39	1.5	384	14.4	130	4.9	2,663	100.0
1997	56	2.1	760	28.6	754	28.4	433	16.3	37	1.4	422	15.9	195	7.3	2,657	100.0
1998	50	1.9	833	31.4	679	25.6	397	15.0	45	1.7	422	15.9	223	8.4	2,649	99.9*

*Total does not sum to 100 because of rounding.

Source: Robinson et al., 2001

very much larger proportion said they relied on barter (25 percent) and growing their own food (16 percent). If we take those relying primarily on purchases and barter as the marketized segment of the sample, it accounts for 56 percent of all respondents. Lim (2005) cites similar results from an unpublished 500-person survey conducted by the South Korean Ministry of Unification that concluded that by the late 1990s ordinary citizens obtained up to 60 percent of their food through unofficial channels. Interestingly, these results correspond roughly to our estimate in chapter 5 of the share of total food nonfarm residents were securing in the market.

The 1998 Good Friends interviews confirm some of the findings of the first set of Johns Hopkins interviews. These interviews asked how families survived following the end of government distribution. The Good Friends surveys on this question also allowed multiple answers, giving us a wider view of household strategies. The dominant coping mechanism was listed as foraging and consumption of inferior foods, with 57 percent reported resorting to these means. Yet 46 percent reported engaging in barter, and nearly 45 percent reported selling assets (with 4 percent even reporting that they had sold their houses). Even though only 5 percent of respondents were farmers, 13 percent reported farming fields in the mountains, and another 6 percent reported collecting herbs to exchange for food.

The Good Friends (2004) interviews asked respondents to estimate the share of households involved in trade in their locales. Nearly 50 percent of respondents answered that more than 90 percent of households engaged in trade; only 20 percent estimated that less than 80 percent of households did. When asked personally if they had engaged in trade, 92.5 percent said that they had. Of this group, 61 percent reported trading in food. These results reflect the fact that many refugees either were, or became, traders. However, their perception of North Korean society is nonetheless revealing: at least by these respondents' estimates, North Korean society had become actively engaged in trade as a matter of survival. In the words of one refugee, "those who could not trade are long dead" (cited in Lankov 2006a:112). Indeed, the figures on the wedge between official and market prices reported in table 5.1 indicate that there were tremendous incentives to channel supplies outside official avenues; these incentives, although attenuated by the July 2002 price reforms, as discussed below, have persisted to a significant degree.

Additional evidence about the process of marketization can be found by considering price trends. The extent of depreciation of the won on the black market is one indicator of the severity of economic distress in North Korea and has been monitored by Chinese scholars and in the Chinese-Korean community;

Snyder (1997) provides some early evidence. The unofficial black market exchange rate soared as the food crisis worsened—from about 90 won per dollar in the early 1990s to over 220 won per dollar in June 1997 (the official exchange rate was 2.2 won to the dollar that year, and average salaries ranged from 100 to 350 won per month). The won/dollar exchange rate in black markets along the Chinese border reached its peak in late fall 1996, at 250 to 280 won per dollar. The black market price of one kilogram of rice quadrupled during the same time frame, to 80 to 90 won per kilogram, and was as high as 150 won per kilogram in October 1996. When put side by side, the evidence on the exchange and rice prices provides an important reminder of the fact that those with access to foreign exchange could protect themselves from the crisis while those locked into won incomes—the vast majority of the urban population—faced debilitating prices on the market.

Policy Reform I: Reforms in the Agricultural Sector

Beginning in the mid-1990s, well before the reforms of 2002, the government initiated a number of piecemeal reforms in the agricultural sector as a response to declining output. Among the policies undertaken was an intensification of double-cropping, an emphasis on the introduction of higher-yield varieties, and a number of specialized campaigns to increase the output of particular foodstuffs, such as potatoes, mushrooms, rabbits, and goats.[7] Some of these policy changes were introduced with technical assistance from the donor community and made perfect sense. An example is the effort to expand potato production, which could be interpreted as a return to a more traditional and environmentally appropriate crop pattern that had been disrupted by policy interventions dating to the 1960s and the ideological campaigns of the 1970s.

Striking in this list of reforms, however, is the prominence of technical fixes, the reliance on exhortation to greater effort, and the dearth of measures that addressed the incentives facing farmers. Indicative of this mind-set was the revival in 1998 of the Nature Remodeling Program as "an important alternative to increased agricultural production" (Kwon and Kim 2003:32). This program had originally been launched in 1976. In the words of Kim Jŏng-il, it would literally bulldoze "in a sweeping manner" the North Korean countryside into fields of "regular shapes like a checkerboard." The intent of the reform was to spur agricultural mechanization and sever the connection between former landowners and the land by changing its physical contours "beyond recognition" (Kim 2000, Foster-Carter 2001). Similarly, his potato, rabbit, and goat projects—even where they might have had technical justification and outside support—were run in the style of mobilization campaigns reminiscent of his father's failed "chicken in every pot" scheme (Noland 2000:box 3.2).

In at least one aspect, however, North Korean agricultural policy during this period did recognize incentive issues. Early land reforms had benefited cultivators and generated an early base of support for the regime. But collectivization—"cooperativization" in North Korean parlance—as well as grain seizures had broken the link to household and individual incentives (Smith 2005b:48–49). In 1996 the government introduced on a limited or pilot project basis in certain areas of the country a reduction of the size of work teams on the cooperatives from roughly ten to twenty-five to seven to ten members, a number that could effectively accommodate family-based teams. This reform was similar in certain respects to the Chinese household responsibility system introduced nearly twenty years earlier that had resulted in a dramatic increase in output. At the same time, the government introduced a system under which production targets would be established according to a moving-average formula rather than arbitrary diktat, thus allowing some predictability in the state's take of the harvest and farmer allotments. The new system would also allow the production team to keep any output over the target either to consume or to dispose of as they wished (Han 2004; Kwon and Kim 2003). As we have discussed, government policy played a crucial role in the onset and deepening of the famine. These policies included the discretionary nature of production targets—and farmers' efforts to evade them and protect themselves from confiscatory policies—as well as the fact that extra production was still sold to the state at stipulated prices.

The initiative to reduce the size of work teams confronted several difficulties, however. First, although it increased individual and family responsibility and effort, decision-making authority did not devolve in a comparable manner. In effect, the new policy amounted to simply pushing grain targets onto work units of smaller size without granting them the corresponding freedom to adjust production techniques, inputs, or the mix of crops. Second, the end of the floods and the increase in aid by no means implied a revival of the industrial economy, on which agricultural production remained dependent. Even if households effectively adjusted for declining production, targets under the new formula were essentially unattainable because of the lack of inputs. As a result, the targets still implied effective confiscation by the state of all production above the level retained on farm for in-kind consumption.

More fundamentally, it is doubtful that the mere announcement of a new target-setting process was enough to reverse farmers' perceptions of government intent; the government had reversed course before. Eventually, the formula, which was based on a moving average of past production, began to reflect plausible targets under the existing input-constrained conditions, not the higher yield pattern of the past. As a result, it held forth the possibility to the cooperative farmers that extra effort would be rewarded. In the short run, however—and continuing through 2005—the changes almost certainly did not fully reverse the hoarding and diversion on the part of the farmers that were a component of their efforts to mitigate political risk.

While the rapid increase in the provision of aid arguably relieved the pressure on North Korea to adopt policy reforms (indirectly crowding out domestic production as well as commercial imports), the donor community also attempted to encourage the adoption of more effective agricultural policies. At the 1998 Agricultural Recovery and Environmental Protection (AREP) meeting organized by UNDP, representatives of the donor community were blunt at to the significance they placed on the importance of changing policies (see, e.g., Babson 1998). But the North Korean interpretation of the crisis continued to emphasize the role of natural disasters and the collapse of foreign trade. The government identified the three priorities of the AREP program as farmland recovery and rehabilitation, the restoration of irrigation capabilities, and emergency improvements to fertilizer production facilities but flatly rejected institutional or incentive reforms. In his introductory remarks to the First Thematic Roundtable on the AREP in 1998, the leader of the North Korean delegation—a vice minister of foreign affairs—argued explicitly that the AREP program would be implemented through existing institutions (Choi 1998).

The process of marketization got a push in July 2002, when the government of North Korea announced major changes in economic policy comprising four central components: microeconomic policy changes, macroeconomic policy changes, and renewed efforts to create special economic zones and secure foreign aid (we take up these reforms in detail in the following sections).[8] From the perspective of agriculture, however, the government continued to describe incentive reforms such as the introduction of smaller work teams and fixed-rate tenancies along the lines of Chinese practices as pilot projects. The evaluation of the inadequacies of North Korea's "within the box" initiatives by a South Korean government think tank is worth citing at length: "Irrigation facilities require streamlining, preferably linked to large gravity-fed networks. More fertilizer alone is not likely to provide sustainable enhancement in agricultural productivity. Other innovative, environmentally friendly agricultural techniques (such as improving soil fertility through green manure, using alternatives to chemical fertilizer, rotating crops, integrating pest management, and instituting policy reforms) need to be put into practice. Double-cropping wheat and barley after rice and maize (cereal after cereal) on already exhausted soils is unsustainable. Introduction of leguminous crops in the crop rotation is vital" (KIEP 2004:104).

In some sense, the policy changes undertaken in July 2002 with respect to agriculture could be interpreted as a belated recognition that earlier incentive reforms had not gone far enough. The most important change introduced at this time was a dramatic increase in the procurement prices of grains. With the famine and chronic food shortages, food prices on the market skyrocketed, while the prices paid to farmers remained constant and the prices paid for the rations that were available through the PDS remained nominal. The price reform raised the state procurement price to roughly 80 percent of the contemporaneous market price. This reform was clearly designed to increase the volume of food entering the PDS and to limit diversion to farmers' consumption, private markets, and other uses, such as the production of liquor, and the reallocation of acreage away from grain to cash crops such as tobacco on the supply side. By implication, it would draw consumers back into state-controlled institutions on the demand side.[9] In parallel, the authorities loosened central planning, allowing some cooperative farms to choose their own crop mixes.

The government also permitted an increase in the size of private plots on cooperative farms from 30 *p'yŏng* (approximately 100 square meters) to 400 *p'yŏng* (1,320 square meters) while at the same time introducing a rental or tax system to compensate the state for the corresponding reduction in the land controlled collectively by the cooperative. Since the rental rate was not set ex ante, however, farmers exhibited reluctance to apply themselves intensively to the cultivation of these plots. Again, the security and credibility of property rights loomed as an important constraint since farmers remained unsure about how much of the output they would be required to surrender to the state (Nam 2004).

The incentives for farmers to route their production through state channels were further weakened by the inflationary spiral set off by the July 2002 policy changes that we take up in the next section. In the year following the July 2002 price increases, the market price of rice and corn, which had been on a generally downward trend since peaking during the famine, more than tripled. The result was that the gap between the state procurement price for grain and the price that farmers could receive if they diverted production to the market increased sharply (figure 7.2). Although the discrepancy between state procurement prices and market prices was not as wide as it was during the prereform period, it was nonetheless substantial.

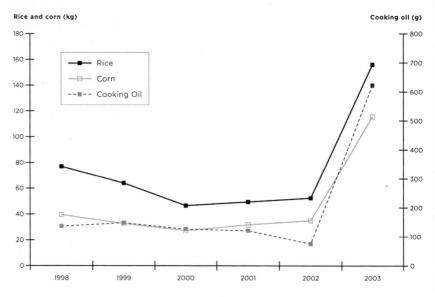

FIGURE 7.2. Price Trends, 1998–2003

The maintenance of yields in the face of dwindling fertilizer inputs suggests that North Korea saw improvements in input-adjusted productivity that might be traced at least in part to the incentive changes introduced after 1996. But the modesty of the changes in incentives—and undoubtedly their lack of credibility—together with an ongoing dearth of complementary inputs contributed to continuing stagnation in output. Despite South Korea's infusions of fertilizer and improved weather, North Korea's agricultural output was still lower in 2005 than in 1990 (figure 2.3). If one accepts the quasi-official figures from the FAO, output remains less than half its peak. It is extremely unlikely that bad weather alone can explain this pattern of stagnation.

Policy Reform II: Industrial Adjustment and Macroeconomic Instability

Although the 2002 reforms made some reference to agriculture, at their core was a wider-ranging reform of prices, wages, and incentives in the industrial sector as well. Whether the intent was to change fundamentally the way the economy operated or simply to improve the functioning of the socialist system is a subject of continuing controversy (see Lee 2002; Y. H. Chung 2003; Frank

2005a; Nam 2003, 2004; Newcomb 2003; Oh 2003; Gey 2004; Noland 2004b; and Kim and Choi 2005). Either way, the July 2002 measures involved a break with the past. From the standpoint of assessing access to food, two aspects of the policy reforms are of particular relevance: the microeconomic reforms in the industrial sector, which affected the demand for food among the urban working class, and the macroeconomic policy changes, which had the effect of generating a sustained high inflation.

The North Korean experience confirms that a successful transition from central planning to market-oriented resource allocation is more complex and challenging in the industrial sphere than in agriculture. This is particularly true in North Korea, where the industrial sector looms large (figure 7.1). Reforms of the industrial sector are important for at least three reasons. First, as we have noted, the North Korean agricultural system was particularly dependent on inputs from agriculture, and the terms of trade between agriculture and industry constitute a critical component of the larger social contract. In the absence of inputs or final consumer goods, there are strong incentives for farmers to bypass the formal channels of intersectoral exchange altogether. Second, developments in the industrial sector were crucial for the demand side of the food story; with marketization, the ability of urban workers to purchase food depends critically on the health of the enterprises in which they work. Perhaps most important, a revived industrial sector is key to North Korea's generating the export earnings needed to finance food imports and to resolve once and for all its chronic food insecurity problem.

The microeconomic reforms had two components. The first was an alteration of state-administered relative prices and wages by administrative fiat, presumably with the intent of aligning them more closely with underlying values or shadow costs. The second change was an alteration of institutional rules and practices with the aim of introducing greater flexibility into decision making at the level of the work unit. This second cluster of changes was by no means the result of a clear reform process but involved a high level of discretion on the part of enterprise managers adapting to declining subsidies and the effective collapse of the planning process.

These changes were both a cause and an effect of the macroeconomic instability that emerged when the reforms were initiated; the reforms gave rise to a high, sustained inflation that continued to plague the country through 2005. In fact, the North Korean experience embodied three analytically distinct changes in prices—a change in relative prices; a one-time jump in the overall price level; and, last, a continuous process of rising prices or inflation—each with a different set of political-economy implications.

Let us begin with the alteration of relative prices: the relationship in the product market between the price of one good, say, rice, and another, such as a television, or in the labor market between wages paid to a miner and those paid to a doctor. In the case of centrally planned economies, these relative prices and wages typically misrepresent underlying scarcities and encourage misallocation of resources, inefficiency, and waste. The alteration of relative prices and wages undertaken in July 2002 could be interpreted as an attempt to bring them into alignment with true, underlying values and thereby improve allocative efficiency. The changes in relative product prices, in particular the prices of staple foods, are evident in the highly uneven pattern of the price changes in the last column of table 7.3. At the same time that the government was changing relative prices in product markets, the authorities were also changing relative wages in the labor market. Certain favored groups such as military personnel, party officials, scientists, and coal miners received supernormal increases in their real wages, while others implicitly suffered a real income loss (table 7.4).

What is unusual about the North Korean case is that the authorities did not simply alter relative wages and prices but also raised the overall price level by roughly 1,000 percent. To get a grasp on the magnitude of these price changes, consider that when the Chinese government raised the price of grains at the start of its reforms in November 1979, the increase was on the order of 25 percent. In comparison, when the North Korean government raised the price of cereals sold through the PDS in 2002, the increase over previous official prices was nearly 40,000 percent or more. Of course, to some extent this change in official prices was simply a recognition of the fact that the PDS had effectively ceased to function, distributing only very small quantities of the total food supply; the reform might therefore be seen as simply bringing the PDS in line with the market. This interpretation is too facile, however, since a number of urban households still depended to at least some extent on the rations they received at official prices, even if the PDS was not the primary source of food.

This second form of price change—the one-time jump in the overall price level—was unnecessary to generate the changes in relative prices that might encourage greater efforts to grow grain or mine coal.[10] Such changes in incentives could have been accomplished by much smaller increases, as illustrated by the Chinese example, where the price of grain was increased by 25 percent, not 25,000 percent.

So why did the North Korean authorities not only change relative prices but engineer an apparently gratuitous hike in the price level? We can see two hypotheses, both turning on the fact that the increase in the price level also decimated the value of local currency holdings. The sympathetic interpretation is that the

TABLE 7.3. State Consumer Prices Before and After the Price Reform of July 1, 2002 (North Korean wǒn)

Product	Unit	Price Before	Price After	Change in %
Bean Paste	kg	0.20	17.00	8,400
Beans	kg	0.08	40.00	49,900
Chicken	kg	18.00	180.00	900
Corn	kg	0.06	24.00	39,900
Herring	kg	10.00	100.00	900
Meals in kindergarten (infants)	monthly	50.00	300.00	500
Pork	kg	17.00	170.00	900
Rice	kg	0.08	44.00	54,900
Soy sauce	kg	0.20	16.00	7,900
Wheat flour	kg	0.06	24.00	39,900
Coal	ton	34.00	1,500.00	4,312
Diesel	Liter	40.00	2,800.00	6,900
Electricity	kWh	0.035	2.10	5,900
Gas	ton	923.00	64,600.00	6,899
Petroleum	liter	40.00	2,800.00	6,900
Beer	bottle	0.50	50.00	9,900
Cigarettes	packet	0.35	2.00	471
Penicillin	ampoule	0.40	20.00	4,900
Bus ticket (urban transport)		0.10	2.00	1,900
Pyong-yang— Ch'ŏngin train fare		16.00	590.00	3,558
Streetcar fare		0.10	1.00	900
Underground ticket		0.10	2.00	1,900
Facial soap		3.00	20.00	567
Laundry soap		0.50	15.00	2,900
Men's sports shoes	pair	3.50	180.00	5,043
Men's suit		90.00	6,750.00	7,400
Men's sneakers	pair	18.00	180.00	900
Spectacles		20.00	600.00	2,900
Winter vest		25.00	2,000.00	7,900
Television set		350.00	6,000.00	1,614

Sources: Y. Chung 2003; Nam and Gong 2004.

TABLE 7.4. Monthly Incomes Before and After the Price Reform of July 1, 2002 (North Korean wŏn)

Occupation	Income Before	Income After	Percentage Change
Party Members and Officials	120–200	850 -3,000	608–1,400
Company manager	250–300	3,500–4,000	1,233–1,300
Company Workers	85–140	1,200–2,000	1,312–1,329
University professors	200–270	4,000–5,000	1,752–1,900
Teachers	80–135	2,400–2, 880	2,033–2,900
Doctor	80–250	1,200–3,000	1,100–1,400
Reporter, Broadcaster	150–200	4,500–6,000	2,900
Miner	130–140	3,000–4,000	2,208–2,757
Services occupation (hairdressers, waiters, etc.)	20–60	1,000–1,500	2,400–4,900
One-star general	247	6,670	2,600
Colonel	219	5,830	2,562
Lieutenant colonel	185	4,610	2,392
Major	163	4,130	2,432
Lieutenant	95	2,970	3,026

Sources: Nam and Gong 2004, KIEP 2004.

North Korean authorities feared so-called monetary overhang. Since the North Korean economy had shrunk so dramatically during the previous decade, the authorities might have feared that citizens had large amounts of cash stuffed in their mattresses. This kind of involuntary savings would have occurred because workers continued to receive wages but in the absence of goods available for purchase. Once the economy began to marketize and goods began to appear in the markets, prices would begin rising as accumulated cash began chasing what goods were on offer. Marketization is often associated with a transitional bout of price increases of this sort. Under this interpretation, the administratively engineered increase in prices was meant to control this process in a way that would reinforce the desired changes in real income for favored groups.

A related but less sympathetic interpretation is that the intent of the price increase was to strike a blow at a disfavored group, namely, the class of traders and black marketeers that had sprung up over the course of the previous decade. To the extent that this group maintained large cash holdings of North Korean won, the huge jump in the overall price level would have the effect of destroying the value of their working capital, potentially crippling their businesses. Historically, socialist governments have periodically used state-administered inflations and their cousins, currency reforms,[11] to target those engaged in economic activity outside state strictures.

The problem for the state was that, having experienced three previous currency reforms, North Korean traders were aware of this political risk and had already begun to operate in U.S. dollars, Japanese yen, and even Chinese yuan. The resulting collapse in the exchange value of the won will be discussed in greater detail below, but the currency was so debased that even North Koreans working on cooperative farms reportedly preferred trinkets as a store of value.[12]

In combination, these measures could therefore be interpreted as attempts not to reform and marketize the economy but rather to buttress the state's position vis-à-vis core state constituencies while reasserting state control by confiscating the assets of newly emergent traders. Unfortunately, these blows aimed at traders may have fallen more squarely on the North Korean masses, especially those in regions and occupations in which opportunities to obtain foreign currencies were limited.

Just as the changes in relative wages and prices did not necessitate a 1,000 percent increase in the price level, in principle, the price-level rise did not necessarily have to generate an ongoing process of inflation, our third analytically distinct price effect; it could have resulted in a one-time jump in the price level. Good economywide estimates of North Korean inflation do not exist, though a growing corpus of data on individual product prices is accumulating. One way of inferring the magnitude of the overall inflation rate would be through the black market exchange rate value of the North Korean won.[13] Although the black market exchange rate is not a perfect proxy for underlying inflation,[14] in a high-inflation environment, movements in the exchange rate are likely to be dominated by inflation differentials. Fragmentary data on the price of foreign exchange indicate that, in the three years after August 2002, the black market exchange rate of the North Korean won depreciated against the U.S. dollar at a relatively steady rate of 7–9 percent monthly, or at an annualized rate of 130–140 percent. Since inflation in the United States over this period was trivial in comparison, this indicator suggests that North Korea experienced ongoing inflation well in excess of 100 percent a year in the three years following the July 2002 policy changes.[15] Other indications of a high-inflation environment include the introduction of a new 10,000 won note in 2003 (5,000 won had previously been the largest denomination in circulation) and *monthly* nominal interest rates of 10–30 percent in the informal market (Lim and Kim 2004, *Chosun Ilbo* 2005).[16]

This ongoing inflation was both a cause and an effect of the problematic adjustment of the industrial sector. The government no doubt continued to be keep important firms afloat by implicit subsidies, either through national or local government budgets or by loans from the central bank. This latter means of support, of course, contributed directly to the inflationary process. State-owned enterprises (SOEs) that cannot meet their payrolls and receive subsidies from the state or indirectly through the accumulation of nonperforming loans with the Central Bank generate excessive monetary growth relative to output. In simple terms, too many won are chasing too few products.

At the same time, the high inflation complicated the transition for SOE managers. We first examine the industrial adjustment experience and then consider how it both effected and was affected by the macroeconomic policy making of the central government.

The North Korean economy had been in decline for more than a decade at the time of the 2002 reforms (figure 7.3), and significant deindustrialization had occurred (figure 7.1).[17] Demand for many of the goods produced by state-owned enterprises had collapsed, and by some accounts the central planning mechanism itself had degraded beyond repair. Major facilities such as the Kim Ch'aek Integrated Iron and Steel Works and the Namp'o Glass Factory were barely operating or had closed completely. In the absence of coherent adjustment policies, officials had been turning a blind eye to unauthorized coping responses by SOE managers (Michell 1994, 1998). Banking and finance had never played a central role in the allocation of resources, but by the mid-1990s a process of financial disintermediation was well under way: the internal payments clearing system had collapsed, and enterprises were reduced to settling transactions in cash or through barter.

With the introduction of the 2002 reforms, SOE managers were instructed that they were responsible for covering their own costs; there would be no more state subsidies. At least initially, it was unclear to what extent managers were sanctioned to hire, fire, and promote workers or to what extent remuneration would be determined by the market as opposed to state directive. Likewise, while the central planners told the enterprises they had to cover costs, the state was continuing to administer output prices. Moreover, in the absence of any formal bankruptcy or other exit mechanism, there was no prescribed method for enterprises that could not cover costs to cease operations. In the absence of a social safety net, it was also unclear how workers from closed enterprises would survive; as in all socialist systems, the core of the social safety net had historically been the employment guarantee, which the state could no longer effectively honor as the industrial sector went into steep decline. In short, man-

Billion won

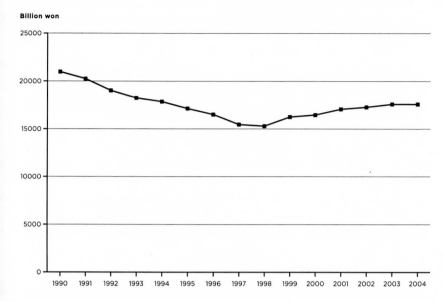

FIGURE 7.3. North Korean GDP (at 1995 constant prices)
Source: Bank of Korea 2005.

agers were told that they were responsible for their enterprises but were given contradictory messages about their scope actually to manage them.

These conditions of fundamental uncertainty undermined enterprise managers' incentives to follow state dictates and encouraged entrepreneurial behavior outside the state plan. Just as the breakdown of the social compact with farmers and households contributed to a de facto marketization from below, so enterprise managers and workers were forced to adapt to a decline in central government support, exploiting the limited autonomy granted to them under preexisting policies and practices.

Two institutional factors were particularly important in this regard; both had originally been introduced to permit limited adaptation to local conditions in the context of the central plan and, as in the case of the PDS, devolved at least some power to the county level. The Taean accounting model, launched in 1961, gave local authorities and enterprises limited autonomy in recalibrating centrally planned directives in the context of local needs. The 1984 "August 3 Campaign for People's Goods" (so named for its date of proclamation by Kim Il-sŏng) sought to increase the availability of consumer goods by mobilizing underutilized labor (housewives, retirees, the handicapped) and waste materials from SOEs at the local level. Neither policy was particularly successful in significantly boosting productivity at the time of its introduction (Oh 1993,

Kim 1994), though in the case of the August 3 movement, sales under the program reportedly reached 13 percent of central plan sales by 1991 (Lee 1991, 1994, 2000).

These initiatives did, however, create a legal and institutional space for using SOE resources in an entrepreneurial or coping fashion as the economy deteriorated in the 1990s (S. C. Kim 1994, 2003, 2006; Lim and Kim 2004; Kim 2005a). In particular, the August 3 measures allowed entrepreneurs (or so-called funding squads) affiliated with SOEs or even government agencies to obtain some political protection in a system with few private property rights. In return, their institutional patrons received a share of the profits generated by what were effectively private initiatives, even entering into multiyear contracts that specified obligations and responsibilities of each party.[18] These contracts included rights of control over assets that were nominally owned by the patron institution as well as the right to transfer these assets at the conclusion of the contract period. Alternatively, individual workers could buy their way out of their obligations to the work unit simply by paying a daily tax to be reclassified as an "August 3" worker; this buyout permitted them to engage in entrepreneurial activity and in effect constituted a means through which labor in declining firms could be productively redeployed (K. J. Kwon 2006). Such arrangements have numerous drawbacks, including the absence of genuine property or contracting rights and the absence of any effective method of appealing to third-party neutrals to resolve the disputes that inevitably arise in business. They did, however, permit a means of reallocating both capital and labor into higher value-added activities.

Entrepreneurship was not limited to funding squads and workers; managers themselves used resources from failing enterprises to establish side businesses either as a legitimate coping mechanism or as a dodge to shed unwanted labor. Others simply stripped assets for barter in China (H. J. Lee 2005), cut wages despite the official wage increase, or closed enterprises altogether. This loosening of central control was in effect ratified in 2004 through directives from the State Planning Commission that granted SOE managers enhanced autonomy (Y. K. Kwon 2006). Quietly, some industrial facilities are being transferred to investors for cash—that is to say, privatized (Kim and Park 2005).

The result of these crisis-driven adaptations has been a considerable decentralization of the industrial economy, with local political authorities and managers playing a more important role. The loosening of the central distribution mechanism is manifest in an increase in direct sales outlets where these ventures sold directly to the public at noncontrolled prices. Recent years have also seen an increase in department stores selling Chinese goods at noncontrolled prices, again paralleling the shift from the PDS to the market in the case of food (Noland 2000, Choi and Koo 2005). The authorities, however, exhibited an ambivalent stance toward both the markets and these other retail outlets, tolerating them as a safety valve but periodically cracking down or banning trade in specific items (Choi and Koo 2006).

As the volume of products passing through these noncontrolled distribution channels increased, domestic trading firms began to arbitrage price differentials across markets, and as a consequence the central planners began to replace fixed prices with ceilings or bands. Yet the North Koreans' discussion of price adjustment has been incoherent, suggesting that prices would simultaneously adjust though the market, adhere to planning guidelines, and be subject to adjustment by the central planners, local governments, and enterprises (Choi and Koo 2005). The authorities announced no mechanism for periodically adjusting state planning prices. As a result, severe disequilibria developed over time, as illustrated by the large wedges between official and market prices for food. At the retail level, state prices are being brought in line with prices observed in the officially sanctioned markets. Because of high ongoing inflation, these sanctioned market prices have been subject to price ceilings that are posted outside the market, subject to enforcement by the police. According to anecdotal accounts, these guidelines are increasingly ignored despite periodic adjustments.

At the same time that the government was attempting to restructure the industrial sector, its inability to secure resources forced it to undertake a fundamental fiscal and financial reform. With the central plan crumbling, the government was no longer able to raise significant revenue through a so-called transactions tax administered by the central planning authorities. Lim (2005) quotes a purported internal North Korean document from October 2001 in which Kim Jŏng-il bemoans the loss of state control over the economy and concludes, "Frankly the state has no money, but individuals have two years' budget worth" (Lim 2005:7).

There are two ways for a state to garner resources: taxes or borrowing. Unable to tax effectively, in March 2003 the government announced the issuance of "People's Life Bonds." The government's announcement states, without irony, that "the bonds are backed by the full faith and credit of the DPRK government," but despite their name these instruments more closely resemble lottery tickets than bonds as conventionally understood. The bonds had a ten-year maturity, with principal repaid in annual installments beginning in year five. There did not, however, appear to be any provision for interest payments, and no money for such payments was budgeted. Rather, for the first two years of the program, the government would hold semiannual drawings (annually thereafter) with winners to receive their principal plus prizes. No information was provided on the expected odds or prize values other than that the drawings were to be based on an "open and objective" principle. Moreover, there is evidence that purchase of the bonds was not altogether voluntary, as committees were established in every province, city, county, institute, factory, village, and town to promote their sale as a "patriotic deed."[19] Both the characteristics of the instrument and the mass campaign to sell it suggest that politics, not personal finance, would be its main selling point. According to Kim (1998), when the government has resorted to lotterylike instruments in the past to deal with monetary overhang problems, they have been unpopular.

The government then attempted to address its underlying fiscal crisis by moving from an indirect system of raising state revenue through transaction taxes levied through the central plan to direct taxation of enterprises based on profits, as one would observe in a market economy. This proved highly problematic. The enterprises did not have the accounting systems to make this shift feasible, nor, for that matter, did the state. For fifty years, the economy had run on the basis of centrally orchestrated quantity planning, not financial profits and losses. Not until March 2003 was accounting legislation enacted, and not until September 2003 was the Tax Collection Agency even organized! Amid this chaos, one tactic was to push responsibility for tax collection down to local governments, which were then supposed to share collections with the center. Not surprisingly, it appears that the local authorities were unwilling and/or unable to carry out these responsibilities. The result has been a chronic gap between what the state spends and what it takes in; the response has been a resort to the printing press, fueling the inflationary process.

In sum, just as there has been a bottom-up process of marketization in other areas—in the emergence of low-level service and retail activities at the household level, in the distribution of food that we take up in the next section—so the industrial sector has undergone a spontaneous and decentralized adjustment process. The contours of this reform are still very difficult to read, since this sector is even less visible to outsiders than other activities such as food distribution. It is almost certain that lower-level political officials are playing an important role in sanctioning, protecting, and defining the scope of the marketization that is taking place. The result is likely to be the kind of apparatchik or crony capitalism familiar to the slow-reforming cases of the former Soviet Union and Eastern Europe: continued subsidization of favored firms coupled with spontaneous privatization and opportunistic behavior in the context of highly uncertain property rights. As one Western diplomat with considerable experience in North Korea put it, when it comes to economic policy, "there is no consistency, no coherency. It's just a tug of war." Such settings are typically characterized by growing inequality, which is highly apparent in access to food.

Food Insecurity I: Marketization and Access to Food

One consequence of the partial reform process we have just described has been a large underemployed industrial proletariat facing sharply falling real wages, no social safety net, and inadequate access to food. Before the standoff over humanitarian assistance in 2005–6, the WFP had begun to conduct household surveys and canvass government officials, both central and local, about these phenomena. They discovered that many factories were running well under capacity and that as a consequence as much as 30 percent of the workforce outside of agriculture was unemployed.

Among those who remained employed in the industrial sector, there was considerable underemployment, and some workers who continued to receive salaries saw their wages cut by 50–80 percent. Women appeared to be among the most seriously affected, with an unemployment rate double that of men. Many of the male redundant workers are redeployed to sanctioned market activities run by their work units or to public works projects. Women were given preferential treatment in obtaining permission to sell in official markets and roadside kiosks. Outside visitors and refugee interviews report a marginally relaxed environment with a bustling small-scale entrepreneurship: wood delivery services, bicycle repair, tailoring, shoe repair, hair cutting, and small vendors, with women represented prominently in these activities (see, e.g., Caritas—Hong Kong 2005b, J. H. Kwon 2006). The prominence of women in these activities could reflect a higher rate of dismissal from formal sector employment or a household division of labor in which men retain formal-sector positions to access remaining benefits, including social services and rations. Writing in 2004, Gey estimated that 6–8 percent of the work force was engaged in such activities, and subsequent refugee interviews suggest it could be much higher.

Prices in North Korea increasingly reflect underlying market scarcities, subject to the proviso that markets remain fragmented and considerable price dispersion across geographic regions persists. Visitors in the immediate postreform period (2003–6) reported an emerging pattern in which the prices for foreign exchange and consumer goods were lower in towns on the Chinese border than in Pyongyang and other inland regions and in which living standards near the border may now exceed those in the capital. In contrast, compared to Pyongyang, prices appeared to be much higher in the hard-hit northeastern industrial port town of Ch'ŏngjin (table 7.5). The exception was foreign exchange: the euro was considerably weaker in Ch'ŏngjin, perhaps reflecting that city's port status and easier access to foreign exchange. This, however, only reinforces the price disparity point: the prices of local goods are even higher in Ch'ŏngjin in comparison to Pyongyang in foreign exchange terms than they are in local currency terms.

Grain prices have always displayed a seasonal pattern, tending to fall in the autumn after the harvest and peak in the spring. The open marketization of grain, however, made these trends even more apparent. Prices also appeared to respond to supply-side shocks. To cite several examples, rice prices fell in June 2003 following the arrival of 400,000 MT of rice donated by South Korea. Indeed, according to the WFP, the mere announcement of a large South Korean aid donation sent prices tumbling in 2005 (Fairclough 2005). In July 2003, the prices of both rice and corn spiked following the closure of the border with China during the SARS scare. Yet another aspect of this phenomenon can be seen from differences in provincial prices that emerged during periods in which the government was collecting local production for the military and banning export to other provinces.

The effect of the marketization of the economy under weak institutions has been to increase the degree of social differentiation within North Korea and contribute to the creation of a new class of mostly urban food-insecure households. The inflation that began in August 2002 was particularly pernicious in this regard, because the market price of food in real terms had been trending downward from the extraordinarily high peaks of the famine years.

TABLE 7.5. Regional price differences (North Korean wŏn)

Item	Pyongyang August 2004	Northern Hamgyŏng Ch'ŏngjin August 26, 2004
Rice (1 kg)	420 (imported)*	900
Corn (1 kg)	200	450–80
Cooking oil (bean oil 1 kg)	1,500	2,000
Egg (hen), 1	45	100
Pork (1 kg)	1,000	2,700
Sugar (1 kg)	470	900
Exchange rate (1 euro)	2,000	1,300

*The actual price of North Korean rice in T'ongilgŏri General Market was 680 won per kg.

Source: Nam n.d.

In principle, the maintenance of the PDS as a mechanism for distributing food could be interpreted as an attempt to maintain the social contract under which everyone is guaranteed a minimum ration. Residents are still issued monthly ration cards; if they do not have sufficient funds to purchase the monthly allotment, it is automatically carried over to the next month. Before the attempt to revive the PDS, declared rations delivered only about half the minimum daily caloric needs and at much higher costs than in the past. According to WFP household surveys in 2004–5, PDS-dependent (in effect, urban) households spent roughly one-third of their income on PDS-supplied food alone, and a typical family of four with one income would spend 40 percent of its budget on PDS-supplied food. Some households surveyed by the WFP reported spending 50–60 percent of their household incomes on PDS food. By 2005, however, the PDS was only supplying households with approximately one-half of an absolute minimum caloric need. If these households are spending one-third of their incomes on PDS food, and we estimate they are spending another third on nonfood essentials, this leaves only one-third of their budgets to cover half their caloric needs through other sources. Market prices are conventionally thought to be three or more times expensive than the PDS. As a result, WFP surveys are finding that households are spending up to 80 percent of total expenditures on food, inclusive of non-PDS sources (WFP 2003b).

How do households cope? What is striking is the continuity in coping behaviors between the high famine period and the current setting, despite a massive increase in food aid. According to the WFP, 40 percent of interviewed households reported receiving food from relatives in rural areas. Between 60 and 80 percent of PDS-dependent (i.e., urban) households and 65 percent of cooperative farm households reported gathering wild foods. Many households and workplaces maintain kitchen gardens, and, as in other cases of economic stress around the world, there are extensive anecdotal reports of households selling or bartering personal belongings for food. According to the WFP, households with a single earner and dependents and PDS-dependent households without access to kitchen gardens are the most vulnerable.

The reality may be even worse, however. One interpretation of the price increases is that they were simply bringing PDS food prices in line with the market. Yet we also have anecdotal evidence that we return to in the conclusion that even the pretense of universalism has been breached and the authorities have significantly reduced the number of households being issued PDS ration cards at all. These reports are fully consistent with refugee surveys from early 2005 (Chang 2006) that document the continuing decline in the share of the population that depends on the PDS as its major source of food. Less than 4 percent of the refugees in China interviewed by Chang "agreed" or "strongly agreed" with the statement that there had been an improvement in food availability since the July 2002 changes were enacted, and 85 percent of these refugees, who admittedly may not be representative of the country as a whole, "agreed" or "strongly agreed" with the statement that North Koreans are voicing their opinions about the chronic food shortage.

What is striking about this emerging picture of contemporary North Korea is just how random or idiosyncratic individual life chances have become. As shown in table 7.4, the initial increase in wages in August 2002 was highly uneven, and for most employees subsequent increases (or decreases) have presumably depended on factors such as the cleverness, deviousness, and general competency of individual enterprise managers under a relatively anarchic process of marketization, the ability of individual enterprise managers to continue to wheedle implicit or explicit subsidies out of the state, and proximity to China as well as underlying economic efficiency. The actual life chances of workers therefore probably depend substantially on idiosyncratic features of their work unit, such as the entrepreneurial capabilities of managers, the nature of the assets in place, and the product markets in which they operate. Clearly, firms that are capable of generating foreign exchange—through whatever means—fare better.

Under conditions of high inflation, access to foreign currency may act as insurance, preserving purchasing power in real terms. Indeed, a process of dollarization appears to be well under way in North Korea, and in certain respects two parallel economies are emerging. In the first, high-quality local products and services (such as North Korean rice or luxury restaurants) and imported goods are bought and sold in foreign exchange. The second is a won-based economy of inferior local products and services. In addition to traditionally privileged senior party officials, those with access to foreign exchange and hence access to the dollarized luxury economy include households with familial or ethnic ties to China and Japan (Lankov 2006a). Subject to systematic discrimination in the past, members of these groups have exploited their transborder connections and surfaced as important beneficiaries of the emerging new order.

In sum, the July 2002 policy changes have created winners and losers. Among the winners have been some enterprise managers, military officers, party officials, and bureaucrats who have used their power and privilege for asset stripping and other forms of entrepreneurial behavior. The more prosperous of the "August 3" workers have in effect successfully exited the state system as well. In the commercial sector, Choi and Koo (2006) describe a hierarchy of traders that exists virtually worldwide: an upper class of dealers in foreign exchange and large-scale distributors, a middle class of wholesalers, and a lower class of market vendors and peddlers. Among the losers have been the industrial proletariat and those who played by the rules and did not engage in market-oriented activities.

Food Insecurity II: The Evidence on Consequences

In chapter 4, we talked about what aid was intended to do and how restrictions on monitoring and diversion to various uses—consumption or sale—might have affected who got assistance. In this chapter, we have talked about the possible consequences of marketization and the reform process and the emergence of new vulnerabilities. The data do not permit us to separate the precise weight of these offsetting effects: the positive benefits of aid versus the adverse effects of the reform. Nor can we say how the North Korean population might have fared under various counterfactual scenarios, for example, with less aid or under different reform scenarios. The best we can do is offer a descriptive snapshot of how vulnerable populations are faring as of 2005, after a decade of humanitarian assistance. What we see is a distressing continuity in the welfare of vulnerable groups.

As relief activities got under way in the mid-1990s, a number of NGOs attempted to do assessments that would size up the scope of the hunger problem, identify the populations in greatest need, and benchmark the effectiveness of their activities in providing relief (see KDI 1999). In 1997 a WFP request to implement a conventional randomized survey was rejected by the North Korean government. Médecins sans Frontières had similarly been denied permission to conduct its own nutritional survey, despite having been assigned responsibility for conducting emergency feeding activities over an extensive geographic area.

The government did consent to a more narrow evaluation of child anthropometric status. In August 1997, the WFP examined 3,965 children under the age of seven from forty government-selected institutions located in nineteen counties in five provinces. The results provided unambiguous evidence of long-term malnutrition. Seventeen percent of the children were wasted (as measured by weight-for-height, signaling short-term malnutrition), and 38 percent were stunted (as measured by height-for-age) and/or underweight (42 percent, measured weight-for-age), measures of longer-term problems (figure 7.4). The age-related figures in particular again suggest that the country's food problems did not begin with the floods of 1995 but were of much longer standing. This

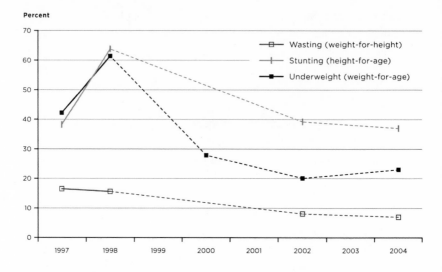

FIGURE 7.4. Child Nutritional Status
Sources: 1997: Katona-Apte and Mokdad 1998; 1998: WFP 1998; 2002: Central Bureau of Statistics (North Korea) 2002; 2004: Central Bureau of Statistics, Institute of Child Nutrition, 2005.

evidence is thus consistent with our interpretation of a secular decline in food availability well before the famine.

As two of the survey's designers observed, the results might not have been representative of the country as a whole or even of the selected institutions. If anything, the sources of bias seemed in the direction of painting a more favorable picture than actually existed, which make the findings even more horrific. The institutions selected were in either the capital or "rice bowl" counties in which conditions were generally believed to be superior. On the day that data was collected, attendance rates at the institutions varied from 21 percent to 100 percent, and there was no way to ensure that local authorities were not deliberately keeping some children away (Katona-Apte and Mokdad 1998).

Some commentators have claimed that the basic anthropomorphic norms embodied in the standards are inappropriate for the Korean population, specifically, that they overstate the expected size of normal Korean children, recalling the debate among nutritionists and anthropologists about the existence of "small but healthy" populations.[20] The implication is that if Korean children are naturally small, the true degree of malnutrition is less than indicated in these figures.

The division of the Korean peninsula and the existence of a large corpus of historical data allow us to do a natural apples-to-apples comparison that does not involve anthropomorphic standards of different races or nationalities. Eberstadt (2001b) reports that the mean heights and weights of the North Korean seven-year-old males measured in the 1998 survey discussed below were 105 centimeters and 15 kilograms, respectively. According to the South Korean National Statistical Office, the comparable figures for South Korean seven-year-olds in that year were 126 cm and 26 kg. This is to say that, if these figures are to be believed, in 1998 seven-year-old North Korean males were roughly 20 percent shorter and 40 percent lighter than their southern counterparts—a gigantic difference that cannot be ascribed to genetic differences or inappropriate norms. Indeed, the North Koreans in 1998 are significantly smaller than the South Koreans in 1965 when the National Statistical Office series begins, and if the Japanese colonial records reported in Yun (1987) are to be believed, smaller than Korean seven-year-olds at any time in the twentieth century.[21] And whatever the validity of the "small but healthy" claim with respect to the level of malnutrition, it should not affect the interpretation of changes in the indicators over time.

As noted above, a second survey of 1,762 children under the age of seven was conducted in September and October of 1998 (WFP 1998). Although involving fewer children than the first venture, it covered a larger geographic area. Two provinces (Chagang and Kangwŏn) that were largely off-limits to the WFP were excluded from the survey, however, as were parts of others, reputedly locations of penal colonies and sensitive military sites. Altogether, eighty-two counties containing roughly 30 percent of North Korea's population were excluded (See figures 4.3—4.5). The sampling procedures appear to have improved markedly over the prior survey, though problems remained. The WFP could not cross-reference its data with that collected by UNICEF and MSF and could not ensure that the households visited were actually the households selected by the survey team (Bennett 1999). Nevertheless, the results of the second survey are generally regarded as more reliable than those of the first despite the much smaller sampling of children.

The second survey recorded a wasting rate of 16 percent, comparable to that observed in the first study. But underweight and stunting rates—indicators capturing chronic malnutrition—were roughly 50 percent higher than the rate observed the previous year (61 percent and 64 percent, respectively). To get some comparative sense of these figures, the results of the 1998 survey implied that the incidence of wasting among children in North Korea was more than double that in Angola, a country in the midst of a thirty-year civil war, and more than 50 percent greater than in Sierra Leone, a country that had collapsed into virtual anarchy.

The North Koreans were reportedly infuriated by the public release of what they regarded as embarrassing information and refused repeated requests by the WFP for a follow-up study (GAO 1999, Snyder 2003b). A subsequent survey was apparently conducted by the North Korean government in 2000 and documented broad improvements in nutritional status, but to our knowledge this study was never publicly released or, as two UN-affiliated analysts put it, "wasn't internationally observed" (Shrimpton and Yongyout 2003:3).

In October 2002, a survey of 6,000 children and 2,795 mothers was conducted by the North Korean Central Bureau of Statistics in collaboration with the North Korean Institute for Child Nutrition. UNICEF and the WFP provided financial and logistical support. Certain geographic regions accounting for roughly 20 percent of the population were excluded, including Chagang and Kangwŏn provinces. The survey results implied extraordinary improvements in nutritional status. The percentage of underweight children fell from 61 to 21 percent. Stunting dropped from 62 to 42 percent, and wasting from 16 to 9 percent. The proportion of low birth-weight babies in the North Korean survey (6.7 percent) was actually lower than that for the United States (7.6 percent) or England and Wales (7.7 percent), as was the reported rate of infant mortality. These improvements were so astonishing as to provoke considerable internal debate about their veracity within the collaborating UN institutions. In the end, the UN agencies decided to accept and disseminate the North Korean report (see Shrimpton and Yongyout 2003, 2004a, 2004b).

The data confirmed the strong regional dimension to the famine that we emphasized in our discussion in chapter 3 (table 7.6). Variation in child and mother nutritional status varied sharply across regions of the country. Stunting and underweight rates reported for the capital of Pyongyang and the port city of Namp'o, for example, were consistently about half that recorded for the province of Yanggang in the northeast. The wasting rate of Pyongyang (4 percent) was a third of that of the worst province, South Hamgyŏng (12 percent).

In October 2004, North Korean authorities with the support of the UN agencies conducted a survey of 4,800 children and 2,109 mothers. Again the survey excluded certain geographical areas and cannot be regarded as necessarily representative of the country as a whole. Indeed, even some areas being served by the WFP were omitted, and the results cannot therefore even be interpreted as representative of areas in which the WFP has operations. Foreign participants in the study registered a variety of complaints with respect to basic lack of quality control over the implementation of the survey, such as the North Korean authorities impeding standard randomization procedures.

TABLE 7.6. Nutritional Status by Region (%)

	Kaesŏng	Namp'o	North Hamgyŏng	North Hwanghae	North P'yong'an	Pyongyang	Yanggang	South Hamgyong	South Hwanghae	South P'yŏng'an	Overall
1997											
Wasting	n.a.	n.a.	n.a.	15.9	n.a.	n.a.	n.a.	15.2	20.1	15.1	16.5
Stunting	n.a.	n.a.	n.a.	47.5	n.a.	n.a.	n.a.	35.9	26.0	53.1	38.2
Underweight	n.a.	n.a.	n.a.	n.a.	n.a.	n.a.	n.a.	n.a.	n.a.	n.a.	n.a.
2002											
Wasting	7.00	4.33	10.68	9.00	6.83	3.68	9.50	12.02	11.00	7.19	8.12
Stunting	44.4	23.2	42.8	39.4	42.4	27.0	46.7	45.5	38.6	42.2	39.2
Underweight	20.7	14.7	20.3	20.7	17.8	14.8	26.5	24.2	20.2	18.7	20.2
2004											
Wasting	n.a.	n.a.	10.0	7.9	6.0	2.8	9.1	10.8	7.6	4.9	7.0
Stunting	n.a.	n.a.	40.0	41.0	41.2	25.9	45.6	46.7	36.7	29.7	37.0
Underweight	n.a.	n.a.	26.6	24.8	21.6	18.8	30.8	29.3	23.4	19.6	23.4

Sources: 1997: Katona-Apte and Mokdad 1998; 2002: Central Bureau of Statistics (North Korea) 2002; 2004: Central Bureau of Statistics, Institute of Child Nutrition, DPRK 2005.

At the national level, the rate of stunting (measured height-for-age), signaling chronic malnutrition, was found to be 37 percent among children under the age of six. This would have marked a slight fall from the previous survey's figure of 42 percent and was well below the 1998 survey's 62 percent, though the comparison is inexact since the previous reports surveyed children under seven while the most recent one used an age ceiling of six. The underweight share (measured weight-for-age) was 23 percent, representing a slight increase from the 21 percent obtained in 2002. Wasting, a measure of acute malnutrition (measured weight-for-height) was 7 percent, down from 9 percent in 2002.

Again, the survey revealed considerable regional variation. For example, the stunting rate in Pyongyang (26 percent) was well below that in the eastern provinces of South Hamgyŏng (47 percent) and Yanggang (46 percent) (figure 7.5). Similarly, underweight rates were roughly 50 percent higher in the northeastern provinces of Yanggang (31 percent) and South Hamgyŏng (29 percent) as compared to southern areas such as Pyongyang (19 percent) and South P'yŏng'an (20 percent) (figure 7.6). Most dramatic were the regional disparities with respect to wasting: the prevalence in Pyongyang (3 percent) was a third or less of that observed in the provinces of South Hamgyŏng (11 percent), North Hamgyŏng (10 percent), and Yanggang (9 percent) (figure 7.7).

How one assesses secular trends at the national level depends very much on the reliability of the first two surveys, done in 1997 and 1998. The 1997 survey is widely acknowledged to have severe deficiencies, and the consensus has been to discount its results. The 1998 survey represents a methodological improvement, but the reported results—implying wide swings in the longer-term markers in comparison to either the survey that preceded it or the one that followed—make it suspect. With respect to another indicator of distress, maternal nutritional status, firm proof of improvement is lacking because the international agencies had not previously examined this issue and the North Koreans have not made their 2002 survey available (Shrimpton and Yongyout 2004b).

(opposite page)

FIGURE 7.5. (*top*) Stunting (2004)
Source: Central Bureau of Statistics, 2005.

FIGURE 7.6. (*bottom*) Underweight (2004)
Source: Central Bureau of Statistics, 2005.

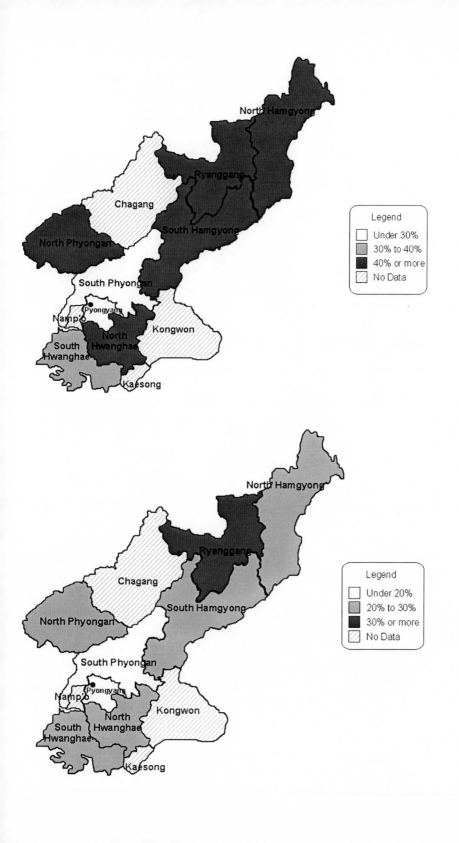

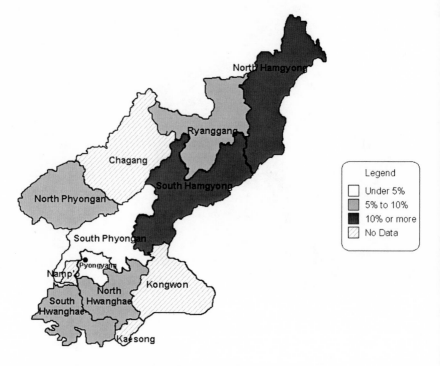

FIGURE 7.7. Wasting
Source: Central Bureau of Statistics, 2005.

There are at least three possible explanations for this anomalous pattern. They are not mutually exclusive. The first explanation is that the 1998 numbers are correct and the subsequent dramatic improvement in child nutritional status can be ascribed to the humanitarian relief effort; we call this "the system worked" interpretation, and it is the view of the North Koreans and the UN agencies (Central Bureau of Statistics 2002, WFP 2003a, Shrimpton and Yongyout 2004a, b). If this interpretation is correct, the improvement in nutritional status in North Korea between 1998 and 2002 is, to our knowledge, without historical parallel. The 2004 figures, however, do not reveal a continuation of the tremendous gains recorded between 1998 and 2002; indeed, the levels of the indicators of chronic malnutrition—stunting and low weight—remain "very high" according to the World Heath Organization (WHO) classification. The problem for supporters of this view is to explain why improvements seem to have stalled after 2002. One possible explanation would be the decline in aid after 2002 that we have described (figure 4.2).

Another would be that the nature of the food problem shifted from the collapse of the PDS to entitlement failures connected with the emergence of a more market-driven distribution process.

A second explanation is that at least some of the reported figures are wrong because of deliberate falsification, or, as one participant in these surveys put it more euphemistically, "they were politically determined." Rather than painting a rosier picture than was in fact the case, the North Korean government initially exaggerated the magnitude of the famine in the mid-1990s in order to secure humanitarian relief. The government then exaggerated the subsequent improvement in nutritional status in order to build political support for continuation of the concessional aid program. In this "fabricated figures" interpretation, the relative constancy of the 2002 and 2004 results that depict high levels of chronic child malnutrition represents a calibrated decision on the part of a North Korean government that wants to maintain access to relief. This interpretation requires that the North Koreans are not only strategic with the use of data and, if one accepts the claims by the UN's statisticians, that they had the capability to fine-tune the data through control over the sample since internal statistical consistency checks should have caught obvious fabrication (Shimpton and Yongyout 2004a).

A third "human error" explanation is that some of the reported figures are wrong, but as a result of design problems and mismeasurement in the various surveys, not strategic calculations. The 1998 survey obtained extremely high stunting and underweight percentages, both in an absolute sense and relative to the much lower wasting percentage. Both of these measures involve age, which could have been misunderstood or misrepresented.[22] According to this "human error" interpretation, the 2002 and 2004 surveys were conducted by the North Koreans who presumably got the ages right, hence the disproportionate improvement in the age-related measures between 1998 and 2002 and the relative stability of the indicators in the 2004 survey that followed.

However we interpret the anomalous trends, the following is clear: after nearly a decade of relief efforts, nutritional status continued to have a pronounced regional component. On average, the favored cities and the more fertile regions of the south consistently displayed far better childhood nutritional status than did other parts of the country, especially the northeast. The continued existence of pronounced regional disparities may, in a backhanded way, give some credence to the "the system worked" interpretation, at least in response to "the figures have been fabricated" view. Yet the damning regional disparities—compounded by continued lack of access to significant regions of the country, together with the testimony of refugees in China that they had not received aid, suggests that neither the normal internal mechanisms for distributing food on a nonconcessional basis nor international aid programs are adequately serving populations in historically low food-production areas. If "the system worked," it did so in an exceedingly narrow sense, at best.

Conclusion and Epilogue: Attempted Retrenchment?

The famine gave rise to de facto or bottom-up marketization as well as reform efforts initiated by the government. These reform efforts present a mixed picture and suggest divisions within the government over the scope and pace of the reform effort. On the one hand, they do reflect some liberalization and increased opportunity for market activity, if only to acknowledge the changed reality that had occurred on the ground in the famine's wake. We also know that official pronouncements, at least, have introduced changes in incentives for cultivators and managers and that at least until the harvest of 2005, the terms of trade had shifted in favor of farmers. To the extent that farmers had been relatively disadvantaged in the past, this is a desirable outcome. Moreover, it was precisely such a shift in relative prices that marked the first phase of the Chinese reforms, unleashing a wave of productivity improvements and rising incomes in the rural sector that ultimately spilled over into industrial activity as well.

In 2005, however, reports began filtering out of North Korea that the state was reneging on the formula determining the share of cooperative grain output to be sold to the state at the official procurement price that remained well below the market price. These reports also suggested that the government was treating grain produced on private plots, in principle purely for free disposal, as cooperative output and subject to forced sale to the state (see, e.g., Y. J. Kim 2005e). These reports were followed by the formal announcement, in the context of a better-than-normal harvest and high levels of South Korean aid, that private trade in grain would be banned starting October 1. The PDS, which had fallen into disuse in most parts of the country, was to be resuscitated, in effect reversing demand-side reforms. In parallel, the government announced that it was expelling international relief agencies that over the previous decade had fed nearly a third of the country.

Moreover, the revived PDS would involve a strongly differentiated price structure, involving a market price; a lower state price for those employed at SOEs; and an additional discount for "good workers." The market price was set at roughly fifteen times that of the state price, apparently approximating the actual difference at the time the policy was enacted (Y. Kwon 2006). The irony that the market price is undefined if markets are banned seems to have escaped the North Korean authorities. The new price structure conveyed large preferences to SOE employees who reported to work (that is, not the "August 3" workers engaged in entrepreneurial activity outside state control).

If diligently implemented, these changes would amount to a fundamental reorganization of the North Korean food economy. By this time, the market, not the PDS, had become the primary institutional mechanism through which North Korean households obtained food. In one fell swoop, the state was criminalizing the market and requiring that families obtain food through a system that had not operated properly, if at all, for over a decade in much of the country. Not only did these policy changes raise important humanitarian issues, but they called also into question the status of the broader reform process.

The most charitable interpretation of these actions is that the government itself had become concerned with the social consequences of allowing food to be allocated solely on the basis of purchasing power in the market. With the supply situation improved as a result of the better-than-normal harvest of 2005 and inflows of aid from South Korea and China, the government was simply moving to rebuild the social safety net (Frank 2005c, Y. Kwon 2006).

A second possibility is that the reorganization of the food economy amounted to an ersatz anti-inflation policy. The previous decade had witnessed a significant decentralization of the economy, penetration of the economy by Chinese consumer goods, and the development of an extensive retail distribution system outside state control. At the same time, the economy had been plagued by high, sustained inflation of at least 100 percent a year. We have argued that this inflationary process fundamentally reflects underlying macroeconomic disequilibria: namely, the state's inability to raise revenues through taxation combined with the maintenance of large expenditures, including SOE subsidies and military outlays.

North Korean policy makers privately shared this concern about inflation but were uncertain about how to respond. They could not control the prices of consumer goods from China (ironically considered a source of deflation elsewhere in the world). Food looms large in consumers' budgets. The lion's share of food is either produced domestically or takes the form of aid that passes directly through state-controlled channels. Ergo, if one wants to control inflation, one must control the food economy. Price controls make little economic sense; they address the symptom of inflation, not its underlying cause. But given the command-and-control nature of the Stalinist economy and the absence, or lack of understanding, of standard macroeconomic policy tools, it is highly plausible that authorities would reach for direct price controls as a tool for stabilizing prices.

Several features of the reform suggest a third interpretation, however: that the revival of the PDS reflected an effort to reassert both economic and political control in the face of ongoing marketization and de facto decentralization of economic decision making. The differentiated price structure, which apparently makes no accommodation for vulnerable groups, is clearly designed to create incentives for workers to return to employment in the state sector. Some commentators hailed this development as a praiseworthy precursor to the resuscitation of the industrial economy (e.g., Lim 2006b). Given the low rates of capacity utilization in the industrial SOEs and the fact that many of these dinosaurs will never be competitive, it is unclear how getting workers to return to their work units would have positive effects. To the contrary, if the exit of workers under the cover of the so-called August 3 measures marked a reallocation of labor to more productive activities, this "reform" would be altogether retrograde or simply punitive.

Instead, an economic measure aimed at reviving the rust belt, the ban on the market, and the revival of the PDS could be seen as a bid to reestablish political control through the food distribution system. The preference given to SOE workers—bound more closely to the state than those operating outside state strictures—would be consistent with an interpretation emphasizing this political motivation. A revived PDS would also empower local party and government officials and provide a mechanism for reconstituting a political network loyal to the central authorities.

At this writing, it is questionable whether the government can actually implement and sustain a policy U-turn. On the demand side, the government has been unable to supply the announced 500–700 gram daily ration (WFP 2005b, Good Friends 2006a). As might be expected under the circumstances, there appears to be a certain degree of unevenness geographically in how diligently the new restrictions are being implemented, and there are anecdotal reports of grain continuing to trade surreptitiously in markets and via private residences. Indeed, Good Friends reports that since the availability of PDS supplies strongly affects market prices, most underground grain dealers maintain good relations with the local Department of Food Policy. Not only do local officials turn a blind eye toward these black market transactions, they are probably involved in the market either as recipients of graft or as direct participants themselves.

On the supply side, it is not clear how widespread the confiscatory grain seizures have been. The critical issue is whether during the next harvest cycle the farmers respond by reverting to their famine-era coping behavior of preharvesting, hoarding, shifting crop mixes away from grains, tending secret plots, and diverting output to illicit markets. There is already some evidence of this kind of coping behavior (Good Friends 2006b). As we documented in chapter 2, when the North Korean authorities engaged in confiscatory seizures in 1995, attempting to extract grain that had already been allocated for farm household consumption, half the North Korean corn harvest "disappeared" the following year. We are not claiming that the events of 2005 are equivalent to the traumatic events a decade earlier. If harvests continue to improve and aid continues to be forthcoming, the policy could be sustained. But the supply response of the farmers during the next harvest cycle could make operating the PDS much more difficult the following year as farmers seek to protect themselves from exploitation. If a standoff between the state and cultivators were to recur, one can imagine at least three possible scenarios. The first scenario would essentially amount to a continuation of the status quo at the beginning of 2006: the market would remain banned, the PDS would operate irregularly, black markets would exist, and farmers would exhibit duplicity in their dealings with the state. Because the market would be underground, its efficiency would be degraded. This outcome is a recipe for the continuation of the chronic nutrition problems documented earlier in this chapter.

A second possibility is that the policy would simply be unsustainable because of some combination of poor harvests, attenuated aid inflows, and coping behavior by the farmers. In this case, the attempt to ban the market and revive the PDS could prove to be little more than a bump on the road to continued reform. The government would quietly acquiesce to the situation that existed from the late 1990s until the fall of 2005, with the market regaining its role as the primary institution for the allocation and distribution of food.

Hopefully, the third possibility will not eventuate, but given the country's history its likelihood cannot be entirely discounted: namely, the recurrence of severe shortages. Farmers would engage in significant hedging behavior by neglecting the official plots, preharvesting, and hoarding. South Korea, China, and perhaps other donors would no doubt respond to signs of shortage. But with the WFP and private NGOs largely excluded from the North Korean countryside, the international community would once again lack information on the distribution of misery and exercise little influence over the allocation of food. Even a recurrence of famine could not be ruled out.

Whether the recent policy changes amount to a U-turn or merely a minor detour remains to be seen. It is clear that the social contract in North Korea has fundamentally changed and that some sort of hybrid market system is increasingly in play in the country. An instructional speech by Kim Jŏng-il made in October 2001 is worth quoting at some length: "There are too many giveaways in our society and more unproductive expenditures than productive ones in the use of the state budget. . . . The state spends millions of won annually in providing its citizens with food supplies . . . as a result, the socialist rationing policies of the past malfunctioned and the society experienced an extreme form of egalitarianism, and it became the norm for people to unlawfully take government property. The [situation] created indolence among the citizens, and decreased efficiency and productivity." At the same time, the Dear Leader acknowledges the flip side of these developments in the emergence of the market. "During the last few years, when the state was unable to supply food efficiently, people began to abandon their jobs and began searching for ways to acquire personal gains [*sic*]"(KIEP 2004:296–97). Herein lies both the hope for the North Korean economy and the current source of vulnerability. With the state unable to provide, markets emerged. But in the absence of social safety nets, significant portions of the urban working class risk continuing poverty, marginalization, and insecure access to food.

CHAPTER EIGHT

Conclusion

North Korea in Comparative and International Perspective

During the 1990s, as many as a million North Koreans died in a famine that ranks as one of the most destructive of the twentieth century. An entire cohort of children was consigned to a myriad of physical and mental impairments associated with chronic childhood malnutrition. This tragedy was the result of a misguided strategy of self-reliance that only served to increase the country's vulnerability to both economic and natural shocks. Slow to respond to crisis—as closed, authoritarian governments so frequently are—the government not only limited effective targeting, monitoring, and assessment of humanitarian assistance but cut off whole portions of the country from desperately needed help just as the famine was cresting. These government actions—and failures to act—are not incidental to the famine and ongoing food shortages; they are central to any explanation of it. The state's culpability in this vast misery elevates the North Korean famine to a crime against humanity.[1]

The famine set in train the marketization of the economy and reforms that hold out at least some hope for the transformation of the country. But through mid-2006, these reforms remained partial and ill-conceived in important respects, and their promise for relieving North Korea's economic distress is thus highly uncertain. Evidence is accumulating that North Korea is changing, but in spite of—not because of—the stance of the government.

We divide our conclusions into two parts. The first explores the implications of our findings for an understanding of North Korea itself. What do the famine and its aftermath imply for the prospects of an economic transition in North

Korea—and a transition to what? What does our understanding of the North Korean economy suggest for the prospects of regime change and for political developments more generally?

Second, we take up in more detail the international implications of our findings. We begin with the humanitarian effort and consider not only how the aid game has worked but also the moral dilemmas of assisting North Korea. Should the international community provide assistance in such a setting? What are the implications of channeling that assistance through multilateral as opposed to bilateral channels? How do donors engage North Korea not only to relieve current suffering but also to assure a more positive future for its citizens?

These questions cannot be posed outside the broader geostrategic context of the Korean peninsula: the complex maze of international politics that has kept the Korean peninsula divided. We close with a consideration of the debate over engagement and the light our findings shed on the second nuclear crisis that began in 2002.

Famine and Reform in North Korea I: The Economic Transition

North Korea experienced severe political and economic shocks in the early 1990s: the collapse of the Soviet Union, a tense standoff with respect to its nuclear ambitions, an uncertain political transition, and a succession of national disasters. From October 2002, the country was once again involved in a dispute with the international community over its nuclear weapons and faced a "hostile policy"—in the regime's trenchant language—not only from the United States but from the increasingly skeptical Japan and European Union as well. All these apparently exogenous shocks contributed to North Korea's economic isolation and posed severe policy challenges to the government. They constitute one explanation, invoked by North Korea and sympathetic outsiders, for the economic collapse of the last fifteen years.

We have argued that these shocks cannot be considered exogenous; rather, they stem from core features of the regime itself, including an economic strategy that contributed to the great famine of the mid-1990s and ongoing food shortages since.

The key to resolving the North Korean hunger problem does not lie in a consideration of agriculture and the food distribution system alone, however; it requires the development of a functioning economy that generates sufficient foreign exchange earnings to purchase needed food on a commercial basis. This argument may strike many as counterintuitive. Food security seems like a reasonable national objective, and some have defended a policy of self-sufficiency for the country (Ahn 2005, Ireson 2006). But food security is rarely, if ever, best achieved through a policy of self-reliance in food production. Particularly given North Korea's basic endowments, most notably the scarcity of arable land, it is highly unlikely that the country is capable of achieving self-sufficiency in food; indeed, the famine and chronic food shortages have proved the point beyond dispute.

The solution to the hunger problem in North Korea is thus intimately tied to the broader question of economic reform. Food security requires North Korea to generate enough foreign exchange through export revenues or borrowing to import bulk grains on a sustainable commercial basis, as Japan, South Korea, and China have done. This problem could probably be solved purely by expenditure switching: shifting the composition of imports away from other priorities. But even taking existing expenditure preferences as given, the improvements in the performance of the export sector needed to address this constraint are modest: the annual import shortfall is not large, in the hundreds of millions of dollars.

Yet relaxing this aggregate supply constraint is not the end of the story. The hunger issues that we have examined are also distributional in nature. Many households in North Korea are now food insecure because the Public Distribution System has broken down and they do not command adequate resources to purchase food in the market. The purpose of the reform process is therefore to reallocate resources, including both capital and labor, in ways that are more conducive to long-run growth. Although we must be concerned with the government's role in ameliorating the impact of inequality on access to food and providing social safety nets, the ultimate solution to the problem is to pursue reforms that raise productivity and incomes.

What is to be done? It is frequently argued that North Korea should pursue the China model, which is regarded as emblematic of a successful outcome but seldom defined. But North Korea differs from China in important ways that will inevitably shape its transition from socialism. We should be cautious about the idea that North Korea is following, or can follow, a Chinese reform path, with or without North Korean characteristics. Unlike China (and another relatively successful reformer, Vietnam), North Korea does not have a large labor-intensive agricultural sector. In terms of the sectoral composition of output and employment, the North Korean economy more closely resembles Romania and parts of the former Soviet Union than it does the agriculture-led Asian reformers.

The existence of a labor-intensive agricultural sector matters for two reasons.

First, because of the relatively simple techniques of production used in such agriculture, considerable productivity improvements can be achieved without an extensive package of ancillary reforms or inputs. Simply removing price distortions and controls on the allocation of acreage to alternative crops and providing some incentives for farmers can go a long way toward increasing output. Similar reforms could no doubt improve agricultural productivity in North Korea as well, and until 2005 the authorities seemed to recognize the importance of moving in this direction.

North Korean farmers, however, are much more reliant on industrial inputs than were their Chinese or Vietnamese counterparts. Productivity in agriculture has been flat over the last decade, suggesting that the incentive reforms may have done little more than stave off an even deeper decline in output. NGO reports note that maize fields were still being guarded in 2006, suggesting that the price reforms have not solved the fundamental problems of diversion. So while improvements in the agricultural terms of trade may have important long-run benefits, they are unlikely to generate Chinese- or Vietnamese-magnitude results without complementary industrial inputs. The success of the reforms in North Korea is thus dependent on developments in the industrial sector.

Increasing productivity in the industrial sector in turn requires a more extensive package of policy supports and, as a consequence, is more difficult to achieve. In China, this sector could be carried by the success of the broader reform effort.[2] In North Korea, by contrast, the weight of the industrial sector is extraordinarily large, and much of it is beyond fixing. The agricultural sector is relatively small, and even with large increases in productivity it will not be the leading sector of a major economic transformation. Effective change will only come from expanding the foreign sector and by allowing urban workers to shift to market-oriented activities, a process that we return to in more detail below.

The second reason that the Chinese or Vietnamese path appears relatively successful is political. In contrast to Eastern Europe and some of the countries of the former Soviet Union, China and Vietnam maintained their authoritarian structure during the course of their economic reforms. Structural conditions arguably made it easier to do so. In a labor-surplus economy, the initial productivity-increasing reforms in agriculture permit a simultaneous increase in agricultural output and a movement of extremely low productivity agricultural labor to the nascent non-state-owned light manufacturing sector. In principle, each of three major groups in the economy can benefit from such a change. The migrants to the emerging light manufacturing sector have higher wages than they did on the farm, as do the remaining farmers, whose average and marginal productivity will increase with higher output generated by fewer farmers. Food prices might initially rise following decontrol of prices, but with a sufficient supply response in agriculture, the incumbent urban proletariat in the old, state-owned heavy manufacturing sector can see an improvement in real wages as the implicit terms of trade between food and industrial products falls. Reform under these circumstances constitutes a happy equilibrium: no large group comes out an obvious loser.

A crucial question for North Korea is whether a labor-abundant agricultural sector was a necessary condition for such a reform path to succeed or whether it was only sufficient. The key factor in the China model is that initial wages in agriculture were extremely low, permitting easy movement into light manufacturing. By contrast, North Korea's industrial sector bears a closer resemblance to conditions in the Soviet Union and some Eastern European countries where industrial workers (and crony capitalists) bitterly opposed economic restructuring, in some cases decisively. These workers not only received relatively high wages through the enterprise but a broad set of social welfare benefits including housing and health care. If an enterprise closed, workers lost not only their jobs but their homes and their access to medical care and even education and foodstuffs as well.[3]

The evidence we have presented suggests that the decline in the industrial sector in North Korea has been so substantial and future opportunities look sufficiently bleak that a positive economic-cum-political dynamic could operate in a more industrialized economy such as North Korea's. If workers at the Kim Ch'aek Iron and Steel Complex are under- or unemployed and are not receiving salaries and benefits, or it is widely believed that the plant is never going to reopen in any case, then the managers, workers, and their representatives in the corridors of power will not oppose reforms that could generate alternative employment. In its second decade of decline, North Korea may have fallen so far that its underemployed industrial proletariat might have become the political equivalent of Chinese surplus agricultural labor: economically available—and even anxious—to be redeployed in new activities and politically lacking in any levers to resist fundamental restructuring.

If this story is correct, then we are once again confronted with the fundamental economic issue of how to raise productivity in a more industrialized economy. The existing literature on North Korea suggests that the current economy is horrendously distorted and that economywide liberalization would have profound affects on the structure of the economy, the composition of output, and the sectoral and geographic distribution of employment (Noland 2000). But what are the new activities into which labor and capital would flow?

Given the country's small size and geographical position, it is clear that the foreign sector should play a much larger role in the North Korean transition than it has to date. North Korea should be exporting its natural resources—as it increasingly is—but also light and medium-tech manufactures. It should import capital goods, intermediate products, and food. The composition of employment would shift toward those emerging export-oriented manufacturing sectors, with literally millions of North Korean workers changing jobs. Given the prevalence of subscale manufacturing establishments and the excessive geographic dispersion of existing facilities, this process of restructuring would have its own distributional consequences. For example, it would involve substantial agglomeration of economic activities in certain areas, as has occurred following reforms in similarly spatially distorted economies such as Russia. Some existing industrial towns could be depopulated, but others with more favorable geographic locations—near ports, near China, or near the road and rail links with South Korea—would expand dramatically. The biggest natural partners would be China, South Korea, and Japan.

Foreign investment would be a fundamental driver of this process of renewal. Foreign firms represent a kind of neural synapse between the latent productive potential of the North Korean economy and external demand in world markets. Foreign firms have the blueprints for the products that the rest of the world wants to buy, as well as the global distribution and marketing networks to make sales happen. One can imagine a wide range of modalities through which this interaction could develop. In the short run, special economic zones, export processing zones, and special industrial parks, such as the ones established or contemplated in Kaesŏng, Sinŭiju, Wŏnsan, and Pyongyang, could form geographically delimited enclaves of foreign investment while the political system adjusted to the enhanced role of foreign investors in the economy. In the longer run, more liberalized policies and practices would allow the spread of such activities throughout the economy as a whole, as occurred in South Korea in the 1960s and 1970s.

The transformation of the North Korean economy would not depend only on the external sector. North Korea is no exception to the tendency of controlled socialist economies to ignore the service sector. Under the current and highly uncertain degree of marketization, we already observe an explosion of small-scale activities such as restaurants, beauty parlors, small shops, and other commercial activities. Closer inspection reveals that these activities are already transforming foreign trade from below, as they participate in growing distribution networks for foreign goods that are increasingly paid for by hard currency earnings from a variety of legal and illicit sources.

Yet North Korea's progress on this path has been at best uneven, and the government has created a number of problems for itself; these barriers are worth reiterating. As documented in chapter 7, the economic policy changes of 2002 unleashed considerable inflation, on the order of 100 percent or more annually. Although the government appears to be making progress on addressing its underlying fiscal and monetary problems, these have by no means been resolved, and some of the solutions pursued—such as the issue of bonds that more closely resemble a lottery and banning the market in grain—do not augur well. Countries that have attempted fundamental reforms in high-inflation environments have generally not fared well. High inflation complicates the policy-making process, magnifies mistakes, and exacerbates distributional conflicts over reform. Inflation also makes it difficult to gauge relative prices and thus deters investment and exchange as well. It is notable that when China, to which North Korea is often compared, introduced its reforms, it faced neither the degree of macroeconomic instability nor the degradation of its planning mechanism that currently confront North Korea.

More fundamentally, the regime faces severe credibility problems. We believe that the substantial marketization from below that has occurred to date has been largely in spite of, rather than because, of government policy. The regime has tolerated the emergence of market activity only grudgingly, and reform efforts have repeatedly been undermined by a zigzagging process that opens up opportunities only to close them down. Reported changes in agricultural policy in the fall of 2005 involving forcible seizures of grain in order to revive the PDS are only the most recent example. Market actors operate in the context of weak and uncertain economic institutions that limit the scope of their business and encourage markets to operate in a netherworld between the legal and the illicit. To date, we have seen few political changes that would buttress private property and contracting rights, and where they have occurred their credibility remains in doubt (Yoon 2005).

Differences in the treatment of local and foreign enterprises reveal the relative weakness of internal forces for the regularization of external economic relations. South Korean small and medium enterprises rendered uncompetitive by rising wages in South Korea are the most natural group of prospective investors in North Korea's manufacturing sector. Individually, these firms lack direct political clout in either Seoul or Pyongyang, and consequently formal institutional rules matter more for them since they have less opportunity for private redress. In this light, the conclusion of bilateral North-South agreements on issues such as taxation and the repatriation of profits could be interpreted as mechanisms for solving these credibility problems. The establishment of the Kaesŏng Industrial

Complex, with the effective imprimatur of the South Korean government and complete with explicit and implicit socialization of risk, also serves this function. Yet even here North Korean behavior has been perplexing. North Korea continuously stalled the completion of the transportation links necessary to make the Kaesŏng project viable, has made wage demands that negate the very advantages in moving to North Korea in the first place, and snubbed South Korean officials during the ceremonial opening of the complex.

At least four nonmutually exclusive hypotheses could explain North Korea's inauspicious policy making to date. The first is that the North Korean authorities are well intentioned but that the failures of economic policy reflect a lack of experience and technical capacity: they literally do not know what they are doing. A second possibility is that the government knows what it should be doing but cannot take the necessary steps because of political stalemate or fear of the political consequences of reform. A third argument focuses on the moral hazard associated with external support: the provision of foreign assistance permits half-measures and temporizing. The fourth possibility is that they know what they should be doing but are discouraged by external constraints such as embargos or sanctions. We take up the first two of these arguments here and return to the external constraints in the following section

There is ample evidence to support the first interpretation, including the well-worn anecdote of North Korean economic policy makers asking a visiting World Bank official what a bond market was. Technical assistance and training may have large payoffs and help avoid some of the more egregious and costly mistakes. The World Bank and International Monetary Fund could play an important role in this regard, as could bilateral technical assistance.[4] Evidence on North Korean receptiveness to such advice is mixed, however, even if we set aside for the moment the issue of Western reluctance that we take up in more detail below. Even the Chinese complain privately about North Korean resistance to outside advice. The government has ultimately been unwilling to accept the degree of openness and transparency that membership in the international financial institutions entails.[5] While it is possible that the partial and vacillating nature of the reforms reflects a necessary learning process, it is also possible that the partial nature of the reforms reflects a deeper political equilibrium.

One possible reason that the reform process would be blocked is that authorities could come to fear the consequences of what had occurred to date and slowly reassert economic control in order to maintain political control. Central government officials would be motivated by the many political liabilities associated with the reforms to date, including growing inequality, the emergence of alternative centers of economic power, and the leakage of ideas and information as a result of increasing trade and investment, particularly and ironically through China (Lankov 2006a). Implicit evidence of these concerns can be seen in, for example, the location of the country's first special economic zone in the highly isolated extreme northeast of the country, or the banning of the private use of cellular telephones after subscriptions began growing rapidly in 2004, or the periodic seizures of contraband videos of South Korean soap operas. Under a more statist scenario, the government would concentrate on resolving the most obvious policy problems, such as the weakness of the tax base and the inadequacy of foreign exchange earnings, while relying on aid inflows from China and South Korea for regime maintenance. Food security could improve in the short run, if, for example the state used its increasing command of resources to reconstitute a social safety net; this could be consistent with the efforts to revive the PDS in October 2005. Such an effort at restoration, however, would ultimately delay a broader reform effort or imply a fragmented and partial process hostage to the regime's perception of political stability.

An alternative political explanation for partial reform may lie not only with the leadership but also with the very economic forces that have been spawned by the reforms to date. North Korea's process of marketization occurred largely in the absence of formal rules and institutions. One route to wider economic changes would build on this start by legalizing, regularizing, and deepening this implicit reform from below. A central problem, however, is that an incumbent set of stakeholders who have acted opportunistically could well oppose the regularization of property rights (for example, enterprise managers engaged in asset stripping or spontaneous privatization) or the introduction of a more coherent and open regulatory environment. Much of this early marketization was allowed to flourish only through corruption and cronyism, which a more open economic environment would dissipate to at least some extent (for example, by eliminating monopoly privileges of various sorts). The stakes are particularly high to the extent that the military is involved in these irregular economic activities, as is surely the case.

In such a setting, reform is uneven or ineffective not because the center is trying to reassert control but because beneficiaries of partial liberalization are sufficiently influential to block further reform (Hellman 1998). This scenario holds forth the possibility of gradually improving economic performance through greater effective reliance on markets. In the absence of offsetting social safety nets, however, such an outcome would continue the trend toward growing inequality and more varied outcomes for individual households, including the possibility of continuing food insecurity.

The interests of the North Korean military are relevant in this regard. The military continues to operate its own parallel economy. With its own trading firms and preferential access to foreign technology and imported goods, the military was well situated to take advantage of the reforms. It now controls a dozen or more conglomerates modeled on East German *Kombinaten* or South Korean *chaebŏl*, depending on one's cultural reference point. Given Kim Jŏng-il's growing reliance on the military, crystallized in the "military-first" politics, economic policy could increasingly reflect the idiosyncratic interests of the military elite itself. This would undoubtedly be a sadly ironic turn of events for an elite raised on the Eighteenth Brumaire of Louis Napoleon. Yet the stance of the military toward the reform process remains a central mystery.[6]

Whether and how the military and the defense-industrial complex participate in the reform process will have a fundamental bearing on the nature and prospects for success of the process of economic development and engagement with the outside world. The case of China is especially relevant here. A key factor behind China's ability to undertake the rapid pace of economic reforms during the first ten to fifteen years of its open door policy was aggressive demilitarization of its economy. The key elements of the Chinese strategy included a concerted effort to shift the output of the military-industrial complex from military to civilian production, the large-scale transfer of military manpower, industrial facilities, and infrastructure to civilian use, and a significant downsizing of the armed forces. At the same time, the political clout of the military in the political process began to decline steadily. Without this extensive and rapid demilitarization of the economy at the outset of reforms, the pace and scale of China's economic liberalization would likely have been much slower and more limited.

In North Korea, the reform effort is taking place without any signs that demilitarization is being seriously considered or pursued; to the contrary. The "military-first" policy suggests that the leadership of the Korean People's Army may view the economic reforms as an opportunity to garner more resources for the military-industrial complex. If this is the case, then the North Korean model of economic development linked with the continued militarization of the state economy has much more in common with the experiences of the Soviet Union during the 1980s than it does with China.

The external environment will play an important role in how these domestic political forces supporting and opposing reform play out. In this regard, the North Korean government faces a complicated environment that is neither wholly supportive nor entirely hostile to the cause of economic reform.

Two important countries, the United States and Japan, impose significant external constraints on North Korea's ability to globalize successfully. Yet its two principal partners, South Korea and China, value political stability above all else and if anything have erred on the side of excessive generosity.[7] As a consequence, the policies of the United States and Japan reduce the prospective payoffs of reform, while those of South Korea and China retard it by enabling North Korea to temporize. These considerations point toward a trajectory of policy that is gradual, partial, and very much tied up with the behavior of external actors.

This outcome is not preordained. If one looks carefully, one can see internal signs of progress. To cite two such examples, the passage of a fiscal law in April 2004 at least holds out the hope that as the new tax system takes hold, the fiscal basis of the state can be reestablished and macroeconomic instability attenuated. In 2006 Kim Jŏng-il visited the economically vibrant cities of southern China and affirmed the "correctness" of the Chinese model; some observers are already hailing this as the beginning of North Korean reforms with Chinese characteristics (Lim 2006b).

With a genuine commitment to reform at the top, China and South Korea providing both resources and technical assistance, and a cooling of diplomatic pressure from the United States and Japan, it is not difficult to imagine a significant rehabilitation of the North Korean economy. Yet such hopes have been dashed in the past: during earlier visits to China, Kim visited Shanghai, praised Chinese reforms effusively, and declared that North Korea "supports the reform policy pursued by the Chinese side," lending a certain air of déjà vu to the 2006 visit (Noland 2001:4). Ultimately, the optimistic scenario rests squarely on the North Korean leadership's willingness to undertake wide-ranging reforms, confident that it can manage this process internally and that the external environment remains fundamentally supportive.

To summarize, the food problem must be seen in the context of wider economic reforms. There is no single route for such reforms, but given North Korea's endowments, an agriculture-led reform process is not likely to be enough; broader changes will be required. These will involve allowing greater freedom for commerce and a reorientation of the economy toward export-oriented activities, facilitated by foreign investment. The failure to pursue this path more aggressively may be due to lack of technical expertise and learning, but it may also be blocked by concerns over political control or the interests of favored groups. To gain a better understanding of these constraints, we turn to a more detailed examination of the country's political prospects.

Famine and Reform in North Korea II: The Political Consequences

We have argued that the food problem in North Korea is ultimately linked to fundamental features of the political system. The system of socialist entitlements, including access to food through the PDS, was determined both directly and indirectly by a complex castelike system in which political loyalty was a key determinant of life chances. We showed how certain regions of the country (most notably the northeast) were particularly disadvantaged vis-à-vis others (Pyongyang) and how these regional differences correlated strongly with other social distinctions (party members versus industrial workers).

We also highlighted the government's response to signs of shortage, the issue that motivates the political theory of famine advanced by Amartya Sen (Dreze and Sen 1989; Sen 2000). We took note of accounts suggesting that the leadership was unaware of the extent of the distress yet also catalog actions by the government that made the food situation worse. These actions included cutting off the northeast from humanitarian access and criminalizing personal movement.

North Korea's tragedy could only have occurred in a system in which the political leadership was both insulated from events on the ground and free to prioritize political control over the welfare of the citizenry. The crisis was therefore systemic, intimately related to the authoritarian structure of government, the absence of accountability to the citizenry, and the denial of political and civil liberties and property rights. At a minimum, these rights include the ability to publicize information—without fear of reprisal—that would have allowed government officials to ascertain the extent of distress. Granting citizens secure property rights, the freedom to trade and engage in private production, and simply the freedom to move would have also had wide-ranging social welfare effects. More expansively, famine and shortages could have been avoided were citizens free to organize collectively in the face of deprivation, confront public officials with their shortcomings, and replace them for failures. In the presence of these rights, neither the great famine nor the ongoing shortages of food would have taken the toll they did.

Yet wishing does not make things so, and simply to trumpet the benefits of regime change does not constitute either a prediction or a policy. If the political characteristics of the country are fundamental to an ultimate resolution of the food situation and of the problem of reform more generally, we need to assess the prospects for political change.

Some humility is warranted. An initial phase of discussion on this issue in the mid-1990s centered on the prospects of regime collapse in the face of international isolation, mounting economic distress, and the problems anticipated with the succession following the death of Kim Il-sŏng in July 1994.[8] In addition to these exogenous shocks, "collapsists" also focused on a number of features of the political system that appeared to signal internal schisms or institutional weaknesses: the apparent decay of political institutions, manifest, for example, in the suspension of Korean Workers' Party Congresses, Supreme People's Assembly (SPA) sessions, and even meetings of the Central Committee; the failure of Kim Jŏng-il to assume his father's titles of president of state and secretary general of the Korean Workers' Party; the absence of mass rallies in support of the Dear Leader; an increase in elite defections, most prominently of former Korean Workers' Party Central Committee member Hwang Chàng-yŏp; and a variety of anecdotal evidence on the public's muted views of Kim Jŏng-il compared to his father.

Predictions of collapse were widespread in the literature (see, however, Noland 1997). In 1995 the American analyst Nicholas Ebersadt wrote, "There is little reason at present to expect a reign by Kim Jŏng-il to be either stable or long" (139). His important book on the topic was called *The End of North Korea* (1999). In an article titled "No Way Out: North Korea's Impending Collapse," South Korean scholar and diplomat Kim Kyung-won wrote that "there is a real possibility that Kim Jŏng-il may find himself on the way out in the next few years, pushed out by reformists or military hardliners." His assessment was shared by fellow academic Ahn Byung-joon, who predicted in widely read articles that the Kim family regime would be short-lived, probably followed by a reformist military coup or the breakup and disappearance of the North Korean state (1994a, b).[9]

We do not cite these accounts to belittle them; all were made by thoughtful analysts and they were not atypical.[10] Nonetheless, at the risk of overestimating the regime's solidity, it is worth considering why North Korea did not collapse.

Evidence of the ability of governments to survive extreme economic distress can be gained by placing North Korea's experience in a broader comparative perspective. Despite the economic collapse we have detailed in this book, the country's experience is not unique. According to figures put together by the Bank of Korea,[11] North Korea experienced a decline in per capita GDP of approximately 25 percent over the twelve-year interval 1990–2002, or about a 2 percent decline annually. The maximum decline of roughly 33 percent (implying a compounded rate of more than 5 percent a year) occurred between 1990 and 1998, before the economy began to stabilize at a lower level of income. According to World Bank data on national economic performance since 1960, forty-two countries other than North Korea have suffered declines of 25 percent or more in per capita income over a twelve-year period, with per capita income falling 50 percent or more in fourteen of these countries.[12]

If North Korea's economic performance is therefore not altogether unusual, its combination of extraordinary crisis and the continuity of authoritarian rule might be. But even this conclusion would be hasty. Cuba is the most obvious comparator: a communist regime led by a charismatic founding leader who endured a devastating economic collapse following the end of the Soviet Union as well as similar if not greater antipathy from the surviving superpower. Among other personalist authoritarian regimes that survived severe crises are Syria under Hafiz and Bashir al-Assad, Haiti under François and Jean-Claude Duvalier, and Romania's Nikolae Ceauçescu, whose fall from power followed a major economic collapse in the context of the wider revolutionary developments sweeping Eastern Europe. What these examples demonstrate is that while deep economic crises may increase the probability of political instability and regime change, they are not necessarily insurmountable obstacles to the retention of power. In none of these cases did regime change coincide with or follow immediately upon the worst economic downturns.

This finding is confirmed by a more systematic crossnational analysis of the determinants of regime change by Noland (2004b). The so-called hazard models used in this study can be calibrated using national data to suggest the likelihood of regime change in any given country and year. According to the most plausible specification of these models, the probability of a North Korean collapse peaked in 1997–98 at around 10 percent and declined to around 5 percent in 2002. Those who predicted that North Korea would experience fundamental political change during the period since 1990 were not making such a bad bet: even in a wider sample of cases, the cumulative hazard rises well above 50 percent over the course of the decade.

By extending these models into the future and making some assumptions about future growth rates, we can estimate some broad, order-of-magnitude probabilities of future regime change; in all of them, the nature of the external environment is a crucial parameter. Under one scenario that might be labeled "cooperative engagement," the Six-Party process succeeds and the diplomatic tensions surrounding North Korea's nuclear program dissipate—at least for a time. North Korea receives higher levels of aid from South Korea, China, Europe, and perhaps even the United States as a result of a comprehensive settlement. Pyongyang normalizes diplomatic relations with Japan and begins to receive postcolonial claim settlements. North Korea joins the multilateral development banks and begins receiving aid from them as well. Under this less threatening environment, the leadership pushes forward with a reform process that, in conjunction with international assistance, permits growth to rebound to its 1999 peak of 6 percent. Under this scenario, the likelihood of regime change falls to less than 1 percent.

In the "neo-con's dream" scenario, the Six-Party Talks fail—or the five powers grow weary of North Korean gambits—and they decide to put the squeeze on the Kim Jŏng-il regime. Aid is cut off, trade declines, growth falls to its previous low of negative 6 percent, and the inexpertly enacted economic policy reforms result in an ongoing high rate of inflation. In the "neo-con's dream," the likelihood of regime change rises to about a one in seven probability. In an even more drastic scenario, which we will call "international embargo," the North Koreans test a nuclear weapon, export fissile material, or engage in some other armed provocation that results in an even more complete economic isolation. Trade and remittances are cut off completely, efforts to trade by sea are met with interdiction, and the country experiences even worse economic performance than was seen during the crisis of the mid-1990s. In these circumstances, the likelihood of regime change could rise to over 40 percent in the first year with a virtual certainty of collapse in the medium run.

These calculations should be taken with the appropriate grain of salt, but they suggest strongly that external economic pressure is not likely to lead to a change of regime anytime soon. The Kim dynasty has already survived the worst of the crisis, and the coordination problems we have highlighted preclude the economic restrictions that would substantially increase the likelihood of regime change. To the contrary: by carefully calibrating its behavior to avoid high-risk outcomes, the North Korean regime could face an international environment that is surprisingly conducive to survival.

So far, we have looked only at the correlation between economic performance and political change, with a focus on the prospects for regime change. But a more nuanced understanding requires a consideration of the mechanisms through which such change might operate and the offsetting political, institutional, and coercive resources the regime can bring to bear.

Haggard and Kaufman (1995:28–32) have suggested three routes through which economic crises weaken the hold of authoritarian leaders: by generating mass protest from below, by reducing support from key economic or business elites, and by generating splits within the coercive apparatus, which always plays a crucial role in the maintenance of power. Why didn't these mechanisms operate as they have in other settings?

With respect to protest from below, famine, recurrent food shortages, and large-scale un- and underemployment would seem a politically lethal mix. But the current regime can draw on two generations of unparalleled political indoctrination and a massive apparatus for internal social control. Accounts of anti-regime activity have surfaced periodically, but usually with the conclusion that they were dealt with swiftly and brutally.[13]

Equally important is the virtual absence of intermediate or civil society institutions that enjoy at least some independence from the state and might thus be capable of channeling discontent into effective political action. A variety of state-controlled associations exist (see KINU 2002:113–17 for an overview), but they are under very tight party control. There is no Solidarity trade union as in Poland. Nor do there exist alternative poles of moral authority such as the Catholic Church that are capable of legitimating dissent, as was the case in the uprising against the martial law regime in Poland and in the "People Power" movement against the dictatorship of Ferdinand Marcos in the Philippines.

An additional constraint on public action concerns information that might provide an outside metric on the society and serve to coalesce opposition. The degree of North Korea's isolation from the outside world has been unusual, although this appears to be changing (Lankov 2005b, 2006a). All televisions and radios are fixed to state channels and have to be modified to receive outside broadcasts.[14] Reading foreign publications or listening to foreign broadcasts—or tampering with TVs or radios for this purpose—is a crime. Leaving the country is also a crime, although that, too, has become an important leak in the dam of outside information flows. Trade with the outside world is increasing access to cultural products from abroad, such as South Korean music and videos.

In addition to these well-documented political and informational controls, it is important not to underestimate the capability of authoritarian regimes to maintain key bases of support even during periods of scarcity. Authoritarian regimes do not survive by coercion alone (Wintrobe 1998). At the top, the North Korean political elite appears relatively coherent and unified, or at least competing factions have been effectively held in check. Kim Jŏng-il's "military first" politics undoubtedly reflected an effort to sustain or shore up the support of the Korean People's Army. We have reports of mutiny within particular units over the last ten years or even more organized challenges within the military hierarchy.[15] But as with episodic social protest, these have been crushed, and we know of no credible evidence that suggests the likelihood of a high-level military challenge to Kim Jŏng-il's rule. Finally, there are no independent sources of economic power that might play a direct political role in challenging the regime, for example, by withholding investment or through capital flight. Despite the widespread distress that began in the 1990s, favored firms such as those linked to the military-industrial complex have been protected and enjoyed access to foreign exchange; indeed, their status has probably even risen under the "military first" politics.

Outside of the core political, military, and economic elite, there are other ways in which the government has moved to forestall opposition. In the absence of rural rebellion, the mobilization of urban publics constitutes the most important threat from below. In North Korea, Pyongyang accounts for perhaps a quarter of the nonrural population, excluding the military. Within the constraints of the economic collapse of the mid-1990s, the regime catered quite assiduously to the needs of its residents. An additional though unknown share of the non-Pyongyang urban population should probably be classified as similarly privileged. An emerging middle class of small-scale entrepreneurs and traders, including Korean Japanese and Korean Chinese, are the beneficiaries of recent marketization and hardly likely to lead the political charge.

Finally, it should be noted that the external environment not only is economically supportive but doesn't pose strong political challenges, either. North Korea's neighbors have not provided sanctuary to anti-Kim political forces that could provide a transnational lever for change. There is little or no evidence of anti-Kim political organizing among the refugees in the Chinese border region, despite growing evidence of political disaffection among them (Chang 2006), and there are certainly no marauding guerilla insurgencies on North Korea's borders. Not only is overt political activity in China limited, but to date there is little prospect for a hole in the fence that would prove fundamentally destabilizing, as occurred in 1989 when Hungary opened its borders and allowed East German refugees to escape to West Germany via Austria. The Chinese authorities have cooperated with North Korean security services to repatriate refugees and have steadfastly refused mounting international pressure to treat fleeing North Koreans as political refugees (Charny 2005). The development of overt political activity aimed at regime change in North Korea, or even a significant increase in refugees, would clearly meet a swift and unequivocal response from Beijing.

Not only has China forestalled a refugee-led destabilization, but South Korea has been increasingly cautious in this regard as well (Lankov 2006b). As the political utility of defectors has declined, as the social composition of defectors has shifted from the elite to more difficult to assimilate workers and farmers, and as the South Korean government has more aggressively pursued a strategy of engagement, Seoul has gradually moved to shut the door.

We are not suggesting that the political situation in North Korea is static. But the focus on collapse scenarios has deterred a more careful consideration of political evolution that falls short of regime change. Given that no communist regime has ever undergone an evolutionary transition to democratic rule, how might North Korea's distinctive brand of authoritarianism evolve?

One route that has been suggested in a number of accounts of "Kim Jŏng-il as reformer" is the transition to a kind of developmental state that bears some resemblance to other East Asian newly industrializing countries, such as Taiwan under the Kuomintang and South Korea under Pak Chŏng-hŭi, or, more logically, to the Chinese path.[16] The potential obstacles to such a course of action created by the dynastic nature of the North Korean regime and the division of the Korean peninsula should not be underestimated. Economic reform that blurs the ideological distinction between the two regimes or widens exposure to South Koreans risks regime delegitimization. Hence it is perhaps no surprise that the regime's initial reaction to the collapse of socialism was unrepentant and open hostility to economic reform, which it interpreted as a crucial—indeed fatal—misstep of Soviet revisionism (Buzo 1999:206–9).

But the initiation of the "military first" politics, which at first blush appeared to signal the ascendance of the most reactionary element of the polity, could allow a reinterpretation of *chuch'e* and significant departures from past practice (Frank 2003, 2005a; Noland 2004b). Current propaganda that emphasizes "military-first" politics to build a "powerful and prosperous country" out of the "barrel of a gun" oddly echoes the "wealthy nation and a strong army" slogan of Meiji-era Japan. Nationalism would be the crucial ideological glue, as it has long been. A skeptical military would be reassured about the reform process, although at the cost of some dilution of the integrity of the reform effort and continuing diversion of resources to the military-industrial complex (Eberstadt 2004; see Cheung 2001 on the Chinese case).

Such a path would not entail political reform in the sense of liberalization but would involve a certain rationalization of the state apparatus and economic decision-making. There is some evidence of such a process occurring as a result of the final consolidation of Kim Jŏng-il's formal political authority in 1998. In July of that year, the tenth SPA elections were held, resulting in a substantial increase in military representation (from 45 to 107 active duty military officers, out of a total of 687). Among a number of other political changes,[17] the new constitution gave the cabinet more responsibility and power to run the economy and the administration, including oversight of the local People's Committees. The economic bureaucracy was both purged and rationalized.

We certainly cannot rule out such a course of development, but we are skeptical. North Korea differs in important ways from the other East Asian developmental states, particularly in the size of the private sector at the onset of reforms and in the somewhat more open, if by no means democratic, political context.

Moreover, North Korea labors under the well-known weaknesses of personalist rule. Such systems suffer not only from the long-run problem of succession but from weak institutionalization, the absence of checks on the leader's discretion, the blurring of the lines between the public and the private, and the tremendous difficulty of making credible commitments to private actors. For example, the apparent rationalization of the state apparatus in the 1998 constitution is obviated by the increasing fusion between key officials in the government and party and higher military echelons and the ability of Kim Jŏng-il to appoint all key economic actors and to override technocratic decision making. Despite discussions of distinct hard-line and reform factions within the government, there is little evidence of real delegation of decision-making power, and in any case the lines of accountability all end in the same place.

The assumption that the beneficiaries of reform to date are private also mischaracterizes the North Korean system and the nature of gradual reforms in a communist context more generally.[18] Partial reforms in communist systems can be highly distorting, favoring small groups of government-connected actors— party cadres, government officials, military officers, and their families—that subsequently become opponents of further reform. The political correlate of such partial reforms is a sort of crony-socialist state characterized by the granting of market opportunities to favored groups, ongoing extortion, and distinct limits on the emergence of a more independent private sector. Far from foreshadowing political reform, such a system requires even more political controls in order to enforce privilege and deter opposition from the economically disenfranchised (Pei 2006).

The fact that Kim Jŏng-il has relied so openly on the military is a particular source of concern. On the one hand, a number of pronouncements suggest that Kim Jŏng-il sees the military-industrial complex as a leading sector for the economy's growth, either through the production and export of weapons or through the involvement of the military or military-linked firms in related sectors, from construction to telecommunications. On the other hand, the favored position of the military suggests that it might end up following the course of the People's Liberation Army in China by moving into altogether unrelated businesses as a payoff for declining fiscal commitments. Tai Ming Cheung (2001) has provided the most detailed analysis of this path in China and shows how military enterprises were involved in corruption, smuggling, and profiteering. Yet in China the party was ultimately able to orchestrate a divestiture of at least some of the military's businesses in the context of a comprehensive program of demilitarization, a prospect that may prove harder in the DPRK, given the relative weakness of the Korean Workers' Party.

An alternative and somewhat more hopeful scenario lies in the de facto decentralization of the political system. To be sure, the central government owns and controls the major enterprises in the country, and there is to date little sign of the sort of formal devolution of policy to provincial and lower-level governments. But as in China and Vietnam, government officials, party cadres, firm managers, and even military officers at lower levels in the chain of command may prove to be agents of change. Attuned to both local needs and profit opportunities, these officials would represent the political-cum-economic forces that have gained from recent marketization and could become a constituency for such activities. Even though the elections for the SPA and local People's Committees are not competitive, it is possible that officials more responsive to local needs have entered the political system through this route. Minxin Pei (2006) makes the argument that these actors are subject to the same incentives as those at the center and could become a force for blocking further reforms and institutionalizing local protection and rent seeking. But at the current juncture these forces are more likely to provide the political foundation for the sort of competitive liberalization and reform from below that played some role in both the Chinese (Montinola, Qian, and Weingast 1995) and Vietnamese reforms.

To summarize, the debate about political change in North Korea has focused for too long on the issue of collapse, ignoring political sources of resilience and failing to consider alternative paths of change within the existing system. It is again important to restate that neither of the scenarios we have sketched here is particularly hopeful with respect to the future evolution of the political system. The "modernization from above" model is associated with a high level of central control. Nor is the more decentralized path we have sketched necessarily conducive to broader political reform. A discouraging feature of recent Chinese political history is that greater economic freedoms have not been associated with greater political freedom, competitiveness, or even the strengthening of civil and political liberties. If there is a relationship between economic growth and democratization, China is a regrettable reminder that such a relationship operates only over the long run.

The International Dimension I: The Dilemmas of Humanitarian Assistance Revisited

What obligations does the international community have to the people of North Korea?[19] The right to food is enshrined most clearly in the Universal

Declaration of Human Rights and article 11 of the International Covenant on Economic, Social and Cultural Rights (ICESCR), to which North Korea has been a party since December 1981. The nature of governments' obligations under the ICESCR has subsequently been clarified through a wide-ranging consultative process, most specifically by the Committee on Economic, Social and Cultural Rights in its General Comment 12 of 1999 (United Nations 1999). The ICESCR does recognize that the right to adequate food can only be realized progressively, but General Comment 12 is clear that states have the obligation to "respect, protect, and fulfill" this right (paragraph 15). Paragraph 6 of the comment is quite explicit on this point: "States have a core obligation to take the necessary action to mitigate and alleviate hunger as provided for in paragraph two of article 11, even in times of natural or other disasters."

These commitments recognize that governments cannot necessarily meet this obligation on their own. The ICESCR and its subsequent interpretation therefore include both an obligation to facilitate (General Comment 12, paragraph 15) and corresponding duties on the part of the international community to assist governments in distress or chronic need (ICESCR Article 11; General Comment 12 paragraph 36).

As we discussed in chapters 4 and 5, the humanitarian response was not as swift as it might have been, held hostage at various points by political calculations. But it did ultimately prove generous. In the decade following the floods of 1995, the international community provided North Korea with over $1.5 billion in food aid alone.

Yet as we also have shown, the North Korean government consistently sought to frustrate transparent, effective humanitarian relief. It is likely that aid is not proffered in a nondiscriminatory manner. Diversion is almost certainly occurring on a large scale, enough food to feed between 3 to 10 percent or more of the North Korean populace. Some of this aid is almost surely consumed by politically connected groups, including the military.[20] The diversion that goes to the market has some positive effects but is also contributing to the creation of a privileged class of state-sector entrepreneurs and their allies and an increasingly stratified society, with a sharp division between those with access to foreign exchange and food and those without.

A crucial first question is whether the international community—viewed as a whole—should provide aid to North Korea at all. A variety of critics—not only in the United States but in Europe and South Korea as well—have argued that aid to North Korea serves to prolong the life of the existing regime (North Korea Advisory Group 1999; Terry 2001; and C. Kang 2005). Some have drawn the conclusion that the goals of policy reform or even regime change would be advanced by coordinated action to cut North Korea off from the international economy and even from external supplies of food (C. Kang 2005).

We agree wholeheartedly that a reformist government or, better still, a peaceful change of regime would be highly desirable. We have also suggested that a coordinated strategy of cutting North Korea off from international assistance would increase the probability of regime change. But there are a number of problems in jumping from the benefits of regime change to a policy of reducing humanitarian assistance. The North Korean government has shown repeatedly its willingness to impose extreme deprivation on its people. The probability that coordinated, wholesale reductions in food aid will lead to improved conditions, policy reform, or regime change remains both uncertain and well below 100 percent.

Moreover, there is little evidence that the coordination required to have the intended (if uncertain) effect is possible given the competing political interests of the donor countries. To the contrary, reductions in multilateral assistance have been matched by increases in bilateral aid from South Korea and China. Thus reductions in aid from any one party must be weighed both against the unlikelihood that such reductions will have their intended effect and the loss of leverage that comes from disengagement.

It is also important to emphasize that the violation of humanitarian norms, the flaws in the aid program, and the problem of diversion do not mean that aid is without positive effects. Aid has had beneficial effects both directly, by increasing overall supply and moderating prices, and indirectly, by encouraging commercialization and the growth of markets.[21] The highest estimates of diversion that we have seen—fully 50 percent going to less-deserving groups or the military—still leave 50 percent of food going to meet the needs of vulnerable groups. Markets have clearly been developing and are likely to continue to do so despite the retrenchment of late 2005.

Most important, the argument for cutting food aid rests on a highly dubious utilitarian logic: that it is morally acceptable to sacrifice the innocent today in the uncertain probability that lives will be saved or improved at some future point. This type of argument flies directly in the face of the fundamental rights that the international community is trying to uphold. We applaud those with the courage to make such a sacrifice for themselves. But we are much less comfortable with the notion that the outside community should make that decision for vulnerable North Korean citizens. It is important to point out that those NGOs who did pull out of North Korea did so in the context of continued aid through the World Food Programme, bilateral donors, and other NGOs. The calculus is very different when considering whether total food aid should be reduced or cut altogether.

If the arguments in favor of continued assistance seem clear, we must simultaneously be clear-headed about the nature of the bargains that have been struck and continually seek to advance the underlying purposes of humanitarian assistance. The donor community must be a voice of conscience for those deprived of the most fundamental right to food. The WFP and its associated donors must:

- continue to highlight government practices that impede the delivery of food to vulnerable groups, including diversion;
- continue to uphold humanitarian principles, including the empowerment of beneficiaries; and
- continue to press for effective assessment that would provide information not only to outsiders but to the North Korean government itself on the nature of the health and nutritional problems faced by its citizens.

Failure to uphold the basic norms of humanitarian assistance risks turning North Korean exceptionalism into the North Korean precedent in dealing with complex humanitarian emergencies.

Although we oppose cutting off food aid, we agree with the critics that the international community must make a concerted and coordinated effort to wean North Korea off humanitarian assistance. This would involve outlining and negotiating a path of reduced aid—subject to reversal in the face of natural disasters—that would point toward self-sufficiency, defined as the capacity to import adequate external supplies on commercial terms. One of our most disturbing findings is the evidence that North Korea seems unwilling to spend scarce foreign exchange on food. We cannot allow this practice to continue and must voice our intent to shift the burden of financing North Korea's food deficit from the international humanitarian community—which is facing pressing needs elsewhere—onto the North Koreans themselves.

A component of this strategy of reducing humanitarian assistance is to couple it with the promise of greater access to development assistance. Such a shift in emphasis would be facilitated by getting North Korea into international organizations such as the World Bank, the International Monetary Fund, and the Asian Development Bank that are capable of providing comprehensive technical assistance in a relatively depoliticized way. As of 2006, membership in the international financial institutions remained hostage to ongoing negotiations on the country's nuclear program. Yet we strongly suspect that North Korea's understanding of participation in these organizations is flawed, and a similar set of ongoing negotiations will be required to make such aid effective. North

Korea's unhappiness with humanitarian assistance has rested to some extent on the invasive nature of external monitoring. But the international financial institutions attach an equal, if not even more onerous, set of conditions to the development lending they do. These range from policy reform, to the monitoring of particular projects, to demands for transparency and accountability in the use of funds and the collection and publication of meaningful data. North Korea will have to recognize and adhere to the norms embodied in these institutions if it expects to avail itself of their benefits.

In thinking through a coherent aid strategy toward a country such as North Korea, the coordination problems cannot be ignored. We have shown that two countries, China and South Korea, have provided concessional sales or grants of food to North Korea largely outside the ambit of the WFP. We have no direct evidence of China's contracts with North Korea but have seen no public evidence that it has conditioned aid either on overall policy reform or more particular principles of programmatic design, implementation, or monitoring. In the case of South Korea, aid has been provided on a concessional basis and, by the admission of the government, with only the most minimal effort to monitor. There are numerous disadvantages in this arrangement. If China and South Korea remain suppliers of last resort, the North Korean government gains the opportunity to weaken the multilateral regime that is in place and to challenge the WFP's most basic mandate; in mid-2005, that is exactly what Pyongyang did by asking the WFP to leave.

In this respect, the policy choices of the South Korean government proved the most problematic. Large, relatively open-ended aid commitments—totaling as much as 90 percent of total WFP needs—had the unintended consequence of undercutting the WFP's attempts to uphold the norms embodied in international agreements to which South Korea is a party. More broadly, we are dubious that a strategy of unconditional economic assistance will have the positive effects, either political or economic, that are postulated. The strategy of engagement was an advance over its predecessors, and we recognize the special circumstances that bind the South and North Korean people together. The open-ended and large-scale delivery of food aid, however, has not advanced the cause of helping North Korea to become more self-reliant in the long run and has even undermined the modest progress in providing more transparent and effective humanitarian relief in the short run. We have therefore argued (Haggard and Noland 2005)—not without controversy— that China and South Korea should channel a greater portion of their concessional food assistance through the WFP. These countries' experience and voice would be of invaluable assistance to WFP operations and would facilitate the coordinated approach needed to reduce North Korea's dependence on humanitarian assistance.[22]

We are fully aware of the ambiguities in the strategy of conditional engagement that we have outlined here, including the fact that North Korea may be unwilling to enter into such a bargain and could call our bluff by once again using its population as a hostage. Strategy, however, does not only involve deciding whether to provide aid or not but continually being on guard for opportunities to press the humanitarian and human rights cause and for gains at the margin.

Yet the issues in this case do not center on food alone. As in most humanitarian disasters, they encompass a wider set of political issues, and on the Korean peninsula, these issues are particularly complex.

The International Dimension II: The Broader Geopolitical Equation

Throughout our discussion—of the economic reforms, of political change, of the humanitarian effort—we have continually been forced back to the plane of high politics: the political and military issues associated with the continuing division of the Korean people into two separate states. Given the structural attributes of the North Korean economy, opening to greater international trade and investment will be central to North Korea's economic revitalization. But no reform initiative will achieve its full potential as long as the country remains a pariah state.

North Korea's external economic relations have always been highly politicized. During the Cold War, it received preferential treatment from the Eastern bloc, while its relations with Western countries were problematic at best (Noland 2000). Following the outbreak of the Korean War in 1950, the United States imposed comprehensive sanctions under the World War I–era Trading with the Enemy Act. These sanctions were partially eased in 1995 as part of the Agreed Framework, and a bilateral agreement on long-range missile testing resulted in the removal of most of the remaining trade restrictions in June 2000.[23] But a few potentially significant ones remain.[24]

Over the course of the second Bush administration—and even before—the United States has also intensified its efforts to squeeze North Korea by depriving it of revenues obtained through illicit activities such as counterfeiting, smuggling, and drug trafficking. Although no actions had been taken under it through the end of 2005, the Proliferation Security Initiative (PSI) threatened coordinated action to interdict shipments of weapons of mass destruction

(WMD) or materials and equipment related to WMD production (Winner 2005). South Korea and China do not participate in the PSI but have cooperated in multilateral efforts to stop illegal activity such as drug trafficking. Given North Korea's limited trade relations, financial sanctions are likely to have more substantial effect. Japan has strengthened its ability to impede remittances to North Korea. And in 2005, the United States threatened an important action against a Macau-based bank, Banco Delta Asia, that had wide-ranging implications for the entirety of North Korea's offshore financial relationships (United States Department of Treasury 2006).

Beyond these measures, North Korea is among the few countries that do not enjoy normal trade relations (NTR) status with the United States; as a result, North Korean exports are subject to the so-called "column two" tariff rates that have their origins in the infamous Smoot-Hawley Tariff Act of 1930. These tariffs tend to be the highest on labor-intensive products such as garments, in which North Korea would presumably specialize. Some countries, notably China, have successfully exported to the United States despite being subject to the higher column two tariffs (though even China eventually gained NTR status, initially on a year-to-year basis).[25] Nevertheless, the effective inability to export to the United States from North Korea represents an important disincentive to firms of any nation contemplating investment in North Korea. Indeed, the issue of whether to treat products made in the Kaesŏng Industrial Complex as "made in South Korea"—and hence eligible for duty-free treatment—has come up in discussions about a U.S.-South Korea free trade agreement, with South Korea pushing for liberal rules of origin and the United States signaling its resistance.

At present, only the terrorism list is a legally—as distinct from politically—binding constraint on U.S. diplomacy.[26] North Korea remains on the U.S. government list of state sponsors of terror, although it is not known to have committed any terrorist acts since 1987 and has subsequently made public statements condemning terrorism and even signed a number of antiterrorism conventions. The willingness of the United States to support North Korea's membership in the multilateral development banks is explicitly tied to third-party allies concerns in this regard. South Korea has indicated that it holds no objection to the removal of North Korea from the terrorism list, but the Japanese abductee issue as well as that of the few aging Japanese Red Army hijackers North Korea continues to harbor are specifically mentioned in the U.S. State Department report on terrorism.[27] Until these issues are settled it is doubtful that the United States will remove North Korea from the list of terror sponsors.

Once they are resolved, both the United States and Japan might drop their opposition to North Korean participation in the international financial institutions. Getting North Korea into the international financial institutions would permit those organizations immediately to begin providing technical assistance to be eventually followed by lending. Furthermore, such a package deal would likely include normalization of relations between Japan and the DPRK and, with it, significant monetary compensation from Japan for postcolonial claims.

In sum, one can imagine a diplomatic breakthrough leading to bilateral financial support and integration into the international financial institutions and greater willingness on the part of private sector firms to invest as sanctions on trade and investment were removed. By raising the payoffs to economic opening, these changes would also presumably cause Pyongyang to begin viewing reform more favorably. But until this happens, North Korea's integration into the world economy will remain somewhat irregular and partial, heavily oriented toward South Korea and China, where these political concerns inhibit the process of economic integration less than they do elsewhere.

So what is the likelihood of North Korea resolving its diplomatic differences with the United States and Japan? It is important to begin by stating the obvious: U.S. policy toward North Korea has been driven overwhelmingly by security considerations on the peninsula and since the late 1980s, if not before, by concern over Pyongyang's nuclear ambitions in particular. The United States has vacillated between strategies of containment and engagement for pursuing these objectives. These two policy orientations are not mutually exclusive as Cha and Kang (2003) show in their thoughtful debate on the issue. But they do rest on contending views of the stability of the military balance on the peninsula and the logic of North Korean behavior.

Those drawn to policies of containment believe that North Korea is weak but dangerous and that the stability of the peninsula cannot be taken for granted (Cha and Kang 2003).[28] More important for our purposes, hawks argue that economic and other concessions tend to strengthen the regime and increase rather than mitigate its tendency to engage in threatening behavior. The result is a form of blackmail in which North Korea effectively demands payment to abide by its international commitments (Downs 1999; Cha and Kang 2003:72–75). Although dubious about the effects of positive incentives (carrots), hawks are not averse to using negative sanctions (sticks) and even threatening the use of force. The reasons appear to rest on the assumption that negative sanctions are more likely to signal resolve and have the intended effect, while material inducements can be misused to support undesirable (read "military") initiatives.

Moreover, a policy of sanctions has the additional benefit of imposing costs on the regime and increasing the probability that it might fall.

Advocates of engagement, by contrast, argue that the military balance is fundamentally stable—that deterrence works—and that there are in any case no politically feasible military options for solving the nuclear issue.[29] When stability has been threatened, it was not only North Korean behavior that was to blame but threats from the United States that left North Korea uncertain about the credibility of American commitments and even about its basic intentions.[30] The core to a settlement therefore resides in maintaining a firm deterrent posture while also providing security guarantees to North Korea that alleviate its insecurity.

Economic integration plays a key role in broader political strategies of engagement. Economic incentives not only build trust and signal peaceful intent but also have direct effects on both the economy and polity that may mute the propensity for conflict and foster change. In particular, increasing economic ties will create vested interests in trade, investment, continuing economic reform, and greater economic openness. Increasing openness is also assumed to have a corrosive effect on the regime's political control by introducing outside sources of information and cultural influence and thus strengthening the independence of civil society. Over the long run, openness fosters growth, which in turn provides the political as well as economic foundation for political liberalization and democratization.

As can be seen, although these approaches hinge largely on contending models of North Korea's military and bargaining behavior, they also rest on important political economy assumptions as well. We have considered these issues with respect to the aid relationship, but they are worth reviewing in the context of the broader strategic context of the period we have considered in this book: the settlement of the first nuclear crisis in 1994, the shift in policy between the Clinton and Bush administrations, and the onset of the second nuclear crisis in October 2002.

Following the first nuclear crisis and the signing of the Agreed Framework, further progress on bilateral relations between North Korea and the United States stalled. In the immediate postframework period, North Korea was distracted by the political transition following the death of Kim Il-sŏng and the extreme economic conditions that characterized the peak famine period. Yet once these immediate challenges had passed, Pyongyang dragged its feet on negotiations that would have institutionalized a final settlement to the Korean War (the so-called Four-Party Talks, 1997–99) while engaging in a string of threatening actions, most notably the failed attempt to place a small satellite into orbit in August 1998. Pakistani intelligence uncovered through the A. Q. Khan network suggests that it was almost certainly during this period—before the election of George W. Bush—that North Korea also moved to acquire technology and equipment for enriching uranium, in direct violation of a number of its international commitments.

From Pyongyang's perspective, however, the Clinton administration had effectively reneged on key commitments under the Agreed Framework as well. Under the deal, the North agreed to freeze and eventually to dismantle its nuclear program in return for two light-water reactors (LWRs), an interim supply of heavy fuel oil, some relaxation of sanctions, and, above all, progress in normalizing political relations with the United States. The Korean Peninsula Energy Development Organization (KEDO) orchestrated the early work on the LWR construction and the United States generally met its commitments with respect to heavy oil shipments and the partial easing of sanctions. But the Clinton administration and the Agreed Framework came under increasing pressure from Republican hawks in Congress after the midterm elections of November 1994. Distracted by other issues, the administration saw little gain from elevating North Korea to a priority issue; from North Korea's perspective, the United States had reneged on the key quid pro quo of normalization.

The missile launch of 1998 triggered a wide-ranging review of policy conducted by former defense secretary William Perry that restated the engagement logic: a settlement of the nuclear and missile issues in return for security guarantees and at least the promise of economic benefits associated with normalization. The so-called Perry Report and the June 2000 North-South summit provided the basis for a flurry of diplomatic activity at the very end of the Clinton administration, including a visit to Pyongyang by Secretary of State Madeleine Albright, and removal of most of the remaining economic sanctions applied administratively under the International Economic Emergency Powers Act, the successor to the Trading with the Enemy Act. But time had run out, and the outgoing administration did not succeed in finalizing a deal to end North Korea's ballistic missile program.

The Bush administration quickly backed away from the Perry approach by initiating an internal review of policy that signaled a more demanding interpretation of the framework and the inclusion of altogether new issues, including conventional force deployments. With the coming of 9/11, everything changed: in rapid succession, North Korea was dubbed a member of the Axis of Evil, and the United States outlined a new counterproliferation strategy that justified preemption and showed that these were not empty threats by confronting Saddam Hussein over weapons of mass destruction and ultimately going to war.

The American revelation that it had evidence of North Korea's uranium enrichment program in October 2002 signaled the onset of the second nuclear crisis. As North Korea quickly escalated the crisis through a series of calculated steps, the United States was in no mood to negotiate, and certainly not directly with North Korea. Nor was it in the mood to reiterate the concessions it had previously made—including a presidential statement under the Clinton administration that the United States did not harbor hostile intent—let alone offer new ones.

While escalating the crisis, the North Koreans were also consistent in stating their demands for reaching an agreement, even if they were vague on the details. In return for addressing the nuclear question, they sought provision of a negative security guarantee from the United States, an end to Washington's hostile policy and a normalization of relations, and the promise not to interfere in North Korea's economic relations, interpreted to mean either with third countries or with the international financial institutions.

China brokered a face-saving solution for both the United States and North Korea by hosting three-party talks that gelled into the Six-Party Talks, also including South Korea, Japan, and Russia. The United States did not table a meaningful proposal through this venue until June 2004. The North Koreans failed to respond, content to proceed with their nuclear activities while hoping that the November 2004 U.S. elections would yield a more pliant set of interlocutors. When the American electorate dashed this hope, the North Koreans suspended their participation in the talks and announced for the first time in February 2005 that they possessed nuclear weapons. A combination of considerable multilateral pressure and substantial economic inducements from South Korea brought the North Koreans back to the negotiating table in July 2005 and produced a statement of principles in September that contained many of the earlier quid pro quos: a promise to dismantle the nuclear program in return for security guarantees, future steps toward normalization, and provision for substantial economic assistance from South Korea and probably China as well. But as of this writing in mid-2006, negotiations remain stalled with no breakthrough in sight.

What does this brief history tell us about the prospects for strategies of containment and engagement? In the absence of credible military options, the strategy of containment would seem to face many of the same coordination problems we have highlighted with respect to humanitarian assistance. The Bush administration clearly saw the Six-Party Talks as a mechanism through which the United States could bring coordinated pressure to bear on North Korea. But China and South Korea bore the immediate risks of North Korean isolation or collapse and had their own strategic and domestic political reasons to be skeptical of U.S. intentions. For those two pivotal countries, the Six-Party Talks were less a mechanism for bringing pressure to bear on North Korea than they were a means of bringing pressure to bear on the United States to be more forthcoming.

Beijing has repeatedly stated its belief that the Korean peninsula should be denuclearized and has quite possibly exerted pressure on North Korea that is not visible from the outside. Yet it has also consistently opposed the strategy of isolating North Korea politically, rejected economic sanctions as counterproductive, and called on the United States to be more cooperative in the negotiations.

Ironically, the problems the United States faces on the South Korean front are arguably more difficult and intractable than the ones they have with China. A growing majority of South Koreans, accustomed to living for decades in the shadow of the North's forward-deployed artillery, do not regard the North as a serious threat. Growing prosperity and confidence in the South have transformed fear and loathing of the North into pity and forbearance.

Deep generational and political changes in South Korea have driven this fundamental shift. In a 2004 public opinion poll, for example, more South Koreans identified the United States than North Korea as the principal threat to peace. The younger the respondent and the higher the level of educational attainment, the wider the gap. Fifty-eight percent of respondents in their twenties and 52 percent of students and white-collar workers polled singled out the United States as the primary threat to peace (*Chosun Ilbo* 2004). Another survey found that more than three-quarters of South Korean students polled actually supported North Korea's development of nuclear weapons (Bong 2003). These changes were both tapped and led by the No government, which ran on a subtly anti-American platform and whose strategy toward North Korea extended the underlying logic of Kim Dae-jung's Sunshine Policy. In one controversial speech in early 2005—a critical moment in the effort to restart the negotiations—President No even argued that South Korea's foreign policy rested on playing a balancing role in the region, presumably between the United States— its nominal alliance partner—and both North Korea and China!

If the case for containment, isolation, and regime change seems weak, it does not necessarily imply that the logic of engagement is airtight. It is true that the 2005 statement of principles seems to embody a clear quid pro quo. As of this writing, it remains a distinct possibility that Pyongyang is playing for time and hoping that the divisions among the five parties over strategy—in effect, the political correlate of the coordination problems we have discussed with respect to humanitarian assistance—will allow it to have the best of both worlds: maintaining its nuclear program while blaming the United States for the necessity of doing so. Indeed, the reticence and outright paranoia evinced by the regime in a decade of dealing with humanitarian aid workers does not augur well for the establishment of a credible verification and monitoring system for its nuclear weapons programs.

That said, the proponents of some form of engagement would seem to be vindicated. The circumstances leading up to the Agreed Framework itself are ambiguous: U.S. signals of a willingness to use force arguably played a role in North Korea's thinking, but the actual deal was made possible by assurances carried to Pyongyang by President Carter and a number of material concessions (the LWRs, commitment to normalize, and at least suggestions of other economic benefits). Republican pressure on the Clinton administration did not appear to have any affect on moving North Korea toward cooperation and did not rest on a coherent alternative strategy. Neither the early years of the Bush administration nor its early management of the 2002 crisis resulted in any progress, either. Financial sanctions may prove more effective than trade sanctions, but only in the context of other economic concessions such as those provided by South Korea: generous food and fertilizer aid, promises of massive electricity assistance, and the initiation of a number of new cooperative ventures.

If a very explicit economic quid pro quo facilitated an agreement to continue to negotiate, some of the softer and longer-term elements of the engagement approach are much more difficult to demonstrate. Moreover, the dilemmas we noted with respect to humanitarian engagement are replicated in the broader political sphere.

The engagement strategy rests on the presumption that the North Korean government places a heavy weight on economic incentives and is sensitive to the costs of both forgone benefits and sanctions. But this reading of North Korean preferences is by no means obvious. It is not clear how much pressure the North Korean government faces to undertake a coherent, wide-ranging economic reform. To the contrary, it is doubtful that this reform will resemble anything like what Western pundits mean by the term. And it is even more dubious that they would lead either directly or indirectly to a relaxation of political controls; indeed, the opposite appears to be the case.

If a strategy of engagement is to have positive effects on North Korea's military and political behavior, those benefits will ironically come in the first instance from North Korea's integration with China and socialization into not a Western but a Chinese model of doing business. U.S., Japanese, and European economic relations with North Korea remain relatively limited, dominated in both the U.S. and European cases by humanitarian assistance and in all three cases constrained by ongoing political tensions over the nuclear question.

South Korea's economic relations with North Korea have grown rapidly over the last decade and over the long run will undoubtedly play an important role in North Korea's economic transformation. But they, too, remain constrained in important ways that limit their transformative effect. North Korea has been more than willing to accept South Korean aid, but investment and trade have been confined to relatively small enclaves such as the Kaesŏng Industrial Complex and the Mount Kŭmgang tourism project. Despite its apparent welcome of South Korean largesse and the limited opening of rail and road links, North Korea is unlikely to allow South Korean business unfettered access to the country. A number of South Korean NGOs have been allowed to operate and are undoubtedly having an effect by flying under the radar and building local alliances. But it is overly optimistic to think that the North Korean authorities will allow these relationships to have serious political consequences.

It is also important to underline crucial silences that have accompanied the engagement approach. North Korea has managed to focus the discussion entirely on the issue of nuclear weapons. But the international community has a range of other interests with respect to North Korea as well: the humanitarian disaster of the last decade, the question of human rights, the growing issue of refugees. The terms of engagement cannot be circumscribed to nuclear weapons and high politics, particularly if we believe that there are close links between political and military behavior and the fundamental nature of the regime.

In short, the same sort of dilemma operates in the political as in the humanitarian sphere. The North Korean regime uses the issue of nuclear weapons to protect itself but also as a bargaining tool to extract gains from engagement. As tempting as it may seem to cut off assistance or to walk away with the hope that an intensification of misery could provoke collapse of the regime, in the end it is unpersuasive to bet increased suffering now against possible gains in an uncertain future. As a consequence, one is forced back into trying to make incremental improvements in the status quo.

We have outlined a variety of policy changes and technical fixes that could contribute to the resolution of food insecurity issues in North Korea—everything from changing the product composition of humanitarian aid, to extending incentive reforms in agriculture, to getting North Korea into the international financial institutions. But these actions, however positive and desirable, ultimately rest on more basic changes. Kang Ch'ŏl-hwan, a North Korean defector and author of a widely read memoir of life in the country's prison system (Kang 2002), recently offered the following metaphor. "If you hold a cow by its hoof, it will starve; if you allow it to roam, it will find grass and eat." This metaphor holds more truth than may appear on its surface. Granting citizens secure property rights and the freedom to trade and engage in private production would have wide-ranging effects, enabling the people of North Korea to do what is best for themselves. This alone is no guarantee of a North Korea permanently free from hunger—there is a role for policy in many dimensions—but the relaxation of social control and establishment of the fundamental rights of a free and open society are a necessary prerequisite.

Appendixes

Illicit Activities

We argued in chapter 2 that the decline in Soviet-Russian and Chinese support and the collapse of the industrial economy provided the government with strong incentives to earn foreign exchange. The government, however, proved largely unwilling or unable to undertake the reforms necessary to do this: expanding exports, encouraging foreign investment, and reestablishing access to international capital markets.

In one important respect, however, this assessment is misleading as the 1990s saw a dramatic expansion of a variety of illicit activities and arms sales. These activities take us beyond the core concerns of this book, but given their sheer scope and magnitude and their growing significance for U.S. policy toward the country after 2002, it is worth providing an overview and some estimates of their size.[1] Moreover, a brief catalog of North Korea's illicit trade provides fascinating insights into the changing nature of the regime. The bulk of these illicit activities appear to have been undertaken at the direction or with the knowledge of the top leadership, although more recent episodes suggest that at least some of these activities are more decentralized in nature and involve complex transnational relations among various state entities and criminal networks of various sorts (Chestnut 2005).

For some time—probably since the inception of the regime—North Korea's diplomatic corps has been under pressure to support the maintenance of foreign missions by earning foreign exchange. One of the simplest ways of doing so is to exploit diplomatic immunity, including most importantly the international conventions that protect the secrecy and integrity of the diplomatic pouch. Erik Cornell (2002:61–62) the first Swedish consular officer in Pyongyang, outlines one of the early cases of such activity in the mid-1970s. Police in all four Scandinavian countries found that North Korean embassies were using their diplomatic tax exemption to purchase alcohol and cigarettes in large quantities and then reselling them on the black market. Far more lucrative, however, was trafficking in drugs. Chestnut (2005:42) documents how total drug seizures went up sharply after 1996, the peak of the famine. She also shows how the personnel involved in these seizures came to include officials outside the foreign ministry (economic and intelligence officials) or individuals without any clear official designation (employees of trading companies), as well as members of Asian criminal organizations that were acting as partners or intermediaries (see also Noland 2000 and Paddock and Demick 2003). From the mid-1990s, North Korea also began to produce drugs for export, beginning with opium but diversifying into methamphetamine following the floods of 1995 (Perl 2005:7–10; Chestnut 2005:52–61). Although drugs almost certainly dominate North Korea's smuggling activity, there is evidence—in the form of diplomatic expulsions—for trade in other sanctioned items, including so-called conflict diamonds from civil war zones in Africa, rhino horns, and ivory (Noland 2000; Chestnut 2005; Asher 2005).

A second major form of illicit activity is counterfeiting. U.S. government officials had long suspected North Korea to be the origin of the so-called supernotes, very high quality counterfeits of $100 bills, that began to appear in 1989. But not until 2005 did a series of criminal cases and Treasury enforcement actions against a Macau bank shed more light on the issue (Meyer and Demick 2005; Perl 2006); Chestnut's study (2005:chap. 4) adds compelling evidence from defector interviews.

As with drug smuggling, the sale of supernotes involves a complex "wholesale" and "retail" distribution chain. A 2005 indictment targeted the leader of the official IRA, Sean Garland, for distributing $28 million in notes in Russia, Belarus, Poland, Denmark, the Czech Republic, and Germany, and two sting operations in the United States resulted in indictments citing $6 million in counterfeit currency. More interesting, however, was a Treasury Department finding that Banco Delta Asia in Macau was a financial institution of primary money laundering concern under the 2001 Patriot Act. Although the bank denied wrongdoing, Macau's lack of crossborder currency reporting requirements had clearly made it a center for North Korea's offshore financial activities. In the wake of the finding and pressure from correspondent banks in Japan, Korea, and Europe, Banco Delta Asia severed connections with roughly forty North Korean individuals or businesses—many believed to be military- or party-related—replaced several managers, and allowed a panel named by Macau's government to administer its operations (Demick and Meyer 2005). Nor has counterfeiting been limited to currency; evidence also exists of North Korean involvement in counterfeiting of cigarettes and pharmaceuticals (Chestnut 2005:93–97).

Much of North Korea's weapons trade is arguably not illicit. Although North Korea continues to sell missiles and base technologies for them that fall under the Missile Technology Control Regime (MTCR), North Korea is not a party to that agreement. The complications arising from this fact were made painfully evident in December 2002, when a Cambodian-registered North Korean ship bound for Yemen was intercepted by Spain in the Arabian Sea carrying fifteen Scud missiles, warheads, and propellant. Although it was later revealed that the missiles were delivered to Libya, at the time the United States chose to release the cargo because Yemen had allied itself with the U.S. in the post-9/11 period. Other customers of North Korean missiles or missile technology include Pakistan, Iran, Egypt, Syria, and Vietnam (Noland 2000, Lintner 2005).

Calculating the size of the illicit sector is even more risky than the other estimates we undertake in this book. For a number of reasons, such trade is likely to be more volatile than other economic activities, and thus an estimate for any given year can be highly misleading. Seizures and arrests that appear to show very large amounts of trade—such as Japanese seizures in 1998–2002 of methamphetamines with a wholesale value of $75 million or the Garland indictment—can be followed by the breakup of networks and a sharp falloff in trade. Large military sales are "lumpy" as well. Successful exports to a particular country do not necessarily generate repeat business. A statement by a U.S. official in 2002 put sales in 2001 alone at $560 million. But this statement, if correct, probably reflects the high point of such sales, as the customer base has subsequently shrunk (Ward 2002, Lintner 2005).

Rather than building up estimates from evidence on seizures or particular military sales, it is probably more sensible to work down from the external accounts of the country. Asher (2005), for example, walks through such an exercise and comes to the conclusion that total criminal activity and military sales in 2003 could have accounted for as much as 35–40 percent of all DPRK trade and an even higher share of total cash earnings. This number is broadly in line with Noland's (2000) earlier estimate of about one-third of all exports, which we use in chapter 2.

The Scope of the Humanitarian Aid Effort

APPENDIX 2.1. Total Humanitarian Assistance, by Sector (millions of US$)

	Food	Agriculture	Health	Water and Sanitation	Education	Coordination and Support Services	Other	TOTAL
1996/7	36.16	4.73	4.02	0.00	0.00	0.06	5.38	50.35
1997/8	243.35	8.83	27.09	1.49	0.00	0.23	11.47	292.46
1998	312.14	7.09	6.35	3.55	0.62	0.30	5.04	335.09
1999	180.82	41.62	10.26	0.27	0.00	0.84	1.99	235.80
2000	150.21	59.03	7.37	0.23	n.a.	1.01	6.36	224.22
2001	270.75	55.52	20.19	0.31	0.18	1.33	29.28	377.59
2002	213.25	70.87	14.68	5.18	0.32	0.84	55.66	360.83
2003	124.02	5.31	24.44	0.95	0.93	0.23	30.79	186.70
2004	128.07	67.41	27.72	10.75	1.72	1.55	63.24	300.49
2005	29.79*	2.33	4.21	1.21	n.a.	1.36	24.64	63.56
Total	1688.59	322.75	146.33	23.96	3.79	7.78	233.86	2427.10

*Value derived from non-WFP-UN-OCHA figure ($107,563) and WFP reported contribution ($29,683,835)

Notes: Does not include China. For 1996–1999, categories listed by UN-OCHA were slightly different: Food security, Coordination, Food aid, Health/Nutrition, Water/Sanitation, Education, and Other.

Row and column totals do not all sum precisely in the original source.

Sources: UN-OCHA, n.d.a.; WFP 2006b.

APPENDIX 2.2. Consolidated Appeal Humanitarian Assistance, by Agency ($US millions)

	WFP	FAO	FAO / UNDP	UNDP	UNICEF	WHO	OCHA (DHA)	UNFPA	NGOs	TOTAL
1996/7	26.21	2.29	0.00	2.28	3.49	0.07	0.06	0.00	0.00	34.39
1997/8	134.34	1.66	1.03	2.50	17.20	1.60	0.06	0.00	0.00	158.38
1998	202.65	0.90	5.12	0.00	5.73	1.17	0.30	0.00	0.00	215.87
1999	177.91	0.00	3.09	0.00	6.16	1.90	0.84	0.00	0.00	189.89
2000	145.58	0.00	3.04	0.00	2.51	1.30	0.68	0.00	0.00	153.10
2001	240.08	0.00	1.84	0.00	3.47	1.57	0.49	0.10	0.42	247.97
2002	206.11*	0.00	1.09	0.00	6.07	2.29	0.60	0.00	3.85	220.01*
2003	117.78	1.36	0.00	0.00	5.98	3.47	0.23	0.11	4.16	133.10
2004	118.86	2.38	0.00	0.00	17.31	5.53	0.53	0.19	6.78	151.58
2005**	-	-	-	-	-	-	-	-	-	-
TOTAL	1,369.53	8.60	15.20	4.78	67.91	18.88	3.80	0.40	15.21	1,504.31

* Includes $99.32 million carried over by the WFP

** No consolidated appeal humanitarian assistance process in 2005

Notes: Additional aid is given by agencies that is not part of the consolidated appeals process. Does not include China.

Source: UN-OCHA n.d.a..

APPENDIX 2.3. Consolidated Appeal Humanitarian Assistance, by Sector (millions of US$)

	Food Aid	Food Security	Health / Nutrition	Water / Sanitation	Education	Coordination	TOTAL
1996/7	26.21	4.57	3.55	0.00	0.00	0.06	34.39
1997/8	134.34	5.80	16.52	1.49	0.00	0.23	158.38
1998	202.65	6.04	2.71	3.55	0.62	0.30	215.87
1999	177.91	3.09	8.01	0.00	0.00	0.84	189.89
2000	145.58	3.04	3.80	0.00	0.00	0.68	153.10
2001	240.08	2.26	4.64	0.31	0.18	0.49	247.97
2002	206.11*	1.53	7.39	4.06	0.33	0.60	220.01*
2003	117.78	2.27	10.93	0.95	0.94	0.23	133.10
2004	120.34	3.00	19.09	6.69	1.73	0.73	151.58
2005	-	-	-	-	-	-	-
TOTAL	1,371.01	31.59	76.64	17.06	3.80	4.17	1,504.31

* Includes $99.32 million carried over by the WFP.

Notes: Does not include China. Food security includes agriculture; Coordination includes capacity building. Row and column totals do not all sum precisely in original source.

Source: UN-OCHA n.d.a.

APPENDIX 2.4. WFP Target Groups, by Appeal

Appeal	Target coverage and populations	Comments
Sept. 1995-June 1996	500,000 flood victims	
June 1996-Mar. 1997	1.58 million total, including: 500,000 flood-affected collective farmers 525,000 children under five (25% of total cohort) 125,000 workers and 425,000 dependents	
April 1997 - Dec. 1997	100,000 MT; total recipients not initially specified, but: 80 percent of aid in support of food-for-work projects in flood-damaged regions 20 percent for children under five	April: Expansion of initial appeal to cover 4.7 million people, including 2.6 million children under age six (100% of cohort) - nutritional support for twelve months through nurseries and kindergartens. July: Further expansion of appeal to increase rations to targeted children and provide special feeding for malnourished children and hospital patients.
1998	7.47 million total, including; 5.52 million children 500,000 hospital patients 500,000 workers (family ration based on two dependents)	Appeals shift to calendar year basis; initial appeal is the largest emergency operation in WFPs history.
1999	8.044 million, including: 1.47 million children 6 months to 4 years; 665,000 5-6 years; 1.362 million primary school; 1.947 million secondary school children	Target reported corresponds to the emergency operation begun in July (EMOP 5959.01), which expands upon the operation that went into effect in January targeting 5.44 million people (EMOP 5959).

(continued)

APPENDIX 2.4. WFP Target Groups, by Appeal (*continued*)

Appeal	Target coverage and populations	Comments
1999 (*continued*)	10,000 orphans 120,000 hospital patients. 500,000 over 60 years old 1.65 million in food for work projects and dependents	March: WFP begins support of local production of fortified biscuits and blended foods.
2000	Same as 1999	Continuation of emergency operation begun in July 1999. September: Additional appeal to cover needs through December.
2001	7,62 total, including: 346,000 pregnant and nursing women 1.312 million nursery children (6 months - 4 years old); 631,000 kindergarten; 1.352 million primary school; 1.850 million secondary school; 6,000 orphans; 24,000 patients in pediatric hospitals 600,000 elderly people 1.5 million in food-for-work projects and dependents	February: WFP approves a special operation to supplement existing program, including increased local production and food-for-work allocations. The WFP establishes more factories to produce special blended foods for babies, biscuits for children, and fortified noodles for pregnant women; 18 operational by end 2001. Program expanded in the wake of spring drought, including supplementary feeding programs in pediatric hospitals. Appeal experiences break in the pipeline in February 2002 and risk of shortfalls due to pace of contributions.

APPENDIX 2.4. WFP Target Groups, by Appeal (*continued*)

Appeal	Target coverage and populations	Comments
2002	6.46 million total, including: 7,000 orphans, 1.36 million nursery children, 650,000 kindergarten, 1.39 million primary school, 676,000 secondary school 357,000 pregnant and nursing women 365,000 elderly 24,000 patients in pediatric hospitals and their mothers 10,000 patients in nutrition rehabilitation centers 300,000 in food-for-work projects and 900,000 dependents 144,000 in need of food safety net during lean season 250,000 contingency provision to assist populations affected by disasters	Growing share of aid is targeted to urban food for vulnerable populations in the Northeast. April: WFP issues urgent appeals to meet shortfalls in targets. May: Shortfalls in donations force cutbacks in rations to one million beneficiaries. September: food distribution halted to some primary schools and kindergartens on the west coast, and cutbacks subsequently spread to the east coast including food-for-work projects and output of WFP factories. July 1: Price reforms introduced.
2003	6.436 million total, including: 1.15 million nursery children (6 months - 4 years old); 577,335 kindergarten; 1.27 million primary school 208,000 pregnant and nursing women 551,000 elderly 22,000 patients in pediatric hospitals and their mothers	In response to the reforms, the WFP is placing still more emphasis on reaching PDS-dependent urban households, including through urban food-for-work projects. Deliveries to target populations erratic due to supplies. In January and February, continuing cutbacks in targets from previous appeal as a result of shortfalls in commitments and deliveries. Programs resume in March as a result of new deliveries, but then once again face cutbacks in July and again in October through December.

(*continued*)

APPENDIX 2.4. WFP Target Groups, by Appeal (continued)

Appeal	Target coverage and populations	Comments
2003 (continued)	725,000 in food-for work projects and 1.45 million dependents	August: DPRK government lends WFP stocks to cover programs (14,000 MT).
	247,000 disaster contingency	
2004	6.15 million total, including:	All core beneficiaries except for 80,000 nursing and pregnant women do not receive rations in January and February. Site visits report drop in school attendance as rations drop. WFP issues urgent appeal to speed or increase donations and feeding is resumed in March.
	984,000 nursery children (6 months - 4 years old); 505,172 kindergarten; 1.14 million primary school	
	297,955 pregnant and nursing women	
	21,000 patients in pediatric hospitals and their mothers	April: Train disaster in Yongch'ŏn followed by new North Korean appeal to UN.
	709,553 elderly, representing 50% of PDS dependants in accessible counties	
	366,634 low-income households, representing 15% of low-income PDS dependants in 17 of the most urbanized counties	
	725,000 in food-for-work projects and 1.45 million dependents	
	111,111 disaster contingency	
2005	6.52 million total, including:	
	2.7 million children in nurseries, kindergartens, primary schools and orphanages	
	300,000 pregnant and nursing women	
	900,000 elderly (PDS dependant)	

APPENDIX 2.4. WFP Target Groups, by Appeal (*continued*)

Appeal	Target coverage and populations	Comments
2005 (*continued*)	360,000 in low-income urban households	
	725,000 in food-for-work projects and 1.4 million dependents	
	100,000 disaster contingency	
2006	1.88 million:	
(proposed)	977,100 mother and child health	
	424,100 school food programs	
	300,000 food for community development	
	100,000 victims of natural disaster	
	76,000 most vulnerable groups	

Sources: FAO/WFP 1995, 1996, 1997, 1998a, 1998b, 1999a, 1999b, 2003, 2004; UN-OCHA n.d.b.

The Marketization Balance Sheet

This appendix describes the marketization balance sheet calculation. We assume that WFP's food-for-work (FFW) program is both outside the PDS and not subject to diversion and that 10–50 percent of non-FFW aid is diverted, or in the notation below d = [.1, .5].

Target PDS is identical to the announced monthly ration (PDS^{mr}) and can be decomposed into FFW and non-FFW aid and the component sourced from North Korean domestic supply. (We do not otherwise distinguish between WFP and non-WFP sources of non-FFW aid.) We have announced monthly ration PDS^{mr}, FFW, and non-FFW aid; we can calculate the part sourced from NK farmers (PDS$_{nk}$) as a residual:

$$PDS = PDS^{mr} = [PDS_{nk} + AID^{non\text{-}FFW}] + AID^{FFW}$$

$$PDS_{nk} = PDS - AID^{non\text{-}FFW} - AID^{FFW}$$

Implicitly we assume that non-FFW aid is not additional, that is, it substitutes for PDS$_{nk}$ without raising the target PDS quantity.

Then we apply the diversion parameter [.1, .5] to the non-FFW aid share (i.e., only aid, not domestically sourced supply, is diverted; this itself is a questionable assumption) to calculate the magnitude of aid that reaches its intended recipients:

$$PDS_{aid} = AID^{non\text{-}FFW} \times (1-d)$$

(Alternatively, we could assume that diversion occurs uniformly across sources of supply, which would have the effect of increasing the estimated degree of marketization.)

We now assume that the government does not compensate for the diverted aid by increasing procurement from the farmers (i.e., the PDS does not deliver in reality what is claimed on paper by the magnitude of the diverted aid).

We know the amount of food retained by farmers for in-kind consumption (INKIND). This allows us to calculate the amount of food intermediated through markets (MKT) as a residual:

$$S = S^{nk} + S^{aid} = D = PDS_{nk} + PDS_{aid} + AID^{FFW} + INKIND + MKT$$

$$MKT = S - PDS_{nk} - PDS_{aid} - AID^{FFW} - INKIND = S - [PDS^{mr} - [AID^{non\text{-}FFW} - AID^{FFW}] - PDS_{aid} - AID^{FFW} - INKIND$$

Note that since PDS_{aid} is a function of diversion, greater diversion (i.e., a larger parameter d) will increase marketization.

APPENDIX 3.1. Marketization, 1999-2003

Basic assumptions

	Population (millions)		
	Total	PDS-share (%)	Ag-share (%)
1999-2003	22.3	71	29

Aid ('000 MT)

	S^{aid}	Targets			AID^{wfp}	$AID^{non-FFW}$	PDS_{aid}		AID^{FFW}	$AID^{non-wfp}$
		WFP total target	WFP FFW target	WFP FFW target / total target (%)			d=0.1	d=0.5		
1999-2003	1,198	583	n.a.	17.3	457	378	1,007	559	79	741

Supply ('000 MT)

	S^{nk}	S^{aid}	S
1999-2003	3,197	1,198	4,395

PDS^{mr} (via the PDCs)

	PDS-dependent population		Average daily PDS ration (g)		PDS^{mr}
	n (millions)	% workers	Workers	Non-workers	('000 MT)
1999-2003	15.8	66.7	279	242	1,538

(continued)

APPENDIX 3.1. Marketization, 1999–2003, (continued)

Basic assumptions

INKIND consumption by farmers

	Ag population		Average daily PDS ration (g)		
	n (millions)	% workers	Ag workers	Ag non-workers	INKIND ('000 MT)
1999-2003	6.5	66.7	583	250	1,112

Demand - ('000 MT)

	PDS	PDS^{mr}	PDS^{nk}
1999-2003	1,538	1,538	340

Marketization ('000 MT)

	d=.1	d=.5
1999-2003	1,856	2,304

Descriptive statistics (%)

	Marketization (producers' perspective)	Marketization (consumers' perspective)		S^{aid} / PDS
		d=.1	d=.5	
1999-2003	83.7	42.2	52.4	77.9

Sources: Population: Bank of Korea; shares: FAO/WFP 1999b, table 6.

NOTES

1. INTRODUCTION

1. Other general accounts of the famine on which we draw throughout this study include Lautze (1996); Kim, Lee, and Sumner (1998); Noland (2000); Goodkind and West (2001); Noland, Robinson, and Wang (2001); Natsios (2001); Woo-Cumings (2002); S. Lee (2003); Noland (2004a); Haggard and Noland (2005); and Smith (2005b).

2. Cumings (1997) provides a highly readable introduction to the whole of Korean history; Oberdorfer (1997) does the same service for the post-1960 era.

3. On North Korea's internal classification system, see Foster-Carter (1994), Hunter (1999), Armstrong (2002), and the Korea Institute for National Unification (KINU) (2004). On the sources of the Kim regime's popular legitimacy, see Park (1998) and Cumings (1997, 2003).

4. There is no technical definition of famine. Most commentators associate the concept with a catastrophic food crisis resulting in an abrupt increase in mass mortality, though this definition is subject to refinement and contestation (Devereux 2000). We will ascribe to the conventional interpretation in our discussion. For a review of theories of famine, see Devereux (1993).

5. Drazen (2002) provides a theoretical model of this interaction, which centers on the concept of "ownership." See also Khan and Sharma (2003).

2. THE ORIGINS OF THE GREAT FAMINE

1. Jagdish Bhagwati pointed out to us that in the context of widespread shortfalls across an entire population living near subsistence, an effort to distribute shortfalls equitably could

in fact result in higher rather than lower famine deaths; see also S. Lee (2005). However, the typical famine pattern is characterized by substantial inequalities across regions in the availability of food, and North Korea seems to fit this pattern, as we will show in chapter 3.

2. The share of the workforce employed in agriculture has risen in recent years as the industrial sector withered and demechanization of agriculture increased manpower requirements in that sector. Moreover, the government has attempted to solve the food problem in part by forcing individuals to return to agricultural work.

3. Total arable land in 1995 amounted to some 2 million hectares, though only some 1.43 million hectares are suitable for cereal and other food grain production. Of the rest, approximately 300,000 hectares were under fruit cultivation, and the remaining 270,000 hectares predominantly under mulberry trees for sericulture (FAO/WFP 1995).

4. According to U.S. Central Intelligence Agency figures, the net flow of resources from the Soviet Union turned negative even before 1990, although these figures probably understate ongoing Soviet subsidies for both fuel and military equipment (CIA 1994).

5. Readers with an economics background will no doubt recognize the more general problem of how to manage a major balance-of-payments adjustment associated with an external shock.

6. While this campaign rose to public prominence in 1990 (Smith 2005b), the former East German ambassador to Pyongyang, Dr. Hans Maretzki, indicates that such campaigns were already under way in the late 1980s (personal communication, May 30, 2005).

7. In August 2000, North Korea merged N'ajin and Sŏngbong into a special municipality called Rasŏn. We, however, will refer to the special district by its more commonly known former name.

8. Admittedly, rapid supply response was probably easier to achieve in Vietnam's labor-intensive agrarian economy than in the more complex and industrialized North Korean economy. But Vietnam had also been through its highly destructive war much more recently than North Korea had.

9. As of 1997, the onset of the period of interest to us here, North Korea had accumulated approximately $11.9 billion of external debt, $4.6 billion owed to Western countries, the remainder to the Soviet Union and China, with the bulk of it owed to the Soviet Union. There was certainly no expectation, however, that the debt to Russia would be repaid at a Soviet-era official exchange rate.

10. Until 1998 the United States, Japan, and South Korea all opposed North Korean membership in the international financial institutions. After the inauguration of Kim Dae-jung as president of South Korea in 1998, the South Korean government changed its position to one of support, though the United States and Japan remained opposed because of continuing concerns about North Korea's nuclear weapons and missile programs. North Korea remains on the U.S. government list of state sponsors of terror, although it is not known to have committed any terrorist acts since 1987 and has subsequently made public statements condemning terrorism. It continues to harbor a few aging Japanese Red Army airline hijackers, however. Under a U.S. law enacted when U.S. airplanes were regularly hijacked to Cuba, the provision of sanctuary to hijackers is one of the specific legal triggers for U.S. opposition to IFI lending. The unresolved cases of Japanese citizens abducted to North Korea were an additional source of tension in the case of Japan, one that assumed greater centrality fol-

lowing Kim Jŏng-il's admission in September 2002 that North Korea had indeed kidnapped Japanese citizens. Additional complications arose because of purported involvement in drug trafficking, counterfeiting, the proliferation of chemical and biological weapons, and human rights abuses, including religious rights, constraining any administration's room to maneuver if so inclined; we take up these issues in appendix 1 and chapters 6 and 8.

11. For unknown reasons, the figures on Chinese grain shipments to North Korea reported by the South Korean Ministry of Unification and the UN's International Food Aid Information System (INTERFAIS) diverge significantly after 1998.

12. Isolation from the outside world reduced genetic diversity of the North Korean seed stock, making plants more vulnerable to disease

13. While the flooding was considerable, the consensus of outside observers was that the government's claims were exaggerated. For example, a UN survey concluded that the flooding displaced 500,000 people, not the 5.4 million the government initially claimed. Michell (1998) observes that the 1995 and 1996 crop losses were insured. Rehabilitation of flood-damaged lands lagged, however, though it is not clear whether this was due to lack of institutional capacity or the use of insurance receipts for other purposes.

14. See, for example, the wide-ranging historical account of the historical origins of the North Korean ideological system in Cumings (2003).

15. See Sigal (1998) on the crisis as an effort to extract concessions from the United States. The key economic demands of the North Koreans related to energy (the provision of light-water reactors) and the normalization of relations and lifting of sanctions rather than food per se.

16. On the commercial initiatives of 1996–97, see Harrison (2002:34). The quality of these initiatives undercut their purported message, however. At least one high-level group was sent out to procure foreign investment, but their road show was ham-handed, and other similar initiatives were marked by abrupt cancellations of meetings with potential investors (Noland 2000).

17. On the first nuclear crisis—from very different perspectives—see Mazarr (1995); Oberdorfer (1997:chaps. 11–14); Sigal (1998); Downs (1999); Harrison (2002, particularly chap. 17); Cha and Kang (2003); Cumings (2003:chap. 2); Harrison (2002); Wit, Poneman, and Galucci (2004).

18. See Woo-Cumings (2002) for an explicit discussion and critique of Sen's ideas in the context of the North Korean famine.

19. Trade statistics indicate that North Korea exported small quantities of niche products such as sea urchins. To the extent that revenues from the sale of these delicacies could be used to purchase bulk grains, such trade would make sense. Whether the revenues were actually spent this way is unknown. There are also allegations that the DPRK resold aid, though even if these are true the magnitudes appear small. Again, if one could sell high-value rice received from donors for lower-cost grains, this would be a sensible tactic—though again there is no evidence that the receipts were actually being spent in this manner.

20. A careful analysis of trade statistics by Eberstadt (1998a) indicates that while commercial imports of bulk grains dropped considerably during the 1990s, North Korea continued to import small quantities of "bread or biscuits," "cakes or pastries," and even "diet infant cereal preparation," presumably to be consumed by the political elite and their offspring.

21. The argument that aid crowded out imports can be extended to domestic supply as well. In the conventional case of a market economy receiving concessional assistance, food aid drives down the price of food and provides a disincentive to cultivators to grow it. During the famine, grain was sold on markets to an increasing extent, and as a result this effect might have operated to some degree. But food aid probably did have a somewhat different crowding-out effect: it relieved the government of the need to adopt more wide-ranging reforms of incentives that would have boosted output. As Scott Snyder observes, "the UN WFP has become an essential crutch upon which North Korea depends for its survival, while facing diminished structural pressure to engage in system reforms" (2003a:8).

22. This counterfactual supply line falls above the baseline by varying amounts depending on the difference between that year's commercial imports and those of 1993.

23. The 2.3 million MT figure was the maximum non–human use figure ever cited by the FAO/WFP (1995). Subsequent FAO/WFP analyses have put nonhuman usage at 1.5 million MT or less, with the most recent assessment putting it at less than 1.2 million MT (FAO/WFP 2004).

24. According to Bermudez (2001), defectors had reported that these stockpiles were enough to sustain the Korean People's Army from six months to three years; this claim would be consistent with the range of estimates cited. Smith (2005b) alleges that as much as 3 million tons of underground war stocks were destroyed in the 1995 floods. We are skeptical of this much larger figure. In terms of the harvest cycle, one would not expect the government to maintain large stocks immediately before the harvest. Moreover, Smith's source is an unpublished paper (Quinones 2002) that mentions the number in passing, in turn ascribing it to unnamed UNDP officials quoting unidentified North Korean officials. In short, this claim appears to be part of the history of North Korean exaggeration about losses. If true, however, it would imply that after four years of dwindling supplies and suppression of consumption and in the face of a widespread famine, the North Korean government was still maintaining "war stocks" equal to 80 percent of the previous year's harvest; such behavior would constitute damning evidence of the regime's culpability in the famine. It should be noted that if the military was maintaining the stocks (i.e., on balance were neither drawing them down nor building them up), then their existence would not affect our analysis of aggregate food availability. The stocks would only have an adverse effect on supply if they were subsequently rebuilt; in that case, the period of stock accumulation would be associated with a corresponding decline in food availability.

3. THE DISTRIBUTION OF MISERY

1. If we treat the PDS as serving the nonagricultural population, then the share is 71 percent, but, as we will show, there were special distribution networks for some party and government officials, and the military had a separate provisioning system, bringing the total covered by the general PDS to approximately 60 percent of the population.

2. Pyongyang was also favored with a higher share of rations in the form of rice as opposed to maize.

3. This point is made in Amnesty International (2004). One of the first studies of the human rights situation in the country is Minnesota Lawyers International Human Rights Committee (1998).

4. Hunter (1999) provides a thorough introduction to the class system. International Federation for Human Rights (2003) and Oh (2003) offer succinct summaries.

5. For an extremely thoughtful and thorough speculation on the "off-limits" counties based on extensive defector interviews, see Martin (2004:557–78).

6. The wavering class accounted for 45 percent, and the hostile class the remaining 27 percent (cited in International Federation for Human Rights 2003:5).

7. This protected core elite consists of perhaps two hundred thousand people or roughly 1 percent of the population, many either blood relatives or descendents of guerillas who fought with Kim Il-sŏng (Lankov 2003).

8. These plots were 95 square meters each in the rural areas and 30 square meters in urban areas, but only where land was available.

9. The quantity allocated per household would depend on the number of dependents and their ages.

10. The cash payments to the cooperative were distributed among the farmers on the basis of work points earned from various duties performed in the cooperative farming process.

11. These points are made both by the two most comprehensive studies of the famine, Natsios (1999) and S. Lee (2003) (see also S. Lee 2005). See also Natsios (2001) for an excellent summary of these incentive issues.

12. There have been persistent rumors that data compiled on defecting North Korean soldiers record a decrease in average size, implying that the onset of the food crisis was sometime in the 1980s. The Korean People's Army reportedly has lowered its minimum height requirement for male conscripts from 150 cm to 125 cm.

13. This is the conclusion of Sen's pioneering book on famines (1981).

14. General accounts of the famine can be found in Snyder (1997); Kim, Lee, and Sumner (1998); Natsios (1999, 2001); Noland (2000:chap. 5); Woo-Cumings (2002); S. Lee (2003, 2005); Smith (2005b).

15. Suk Lee (2003, 2005) argues that the government in fact did this.

16. For example, the claim appears to be supported by systematic survey evidence and refugee testimonials of the collapse of the PDS in the eastern provinces, but this collapse could have resulted from other sources. Hwang Chang-yŏp, the highest-ranking political official ever to defect from the country, has claimed that even sensitive personnel such as weapons scientists were dying (Natsios 2001:203), but many of his other claims have been called into question. Natsios (2001) argues that triage is plausible because of historical animosity between the eastern and western provinces. Suk Lee (2003:237) cites Ahn (1996:251) to the effect that the party gave a direct order not to ship grain to the northeast, but Ahn in fact does not make such a claim.

17. See Ellman (2000), who distinguishes between a food-availability famine in which there is no feasible allocation of grain that would prevent hunger or starvation and one in which food has declined but could be redistributed.

18. This figure is revealing, however, because the allocations suggested by the FAO/WFP crop assessments fell well below that.

19. This exercise is subject to one objection: that the distribution of the population in different entitlement categories may vary. We ignore this, although it is the most obvious explanation for Pyongyang's consistently higher share.

20. Namp'o and Kangwŏn also fared poorly with respect to PDS distribution, but as a port city Namp'o almost certainly had a more developed black market than did the cities in the northeast. See Smith (2005b:83–86).

21. These data reflect the occupation not of respondents but of their families.

22. Intriguingly, women tend to fare better than men during famines, but the biological and sociological bases for this advantage are not well understood (Macintyre 2002).

23. Good Friends (1998) also presents estimates of mortality that show the classic U-shape pattern—high among infants and the elderly—but at rates that are outside the bounds even of famine conditions.

24. Eberstadt (1998b) takes a somewhat different tack in estimating famine-related deaths. Noting the fact that the size of the Supreme People's Assembly did not change between 1990 and 1998, despite the fact that each member is supposed to represent a fixed population (30,000), Eberstadt argues that three million people were "missing" during this period. Although this novel calculation gains some external validation from other estimates, it rests on the assumption that the North Korean government in fact stuck precisely to the fine points of its constitution, an assumption that strains credulity.

4. THE AID REGIME

1. Overviews of the multilateral aid process can be found in Natsios (1999:chap. 8); Bennett (1999); Noland (2000); Smith (2002); Flake and Snyder (2003); J. Lee (2003); Reed (2004); and Manyin (2005).

2. The relatively small shares devoted to coordination and other purposes almost certainly were in support of the food distribution effort as well.

3. The WFP planning and appeal process closely mirrors that of the CAP. The WFP, working in conjunction with the Food and Agricultural Organization (FAO) dispatches Emergency Assessment teams to the affected country to investigate how much food aid is needed, for how many beneficiaries, and how the food can be most effectively delivered. The WFP then draws up an Emergency Operation (EMOP), including a plan of action and a budget. This plan lists who will receive food aid, what rations are required, the type of transport WFP will use. and which humanitarian corridors lead to the crisis zone. This assessment and planning process feeds into the formulation of an appeal, which depends entirely on voluntary contributions from governments, in the form of either food aid or cash for the purchase of food from third parties. As funds and food start to flow, the WFP and OCHA logistics teams oversee the movement of food from its point of embarkation to the ultimate recipients.

4. The representative of one NGO with a long-time involvement with North Korea may have inadvertently demonstrated this political capture phenomenon when she observed that, "while the DPRK authorities have not fully accepted the concept of nongovernmental aid agencies operating on a long-term basis in their country, there is an understanding now that

NGOs in many countries have a strong voice and thus can be quite influential" (quoted in Flake [2003:40]).

5. The most prominent of these exercises is the Inter-agency Code of Conduct arising out the Sphere Project (2004), and later, in recognition of the absence of a formal accountability mechanism, the establishment of the Humanitarian Accountability Project International (Young et al. 2004).

6. The humanitarian principles included knowledge about the overall humanitarian situation in the country according to assessed needs; assurance that humanitarian assistance reaches sectors of the population in greatest need; access for assessment, monitoring, and evaluation; distribution of assistance only to areas where access is granted; protection of the humanitarian interests of the population; support to local capacity building; beneficiary participation in program planning and implementation; adequate capacity in terms of international staff; and guarantees of the health and safety needs of the international humanitarian community.

7. UNICEF established a resident office in January 1996, and the World Health Organization in late 1997. The European Commission opened an office in 1997, and several European countries also established resident offices. A number of NGOs proved more nimble, but they too faced start-up costs and resistance from the North Korean government. Excellent analyses of the NGOs are contained in Smith (2002); Flake and Snyder (2003); Reed (2004).

8. A thorough discussion of these coordination issues is contained in Flake (2003) and included the formation of a North Korea working group, which coordinated functions taken on by InterAction in the United States, and the establishment of the Food Aid Liaison Unit in Pyongyang, which represented mostly Canadian and European NGOs and worked with the WFP.

9. The most respected European consultancy on North Korea stated flatly in July 1994: "We have been unable to find anyone in the DPRK who is starving" (Euro-Asian Business Consultancy 1994). Similarly, an assessment conducted in March and April 1996 funded by the British Overseas Development Administration concluded that there did not appear to be widespread malnutrition, although certain groups were deemed vulnerable (Nathanail 1996:5).

10. The December 1995 assessment states, "There is a need for both emergency and project and program food assistance as well as support for the rehabilitation of the agriculture sector to raise production to more normal levels" (FAO/WFP 1995).

11. Typically, parents supply a daily ration of 100 grams per day to nurseries, kindergartens, and schools for their children, a very large share of total allocation through the PDS (WFP 2003c).

12. The WFP admits this specifically (WFP 2003b).

13. NGOs have been subject to similar obstacles, and we note the distinctive constraints, but some have been more successful in adapting than others. As a result, the characterization of North Korean behavior that we offer may not hold universally; some NGOs may have effectively gained better access than we describe here by keeping their heads down and developing relationships at the local level.

14. We constructed the map for 1995–96 by excluding four provinces altogether (Chagang, Yanggang, North and South Hamgyŏng).

15. The bargaining power of the government is considerably greater vis-à-vis NGOs. The North Korean government routinely denies access to NGOs in the absence of a precommitment to a target aid level and has shown reluctance to issue long-term or multiple entry visas. Once a program has been agreed on, NGOs also depend on government-appointed staff, a problem we discuss in more detail below.

16. All official visits (including calls on North Korean officials in Pyongyang) are included in these totals. In June 2003, there was a revision in the way food-for-work visits were counted: the WFP started to count visits to beneficiaries, work sites, and PDCs separately. As food-for-work visits were a relatively small share of the total, this difference does not affect the totals substantially and is any case justified.

17. Deliveries for NGOs handled by the WFP's Food Aid Liaison Unit (FALU) follow the same format. See Caritas—Hong Kong (2005a) for a description.

18. The North Koreans' revision of their baby formula proposal to encompass a much larger number of institutions after diversion was detected is notable in this regard.

19. The following draws on the March 31, 2005, press conference with Tony Banbury, WFP regional director for Asia (see Banbury 2005).

20. The following draws on USAID (2005) and subsequent private correspondence with WFP staff.

21. In fact, the distinction between the two forms of engagement is not crystal clear: the WFP had been operating food factories and food-for-work programs, which might be thought of as having a development assistance component.

22. Jan Egeland, the United Nations emergency relief coordinator, described halting humanitarian aid as "potentially disastrous" and pointed to nutritional surveys documenting chronic widespread malnourishment and the widening gap in stature between North and South Koreans (Brooke 2005). These surveys are discussed in detail in chapter 7.

5. DIVERSION

1. MSF interviews conducted in August 1998 reported specifically that foreign aid was diverted to the military and "executives," although the three accounts making this allegation use suspiciously similar language and do not appear to rest on firsthand accounts (MSF 1998).

2. There are also periodic allegations of aid being resold abroad. In one such case, a Thai senate committee concluded that rice sold to North Korea on concessional terms had been diverted to West Africa instead (*Joongang Ilbo* 2002). However, we have not come across evidence that foreign diversion is a central aspect of the North Korean story, as food exports were, for example, during the great Irish famine.

3. As Caritas—Hong Kong observes, "With a market economy developing, the chances that food and non-food donations are sold or bartered increase" (Caritas—Hong Kong 2005a:11), and "no doubt with more market activities—some cities now have apparently official bartering centers—the risk that donations are sold or bartered is increasing" (Caritas—Hong Kong 2005b:4).

4. The story is complicated by the ability to store food. In this case, the ability to stock-

pile will attenuate the impact on market prices, reducing the gains to third-party consumers and reducing the losses to cultivators. Just such a case is reported in an interview with a defector (*Daily North Korea* 2006) who describes how a shipment of South Korean food aid lowered market prices initially but aid was quickly diverted by the military or bought up by speculators with the intention of reselling it at a later point in time.

5. Certainly the most vociferous in this regard was Fiona Terry, a researcher for MSF, who repeatedly invoked refugee interviews to suggest that food was not getting to its intended targets but was being diverted (Terry 2001).

6. As we have seen, the PDS was collapsing for a complex set of reasons that included a drop in overall production, regional shortages, farmers' hoarding and diversion, the break-down of the transportation system, the emergence of black markets, and the fact that food aid was squeezing out rather than complementing commercial imports. Moreover, the humanitarian allotments to particular regions constituted only the best guesses of the aid community as to what actual needs were.

7. In reality, the state is presumably factoring in diversion when setting its procurement targets.

8. As observed in chapter 3, the PDS is decentralized, with local officials coordinating supply and demand within their jurisdictions to a significant extent. We assume that this bureaucratic regime more effectively deters diversion to the market of locally procured supply than aid. If one relaxes this assumption and posits that locally procured food is also diverted to the market, then such diversion will increase the revealed degree of marketization associated with that level of diversion. Alternatively, it will imply less diversion associated with a particular degree of marketization, since a greater quantity base is subject to diversion.

6. THE POLITICAL ECONOMY OF AID

1. For a review of this issue from somewhat different perspectives, see Cha and Kang (2003) and Manyin (2005).

2. Manyin summarizes concisely: "Following North Korea's invasion of the South in June 1950, the United States imposed a nearly complete economic embargo on the DPRK. In September 1999, President Clinton announced that the United States would ease economic sanctions against North Korea affecting most trade and travel. Today, trade and related transactions are generally allowed for other than dual-use goods (i.e., items that may have both civilian and military uses). U.S. citizens may travel to North Korea; there are no restrictions on the amount of money one may spend in transit or while there" (2005:27). Nonetheless, commercial transactions between the two countries are trivial.

3. North Korea received heavy oil shipments while light water reactors were being constructed, nominally to compensate for the power lost by the closure of the 5MW(e) reactor in Yŏngbyŏn, as well as the cessation of construction of a 50MW(e) reactor in Yŏngbyŏn and a 200MW(e) reactor in T'aech'ŏn under the terms of the Agreed Framework. However it is conceived, this aid clearly constituted a major source of support for the North Korean economy, which had seen both Soviet/Russian and Chinese supplies of fuel shift from friendship prices to hard currency ones.

4. These included the conditions that South Korea did not oppose the aid, that previous aid had not been diverted, that North Korea's military stocks had been tapped to address the crisis, and that the WFP would guarantee that future aid would not be diverted. On this important and still-controversial early history, see Natsios (2001:168–71, 182–86); Noland (2000:186–87); Flake (2003) (on the NGO community); and Hathaway and Tama (2004) (on the legislative politics).

5. Most notable in this regard were a GAO report in October 1999 and the House of Representatives North Korea Advisory Group report of a month later. Both of these reports underlined the weakness of the monitoring regime and repeated evidence of various sorts that diversion to the military was occurring.

6. The comment was made in a press conference with Swiss president Adolf Ogi. The Swiss were one of the earliest and most generous European providers of aid (Deutsche Presse Agentur 2000).

7. In both cases, the announcements also referred to marginal improvements in North Korea's cooperation with the WFP on access and monitoring.

8. For criticisms of the legislation from different perspectives, see Smith (2004) and particularly Chung (2004), which argues (apparently without irony) that "the North Koreans perceive human rights as 'human rights in our own style,' characterized by socialism and communitarianism. From this perspective, freedom of religion and conscience of individuals and political freedom can be sacrificed to some degree for the sake of the greater good of the majority" (76).

9. In particular, the Proliferation Security Initiative (PSI) sought to establish the international legal authority and military capacity to interdict suspected proliferation efforts. The PSI did not directly affect the aid regime but served more as a reminder of hardening attitudes toward North Korea among some major aid donors. In addition, the U.S. government took a number of actions to curtail North Korea's illicit activities, most notably the counterfeiting of U.S. currency; we take these up in chapter 8.

10. The most comprehensive treatment of the Japan–North Korea relationship is Hughes (1999). See also Lind (1997); Hughes (2002, 2005); Manyin (2003, 2005:24); International Crisis Group (2005); and Lintner (2005:chap. 7). We are also thankful to Christopher Hughes for his comments on this section and to Amanda Hayes and Takeshi Nagasawa.

11. Crucial in this regard was an unofficial visit by a Liberal Democratic Party–Japan Socialist Party delegation led by LDP kingmaker Shin Kanemaru in (1990). On this earlier history, see Hughes (1999:51–112).

12. The size of these remittances has been the subject of substantial speculation, but Lintner's assessment—that they amounted to tens of millions annually through the early 2000s—seems plausible (2005:162). Hughes (2005) offers more recent estimates, following closer investigation of the issue by Japanese authorities, of approximately $32 million in 2002 falling off to about $23 million in (2003). In addition to these financial flows, Hughes (2005) estimates that North Korea had defaulted on approximately $900 million of loans to Japanese banks in the 1970s. See also Lind (1997).

13. Japan insisted that the aid extended following normalization in 1965 in no way reflected reparations for damage inflicted during World War II but was simply a settlement of outstanding property claims. Figures on the order of $10 billion have been floated in discussions of a package for North Korea (Noland 2004a).

14. For an intriguing account of the political economy of the missile program in North Korea, see Pinkston (2003).

15. From 2002 the Japanese government started to crack down on illicit activities of the previously powerful General Association of Korean Residents in Japan (Chosen Soren in Japanese; Ch'ongnyŏn in Korean), tightened supervision of its affiliated credit union, and removed some of the organization's tax privileges. The government gained legal authority to control remittances, pressured several banks to limit them, and passed legislation in conjunction with the American-led Proliferation Security Initiative effectively to limit North Korean maritime connections. Japanese authorities began subjecting North Korean vessels to detailed safety inspections that they could not pass and requiring insurance that they could not afford. The government also took a variety of trade-related actions, such as requiring labeling of North Korean imports as such, a move proposed by those encouraging a boycott. See Lintner (2005:chap. 7) and particularly Hughes (2005).

16. We are indebted to Yeon-kyeong Kim for her research on this section, as well as to extensive interviews with South Korean officials and detailed comments from Chung-in Moon.

17. Figure 5.2 reports data for commercial trade, that is, excluding aid. South Korean sources sometimes incorrectly count aid (including items such as U.S.-financed heavy oil deliveries under the 1994 Agreed Framework) as exports to North Korea. The series reported in figure 5.1 also nets out processing-on-commission (POC) trade, in which components are sent to the North for assembly and then reexported. Under normal accounting conventions, these reexports are not counted as exports of the processing country. Until recently, however, there has been no direct route through which South Korean firms could ship components to the North; everything was trans-shipped via China. As a consequence, there is probably some erroneous double-counting of these trans-shipments as Chinese exports to and imports from North Korea.

18. The evolution of South Korea's aid policy can be tracked through the Ministry of Unification's monthly *Overview of Intra-Korean Exchanges and Cooperation* at www.unikorea. go.kr/en/index.jsp.

19. South Koreans are at the dock when food is delivered, but no distribution plan is decided in advance; the North Korean authorities provide a distribution plan thirty days after food has arrived. Monitoring takes place at a small number of sites by four-person teams chosen by the South Koreans from a list provided by their North Korean counterparts. From 2004 the South Koreans were permitted to station roughly forty people in North Korea. The number of visits is low, however; in 2004 the WFP conducted more site visits in a typical week than the South Koreans did in the entire year. South Korea does not audit the disposition of its aid beyond visual confirmation that rice is indeed stored in the public distribution center under inspection.

20. The following draws on personal communication with Im Wŏn-hyŏk, particularly on events during 1997.

21. An accessible introduction to the domestic politics of the Sunshine Policy, emphasizing consistent resistance by the opposition Grand National Party, can be found in Levin and Han (2002).

22. For an overview of these efforts see O. Chung (2003). An unexpected by-product of this approach to aid has been an increasing number of visits by South Koreans to the North

in conjunction with these programs. In 1998 thirty-four people visited, and forty-nine in 1999. Thereafter, however, the numbers rise and in 2003 exceeded fifteen hundred. This is still a relatively small number, of course, but recall that at its peak the WFP only had fifty-one resident staff in the whole country.

23. As early as 1998, members of the Hyundai group committed to payments of nearly $1 billion over seven years (1998–2005) for the rights to develop tourism at Mount Kŭmgang in North Korea. In a meeting purportedly held a month before the breakthrough North-South summit in 2000, South Korean officials and a representative of the Hyundai group met and promised payments of $500 million to secure business rights for the company in North Korea. But this promise was commingled with government money. In February 2003, Kim Dae-jung, who had won the Nobel Prize for his policy toward the North, admitted publicly that government payments were part of the summit deal and were not legal. Several of his aides, including his national security adviser, were eventually convicted, but President No Mu-hyŏn effectively blocked further investigation before it reached Kim personally.

24. Of particular importance with respect to commercial policy were agreements reached in December 2000 on investment guarantees, prevention of double taxation, settlements, and conflict resolution. As of early 2005, the main cooperation projects were the Mount Kŭmgang tourism project, the Kaesŏng Industrial Complex, and an ambitious program to connect both railroads and roads on the east and west coasts of the peninsula. These projects were expanded after June 2005, as we detail below.

25. It is again important to underscore that this humanitarian assistance was in addition to the highly controversial private payments by South Korean groups and the illegal public payments.

26. Good Friends (2005) estimates that 30 percent of aid is diverted to the military and another 10 percent to industrial enterprises in the military-industrial complex. The Good Friends statement also noted—as we have—that the remainder of the aid is channeled through the PDS and thus allocated on the basis of the priorities of those officials, which included workers on major construction projects and railway workers. Last in priority is "general" food distribution (3).

27. These commitments can be seen in the agreement reached following the tenth meeting of the economic cooperation committee, described in Rhee (2005), which also contains quite frank assessments of the continuing limits on commercial relations.

28. The following draws on overviews of the European aid experience in Berkofsky (2003), the EC's useful "Country Strategy Paper" (European Commission 2001), and recently completed evaluation of the ECHO program in Dammers, Fox, and Jimenez (2005). A useful overview of the broader EU–North Korean relationship is Frank (2002); we are thankful to the author for his comments on this section as well. An outstanding review of the stormy relationship between European NGOs and North Korea can be found in Schloms (2003). We are particularly thankful for comments by Maria Castillo-Fernandez.

29. The non-EU European share is accounted for by Iceland, Liechtenstein, Monaco, Norway, Poland, Russia, and Switzerland. Russia made its first contribution to the WFP ($10 million) in 2003.

30. As in South Korea, a certain share of European Commission assistance is channeled through NGOs. See Schloms (2003).

31. It is striking that the two major European countries that have withheld assistance are also the continent's two nuclear powers.

32. The political dialogue at the EC level began in December 1998 and with a succession of EU parliamentary delegations as well. The new approach was set out in the council conclusions of October 9 and November 20, 2000. On the possible role of Europe in the security process, see Heiskanen (2003). In January 2003, as the second nuclear crisis was breaking, the European Parliament called on the commission to consider convening a multilateral conference on the full range of issues on the peninsula. This approach had roots in earlier efforts to define a role for Europe in Korea but was superseded by political developments.

33. The Europe Aid Co-Operation Office was set up in January 2001 to oversee projects funded by the EC budget and European Development Fund.

34. Food aid is not channeled through the ECHO program but through the food security budget line; since the report is evaluating ECHO efforts, it does report on food aid issues but includes a parenthetical discussion. It is quite possible that monitoring issues are not as severe in the functional project areas because of the need for ongoing contact with beneficiaries and coordination with NGOs.

35. For example, it finds that "[there are] particularly positive aspects to the food aid programme that are almost unique to DPRK. These include the implementation of the targeting system through institutions such as nurseries and kindergartens and the local production of fortified food. The targeting system, based on data made available by the government, provides WFP with a picture of the groups that require food aid, though not complete beneficiary lists" (Dammers, Fox, and Jimenez 2005:31).

36. The following draws extensively on Kim (2005) and research by Erik Zhang for a project with Tai Ming Cheung on China–North Korea economic relations. For broader overviews of the relationship, see Scobell (2004); Wu (2005); and International Crisis Group (2006).

37. Our interviews with Chinese scholars found that they were themselves divided on how to interpret this crucial event. Possible economic explanations for this fall-off are continuing shortfalls in Chinese production, conflicts over Chinese trade duties, and the onset of Chinese disaffection with North Korean failure to pay for commodities shipped as the crisis deepened. An alternative political explanation, however, is high-level Chinese political disaffection with Kim Jŏng-il and a general deterioration in relations. This disaffection had two possible sources. One was North Korea's initial effort to marginalize China in the context of the first nuclear crisis, a strategy that Kim and Lee (2002) refer to as the "two plus zero" approach of dealing directly with the United States. The second source of disaffection has to do with economic strategy. Premier Li Peng came close to criticizing North Korea publicly at the time aid was extended in 1996. Since then, Chinese contempt for North Korea's failure to reform has become increasingly open. See for example, Mansourov (2003).

38. These numbers do not reflect total humanitarian assistance; such assistance might reasonably pass through other channels given the capabilities of national aid bureaucracies to provide technical assistance.

39. For a more detailed overview of these issues, see Haggard and Noland (2005) and our exchange with the South Korean Ministry of Unification on these questions at www.hrnk.org/.

7. COPING, MARKETIZATION, AND REFORM

1. Many of the countries of the former Soviet Union represent hybrid cases in this political aspect, since reforms were launched under largely unreformed Communist parties, albeit with some political liberalization.

2. The data in reported in figures 7.1 and 7.3 should be viewed with skepticism: there would be significant conceptual difficulties associated with measuring value added in a planned socialist economy as distorted as North Korea's even if one had access to the normal complement of data. The Bank of Korea estimate of North Korean national income is reportedly constructed by applying South Korean value-added weights to physical estimates of North Korean output derived through classified sources and methods, though a classified North Korean input-output table exists and may have been used to do this computation in recent years. This raises a variety of concerns: that the reliance on physical indicators may signal an overemphasis on the industrial sector (where output is relatively easy to count) relative to the service sector; that prerelease discussions may imply interagency bargaining and a politicization of the estimate; and that the methods through which the figures are derived are not subject to independent verification. At times, analysts have even questioned the veracity of the South Korean estimates. See Noland (2001) for further elaboration.

3. The amended constitution of 1992 stipulated that the National Defense Commission was the supreme command of the military. Kim was "elected" NDC chairman in 1993 and reelected in 1998 and again in 2003 by the SPA.

4. As one would expect, the internal security organization of the DPRK is large and complex. In addition to the State Security Department, which provides internal intelligence functions, the police are organized on a highly centralized military model in the Ministry of People's Security. Moreover, the regime clearly drew on a large pool of reservists (the Workers-Peasants Red Guard) for a variety of internal security and economic functions during the 1990s; Bermudez (2001) estimates the size of this reserve force, made up largely of veterans, at over four million (162). Thus, quite apart from the specific tasks these groups undertake, the "military first" politics clearly appeals to very large groups within society quite apart from the regular military forces: reservists, paramilitary groups, intelligence forces, and police. See Bermudez 2001 and the excellent study of the Ministry of People's Security by Chon (2004). We are also indebted to Park Syung Je for conversations on this point.

5. On the refugee problem, see Human Rights Watch (2002); Kim (2002); Charny (2004); Lankov (2004); Lee (2004); Haggard and Noland (2006). On the quantitative estimates, see Noland (2000) and KINU (2004).

6. In 2004 the SPA passed revisions to the criminal code. The revisions could be interpreted as an attempt to bring the penal code in line with the changes that had occurred in North Korea over the previous decade, for example, by indicating what kinds of economic activity were legal and which were not. Sentencing was also revised, with the categories including "unlimited-term correctional labor," "limited-term correctional labor," and the euphemistically named "labor training" (KINU 2005; Yoon 2005).

7. A chronology of agricultural reforms derived from North Korean pronouncements finds references to increasing production of various foodstuffs through the application of the "*chuch'e* farming method" in every year between 1995 and 2000 (Kwon and Kim 2003:table 2).

8. These changes were preceded by constitutional revisions in 1998 that introduced such concepts as private property and profit, if in the context of an otherwise thoroughly orthodox elaboration of a planned socialist economy, and a comprehensive law on central planning enacted the following year that criminalized nonsanctioned economic activities (Lim and Kim 2004). See Noland (2004b), Kim and Choi (2005), and Frank (2005a) for comprehensive evaluations of the policy changes and speculation about the possible reasons for their introduction. The Kaesŏng Industrial Complex was the most obvious example of the tactic of establishing special zones. Pyongyang's botched rapprochement with Tokyo, described in the previous chapter, is the most obvious example of aid seeking.

9. One member of a delegation that visited the Mansfield Foundation in Washington, D.C., in late 2002 made this explicit: "If the official price of grain is the same as in the markets, people will have no incentive to sell grain in the markets."

10. For example, in March 2003, Kang Kyŏng-sun, director of North Korea's State Price Determination Bureau, declared "80% of the standard wage will be guaranteed if 80% of the plan is achieved, and 200% of the wages will be guaranteed if 200% of the plan is achieved" (quoted in Kim and Choi 2005:16).

11. In a currency reform, residents are required to turn in their existing holdings—subject to a ceiling—for newly issued notes; the ceiling on the ability to convert is what makes such reforms confiscatory. In July 2002, the blue won ("foreigner's won") foreign-exchange certificates were replaced by the normal brown ("people's") won, though it is unclear if the latter were formally convertible into foreign currency. The other shoe dropped in December 2002, when the authorities prohibited dollar holdings and required that all residents, foreign and domestic alike, would have to exchange dollars for euros, which the central bank in fact did not have.

12. Echoing the monetary theory of Chicago-school bluesman Willie Dixon, who, observing the likenesses on American paper currency, opined, "Everybody loves them dead presidents," one North Korean refugee in China was reported to have expressed its international finance equivalent: "[George] Washington is better than Kim Il-sŏng."

13. According to the South Korean government, despite the government's December 2002 announcement prohibiting the use of U.S. dollars, most foreign exchange in North Korea is held in this currency, with the remainder roughly divided between Japanese yen and Chinese yuan.

14. It could vary for other reasons such as the risk or penalties associated with what is technically criminal behavior.

15. Frank (2005b), on the basis of casual observations in Pyongyang, concluded that between July 2002 and October 2005, the annual rate of inflation was roughly 215 percent; Y. Kwon (2006) estimates it at more than 300 percent annually since August 2002.

16. According to Lim and Kim (2004), lenders are typically backed by organizations such as the Korean People's Army or the People's Security Agency for obvious reasons relating to the collection of debts.

17. To reiterate an earlier warning, this data should be viewed with caution. There are significant conceptual difficulties associated with measurement, and the South Korean authorities derive their estimates from unknown sources and methods.

18. Kim (2005a, b, c, d) and Kim (2006) provide fascinating examples of the symbiotic relationship among entrepreneurs, their patron SOEs, and the parasitic state officials who

regulate economic activity. Indeed, Kim (2005a) documents how, at least in some cases, entrepreneurs who affiliated with government offices received preferential tax treatment.

19. The discussion in Y. H. Chung (2003) suggests that purchases of the bonds may be compulsory. According to another account, while purchases are not mandatory, the authorities use purchases as "a barometer of the buyers' loyalty and support for the party and the state" (ITAR-Tass 2003).

20. See Seckler (1980) for the original exposition of this now discredited hypothesis and Pelto and Pelto (1989), Martorell (1989), and Beaton (1989) for critiques.

21. The 1998 survey reports the worst outcomes on nutritional status, and it would have been desirable to compare the sample means of subsequent surveys to those obtained in 1998. Unfortunately, the WFP was unwilling to supply the comparable data, making evaluation of changes over time—either positive or negative—in this particular dimension impossible to assess.

22. In traditional Korean society, a baby is considered to be one year old at birth. It could be that there was cultural miscommunication among the North Korean anthropometrists, the North Korean respondents, and the foreign participants from the UN agencies and the EU who, given North Korean practices, could be assumed not to speak Korean. This could have led to misinterpretation of parental responses to questions about the children's ages, resulting in a systematic overestimation of the ages of the children in their sample, hence the shocking figures on the age-related measures. However, the questionnaire asks for both the date of birth and the age in months and years; it should have been possible for the enumerators to maintain internal consistency.

8. CONCLUSION

1. G. Kang (2005) sets out the case for prosecuting Kim Jŏng-il in the International Criminal Court.

2. As Lau, Qian, and Roland (2000) observe, additional institutional changes, such as the maintenance of a dual price system in the context of reforms of the central planning mechanism, might have yielded additional benefits, and some argue that a similar process of growing around the plan is under way now in North Korea (e.g., Lim 2006), though we suspect that macroeconomic instability is so great and the planning mechanism so degraded in contemporary North Korea that this channel is unlikely to produce large effects.

3. These considerations were reinforced in economies like Russia's by the excessive spatial dispersion of economic activity and the prevalence of company towns, which reduced the opportunities for alternative employment or access to alternative networks of support.

4. Among such programs have been a variety of Chinese technical support programs, U.S.-supported legal training conducted in China, and Vietnamese programs on economic reform, as well as Swedish-supported economic policy training programs conducted in Vietnam. Australia has supported an economics educational initiative, and the EU has supported visits to North Korea by a number of former economic policy makers from its new Central European members.

5. Rather, it has favored technical assistance and training that can be gained under highly

controlled circumstances. Although the impact of these sorts of programs and exchanges is difficult to document, they are potentially important not only in the design of reforms but in negotiating with foreigners, whether in the international financial institutions or in the private sector. Yet while such interactions might be helpful in the long run, China introduced its reforms without access to such supports, and indeed we can attest from personal experience that at least through the mid-1980s some senior Chinese officials betrayed very hazy notions of the operations of a market economy. This interpretation of what has gone wrong to date may have a relatively hopeful interpretation.

6. On the one hand, some foreign visitors have hypothesized a hard-liner/reformer split in the government, with military leaders at the core of the hard line (Harrison 2002). These groups see little point in engaging the United States and other parties on the nuclear issue, prioritize spending on the military over the reform process, and favor tight economic as well as political controls. These arguments have been deployed in support of deeper engagement with the country—which we support—yet we have some doubt about their veracity. In particular, it is almost certain that the emerging market economy is deeply penetrated by state actors of various sorts, including the military; no other groups would be able to engage in large-scale trade or control substantial foreign exchange.

7. In December 2004, President No Mu-hyŏn observed, "The Chinese government is providing assistance to the North because it will be completely out of control if a serious political crisis happens in North Korea and refugees literally pour into Chinese territory. South Korea doesn't want to see the North Korean government collapsing either because that situation would lead to a huge influx of North Korean refugees. For this reason, China and South Korea are in a kind of desperate position to help the North pursue reform and opening" (Kim 2004). See also Shin, Chun, and Ser (2005). The South Korean public appears ambivalent on this score: a 2005 poll conducted by the East Asia Institute found declining interest in unification; more than 30 percent of those surveyed were unwilling to pay any additional taxes to support unification, while another 40 percent were willing to pay less than $100 a year to support North Korea's development before unification (N. Lee 2005).

8. Despite its popularity in discussions of North Korea, the term "collapse" does not have any clear meaning in economics beyond some unspecified but large decline in overall output. By any threshold, the North Korean economy certainly collapsed in the 1990s. The term does not have a precise meaning in political science, either. It is most plausibly invoked in a revolutionary setting in which an incumbent regime is altogether incapable of maintaining political and social control and is replaced by a challenger or nominally maintains power but in the context of sustained civil conflict or war, so-called state failure. It is not a good metaphor for political changes that occur as a result of challenges from within the regime, such as a coup d'état, or from some other sort of evolutionary change.

9. These judgments were affirmed by the one attempt we know of to model the process of transition formally; see Bueno de Mesquita and Mo (1997). Employing a repeated game model calibrated to 1996 that predicted outcomes on the basis of the potential power of each actor, each actor's policy positions, and the salience each ascribed to the issue of political reform, the authors concluded that "Kim Jŏng-il's hold on power is tenuous" (26) and that North Korea was entering "a period of significant political instability" (25). See also Collins (1996) and Pollack and Lee (1999).

10. When forty-eight analysts were queried in a poll conducted by Lee Young-sun in 1995 about the prospects for Korean unification through a North Korean collapse and its absorption by the South, the modal response (29 percent) was that such change would occur in the period 2001–2005, with cumulatively 40 percent of respondents expecting it to transpire by this time, and 60 percent expecting it by 2010 (Lee 1995). A similar survey the following year undertaken by the *Joongang Ilbo* found that 16 percent expected North Korean collapse within five years (i.e., by 2001), while an additional 28 percent expected it to occur by 2006. Only one of the fifty respondents doubted that North Korea would ever collapse. An informal poll of another group of scholars in September 1997 reached a similar conclusion: roughly one-third of the participants expected North Korea's collapse within five years (i.e., by 2002), with the remainder splitting between those expecting the maintenance of a "hard" state and those anticipating significant reform (Noland 1998).

11. To reiterate the cautions from chapter 7, the South Korean estimates of North Korean activity should be regarded as rough guesses: the North Koreans to do not report the relevant underlying data, and there are enormous conceptual and measurement challenges associated with inferring it from the outside. See Noland (2001) for further discussion.

12. Many of these were oil exporters, and their declining fortunes were therefore explicable in terms of commodity price movements rather than general policy failings.

13. Becker (2005:197–202) provides a useful catalog of these incidents, although he includes antiregime behavior that might have largely economic motives such as stripping of state assets.

14. A 2004 survey of two hundred recent defectors found that for 19 percent, foreign radio broadcasts such as Korea Broadcasting System, Radio Liberty, Voice of America, and Radio Free Asia were their main source of news. Twenty-one percent knew someone who had modified his or her North Korean fixed-tuner radios to listen to foreign broadcasts, and more than half reported knowing someone who had been punished for listening to unauthorized broadcasts. None reported receiving information through foreign newspapers. There is no way of knowing how representative these defectors are of the general public.

15. See Martin (2004:545) for a defector account of a plot within the Ministry of the People's Armed Forces dating to 1989. Oberdorfer (1997:375) and Becker (2005:199–201) report on a plot within the Korean army's Sixth Corps, headquartered not coincidentally in Ch'ŏngjin in the northeast and taking place at the height of the famine in 1995; the offending units were purged, disbanded, and merged.

16. There are other historical precedents, of course, including the Meiji Restoration and the founding of modern Turkey under Mustafa Kemal; in both of these circumstances as well, revolutionary changes were justified as responses to external threats.

17. The new constitution clearly weakened the institutional status of the Korean Workers' Party, a marked contrast to the Chinese model. Choi is worth quoting at length on this point, since his assessment is still true as of 2006:

> A party congress has not been held since the sixth party congress in 1980. According to the Party Act, a party congress is supposed to be held every five years. The plenum of the Central Committee has not been held since the twenty-first plenum in December 1993. The plenum, which has the right to elect the secretary-general, was not held even when Kim Jŏng-il became the party's secretary-general in October 1997.

Instead, Kim Jŏng-il was endorsed by both the Central Committee and the Central Military Committee. For the first time in the history of North Korea's communist party, a plenum also was not held before the first session of the 10th SPA. It is also suspected that Secretariat and Politburo meetings have not been held since Kim Il-sŏng's death. (1999:9)

18. Hellman (1998) was the first to make the point. Pei (2006) elaborates it in the context of the Chinese case.

19. This discussion draws extensively on the thorough treatment of the international legal issues in Amnesty International (2004).

20. As we noted in chapter 5 and want to underline again here, the ethical issues surrounding diversion to the military are not straightforward. The North Korean army is a conscript force, and we have ample evidence that lower-level military personnel have not received adequate rations in the past.

21. The modest improvement in nutritional status that we detail in chapter 7 does not mean that delivered aid is ineffective; it only demonstrates the uphill battle the humanitarian community must fight in a context where other features of the system make it difficult to be effective. In the absence of food aid, nutrition status would certainly have been worse still.

22. Given that most food aid passes through official channels, we have not addressed the outstanding and innovative work by the variety of NGOs that have worked in North Korea. A handful of influential organizations have taken the decision to leave; others have stayed in the hope of continuing to do effective work. A number of them have adopted innovative strategies that manage to provide assistance while also serving to advance the cause of basic human rights and the empowerment of the people whom they serve. To the extent that NGOs focus not only on their humanitarian mission but also on the empowerment of their constituencies, their activities constitute a low-profile channel of social transformation.

23. U.S. importers of DPRK products are required to obtain prior approval from the U.S. Treasury's Office of Foreign Assets, certifying that the products were not produced by North Korean entities designated as having engaged in missile proliferation. Subject to this condition, approval is routine. U.S. government officials report that they receive only a handful of such requests each year. The relaxation of sanctions tied to a specific political agreement is intentionally reversible: the trade restrictions remain off as long as North Korea maintains the missile moratorium; if missile testing is resumed, sanctions could be reimposed.

24. Probably the most important of these are restrictions on the sale of potential military-use items under the multilateral Wassenaar Arrangement to which both the United States and South Korea are parties. Under the existing regulations, South Korean firms attempting to establish operations in Kaesŏng initially encountered difficulty outfitting their establishments with basic computer and telecommunications equipment, though the incumbent firms appear to have surmounted this obstacle.

25. Even if the DPRK should obtain NTR status, the United States would likely classify it as a nonmarket economy and subject it to onerous antidumping rules on the Chinese template.

26. With respect to narcotics, the State Department has declined to list the DPRK as a major producer or trafficker in illicit drugs, so this provision at present is not binding. The DPRK government is probably the world's worst abuser of human rights, and it would be

hard to certify North Korean human rights practices under any meaningful criteria. But under current U.S. law, the executive probably can act with more discretion with respect to the human rights requirements than those relating to other concerns. Labor practices at the Kaesŏng Industrial Complex have already emerged as a subject of controversy in the proposed U.S.-Korea free trade agreement (Yonhap 2006).

27. Under a law enacted when U.S. airplanes were regularly hijacked to Cuba, the provision of sanctuary to hijackers is one of the specific legal triggers for U.S. opposition to international financial institution lending.

28. In particular, Cha draws on power transition theories to suggest that there are plausible conditions under which North Korea could be tempted to launch a preemptive strike despite its weakness. Yet, as he admits, the conditions under which this would occur are when North Korea believes with a high probability that it will be forced to fight in the future on worse terms than it would fight in the present, a parameter determined almost entirely by North Korea's perception of external threats.

29. The fundamental military problems include lack of knowledge about the precise location of weapons and facilities but even more important the forward-deployment of North Korean military forces, the vulnerability of Seoul to conventional attack, and the corresponding South Korean resistance to military options.

30. The staunchest defenders of this position have been Leon Sigal (e.g., Sigal 1998) and Selig Harrison (2002). See also Cumings (2003:43–102) and McCormack (2004).

APPENDIX I

1. Of particular importance is the outstanding monograph by Sheena Chestnut, "'The Soprano State'" (2005), which does the service of collating information from a wide range of public sources.

REFERENCES

Agence France Presse. 1996. "China Revives 'Friendly Prices' to Help North Korea." July 13.
———. 2005. "North Korea Wants UN Development Assistance, Not Humanitarian Aid: WFP." October 31. www.reliefweb.int/rw/RWB.NSF/db900SID/EKOI-6HP8YC? OpenDocument. Accessed November 1, 2005.
———. 2006. "South Korea Doubles Fund for Aid to North Korea." January 18.
Ahn, Byung-joon. 1994a. "The Man Who Would Be Kim." *Foreign Affairs* 73, no. 6: 94–108.
———. 1994b. "Korea's Future after Kim Il-sung." *Korea and World Affairs*, Fall: 442–72.
Ahn, Christine. 2005. "Famine and the Future of Food Security in North Korea." Policy Brief no. 11. San Francisco: Food First/Institute for Food and Development Policy.
Ahn, Jong Chul. 1996. "Maintaining Social Structure and the Food Problem in North Korea." *Korean Northeast Collection of Treatises* 3 (December): 1–24 (in Korean).
Albright, Madeleine. 2003. *Madame Secretary.* New York: Miramax.
Amnesty International. 2004. "Starved of Rights: Human Rights and the Food Crisis in the Democratic People's Republic of Korea (North Korea)." web.amnesty.org/library/index/engasa240032004. Accessed March 1, 2006.
Appadurai. A. 1984. "How Moral Is South Asia's Economy? A Review Article." *Journal of Asian Studies* 43:481–97.
Armstrong, Charles. 2001. "The Nature, Origins, and Development of the North Korean State." In Samuel Kim, ed., *The North Korean System in the Post-Cold War Era.* New York: Palgrave.
———. 2002. *The North Korean Revolution.* Ithaca: Cornell University Press.
Asher, David L. 2005. "The North Korean Criminal State, Its Ties to Organized Crime and Possibility of WMD Proliferation." Nautilus Institute Policy Forum Online 05–92A. November 15. www.nautilus.org/for a/security/0592Asher.html. Accessed March 1, 2006.

Associated Press. 1993. "Defector Cites Growing Unrest in North Korea." August 24.

———. 1998. "French Aid Workers Report Cannibalism in Famine-Stricken North Korea." April 15.

Babson, Bradley O. 1998. "Roundtable on Agricultural Recovery and Environment Protection in DPRK: Statement by the World Bank." Paper presented at the Thematic Roundtable Meeting on Agricultural Recovery and Environment Protection (AREP) for the Democratic People's Republic of Korea (DPRK), Geneva, May 28–29. Photocopy.

Banbury, Anthony. 2005. "World Food Programme Press Conference on the DPRK." *NAPSnet Daily Report*, March 31. www.nautilus.org/napsnet/sr/2005/0528A_Banbury.html. Accessed March 1, 2006.

Bank of Korea. 2005. "GDP of North Korea in 2004." Press release. May 31.

Beaton, George H. 1989. "Small but Healthy? Are We Asking the Right Questions?" *Human Organization*. 48, no. 1: 30–39.

BBC Summary of World Broadcasts. 1994. "China Reportedly Expands Economic Aid to Pyongyang." September 8.

Becker, Jasper. 1996. "The Starvation of a Nation." *South China Morning Post*, February 4.

———. 1997a. "Letters Highlight Horror of Famine: Victims Caught in Desperate Struggle for Help as Worst Feared to Be Yet to Come." *South China Morning Post*, May 12.

———. 1997b. "'Million Dead' in North Korean Famine." *South China Morning Post*, September 30.

———. 1997c. "North Koreans Turning to Cannibalism." *South China Morning Post*, October 1.

———. 1998a. "Horror of a Hungry Country." *South China Morning Post*, February 15.

———. 1998b. "Food for Hungry Stolen by Army." *South China Morning Post*. April 11.

———. 2005. *Rogue Regime: Kim Jong Il and the Looming Threat of North Korea*. New York: Oxford University Press.

Bennett, John. 1999. "North Korea: The Politics of Food Aid." RRN Network Paper 28. London: Overseas Development Institute.

Berkofsky, Axel. 2003. *EU's Policy Towards the DPRK: Engagement or Standstill?* Brussels: European Institute for Asian Studies.

Bermudez, Joseph S., Jr. 2001. *Shield of the Great Leader: The Armed Forces of North Korea*. London: I. B. Tauris.

Bong, Young-shik. 2003. "Anti-Americanism and the U.S.-Korea Military Alliance." In Korea Economic Institute, ed., *Confrontation and Innovation on the Korean Peninsula*. Washington, D.C.: Korea Economic Institute.

Brooke, James. 2005. "North Korea Says Bumper Crop Justifies Limits on Aid." *New York Times*, October 6.

Bueno de Mesquita, Bruce and Jongryn Mo. 1997. "Prospects for Economic Reform and Political Stability." In Thomas H. Hendriksen and Jongryn Mo, eds., *North Korea After Kim Il Sung*. Stanford, Calif.: Hoover Institution.

Burnside, Craig and David Dollar. 1997. "Aid, Policies, and Growth." Policy Research Working Paper 1777. Washington, D.C.: World Bank.

Buzo, Adrian. 1999. *The Guerilla Dynasty: Politics and Leadership in North Korea*. Boulder, Colo.: Westview.

Caritas—Hong Kong. 2005a. "SOA 11/2005: Emergency Appeal for the Ongoing Food and Health Crisis in the Democratic People's Republic of Korea (DPRK) for the Period April 2005 to March 2006." Hong Kong: Caritas—Hong Kong.

———. 2005b. "DPRK Trip Report 23 July to 13 August 2005." Hong Kong: Caritas—Hong Kong. August 25.

Central Bureau of Statistics (North Korea). 2002. "Report on the DPRK Nutrition Assessment 2002." November 20.

Central Bureau of Statistics, Institute of Child Nutrition, DPRK. 2005. "DPRK 2004 Nutrition Assessment Report of Survey Results." February.

Central Intelligence Agency. 1994. *Handbook of Economic Statistics*. Washington, D.C.: CIA.

Cha, Victor D. and David C. Kang. 2003. *Nuclear North Korea: A Debate on Engagement Strategies*. New York: Columbia University Press.

Chang, Yoo-nok. 2006. "Preliminary Survey Results on Access to Food in North Korea." Unpublished.

Charny, Joel. 2005. *Acts of Betrayal: The Challenge of Protecting North Korean Refugees in China*. Washington, D.C.: Refugees International.

Charny, Joel R. 2004. "North Koreans in China: A Human Rights Analysis." *International Journal of Korean Unification Studies* 13, no. 2: 74 –97.

Chestnut, Sheena E. 2005. "The 'Soprano State?': North Korean Involvement in Criminal Activity and Implications for International Security." Honors Program for International Security Studies, Center for International Security and Cooperation, Stanford University, May 20.

Cheung, Tai Ming. 2001. *China's Entrepreneurial Army*. Oxford: Oxford University Press.

Cho, Myung Chul and Hyoungsoo Zang. 1999. "The Present and Future Prospects of the North Korean Economy." KIEP Working Paper 99–07. Seoul: Korea Institute for International Economic Policy. June 25.

Choi, Bong Dae and Kab Woo Koo. 2005. "North Korea's State Ration System." *NAPSnet Daily Report*. November 3. www.nautilus.org/napsnet/sr/2005/0589Choi_Woo.html. Accessed November 3, 2005.

———. 2006. "North Korean Market Activities in the 1990s." ICNK Forum No. 06-3-14-1. Seoul: Institute for Far Eastern Studies, Kyungnam University.

Choi, Jinwook. 1999. "Changing Relations between Party, Military and Government in North Korea and their Impact on Policy Direction," unpublished manuscript, Korea Institute on National Unification.

Choi, Su Hon. 1998. "Statement by H.E. Choi Su Hon, Vice Minister of Foreign Affairs, to the Thematic Roundtable Meeting on Agricultural Recovery and Environmental Protection (AREP) for the Democratic Republic of Korea (DPRK)." Paper presented at the Thematic Roundtable Meeting on Agricultural Recovery and Environment Protection (AREP) for the Democratic People's Republic of Korea (DPRK), Geneva, May 28–29. Geneva. May 28–29.

Chon, Hyun Joon. 2004. *A Study of the Social Control System in North Korea: Focusing on the Ministry of People's Security*. Seoul: Korea Institute for National Unification.

Chosun Ilbo. 2004. "U.S. More Dangerous than NK? Most Seem to Think So." January 2.

———. 2005. "Loan Sharks Prosper in N. Korea." 24 November. english.chosun.com/cgi-binn/printNews?id=2005112400. Accessed November 29, 2005.

Chung, Oknim. 2003. "The Role of South Korea's NGOs: The Political Context." In L. Gordon Flake and Scott Snyder eds., *Paved With Good Intentions: The NGO Experience in North Korea*. Westport, Conn.: Praeger.

Chung, Tai-Uk. 2004. "Beyond the Limits of Intervention? The Dilemma of the North Korean Human Rights Act." *East Asian Review* 16, no. 3 (Autumn): 75–86.

Chung, Yun Ho. 2003. "The Prospects of Economic Reform in North Korea and the Direction of Its Economic Development." *Vantage Point* 26, no. 5 (May): 43–53.

City Population. 2003. *City Population—North Korea: City Population—Cities, Towns, and Provinces—Tables and Maps.* August 31, 2003. www.citypopulation.de/KoreaNorth. Accessed March 16, 2006.

Collins, Robert. 1996. "Patterns of Collapse in North Korea." *The Combined Forces Command C5 Civil Affairs Newsletter.* Seoul, Korea. January.

Conquest, Robert. 1986. *The Harvest of Sorrow: Soviet Collectivization and the Terror-Famine.* London: Pimlico.

Cooley, Alexander and James Ron. 2002. "The NGO Scramble." *International Security* 27, no. 1: 5–39.

Cornell, Erik. 2002. *North Korea Under Communism: Report of an Envoy to Paradise.* New York: Routledge Curzon.

Cumings, Bruce. 1997. *Korea's Place in the Sun.* New York: Norton.

———. 2003. *North Korea: Another Country.* New York: New.

Daily North Korea. 2006. January 13.

Dammers, Chris, Patrick Fox, and Michelle Jimenez. 2005. *Report for the Evaluation of ECHO's Actions in the Democratic People's Republic of Korea 2001–2004.* United Kingdom: Agua Consulting.

Deutsche Presse Agentur. 2000. "Cohen: US Food Aid Supports North Korean Military." July 28.

Devereux, Stephen. 1993. *Theories of Famine.* London: Harvester Wheatsheaf.

———. 2000. "Famine in the Twentieth Century." IDS Working Paper 105. Sussex: Institute of Development Studies.

———. 2001. "Sen's Entitlement Approach: Critiques and Counter-Critiques." *Oxford Development Studies* 29, no. 3: 245–63.

de Waal, Alex. 1997. *Famine Crimes: Politics and the Disaster Relief Industry in Africa.* Bloomington: Indiana University Press.

Donga Ilbo. 1994. "Food Requested from China to Secure Stable Foundation of Kim Chong-Il's System." September 17.

Downs, Chuck. 1999. *Over the Line: North Korea's Negotiating Strategy.* Washington, D.C.: AEI.

Drazen, Allan. 2002. "Conditionality and Ownership in IMF Lending: A Political Economy Approach." Unpublished manuscript.

Dreze, Jean and Amartya Sen. 1989. *Hunger and Public Action.* Oxford: Oxford University Press.

————, eds. 1991. *The Political Economy of Hunger: Entitlement and Well-Being.* New York: Oxford University Press.

Easterly, William, Ross Levine, and David Roodman. 2003. "New Data, New Doubts: Revisiting 'Aid, Policies, and Growth.'" Working Paper 26. Washington, D.C.: Center for Global Development.

Eberstadt, Nicholas. 1995. *Korea Approaches Reunification.* Armonk, N.Y.: M. E. Sharpe.

————. 1998a. "North Korea's Interlocked Economic Crises." *Asian Survey* 38, no. 3: 203–30.

————. 1998b. "Development, Structure, and Performance of the North Korean Economy: Empirical Indications." Paper presented at the conference "Developing Social Infrastructure in North Korea for Economic Cooperation Between the North and the South," Seoul, Korea, November 9–10.

————. 1999. *The End of North Korea.* Washington, D.C.: American Enterprise Institute.

————. 2000. "'Our Own Style of Statistics': Availability and Reliability of Official Quantitative Data for the Democratic People's Republic of Korea." *The Economics of Korean Reunification* 5, no. 1: 68–93.

————. 2001. "Socio-Economic Development in Divided Korea: A Tale of Two 'Strategies.'" Harvard Center for Population and Development Studies Working Paper Series, vol. 11, no. 5. Cambridge: Harvard School of Public Health. April. www.hsph.harvard.edu/hcpds/wpweb/Eberstadt%20wp11.05.pdf. Accessed November 1, 2005.

————. 2003. "DPRK Trade Statistics Spreadsheet." Personal communication.

————. 2004. "The Persistence of North Korea." *Policy Review* 127 (October–November). www.policyreview.org/oct04/eberstadt.html. Accessed March 1, 2006.

Eberstadt, Nicholas and Judith Banister. 1992. *The Population of North Korea.* Berkeley, Calif.: Institute of East Asian Studies.

Eberstadt, Nicholas, Marc Rubin, and Albina Tretyakova. 1995. "The Collapse of Soviet and Russian Trade with North Korea, 1989–1993: Impact and Implications." *Korean Journal of National Unification* 4:87–104.

Ellman, M. 2000. "The 1947 Famine and the Entitlement Approach to Famines." *Cambridge Journal of Economics* 24:603–30.

Euro-Asian Business Consultancy. 1994. "DPRK: What Happens Next? Strategy Under Uncertainty." Seoul: Euro-Asian Business Consultancy.

European Commission. 2001. "The EC–Democratic People's Republic of Korea (DPRK) Country Strategy Paper 2001–2004." Brussels: European Commission External Relations. europa.eu.int/comm/external_relations/north_korea/csp/index.htm. Accessed 26 April 2005.

Fairclough, Gordon. 2005. "North Korea Poses Aid Puzzle." *Wall Street Journal,* September 16.

Flake, L. Gordon. 2003. "The Experience of U.S. NGOs in North Korea." In L. Gordon Flake and Scott Snyder, eds., *Paved with Good Intentions: The NGO Experience in North Korea.* Westport, Conn.: Praeger.

Flake, L. Gordon and Scott Snyder, eds. 2003. *Paved with Good Intentions: The NGO Experience in North Korea.* Westport, Conn.: Praeger.

Food and Agricultural Organization (FAO). 1996. "Report of the World Food Summit, 13–17 November 1996, Rome, Italy." www.fao.org/documents/show_cdr.asp?url_file=/docrep/003/w3613e/w3613e00.htm.

———. 2003. *The State of Food Insecurity in the World 2003*. Rome: FAO.

Food and Agricultural Organization and World Food Programme (FAO/WFP). 1995. "Special Report—FAO/WFP Crop and Food Supply Assessment Mission to the Democratic People's Republic of Korea." December 22. www.fao.org/documents/show_cdr.asp?url_file=/docrep/004/w0051e/w0051e00.htm. Accessed April 27, 2005.

———. 1996. "Special Report—FAO/WFP Crop and Food Supply Assessment Mission to the Democratic People's Republic of Korea." December 6. www.fao.org/documents/show_cdr.asp?url_file=/docrep/004/w3690e/w3690e00.htm. Accessed April 27, 2005.

———. 1997. "Special Report—FAO/WFP Crop and Food Supply Assessment Mission to the Democratic People's Republic of Korea." November 25. www.fao.org/documents/show_cdr.asp?url_file=/docrep/004/w7289e/w7289e00.htm. Accessed April 27, 2005.

———. 1998a. "Special Report—FAO/WFP Crop and Food Supply Assessment Mission to the Democratic People's Republic of Korea." June 25. www.fao.org/documents/show_cdr.asp?url_file=/docrep/004/w9066e/w9066e00.htm. Accessed April 27, 2005.

———. 1998b. "Special Report—FAO/WFP Crop and Food Supply Assessment Mission to the Democratic People's Republic of Korea." November 12. www.fao.org/documents/show_cdr.asp?url_file=/docrep/004/x0449e/x0449e00.htm. Accessed April 27, 2005.

———. 1999a. "Special Report—FAO/WFP Crop and Food Supply Assessment Mission to the Democratic People's Republic of Korea." June 29. www.fao.org/documents/show_cdr.asp?url_file=/docrep/004/x2437e/x2437e00.htm. Accessed April 27, 2005.

———. 1999b. "Special Report—FAO/WFP Crop and Food Supply Assessment Mission to the Democratic People's Republic of Korea." November 8. www.fao.org/documents/show_cdr.asp?url_file=/docrep/004/x3691e/x3691e00.htm. Accessed April 27, 2005.

———. 2003. "Special Report—FAO/WFP Crop and Food Supply Assessment Mission to the Democratic People's Republic of Korea." October 30. www.fao.org/documents/show_cdr.asp?url_file=/docrep/006/j0741e/j0741e00.htm. Accessed April 27, 2005.

———. 2004. "Special Report—FAO/WFP Crop and Food Supply Assessment Mission to the Democratic People's Republic of Korea." November 22. www.fao.org/documents/show_cdr.asp?url_file=/docrep/007/j2972e/j2972e00.htm. Accessed 27 April 2005.

Food and Agricultural Organization Statistical Databases (FAOSTAT). n.d. Database. Geneva: Food and Agricultural Organization of the United Nations. faostat.fao.org.

Foster-Carter, Aidan. 1994. "Korea: Sociopolitical Realities of Reuniting a Divided Nation." In Thomas H. Hendricksen and Kyong-soo Lho, eds., *One Korea?* Stanford: Hoover Institute Press.

———. 2001. "The Great Bulldozer." *Far Eastern Economic Review*, April 19.

Frank, Ruediger. 2002. "EU–North Korean Relations: No Effort Without Reason." *International Journal of Korean Unification Studies* 11, no. 2: 87–119.

———. 2003. "The End of Socialism and a Wedding Gift for the Groom? The True Meaning of the Military First Policy." www.nautilus.org/DPRKbriefingbook/transition/Ruediger_Socialism.html. Accessed September 15, 2005.

————. 2005a. "Economic Reforms in North Korea (1998–2004): Systemic Restrictions, Quantitative Analysis, Ideological Background." *Journal of the Asia Pacific Economy* 10, no. 3: 278–311.

————. 2005b. "International Aid for North Korea: Sustainable Effects of Waste of Resources?" Policy Forum Online 05-100A. December 15. www.nautilus.org/fora/security/05100Franks.html. Accessed March 1, 2006.

————. 2005c. "North Korean Markets and the Reactivation of the Public Distribution System: Dialogue Between a Pessimist and an Optimist." Policy Forum Online 05-81A. October 6. www.nautilus.org/fora/security/0581Frank.html. Accessed March 1, 2006.

General Accounting Office (GAO). 1999. "Report to the Chairman, Committee on International Relations, House of Representatives, Foreign Assistance: North Korea Restricts Food Aid Monitoring," Washington, D.C.: GAO, October.

General Affairs and External Relations Council (GAERC). 2002. "Korean Peninsula-Council Conclusions." November 19. europa.eu.int/comm/external_relations/north_korea/intro/gac.htm#nk180303. Accessed March 21, 2006.

Gey, Peter. 2004. "North Korea: Soviet-style Reform and the Erosion of the State Economy." *Dialogue and Cooperation*, no. 1. www.fesspore.org/pdf/D+C%201-2004/5-Gey.pdf.

Good Friends. 1998. "The Food Crisis of North Korea Witnessed by 1,694 Food Refugees." December. www.goodfriends.or.kr/eng/report/1019e.htm. Accessed March 15, 2005.

————. 1999. "Report on Daily Life and Human Rights of North Korean Food Refugees in China." Seoul: Good Friends Center for Peace, Human Rights and Refugees, June.

————. 2004. "Human Rights in North Korea and the Food Crisis." Seoul: Good Friends Center for Peace, Human Rights and Refugees, March.

————, 2005. "North Korea Today." Seoul: Korea, January.

————. 2006a. *North Korea Today*, no. 12. Seoul: Korea, February.

————. 2006b. *North Korea Today*, special issue. Seoul: Korea, February.

Goodkind, Daniel and Lorraine West. 2001. "The North Korean Famine and Its Demographic Impact." *Population and Development Review* 27, no. 2: 219–38.

Haggard, Stephan and Robert R. Kaufman. 1995. *The Political Economy of Democratic Transitions*. Princeton: Princeton University Press.

Haggard, Stephan and Marcus Noland. 2005. *Hunger and Human Rights: The Politics of Food in North Korea*. Washington D.C.: U.S. Committee for Human Rights in North Korea.

Haggard, Stephan and Marcus Noland, 2006, *The North Korean Refugee Crisis: Human Rights and International Response*. Washington D.C.: U.S. Committee for Human Rights in North Korea.

Han, Paul S. 2004. "Report on Critical Dimensions and Problems of the North Korean Situation (1996–2004)." *Peace Economics, Peace Science and Public Policy* 10, no. 3. www.bepress.com/peps/vol10/iss3/4/. March 1, 2006.

Harrison, Selig. 2002. *Korean Endgame: A Strategy for Reunification and U.S. Disengagement*. Princeton: Princeton University Press.

Harrold, Michael. 2004. *Comrade and Strangers: Behind the Closed Doors of North Korea*. Chichester: Wiley.

Hathaway, Robert and Jordon Tama. 2004. "The U.S. Congress and North Korea during the Clinton Years." *Asian Survey* 44, no. 4 (September–October): 711–33.

Hawk, David. 2003. *The Hidden Gulag*. Washington, D.C.: U.S. Committee for Human Rights in North Korea.

Heiskanen, Markku. 2003. "A Multilateral Scenario for Korea: The Role of the European Union." *NAPSnet Daily Report*, March 25. www.nautilus.org/fora/security/0324A_Heiskanen.html. Accessed March 1, 2006.

Hellman. Joel. 1998. "Winners Take All: The Politics of Partial Reform in Postcommunist Transitions." *World Politics* 50, no. 2: 203–34.

Hollinger, Richard C. and Jason L. Davis. 2003. *2002 National Retail Security Survey Final Report*. Gainesville: Security Research Project, Department of Sociology, University of Florida.

Hughes, Christopher W. 1999. *Japan's Economic Power and Security: Japan and North Korea*. London: Routledge.

———. 2002. "Japan–North Korean Relations from the North-South Summit to the Koizumi-Kim Summit." *Asia-Pacific Review* 9, no. 2: 61–78.

———. 2005. "Japan–North Korea Relations and the Political Economy of Sanctions." University of Warwick. Unpublished manuscript.

Human Rights Watch. 2002. *The Invisible Exodus: North Koreans in the People's Republic of China*. New York: Human Rights Watch.

Humanitarian Development Resource Center for DPR Korea, "WFP Monthly Reports." 2004. www.humanitarianinfo.org/DPRK/infocentre/reportswfp/index.asp. Accessed March 1, 2006.

Hunter, Helen-Louise. 1999. *Kim Il-sŏng's North Korea*. Westport, Conn.: Praeger.

International Crisis Group. 2005. *Japan and North Korea: Bones of Contention*. International Crisis Group Asia Report No. 100. Brussels: International Crisis Group.

———. 2006. *China and North Korea: Comrades Forever?* International Crisis Group Asia Report No. 112. Brussels: International Crisis Group.

International Federation for Human Rights. 2003. *Misery and Terror: Systematic Violations of Economic, Social and Cultural Rights in North Korea*. International Federation of Human Rights Report No. 374/2 (November). Paris: International Federation of Human Rights.

International Federation of Red Cross and Red Crescent Societies (IFRC). 2000. *World Disaster Report 2000*. Geneva: IFRC. www.ifrc.org/publicat/wdr2000/wdrconte.asp. Accessed April 27, 2005.

International Monetary Fund. 2005. *Direction of Trade Statistics*. Washington, D.C.: International Monetary Fund, June.

———. 2006. *Direction of Trade Statistics*. Washington, D.C.: International Monetary Fund, February.

Ireson, Randall. 2006. "Designing Food Security in North Korea: Designing Realistic Possibilities." Shorenstein Asia-Pacific Center Working Paper. Stanford: Shorenstein Asia-Pacific Research Center, February. iis-db.stanford.edu/pubs/21046/Ireson_FoodSecurity_2006.pdf. Accessed March 27, 2006.

ITAR-Tass. 2003. "Bonds Are Being Issued for Sale Mainly to Wealthy." May 23. Translation by KOTRA, 27 May 2003. KOTRA–North Korea Team, Lee Chang-hak. crm.kotra.or.kr/main/common_bbs/bbs_read.php3?board_id:21&pnum=899826&cnu. Accessed June 6, 2003.

Japan Economic News Wire. 1997. "China Asks International Community to Give Food Aid to N. Korea." April 18.

Joongang Ilbo. 1996. "Scholars Polled on NK Future." September 22.

———. 2002. "Thai Senate Raises Suspicions on Rice Exports to North." May 22.

———. 2004. "Roh Says North Korea Will Not Collapse." December 6. service.joins. com/asp/print_article_english.asp?aid=2501003&esectcode=e_politics. Accessed March 1, 2006.

Kang, Chol-hwan. 2002. *The Aquariums of Pyongyang.* New York: Basic.

———. 2005. "Give Us An 'Eclipse Policy.' " *Wall Street Journal,* July 14.

Kang, David. 2003. "International Relations Theory and the Second Korean War." *International Studies Quarterly* 47:301–24.

Kang, Grace M. 2005. "A Case for the Prosecution of Kim Jong Il for Crimes Against Humanity, Genocide, and War Crimes." Unpublished paper. Beijing: Renmin University.

Katona-Apte, Judit and Ali Mokdad. 1998. "Malnutrition of Children in the Democratic People's Republic of North Korea." *Journal of Nutrition* 128:1315–19.

Khan, Mohsin and Sunil Sharma. 2003. "IMF Conditionality and Country Ownership of Adjustment Programs." *World Bank Research Observer* 18, no. 2 (Fall): 227–48.

Kim, Ilpyong J. 2006. "Kim Jong Il's' Military First Politics." In Young Whan Kihl and Hong Nack Kim, eds., *North Korea: the Politics of Regime Survival.* Armonk N.Y.: M. E. Sharpe.

Kim, Jeongnim. 2002. "Forceful Repatriation of North Korean Refugees and Their Punishment." Paper prepared for the Second International Conference on North Korean Human Rights and Refugees, Seoul, Korea, December 8. www.nkhumanrights.or.kr/ inter_eng_02.html. Accessed March 1, 2006.

Kim Jŏng-il. 1996. "On the 50th Anniversary of Kim Il Sung University." December 7. www. kimsoft.com/korea/kji-kisu.htm. Accessed March 1, 2006.

———. 2000. "Improving the Layout of the Field Is a Great Transformation of Nature for the Prosperity of the Country, a Pacific Work of Lasting Significance." *People's Korea* (Tokyo), December 21.

Kim, Jung-Hun. 2004. "President Roh 'Virtually No Possibility of a North Korean Collapse.' " *Donga Ilbo,* December 6. english.donga.com/srv/service.php3?biid=2004120645538. Accessed March 1, 2006.

Kim, Kyung-won. 1996. "No Way Out: North Korea's Impending Collapse." *Harvard International Review* 18, no. 2 (Spring): 22–71.

Kim, Pyung-joo. 1998. "Monetary Integration and Stabilization in the United Korea." In Il SaKong and Kwang-suk Kim, eds., *Policy Priorities for the Unified Korean Economy.* Seoul: Institute for Global Economics.

Kim, Samuel S. and Tai Hwan Lee. 2002. "Chinese–North Korean Relations: Managing Asymmetrical Interdependence." in Samuel S. Kim and Tai Hwan Lee, eds., *North Korea and Northeast Asia.* Lanham: Rowman and Littlefield.

Kim, Sung Chull. 1994. "Is North Korea Following the Chinese Model of Reform and Opening?" East Asia Institute Reports. New York: East Asia Institute, Columbia University, December.

———. 2003. "Fluctuating Institutions of Enterprise Management in North Korea: Prospects for Local Enterprise Reform." *Journal of Communist Studies and Transition Politics* 19, no. 1: 10–34.

―――. 2006. *North Korea Under Kim Jong-il*. Albany: SUNY Press.

Kim, Woon-keun, Lee Hyun-ok, and Daniel A. Sumner. 1998. "Assessing the Food Situation in North Korea." *Economic Development and Cultural Change* 46, no. 3: 519–34.

Kim, Yeri. 2005. "China–North Korea Relations." Graduate School of International Relations and Pacific Studies, University of California, San Diego. Unpublished manuscript.

Kim, Young-hoon. 2001. "The AREP Program and Inter-Korean Agricultural Cooperation." *East Asian Review* 13, no. 4 (Winter): 93–111.

Kim, Young-jin. 2005a. "Rice Merchants Increasing in North Korea." *Daily North Korea,* February 7.

―――. 2005b. "North Koreans Bet Lives in Markets." *Daily North Korea*, April 12.

―――. 2005c. "Interview with the Victim." *Daily North Korea*, October 6.

―――. 2005d. "An Employee from the Emperor Hotel in Rajin Out to Do Business in the Marketplace." *Daily North Korea,* November 14.

―――. 2005e. "NK State Forfeit of Privately Farmed Food." *Daily North Korea*, September 26.

Kim, Young Jin and In Ho Park. 2005. "North Korean State Enterprises, Handed Over to Individuals with Fee." *Daily North Korea*, April 20.

Kim, Young-yoon and Soo-young Choi. 2005. *Understanding North Korea's Economic Reforms*. Seoul: Center for the North Korean Economy, Korean Institute for National Unification.

Kirk, Mark, Peter Brookes, and Maria Pica. 1998. "Stafdel Report Final: Mission to North Korea and China August 11–23, 1998." Washington, D.C.: International Relations Committee, U.S. House of Representatives, 31 August. Photocopy.

Kirk, Mark and Amos Hochstein. 1997. "Trip Report Regarding the Food Situation in North Korea." Washington, D.C.: International Relations Committee, U.S. House of Representatives.

Knack, Stephen. 2000. "Aid Dependence and the Quality of Governance." World Bank Development Research Group Working Paper 2396. Washington, D.C.: World Bank, July.

Koh, Byung Chul. 2005. "'Military-First Politics' and Building a 'Powerful and Prosperous Nation' in North Korea." *Nautilus Policy Forum Online*, PFO-05-32a, April 14. www.nautilus.org/fora/security/0532AKoh.html. Accessed March 1, 2006.

Korea Development Institute (KDI). 1999. *Nutritional Problems of North Korean Children*. Seoul: KDI.

Korea Institute for International Economic Policy (KIEP). 2004. *North Korea Development Report 2003/04*. Seoul: KIEP.

Korea Institute for National Unification (KINU). 2002. *White Paper on Human Rights in North Korea 2001*. Seoul: KINU.

―――. 2004. *White Paper on Human Rights in North Korea 2004*. Seoul: KINU.

―――. 2005. *White Paper on Human Rights in North Korea 2005*. Seoul: KINU.

Korean Buddhist Sharing Movement (KBSM). 1998. *Witnessed by 1,019 Food Refugees*. Seoul: Korea Buddhist Sharing Movement, June.

Korean Ministry of Unification. 2005. "The South Korean Government's Efforts on Resolution of Humanitarian Issues." Issues in Focus. November 28. www.unikorea.go.kr/index.jsp. Accessed June 8, 2006.

———. 2006. "Updated Statistics on Inter-Korean Contacts, Reunion of Separated families, Humanitarian Assistance and North Korean Defectors (as of the End of Dec, 2005)." Facts and Figures. January 1. www.unikorea.go.kr/index.jsp. Accessed June 8, 2006.

Kornai, Janos. 1992. *The Socialist System: The Political Economy of Communism.* Princeton: Princeton University Press.

Kwon, Jeong Hyun. 2006. "Hamheung City, 90% of the Families Dependent on Private Businesses for Living." *Daily North Korea*, January 24.

Kwon, Tai-jin and Kim Young-hoon. 2003. "Agricultural Policy Changes in North Korea and Inter-Korean Cooperation." *Journal of Rural Development* 26 (Summer 2003): 19–52.

Kwon, Young-kyong. 2006. "An Analysis of Trends in North Korea's Economic Reforms in Recent Years." *Vantage Point* 29, no. 2: 44–55.

Kyodo News Service. 1999. "President Meets North Korea Parliament Head, Premier Offers Food Aid." June 4.

———. 2004. "China Seeks Kim Jong Il Visit, Will Increase Aid." July 18.

Lam, Willy Wo-Lap. 2003. "Time to Act, China Tells N Korea." CNN International. August 25. edition.cnn.com/2003/WORLD/asiapcf/east/08/24/willy.column/index.html. Accessed June 1, 2006.

Lankov, Andrei. 2002. *From Stalin to Kim Il Sung: The Formation of North Korea. 1945–1960.* New Brunswick: Rutgers University Press.

———. 2003. "Pyongyang: Rules of Engagement." *Pacific Review* 16, no. 4: 617–26.

———. 2004. "North Korean Refugees in Northeast China." *Asian Survey* 44, no. 6: 856–73.

———. 2005a. *Crisis in North Korea: The Failure of De-Stalinization, 1956.* Honolulu: University of Hawaii Press.

———. 2005b. "Welcome to Capitalism, North Korean Comrades." *Asia Times Online.* December 14, 2004. www.atimes.com/atimes/Korea/FL14Dg01.html. Accessed via www.nautilus.org/fora/security/0501A_Lankov.html, June 15, 2006.

———. 2006a. "The Natural Death of North Korean Stalinism." *Asia Policy* 1:95–122.

———. 2006b. "Bitter Taste of Paradise: North Korean Refugees in South Korea." *Journal of East Asian Studies*, forthcoming.

Lau, Lawrence J., Yingi Qian, and Gérard Roland. 2000. "Reform Without Losers: An Interpretation of China's Dual-Track Approach to Transition." *Journal of Political Economy* 108, no. 1: 120–43.

Lautze, Sue. 1996. "North Korea Food Assessment (May–June 1996)." Washington, D.C.: U.S. Agency for International Development, June 6. www.reliefweb.int/rw/rwb.nsf/db900SID/ACOS-64CD8S?OpenDocument. Accessed November 15, 2005.

———. 1997. "The Famine in North Korea: Humanitarian Responses in Communist Nations." Cambridge: Feinstein International Famine Center, Tufts University, June.

Lee, Chan-woo, Tsutomu Nakano, and Makoto Nobukuni. 1995. *Estimate of the Supply and Demand for Grain in the Democratic People's Republic of Korea: 1995.* Niigata, Japan: Economic Research Institute for Northeast Asia (ERINA), Research Division, July. Photocopy.

Lee, Eon Jeung. 2005. "Japanese Food Aid Sold in Markets in North Korea." *Daily North Korea*, June 21.

Lee, Hyun Joo. 2005. "North Korean People Smuggle Out Metal Scraps Taken Away from Factory Facilities." *Daily North Korea*, December 2.

Lee, Hy-sang. 1991. "Inter-Korean Cooperation: Realities and Possibilities." In Steven W. Mosher, ed., *Korea in the 1990s*. New Brunswick, N.J.: Transaction.

———. 1994. "Economic Factors in Korean Reunification." In Kihl Young-whan, ed., *Korea and the World*. Boulder: Westview.

———. 2000. *North Korea: Strange Socialist Fortress*. Westport, Conn.: Praeger.

Lee, Jong-woon. 2003. "Outlook for International Agency Assistance for North Korea." *Korea Focus* 11, no. 5: 77–93.

Lee, Jung-chul. 2002. "The Implications of North Korea's Reform Program and Its Effects on State Capacity." *Korea and World Affairs* 26, no. 3: 357–64.

Lee, Keun-soon. 2004. "Cross-Border Movements of North Korean Citizens." *East Asian Review* 16, no. 1 (Spring): 37–54.

Lee, Nae-Young. 2005. "Changing S. Koreans' Perception Toward the Reunification." *Joongang Ilbo*, October 13.

Lee, Suk. 2003. *Food Shortages and Economic Institutions in the Democratic People's Republic of Korea*. Ph.D. diss., Department of Economics, University of Warwick, Coventry, U.K.

———. 2005. *The DPRK Famine of 1994: Existence and Impact*. Studies Series 05-06. Seoul: Korea Institute for National Unification.

Lee, Young-Hoon. 2005. "An Analysis of the Effect of North Korea's International and Inter-Korean Trade on Its Economic Growth." September 5. The Bank of Korea—Publications. www.bok.or.kr/index.jsp. Accessed June 1, 2006.

Lee, Young-sun. 1995. "Is Korean Unification Possible?" *Shin Dong-A Monthly*, May (in Korean); *Korea Focus* 3, no. 3 (May/June): 5–21 (in English).

Lee, Young Hwa. 2005. "Aids [*sic*] to North Korean Never Reach the People." *Daily North Korea*, May 2.

Levin, Norman D. and Yong-Sup Han. 2002. *Sunshine in Korea: The South Korean Debate About Policies Toward North Korea*. Santa Monica: RAND.

Lim, Kang-Taeg and Sung Chull Kim. 2004. "The Unofficial Exercise of Property Rights in North Korea." Studies Series 04-04. Seoul: Korea Institute for National Unification.

Lim, Phillip Wonhyuk. 1997. "North Korea's Food Crisis." *Korea and World Affairs*, Winter: 568–85.

Lim, Wonhyuk. 2005. "North Korea's Economic Futures: Internal and External Dimensions." Washington, D.C.: Brookings Institution. http://brookings.edu/fp/cnaps/events/lim_20051102.pdf. Accessed December 15, 2005.

———. 2006a. "Common Myths about Food Aid in North Korea." Washington, D.C.: Brookings Institution, February 10. Unpublished paper.

———. 2006b. "Kim Jong Il's Southern Tour: Beijing Consensus with a North Korean Twist." Washington, D.C.: Brookings Institution, February. Unpublished paper.

Lind, Jennifer. 1997. "Gambling with Globalism: Japanese Financial Flows to North Korea and the Sanctions Policy Option," *Pacific Review* 10, no. 3: 391–406.

Lintner, Bertil. 2005. *Great Leader, Dear Leader: Demystifying North Korea under the Kim Regime*. Chiang Mai, Thailand: Silkworm.

McCarthy, Thomas. 2000. "CARE's Withdrawal from North Korea." Nautilus Policy Forum Online PFO 00–03A. April 26. www.nautilus.org/fora/security/0003A_McCarthy.html. Accessed March 2, 2006.

McCormack, Gavin. 2004. *Target North Korea: Pushing North Korea to the Brink of Nuclear Catastrophe*. New York: Nation.

Macintyre, Kate. 2002. "Famine and the Female Mortality Advantage." In Tim Dyson and Cormac Ó Gráda, eds., *Famine Demography*. Oxford: Oxford University Press.

Mansourov, Alexandre Y. 2003. "Giving Lip Service with an Attitude: North Korea's China Debate." Honolulu: Asia-Pacific Center for Security Studies Special Assessment, December.

Manyin, Mark E. 2003. "Japan–North Korea Relations: Selected Issues." Washington, D.C.: Library of Congress Congressional Research Service, November 26.

———. 2005. "Foreign Assistance to North Korea." In *CRS Report for Congress*. Washington, D.C.: Congressional Research Service, May 26.

Manyin, Mark E. and Ryun Jun. 2003. "U.S. Assistance to North Korea." Washington, D.C.: Library of Congress Congressional Research Service, March 17.

Martin, Bradley K. 2004. *Under the Loving Care of the Fatherly Leader: North Korea and the Kim Dynasty*. New York: Thomas Dunne.

Martorell, Reynaldo. 1989. "Body Size, Adaptation, and Function." *Human Organization* 48, no. 1: 15–20.

Mazarr, Michael J. 1995. *North Korea and the Bomb: A Case Study in Nonproliferation*. New York: St. Martin's.

Médecins sans Frontières (MSF). 1998. "MSF Calls on Donors to Review Their Aid Policy Towards DPRK." September 30. www.msf.org/countries/page.cfm?articleid=712831efec70–11d4-b2010060084a6370. Accessed April 27, 2005.

Meyer, Josh and Barbara Demick. 2005. "U.S. Accuses North Korea of Conspiracy to Counterfeit." *Los Angeles Times*, December 18.

Michell, Anthony. 1994. "Report." Seoul: Euro-Asian Business Consultancy.

———. 1998. "The Current North Korean Economy." In Marcus Noland, ed., *Economic Integration on the Korean Peninsula*. Washington, D.C.: Institute for International Economics.

Ministry of Unification (South Korea). 2003. *The Policy for Peace and Prosperity*. Seoul: Ministry of Unification.

Minnesota Lawyers International Human Rights Committee. 1998. *Human Rights in the Democratic People's Republic of North Korea*. Minneapolis: Minnesota Lawyers International Human Rights Committee.

Montinola, Gabriella, Yingyi Qian, and Barry Weingast. 1995. "Federalism, Chinese Style: The Political Basis for Economic Success in China." *World Politics* 48, no. 1 (October): 50–81.

Moon, Chung-in. 2004. "Managing Collateral Catastrophe: Rationale and Preconditions for International Economic Support for North Korea." In Ahn Choong-yong, Nicholas Eberstadt, and Lee Young-sun, eds., *A New International Engagement Framework for North Korea*. Washington, D.C.: Korea Economic Institute.

Nam, Sung-wook. 2003. "Moves Toward Economic Reforms." *Vantage Point* 26, no. 10: 18–22.

———. 2004. "Food Security in North Korea and Its Economic Outlook." Department of North Korean Study, Korea University.

———. 2005. "Future Prospects of North Korean July Economic Reforms and Implication from the Perspective of Comparative Socialism." Seoul: Korea University. Unpublished paper.

Nam, Sung-wook and Sung-young Gong. 2004. "The Effects of the Price and Wage Increases of 2002 on Production and Consumption." Seoul: Korea University. Unpublished paper.

NAPSnet Daily Report. 2001. "Food AID for DPRK." July 9.

Nathanail, Lola. 1996. "Food and Nutrition Assessment: Democratic People's Republic of Korea." Report to the World Food Programme from the Save the Children Fund, UK, March 16–April 24.

Natsios, Andrew. 1999. "The Politics of Famine in North Korea." *Special Report.* Washington, D.C.: United States Institute of Peace, August 2.

———. 2001. *The Great North Korean Famine.* Washington, D.C.: U.S. Institute for Peace.

———. 2003. "Testimony." Committee on Foreign Relations, Subcommittee on East Asian and Pacific Affairs, U.S. Senate, June 5. www.usaid.gov/press/speeches/203/ty030605.html.

Newcomb, William. 2003. "Reflections on North Korea's Economic Reform." In *Korea's Economy 2003*, vol. 19. Washington, D.C.: Korea Economic Institute of America.

Noland, Marcus. 1997. "Why North Korea Will Muddle Through." *Foreign Affairs* 76, no. 4: 105–18.

———. 1998. "Introduction" Marcus Noland, ed., *Economic Integration on the Korean Peninsula.* Washington, D.C.: Institute for International Economics.

———. 2000. *Avoiding the Apocalypse: The Future of the Two Koreas.* Washington, D.C.: Institute for International Economics.

———. 2001. "Between Collapse and Revival: A Reinterpretation of the North Korean Economy." http://www.iie.com/publications/papers/noland0201–2.htm

———. 2004a. *Korea After Kim Jong-il.* Washington D.C.: Institute for International Economics.

———. 2004b. "Famine and Reform in North Korea." *Asian Economic Papers* 3, no. 2: 1–40.

Noland, Marcus, Sherman Robinson, and Tao Wang. 2001. "Famine in North Korea: Causes and Cures." *Economic Development and Cultural Change* 49, no. 4.

North Korea Advisory Group. 1999. "Report to the Speaker U.S. House of Representatives." Washington, D.C.: North Korea Advisory Group, November.

Oberdorfer. Don. 1997. *The Two Koreas.* Reading, Mass.: Addison-Wesley.

Oh, Seung-yul. 1993. "Economic Reform in North Korea: Is China's Model Relevant to North Korea?" *Korean Journal of National Unification* 2:127–51.

———. 2003. "Changes in the North Korean Economy: New Policies and Limitations." *Korea's Economy 2003*, vol. 19. Washington, D.C.: Korea Economic Institute of America.

Oh, Kang Don and Ralph C. Hassig. 2000. *North Korea through the Looking Class.* Washington D.C.: Brookings Institution Press.

Okamoto, Katsuo, Shuji Yamakawa, and Hiroyuki Kawashima. 1997. "Estimation Method of Flood Damage to Rice Production." GIS Development. www.gisdevelopment.net/ aars/acrs/1997/ts3/ts3006.asp. Accessed November 18, 2005.

Okonogi, Masao. 1994. "North Korean Communism: In Search of Its Prototype." In Dae-Sook Suh, ed., *Korean Studies: New Pacific Currents.* Honolulu: Center for Korean Studies.

Paddock, Richard C. and Barbara Demick. 2003. "N. Korea's Growing Drug Trade Seen in Botched Heroin Delivery." *Washington Post*, May 21.

Park, Han S. 1998. "Human Needs, Human Rights, and Regime Legitimacy." In Moon Chung-in, ed., *Understanding Regime Dynamics in North Korea.* Seoul: Yonsei University Press.

Pei, Minxin. 2006. *China's Trapped Transition.* Cambridge: Harvard University Press.

Pelto, Gretel and Pertti J. Pelto. 1989. "Small but Healthy." *Human Organization* 48, no. 1: 11–15.

Perl, Raphael. 2005. "Drug Trafficking and North Korea: Issues for U.S. Policy." CRS Report to Congress. Washington, D.C.: Congressional Research Service, March 4.

———. 2006. "North Korean Counterfeiting of U.S. Currency." CRS Report to Congress. Washington, D.C.: Congressional Research Service, March 22.

Pinkston, Daniel A. 2003. "Domestic Politics and Stakeholders in the North Korean Missile Development Program." Monterey: Center for Nonproliferation Studies, Monterey Institute of International Studies.

Pollack, Jonathan and Chung-min Lee. 1999. *Preparing for Korean Unification.* Santa Monica: RAND.

Powell, John. 2002. "Testimony Before the Subcommittee on East Asia and the Pacific House International Relations Committee." wwwa.house.gov/international_relations/107/ powe0502.htm. Accessed June 18, 2005.

Powers, Samantha. 2002. *The Problem from Hell: America and the Age of Genocide.* New York: Basic.

Quinones, C. Kenneth. 2002. "Chapter II: The American NGO Experience in North Korea." Washington, D.C.: Mansfield Foundation. Unpublished paper.

Ravallion, Martin. 1987. *Markets and Famines.* Oxford: Clarendon.

Reed, P. Edward. 2004. "Unlikely Partners: Humanitarian Aid Agencies and North Korea." In Ahn Choong-yong, Nicholas Eberstadt, and Lee Young-sun, eds., *A New International Engagement Framework for North Korea?* Washington, D.C.: Korea Economic Institute of America.

Reuters. 2005. "WFP to Stop Feeding North Koreans This Month." December 15. www. alertnet.org/thenews/newsdesk/PEK50084.htm. Accessed December 15, 2005.

Rhee, Bong-jo. 2005. "Policy on Inter-Korean Cooperation and Exchanges." *Korea Policy Review* 1, no. 2 (August): 16–20.

Robinson, W. Courtland, Myung Ken Lee, Kenneth Hill, and Gilbert Burnham. 1999. "Mortality in North Korean Migrant Households: A Retrospective Study." *Lancet* 354 (July–December): 291–95.

———. 2001. "Demographic Methods to Assess Food Insecurity." *Prehospital and Disaster Medicine* 16, no. 4 (October–December): 286–92.

Roland, Gérard. 2000. *Transition and Economics: Politics, Markets, and Firms.* Cambridge, Mass.: MIT Press.

Russell, Sharman Apt. 2005. *Hunger: An Unnatural History.* New York: Basic.

Schloms, Michael. 2003. "The European NGO Experience in North Korea." In L. Gordon Flake and Scott Snyder, eds., *Paved with Good Intentions: The NGO Experience in North Korea.* Westport, Conn.: Praeger.

———. 2004. *North Korea and the Timeless Dilemma of Aid.* Munich: Lit.

Scobell, Andrew. 2004. *China and North Korea: From Comrades-in-Arms to Allies at Arms Length.* Carlisle, Pa.: Strategic Studies Institute, U.S. Army War College.

Seckler, David. 1980. "Malnutrition: An Intellectual Odyssey." *Western Journal of Agricultural Economics* 5 (December): 219–27.

Sen, Amartya K. 1981. *Poverty and Famines: An Essay on Entitlement and Depression.* Oxford: Clarendon.

———. 2000. *Development as Freedom.* New York: Anchor.

Shin, Chang-Woon, Young-gi Chun, and Myo-ja Ser. 2005. "Koreans Sober about Unification." *Joongang Daily*, October 31.

Short, Philip. 2004. *Pol Pot: Anatomy of a Nightmare.* New York: Henry Holt.

Shrimpton, Roger and Yongyout Kachondham. 2003. "Analysing the Causes of Child Stunting in DPRK." October. www.unicef.org/dprk/further_analysis.pdf. Accessed October 18, 2005.

———. 2004a. "Food and Nutrition in the Democratic People's Republic of Korea: Children's Nutritional Status." North Yorkshire, U.K. Unpublished paper.

———. 2004b. "Food and Nutrition in the Democratic People's Republic of Korea: The Nutritional Status of the Mothers of Young Children." North Yorkshire, U.K. Unpublished paper.

Sigal, Leon V. 1998. *Disarming Strangers: Nuclear Diplomacy with North Korea.* Princeton: Princeton University Press.

Smith, Hazel. 2002. "Overcoming Humanitarian Dilemmas in the DPRK (North Korea)." In *United States Institute for Peace Special Report 90.* Washington, D.C.: U.S. Institute for Peace, July.

———. 2004. "Brownback Bill Will Not Solve North Korea's Problems." *Jane's Intelligence Review* (February): 42–45.

———. 2005a. "Disintegration and Reconstitution in the Democratic People's Republic of Korea." In Simon Chesterman, Michael Ignatieff, and Ramesh Thakur, eds., *Making States Work: State Failure and the Crisis of Governance.* New York: United Nations University Press.

———. 2005b. *Hungry for Peace: International Security, Humanitarian Assistance, and Social Change in North Korea.* Washington D.C.: United States Institute of Peace Press.

Smith, Heather. 1998. "The Food Economy: Catalyst for Collapse?" In Marcus Noland, ed., *Economic Integration of the Korean Peninsula.* Washington, D.C.: Institute for International Economics.

Smith, Heather, and Yiping Huang. 2003. "Trade Disruption, Collectivisation and Food

Crisis in North Korea." In Peter Drysdale, Yiping Huang, and Masahiro Kawai, eds., *Achieving High Growth: Experience of Transitional Economies in East Asia.* London: Routledge, forthcoming.

Snyder, Scott. 1996. "A Coming Food Crisis on the Korean Peninsula? The Food Crisis, Economic Decline and Political Considerations." United States Institute of Peace Special Report 19. October. www.usip.org/pubs/specialreports/early/korea96.html. Accessed December 15, 2004.

———. 1997. *North Korea's Decline and China's Strategic Dilemmas.* Washington, D.C.: United States Institute for Peace, October.

———. 1999. *Negotiating on the Edge.* Washington, D.C.: U.S. Institute for Peace.

———. 2003a. "The NGO Experience in North Korea." In L. Gordon Flake and Scott Snyder, eds., *Paved with Good Intentions: The NGO Experience in North Korea.* Westport, Conn.: Praeger.

———. 2003b. "Lessons of the NGO Experience in North Korea." In L. Gordon Flake and Scott Snyder, eds., *Paved with Good Intentions: The NGO Experience in North Korea.* Westport, Conn.: Praeger.

Sphere Project. 2004. *Humanitarian Charter and Minimum Standards in Disaster Response.* Geneva: Sphere Project.

Struck, Doug. 2003. "Opening a Window on North Korea's Horrors." *Washington Post,* October 4.

Suh, Dae-Sook. 2002. "Military-First Politics of Kim Jong Il." In Byung Chul Koh, *The Korean Peninsula in Transition: The Summit and Its Aftermath.* Seoul: Institute for Far Eastern Studies.

Svensson, Jakob. 1999. "Aid, Growth, and Democracy." *Economics and Politics* 11, no. 3: 275–98.

———. 2000. "Foreign Aid and Rent-Seeking." *Journal of International Economics* 51, no. 2: 437–61.

Takahara, Kanako. 2004. "WFP Better Able to Monitor food in North Korea." *Japan Times,* October 27.

Terry, Fiona. 2001. "Feeding the Dictator." *The Guardian,* August 6.

United Nations. 1999. "Substantive Issues Arising in the Implementation of the International Covenant on Economic, Social and Cultural Rights: General Comment 12." E/C.12/1999/5. Geneva: United Nations Committee on Economic, Social and Cultural Rights.

United Nations Commission on Human Rights. 2001. *Report on the Special Rapporteur on the Right to Food, Mr. Jean Ziegler, Submitted in Accordance with Commission on Human Rights Resolution 2000/10.* Geneva: U.N. Commission on Human Rights, February 7.

United Nations Commodity Trade Statistics Database (UN-COMTRADE). 2005. Database. unstats.un.org/unsd/comtrade/. Accessed April 2005.

United Nations Development Program (UNDP). 1998. Paper presented at the Thematic Roundtable Meeting on Agricultural Recovery and Environment Protection (AREP) for the Democratic People's Republic of Korea (DPRK), Geneva, May 28–29. Photocopy.

United Nations General Assembly. 1948. "Universal Declaration of Human Rights." www.un.org/Overview/rights.html. Accessed June 15, 2005.

———. 1966. "International Covenant on Economic, Social, and Cultural Rights." www. unhchr.ch/html/menu3/b/a_cescr.htm. Accessed June 15, 2005.

United Nations Office for the Coordination of Humanitarian Affairs (UN-OCHA). "Financial Tracking Service." ocha.unog.ch/fts/index.aspx. Accessed April 18, 2005, and February 21, 2006.

———. N.d.b. "The Consolidated Appeals Process." ochaonline.un.org/webpage. asp?Site=cap. Accessed April 27, 2005.

United States Agency for International Development (USAID). 2005. "Report on U.S. Humanitarian Assistance to North Koreans." Washington, D.C.: USAID, April 15. www. usaid.gov/our_work/humanitarian_assistance/nkhra.html. Accessed April 27, 2005.

United States Department of State. 2005. *Country Reports on Human Rights Practices, North Korea*. Washington, D.C.: U.S. Department of State, February 28.

United States Department of Treasury. 2006. "Finding that Banco Delta Asia SARL is a Financial Institution of Primary Money Laundering Concern." www.fincen.gov/finding_banco.htm. Accessed January 24, 2006.

United States House of Representatives. 1999. "North Korea Advisory Group Report to the Speaker U.S. House of Representatives." November. www.fas.org/nuke/guide/dprk/nkag-report.htm. Accessed April 14, 2005.

Walker, Peter. 1989. *Famine Early Warning Systems: Victims and Destitution*. London: Earthscan.

Ward, Andrew. 2002. "US Accuses North Korea of Narcotics Trade." *Financial Times*, December 4.

Williams, James H., David von Hippel, and Peter Hayes. 2000. "Fuel and Famine: Rural Energy Crisis in the Democratic People's Republic of Korea." Institute on Global Conflict and Cooperation. IGCC Policy Papers. March 1. http://repositories.cdlib.org/igcc/PP/pp46. Accessed June 1, 2005.

Winner, Andrew C. 2005. "The Proliferation Security Initiative: The New Face of Interdiction." *Washington Quarterly* 28, no. 2 (Spring): 129–43.

Wintrobe, Ronald. 1998. *The Political Economy of Dictatorship*. New York: Cambridge University Press.

Wit, Joel S., Daniel B. Poneman, and Robert L. Galucci. 2004. *Going Nuclear: The first North Korean Nuclear Crisis*. Washington, D.C.: Brookings Institution Press.

Woo, Seongji. 2004. "North Korea's Food Crisis." *Korea Focus* 12, no. 3: 63–80.

Woo-Cumings, Meredith. 2002. "The Political Ecology of Famine: The North Korean Catastrophe and Its Lessons." Asia Development Bank Institute. www.adbi.org/research-paper/2002/01/01/115.political.ecology/. Accessed April 27, 2005.

World Food Programme (WFP). 1996. "WFP Expands Operations in North Korea." Pyongyang: WFP Update, July.

———. 1997. "WFP to Deliver First Food Aid Directly to Hard-hit Northeast of North Korea." Pyongyang: WFP Update, July.

———. 1998. "Nutritional Survey of the DPRK." Geneva: WFP, November.

———. 2002a. *The WFP DPR Korea Monthly Update*, no. 39. Pyongyang: WFP, April.

———. 2002b. *The WFP DPR Korea Monthly Update*, no. 40. Pyongyang: WFP, May.

———. 2002c. *The WFP DPR Korea Monthly Update*, no. 46. Pyongyang: WFP, November.

———. 2003a. "Child Nutrition Survey Shows Improvements in DPRK but UN Agencies Concerned about Holding onto Gains." Pyongyang/Geneva, February 20. www.unicef.org/media/media_1822.html. Accessed June 27, 2006.

———. 2003b. "Public Distribution System (PDS) in DPRK." Pyongyang: DPR Korea Country Office, May 21.

———. 2003c. *The WFP DPR Korea Monthly Update*, no. 48. Pyongyang: WFP, January.

———. 2004. *The WFP DPR Korea Monthly Update*, no. 60. Pyongyang: WFP, January.

———. 2005a. *The WFP DPR Korea Monthly Update*. Pyongyang: WFP, January 31.

———. 2005b. *Emergency Report n. 48 25 November 2005*. www.wfp.org/english/?n=34&Key=6. Accessed November 29, 2005.

———. 2006a. *Projects of Executive Board Approval: Agenda Item 8. Protracted Relief and Recovery Operation—Democratic People's Republic of Korea 10488.0.* WFP/EB.1/2006/8/3. Geneva: WFP, February 3.

———. 2006b. "Resourcing Update: Summary Chart Detailing Confirmed Contributions to Emergency Operations Through the World Food Programme of the United Nations." February 27. www.wfp.org/appeals/flash_appeals/index.asp?section=3&sub_section=1#. Accessed June 8, 2006.

World Food Programme International Food Aid Information System (WFPINTERFAIS). 2004. "Food Aid Flows 2003." Geneva: World Food Programme, May. www.wfp.org/interfais/. Accessed April 27, 2005.

———. 2005. "2004 Food Aid Flows." Geneva: World Food Programme, May. www.wfp.org/interfais/index2.htm#. Accessed March 13, 2005.

Wu, Anne. 2005. "What China Whispers to North Korea." *Washington Quarterly* 28, no. 2 (Spring): 35–48.

Yang, Dali L. 1996. *Calamity and Reform in China: State, Rural Society, and Institutional Change since the Great Leap Famine*. Stanford: Stanford University Press.

Yonhap. 2006. "U.S. Labor Group Shows Concern over Kaesong Workers' Conditions." March 14. english.yna.co.kr/Engnews/20060315/430100000020060315092142E7.html. Accessed March 16, 2006.

Yoon, Dae-Kyu. 2005. "Analysis of Changes in the DPRK Criminal Code." Seoul: IFES, 31 January.

Young, Helen, Anna Taylor, Sally-Anne Way, and Jennifer Leaning. 2004. "Linking Rights and Standards: The Process of Developing 'Rights-based' Minimum Standards on Food Security, Nutrition, and Food Aid." *Disasters* 28, no. 2: 142–59.

Yun, Nam-sik. 1987. *Physique in (South) Korea*. Seoul: Ehwa Women's University Press.

Ziegler, Jean. 2002. "Economic, Social, and Cultural Rights: The Right to Food." Report by the Special Rapporteur on the Right to Food. Commission on Human Rights, 58th sess., E/CN.4/2002/58. Geneva: United Nations Economic and Social Council.

INDEX

Accion Contra la Faim, 87
Agreed Framework (1994), 32, 50, 131, 137, 233, 240, 236–237
agriculture: capital intensity of, 26, 37, 56–57, 171, 177, 180; cooperative farming, 25–26, 31, 52–53, 56–57, 72, 122–123, 170, 172, 177–179, 185, 193, 204, 267; irrigation, 26, 57, 178; labor intensity of, 211–212; militarization, 111, 170; special production campaigns, 176–177; production targets, 177–178; productivity, 179–180, 212; reforms in, 212, 218, 241; sustainability 178–179. *see also* Production, agricultural
Ahn, Byung-joon, 221
Albright, Madeline, 134, 237
Asian Development Bank, 30, 231
August 3 Campaign for People's Goods, 187, 206; workers, 194, 205

Banbury, Anthony, 101, 105, 119, 270
Banco Delta Asia, 234, 246
Bertini, Catherine, 94, 95, 108

CARE, 88

Carter, James E., 240
Cheung, Tai Ming, 227
China: People's Liberation Army (PLA), 227; reform in, 5, 166, 211, 212, 218, 227–228; as reform model, 15, 215, 218, 225, 240; relations with North Korea, 9, 27, 128, 154–160, 225, 232; relations with South Korea, 155; relations with United States 234; trade with North Korea, 31
Christopher, Warren, 130
chuch'e, 4, 24, 26, 38, 226, 276n7
Cohen, William, 134
collectivization, 25, 26
Consolidated Appeals Process (CAP), 82–84, 150, 251–252
Cornell, Erik, 246

Deng, Xiaoping, 158
diversion: 14, 108–125; decentralized diversion, 110; deterrents, 115, 179, 204; effects, 114; estimates 109, 115, 117–18, 121–124; evidence of 117–121; incentives for, 14, 109, 112, 115, 175, 179, 204; to markets, 112, 172; and market

diversion (*continued*)
development, 109, 121; models of, 112–114,

Dreze, Jean, 3, 21, 40, 220

Eberstadt, Nicholas, 27–28, 45–46, 156, 197, 226, 265n20, 268n24
entitlements, xv, xvii–xviii, 9–10, 21–24, 35, 44. *see also* North Korea – entitlements
European Commission Humanitarian Aid Office (ECHO), 150, 153
European Union: 84, 127; relations with North Korea, 149, 154
export processing zones, 28–29, 145, 178, 214–217, 234, 277n8

famine: causes of, 1, 6–11, 21–50, 89–90, 220; coping behavior, 15, 165, 170–171, 193; coping strategies, 111; death toll, 1, 3, 7–8, 11, 45, 56, 70, 73–76, 166, 209; effect on rural population, 24–25, 61, 71, 72, effect on urban population, 24–25, 61, 70–71, 72; and genocide, 2; origins of, 3; regional differences, 70; theories of, 68, 220; triage, 64, 70, 94; weather and, 23–24, 50, 57, 67, 72. *see also* food, humanitarian assistance, malnutrition, Public Distribution System, weather
farmers: 14, 16, 22, 56–57, 61, 72; coping behavior, 57, 61, 64, 66, 67, 111, 207; actions in response to famine, 57; grain recollection from 63; and PDS, 58
farmers' markets, 172–173
fertilizer: as agricultural input, 26, 32–33, 36, 57; as aid, 142, 144, 146–148, 153, 240; production of, 26, 32–33, 63, 84, 178, 180
Flood Damage Rehabilitation Committee (FDRC), 34, 89, 96–97, 102, 118
floods, 2, 8–10, 23–24, 34, 37, 65–66, 90, 177, 195, 229
food: availability, 1, 22–24; balance sheet, 10, 37, 41, 42, 50; distribution 9, 21, 46, 65, 193, 204, 210; diversion by

farmers, 57, 64, 68, 123, 181, 207, 260; diversion to military, 2, 53, 229, 230; emergency response, 65–66; entitlement to, 21–24; human need, 60, 66, 193, 229; minimum human need, 43–46; normal human demand, 46–47, 50; normal total demand, 47; pricing, 193, 204–205; production estimates for, 36, 65–68; rationing, 62, 206; security, 206, 210–211, 217, 241; self-sufficiency, xviii, 8, 23, 24–26, 52–53, 211, 231; supply estimates, 35, 50, 122; trading in, 173–175. *see also* marketization
Food and Agricultural Organization (FAO), 34, 42, 45, 59, 72
food for talks, 131–134, 137–140, 148–149, 160; 238–239
foreign aid; *see* humanitarian assistance
foreign exchange, 23, 27, 29–31, 44, 48, 50, 172, 176, 185, 191–192, 194, 210–211, 245
Four-Party Talks, 131–236

Good Friends, 71, 74, 117, 169, 175, 206. *see also* Korean Buddhist Sharing Movement
Goodkind, Daniel, 75
Hall, Tony, 130
Hamgyong: North, 41, 58, 62–64, 69, 70, 74–75, 100, 192, 199–201; South, 58, 62–64, 70, 198–201
Harrison, Selig, 39
Hong, Song-nam, 156
Hu Jintao, 158
humanitarian assistance: 44, 50, 66–67, 73, 80–161, 250–257; access limitations, 88–89, barriers to, 2, 11, 13, 24, 269; bilateral, 12, 14, 66, 70, 80–86, 144, 146–148, 210, 230; coordination, 11, 15, 17, 84–85, 88, 127–129, 144, 149, 160–161, 222, 223, 230, 232–233; debate over, 13, 17, 89, 129, 210; delivery of, 102–104; difficulties with, 5, 11–12, 108, 216, 228–233; distribution mechanisms, 92; diversion of, 103–104, 108–125, 144, 229, 260; donor fatigue,

81; donor motivation, 3, 12, 14–15, 23, 79, 126–127, 229; efficacy, 13, 17; ethics of, 12, 17, 64, 87, 111, 281n20; focus on vulnerable populations, 10, 13, 91–92, 111, 118, 166, 195, 230, 253–257; forms of, 229, 260; goals of, 13, 14–15, 17; institutions, 17, 64; and marketization, 112–125; monitoring, 79, 82, 209; multilateral, 79, 230; negotiating, 105; norms, 85–88, 230, 232; obligations, 228–233; political economy of, 126–161, 236; strategies for reducing, 231; regional restrictions, 89; strategy, 12, 90, 232–233; targeting, 13, 118, 121, 166, 209, 230, 254–257; volatility of, 127, 135–136. *see also* diversion; marketization; monitoring; NGOs
—from China, 5, 14–15, 17, 31–32, 85, 110, 122, 127, 129, 132, 155–161, 207, 211, 219, 232; from European Union, 3, 23, 79, 81, 103–104, 108–127, 229; from Japan, 15, 30, 37, 119, 126, 127, 136–140; from South Korea, 14, 17, 62, 79, 119, 122, 148–149, 155, 192, 205, 217, 219, 222, 230, 232, 238, 240, 274n25, 279n2; from United States, 14–15, 32, 90, 119, 127–136, 139–141, 145, 148, 160–161, 237
humanitarian principles, 88, 99–100, 145, 231, 269n6
Hwang, Chang-yop, 73, 221, 267n16
Hwanghae Iron and Steel Works, 171

Inter-Korean Economic Cooperation Promotion Committee, 146, 147
International Atomic Energy Agency (IAEA), 38
International Covenant on Civil and Political Rights, 169
International Covenant on Economic, Social and Cultural Rights (ICESCR—1966), 11, 23, 229
International Federation of Red Cross and Red Crescent Societies (Red Cross), 119, 144–146
International Financial Institutions (IFIs),

17, 30, 216, 231–232, 235, 238, 241, 264n10, 279n5
International Fund for Agricultural Development, 84
International Monetary Fund (IMF), 13, 30, 216, 231

Japan: 127, 226; abduction of Japanese citizens, 139; colonialism, 137, 222; Koizumi administration, 139; Mori administration, 139; North Koreans in, 136; relations with North Korea, 129, 136–140, 218, 234–235; relations with South Korea, 137

Kaesong, 29, 52, 67–68, 93, 100, 145, 214, 216, 234, 241, 274, 277
Kang, Ch'ol-hwan, 241
Kang, Myong-do, 41
Kang, Song-san, 41
Khan, A. Q., 237
Kim Ch'aek Integrated Iron and Steel Works, 186, 213
Kim, Dae Jung, 15, 141, 145, 239. *see also* Sunshine Policy
Kim, Il-song, 4, 6, 24, 41, 155, 156, 167, 221, 236
Kim, Jong-il: 4, 17, 39, 139, 148, 158, 226; December 1996 speech, 40–41, 67, 111, 169, 171, 173; and military, 40, 218, 221, 224, 227; October 2001 document, 189; October 2001 speech, 208
Kim, Kyung-won, 221
Kim, Yong Sam: 141, 145; and foreign aid, 137
Kim, Young Nam, 158
Korea, Democratic People's Republic of, *see* North Korea
Korea, division of peninsula, 4, 8. *see also* Korea, unification
Korea, Republic of, *see* South Korea
Korean Buddhist Sharing Movement (KBSM), 58, 70, 145. *see also* Good Friends

Korean Peninsula Energy Development
    Organization (KEDO), 130, 134, 137,
    139, 217
Korean War, 4, 24, 25, 233, 236
Korean Workers' Party (KWP), 6, 24, 55,
    168, 221, 227

Laney, James, 131
Lautze, Susan, 48
Lee, Suk, 75
let's eat two meals a day, 27, 58
Li, Peng, 156

malnutrition, 2, 76, 167, 195–204, 209; *see
    also* stunting, underweight, wasting
marketization: 3, 14, 15, 22, 161, 165–208,
    209, 214, 215, 217, 230, 259–262; arbi-
    trage, 114, 189; attempts to curb, 189;
    bartering and, 173–175; price trends,
    175–176; role of women in, 191
Médicins du Monde, 87
Médicins sans Frontières (MSF), 75, 87–88,
    118, 195, 197
military first politics, 5, 39, 166, 218,
    224–225, 226
Missile Technology Control Regime
    (MTCR), 247
monitoring: 2, 12, 65, 82, 86, 92–107, 109,
    115–117, 144, 232, 239; restrictions on, 13,
    94–107
mortality: 72–76; births forgone, 74, 75;
    elderly 73; excess deaths, 74; infant, 73,
    198

N'ajin-Sonbong, 28–29
Namp'o Glass Factory, 186
Natsios, Andrew S., 74, 170
natural disasters: as cause of famine, 231;
    damage from, 34, 66, 67
NGOs: 12, 73, 117–119, 134, 146, 153, 241;
    cessation of aid, 80; eviction of, 93, 105,
    207; humanitarian activities of, 143–144,
    151–152; and humanitarian principles,
    85; restrictions on, 96; withdrawals of,

87–88, 98, 129, 230
North Korea: agricultural policy, 8–10,
    22, 26, 49, 177, 179, 210; agricultural
    production, 34, 37, 56; aid dependence,
    81; black market in, 206, 207; civil
    society in, 224; collapse of, 133, 210,
    221, 225, 239, 241; consumer prices in
    16, 181–184, 188, 191–193; cooperativiza-
    tion in, 177; crony capitalism in, 190;
    currency reform, 185; debt, 30; domestic
    food production, 9, 79, 81; domestic
    politics in, 168, 216, 224, 226–227, 228;
    economic mismanagement, 29, 181–182,
    205, 221; economic performance,
    221–222; economic structure of, 2, 5,
    24, 27, 233, 247; engagement with, 15,
    134, 210, 222, 232, 236, 238, 239–242;
    entitlements in, 2, 10, 35, 42, 51, 52, 53,
    55, 62, 114, 166, 203, 220; entrepreneur-
    ship, 188, 194–195; exchange rates, 185;
    exports, 29, 214, 234; external relations
    of, 27–29, 30, 214, 215–216, 218, 223,
    225, 233–242, 245–247; fiscal crisis,
    189–190; floods in, 37; food distribution
    48, 51; food shortages, 37; food supply
    in, 9–10, 67, 208, 231, 259–260; foreign
    investment in, 214; grain production,
    37, 49, 62; human rights in, 18, 135,
    150, 154, 265n10, 272n8, 282n26; illicit
    activities, 5, 31, 214, 233–234; 245–247;
    imports, 9, 14, 27, 31, 42, 211; industry,
    177, 181, 186–187, 212, 214, inflation in,
    16, 181, 185–186, 190, 205, 215; internal
    migration, 169; isolation of, 224; land
    reform in, 25, 177; local officials in,
    102–104; macroeconomic instability,
    180–191, 219, 278n2; markets in, 3, 109,
    112–125; military, 5, 49, 56, 104, 109, 120,
    155, 168–170, 217, 218, 224, 226–227,
    235, 236, 247; missile sales, 5, 31, 50, 247;
    National Defense Commission (NDC)
    168; Nature Remodeling Program, 176;
    nuclear program, 3, 5, 210, 222, 223, 235,
    237–241; occupational stratification, 22,

24, 53, 55, 71, 165, 182, 220, 227; political and administrative structure, 1, 3, 6, 10, 52, 53, 220–221, 223, 227–228; political dissent in, 224–225; political elite in, 55–56; political prisoners, 6, 54, 55; political stratification, 10, 165; prison camps, 5, 17, 169–170, 214; procurement prices, 179; reform in (*see* reform); regime change in, 240–242; regional stratification, 10, 65, 114, 191–192, 194, 200, 203, 209, 214, 220, 225; relations with China, 9, 27, 154–160, 218, 222, 232; relations with European Union, 149–154, 222; relations with Japan, 218, 222, 234–235; relations with Russia, 9; relations with South Korea, 1, 140–149, 215–216, 218, 222, 232, 239, 241 (*see also* unification); relations with Soviet Union, 27; relations with United States, 32, 130–136, 218, 222, 234–235, 236–238; responses to food shortage, 33, 34, 38, 39, 50, 67, 126, 170, 220; rural population, 122; sanctions against, 129; security environment, 5–6, 17, 38, 40, 50, 235, 275n4; social stratification, 4, 16, 192, 217, 229; state-owned-enterprises (SOEs), 186–188, 194, 204–205, 206, 217; trade with China, 31; transportation system, 62, 63, 64, 65, 103, 119–120; unemployment, 191, 213, 223; urban vs. rural residence 53, 63; wages in, 16, 182–185, 191, 194, 212–213, 216
No, Mu-hyon, 15, 141, 147, 239
No, T'ae-wu, 136, 141
Nordpolitik, 136
North Korean Human Rights Act, 135, 136
North Korean Institute for Child Nutrition, 198
North Korean People Urgent Action Network (RENK), 119
nuclear crisis (2002), 134, 154, 238
Nuclear Non-Proliferation Treaty (NPT), 40, 129
Nunn, Sam, 131

OPEC, 84
Oxfam, 88

Pak, Chong-hŭi, 226
People's Life Bonds, 189–190
Perry, William, 237
Powell, John, 110
productivity: 208, 211; agricultural, 32, 178, 180, 204, 212–213; industrial, 187
Proliferation Security Initiative (PSI), 233
Public Distribution Center (PDC), 52, 54, 92, 105
Public Distribution System (PDS): 9, 10, 13, 16, 24, 26, 51, 52, 53, 72, 167, 207, 220, 259–262; and aid distribution, 92, 144, 153; breakdown 58, 59, 60, 67–68, 71, 173, 182, 193, 203, 211; daily grain rations, 58, 59; dependency on, 193, diversion from, 109, 120, 122, 172; and marketization, 114, 122–124; ration allocation, 53, 258–262; regional differences, 68–69; revival of, 204, 206, 215, 217; rural dependency on, 63; and rural people, 56, urban residents and, 58, 63, 91, 255

Ragan, Richard, 106
ration cards, 106, 193
reform: agricultural, 31, 33, 166, 176–180; economic, 3, 166, 180–191, 205, 211, 212–214, 216–218, 226–228, 233–242, 245; obstacles to, 215; political, 3, 17, 166, 206–208, 209–210, 215–217, 220–228, 232, 236, 245
refugees: 65, 110, 173, 191, 241; access to food, 120; in China, 6, 70, 156, 160, 169–170, 225; from famine, 193; and mortality reports, 73; regional origins, 72, 74; and trade, 175; views of North Korea, 129
RENK (see North Korean People Urgent Action Network)
Robinson, W. Courtland, 59, 74, 173–175
Russia: reforms in, 166; relations with North Korea, 9 (*see also* USSR)

sanctions: 38, 129, 140, 216, 223, 230, 233, 234, 235, 237, 239, 240–241

Sen, Amartya, xv–xix, 2, 8, 21, 40, 220

Simon, Paul, 130

Six-Party Talks, 16, 140, 148, 149, 158, 222, 223, 238

Smith, Heather, 37, 46

socialism: 205, 211, 220; collectivization, 177; and famine, 1, 12, 22–26; grain procurement system, 57; reform in, 166, 180

South Korea: aid commitments to North Korea, 140–149; assistance to North Korea, 127, 240; *chaebol* 218; democratization in, 136; domestic politics, 148, 215, 239; Inter-Korean Cooperation Fund, 145–146; Ministry of Unification, 34, 37, 144, 147, 173; relations with Japan, 137; relations with North Korea, 1, 129, 140–149, 215–216, 218, 225, 232, 239, 241; relations with United States, 234, 239

stunting, 76, 195, 197–203

Sunshine Policy, 141, 144, 147, 150, 153, 239

Supreme People's Assembly (SPA), 221, 226, 228

terrorism, 234

Three Revolutions Team Movement (1973), 26

Treaty on the Non-Proliferation of Nuclear Weapons, 16

underweight children, 195, 197–203

unification, 15, 144, 147

United Nations, 16

United Nations Agricultural Recovery and Environmental Protection (AREP), 84, 178

United Nations Development Program (UNDP), 84, 88, 178

United Nations International Children's Educational Fund (UNICEF), 197

United Nations Office for the Coordination of Humanitarian Affairs (OCHA), 88, 105

United States Agency for International Development (USAID), 119, 134

Universal Declaration of Human Rights, 11, 169, 228–229

United States: Bush administration, 134, 135, 136, 139, 233, 236, 237; Clinton administration, 130, 134, 146, 236, 237–238, 240; debate over North Korea policy, 235–236, 237–239; Department of Agriculture (USDA) 34, 37, 42; International Emergency Powers Act, 237; list of state sponsors of terrorism, 234; normal trade relations (NTR) status, 234; relations with China, 234; relations with North Korea, 32, 130–136, 218, 234–235, 236–238; relations with South Korea, 234, 239; Trading With the Enemy Act, 233, 237; Treasury Department, 246

Soviet Union: 222; collapse of, 27, 31, 155, 160; crony capitalism in, 213; reform in, 211, 212, 213, 226; relations with North Korea, 27

Vietnam, 166, 211, 212, 228

wasting, in children, 195, 197–203

weapons of mass destruction (WMDs), 233–234, 237

weather: 8, 9, 11, 25, 49, 98, 180; and famine, 23–24, 50, 57, 67, 72

West, Lorraine, 75

World Bank, 30, 216, 231

World Food Programme: 12, 45, 66, 72, 79–107; access, 93–94; aid delivery, 102–104; aid distribution, 59, 161; aid targeting, 253–257; and diversion, 117; appeals to by North Korea, 37, 38; exclusion from North Korea, 207, 232; mission of, 82, 230–231; norms 85, 88; operat-

ing procedures, 87; relief effort design, 17; reporting obligations, 87; response to monitoring restrictions, 94–102, 105–107; supply sources, 14, 42, 60
World Food Summit (1996), 11

World Health Organization (WHO), 202
World Trade Organization (WTO), 155

Zhu, Rongji, 158
Ziegler, Jean, 89–90, 108